A Manual of Mystical Theology, or, The Extraordinary Graces of the Supernatural Life Explained

A MANUAL OF MYSTICAL THEOLOGY

Nihil Obstat:
JOSEPH SMITH, C.P.,
Censor Deputatus.

Imprimatur:
✠ HERBERTUS CARDINALIS VAUGHAN,
Archiepiscopus Westmonast.

Die 28, Aprilis, 1903.

A MANUAL OF MYSTICAL THEOLOGY

OR

The Extraordinary Graces of the Supernatural Life Explained

BY THE

REV. ARTHUR DEVINE
PASSIONIST

AUTHOR OF 'CONVENT LIFE,' 'A MANUAL OF ASCETICAL THEOLOGY,' ETC.

R. & T. WASHBOURNE
4 PATERNOSTER ROW, LONDON
BENZIGER BROS.: NEW YORK, CINCINNATI AND CHICAGO
1903

PREFACE

THE present volume completes the series of theological works which the author proposed to himself, and which for some years he has been giving to the public at intervals. It is a companion volume to his recent work, 'A Manual of Ascetical Theology.' The one may be regarded as the basis of the other, as Christian asceticism is the basis of true mysticism, which always supposes real and solid piety, without which we shall have false mysticism and false mystics. These two branches of theological science, though depending upon each other and united, inasmuch as they both rest upon the same principles, and the one is a continuation of the other, may well be kept distinct in their treatment and exposition. In 'Ascetical Theology' the nature of the ordinary supernatural life of the soul is explained, and rules are given for the direction of all pious souls tending to perfection according to the ordinary way of Christian asceticism, by the practice of the theological and moral virtues. The object of mystical theology is to treat of the extraordinary graces of the supernatural life of the soul, and to give the rules for the direction of souls who by the special favour of God are called to perfection by the extraordinary way of mysticism. It has also to deal with some mystical phenomena by which God's predilection for these souls is manifested, such as visions, locutions, revelations, prophecies, and miracles. The two together—that is, ascetical and mystical theology—embrace the whole Catholic doctrine of the Church as taught and explained by theologians and spiritual writers, with regard to Christian perfection and sanctity, and the means necessary to co-operate with the ordinary and extraordinary graces of God conferred upon souls in this life

The order followed in this work is that of the compendium of J B. Scaramelli's 'Mystical Directory' by Rev. F. V. Voss, priest of the Congregation of the Sacred Hearts of Jesus and Mary The work is divided into four parts

Part I. deals with mystical theology in general, with contemplation in general, its division, its objects, its causes or principles, and its effects or fruits.

Part II. is devoted to the preparation and dispositions required for contemplation. This part embraces the subjects of prayer and meditation, mortification, active and passive purification

Part III. introduces the reader to the consideration of the various degrees of contemplation, and conducts him from the first to the last degree of this sublime and infused manner of prayer. Scaramelli has been followed in the arrangement of the degrees of contemplation, both in their order and number, as in the arrangement of the four parts of the work.

Part IV goes outside infused contemplation, and treats of mystical phenomena which are distinct from contemplation, yet connected with it, because they more frequently take place during it than at other times, and because such favours are bestowed more frequently upon contemplatives than others.

It may appear somewhat irregular to consider contemplation in itself before treating of the preparation which usually precedes it. In this the example not only of Scaramelli, but of other recent authors, as Ribet and Lejeune is followed, and the arrangement, is justified by the following reasons: In the first place, it is necessary to introduce into a work on mystical theology the trials which prepare the soul for contemplative prayer, because these are full of dangers and practical difficulties, and their knowledge is of great importance in the direction of souls. Then they are dealt with, in the second place, because the knowledge of these preliminaries throws but little light on the subject of contemplation itself, whilst the knowledge of contemplation makes their meaning clearer, more precise and easier; and in adopting this order the rules of demonstration are observed by proceeding from that which is better known to that which is more obscure. Besides, contemplation is the end or term, and the purifying trials are the way and the means; now, the way cannot be well chosen if we do not know our journey's end, and the means have signification and justification only in so far as they are ordained to the end.

The sources whence the materials for the compilation of a work of this nature may be drawn are various, and both ancient and modern. The writer has fully availed himself of the aid of the best standard authors at his disposal, and due reference is made to these authors and to their works in the footnotes throughout the volume. Besides Scaramelli some others deserve special mention, who have been used as guides in much that has been treated of. These are, amongst English authors, the Benedictine Father Baker and the Carthusian W. Hilton. The 'Sancta Sophia,' or 'Holy Wisdom,' of the former, and the 'Scale of Perfection' of the latter, have been of invaluable service, and the author has learnt much and taken much from these sources.

Benedict XIV.'s treatise on 'Heroic Virtue' has also been largely used, and reliance has been placed on the authority of that work for most of the opinions expressed and the doctrine taught with regard to mystical phenomena distinct from contemplation, treated of in Part IV of this book. St John of the Cross and St Theresa have been the author's principal companions throughout the whole of his work, and they were almost his only guides in treating of the higher degrees of contemplation. Special acknowledgment is due to Schram's 'Theologia Mystica' and to the 'Principles of Religious Life,' by the Very Rev. F. C. Doyle, O.S.B., for the elucidation of some difficult points on the subject of prayer and contemplation, and to the latter work especially for the schemes or methods of prayer which that author has drawn out so clearly and accurately. The recent French works by M. J. Ribet, M l'Abbé P Lejeune, and that by Dom B. M. Maréchaux, frequently quoted, deserve special attention and recommendation. In following their method of treatment and of thought and expression, the author has endeavoured to adapt his work to all modern requirements in this order of the spiritual life which belongs to every age of the Church, and the knowledge of which is as suitable, as necessary, and as advantageous, in our own day as it has ever been in the past

As may easily be seen, it has not been the intention or pretension of the author to produce a new and original work, but simply to give in one volume a résumé, as far as possible, of all that others, who were able to speak and write from experience, have taught in their many important and well-arranged works concerning the various subjects which come under the title of mystical theology.

It is true that this branch of theology does not apply to all souls All have to be guided to perfection according to the rules of moral theology, very many according to the rules of ascetical theology, and some privileged souls, called by God to walk in the extraordinary way of perfection, are to be guided according to the rules of mystical theology. From the fact that mystical theology applies only to the few, and that souls led by extraordinary ways are the exception, the necessity and the utility of this science may be concluded. It is only when extraordinary cases arise that directors of souls and the souls themselves need special advice, special instruction, and very special care and guidance, and that the need of books of this kind is felt Besides, mystical theology has its own value from a doctrinal and devotional point of view, apart from its experimental aspect. It is calculated to lead souls to God, and to occupy them with that which is the most sublime and the most noble object of their aspirations

Cardinal Wiseman, in his preface to the English edition of the works of St. John of the Cross, thus expresses himself:

'God and His attributes present more perfect claims, motives and allurements, and more full gratification, repletion, and reward to earnest and affectionate contemplation, than any other object or subject. How much soever the mathematician may strain his intellect in pursuit of the true, however the poet may luxuriate in the enjoyment of the beautiful, to whatsoever extent the moralist may delight in the apprehension of the good in its recondite quintessence, none of these can reach, in his special aim and longing, that elevation and consummation which can be attained in those of all three by one whose contemplation is directed to the Infinite in Truth, in Beauty, and in Goodness.

'Why, then, should not this so comprehensive and so grand a source of every mental enjoyment become a supreme, all-exhausting, and sole object of contemplative fruition? Why should not some, or, rather, many, minds be found which have selected this as their occupation, their solace, their delight, and found it to be what none other can of its nature be—inexhaustible? Everything else is measurable and fathomable, this alone unlimited.

'Thus, if there be no repugnance to such a choice being made in the aim of contemplation, it is natural to expect conditions and laws in its attainment analogous to what we find when the mental powers have selected for their exercises some inferior and more restricted object. There will be the same gradual and often slow course of training, the same difficulty of fixing and concentrating the thoughts, till by degrees forms and intermediate steps are dispensed with; when the mind becomes passive, and its trains of thought seem spontaneous and incoming rather than worked out by elaborating processes.

'This state, when God is the sole occupier of thoughts, represents the highest condition of contemplation, the reaching of which mystical theology professes to direct.'[1]

The Seraphic Doctor St. Bonaventure defines mystical theology: 'The extension of the love of God by the desire of love'—*Mystica theologia idem est quod extensio amoris in Deum per amoris desiderium* ('De Myst. Theolog.' in prologo). Man here on earth, according to the first and greatest commandment, should love God with his whole heart, mind and soul, and with all his strength. Mystical theology is a science and experience that increases, extends, and perfects this love of God, and this it does by the desires of the heart—desires that are fervent, assiduous, and persevering—and this is what the holy Doctor means by the desire of love. He who desires sincerely and fervently to love God and to make others love Him, who endeavours to increase each day in his soul that love of God in order to become transformed into the perfect image of Jesus Christ, and who remains thus closely united to God here on earth, awaiting in purity and peace of conscience the perfect and incomprehensible union enjoyed by the Saints in bliss: this is the man who possesses, or who is best disposed to possess mystical theology, and to

[1] Preface to the Works of St John of the Cross, pp. xvii, xviii

enjoy the graces and effects of infused contemplation in all its degrees, and especially in the highest degrees of the perfect spiritual union which it establishes between the soul and God

A. D.

St. Joseph's Retreat,
    Highgate, London, N.,
Feast of Corpus Christi, June, 1903

CONTENTS

PART I

MYSTICAL THEOLOGY AND CONTEMPLATION IN GENERAL

CHAPTER		PAGE
I	MYSTICAL THEOLOGY: ITS MEANING, OBJECT AND DIVISION	3
II	THE THREE KINDS OR STATES OF THE SPIRITUAL LIFE	20
III	ON CONTEMPLATION IN GENERAL	28
IV	VARIOUS SPECIES OF CONTEMPLATION	37
V	THE OBJECTS OF CONTEMPLATION	48
VI	THE OBJECTS OF CONTEMPLATION (*continued*)	62
VII	THE OBJECTS OF CONTEMPLATION (*continued*)	76
VIII	THE CAUSES AND PRINCIPLES OF CONTEMPLATION	90
IX	THE SUPERIOR FACULTIES OF THE SOUL AS THE CAUSES OR PRINCIPLES OF CONTEMPLATION	101
X	THE PRINCIPLES AND CAUSES OF CONTEMPLATION ON THE PART OF GOD	116
XI	THE PRINCIPLES AND CAUSES OF CONTEMPLATION ON THE PART OF GOD (*continued*)	128
XII	THE EFFECTS AND FRUITS OF CONTEMPLATION	142
XIII	THE DURATION OF CONTEMPLATION AND ITS CESSATION	156

PART II

ON PREPARATION FOR CONTEMPLATION

CHAPTER		PAGE
I	THE DISPOSITIONS OF SOUL REQUIRED FOR CONTEMPLATION. SOLITUDE REQUIRED FOR CONTEMPLATION	169
II	PRAYER CONSIDERED AS A PREPARATION FOR CONTEMPLATION	180
III	VOCAL PRAYER A PREPARATION FOR CONTEMPLATION	190
IV	MEDITATION OR MENTAL PRAYER AS A PREPARATION FOR CONTEMPLATION	201
V	INTERNAL AFFECTIVE PRAYER (FATHER BAKER)	216
VI	ON MORTIFICATION IN GENERAL	228
VII	BODILY MORTIFICATION OR CORPORAL AUSTERITIES	238
VIII	PURIFICATIONS—ACTIVE AND PASSIVE	253
IX	ACTIVE PURIFICATIONS (*continued*)	268
X	PASSIVE PURIFICATIONS	280
XI	PASSIVE PURIFICATION OF THE SENSES (*continued*)	290
XII	PASSIVE PURIFICATIONS OF THE SENSES CAUSED BY SECONDARY AGENTS	305
XIII	THE PURIFICATION OF THE SENSES BY TRIALS FROM NATURAL CAUSES	323
XIV	THE PASSIVE PURIFICATION OF THE SPIRIT	338
XV	THE PASSIVE PURIFICATION OF THE SPIRIT (*continued*)	355

PART III

THE DEGREES OF CONTEMPLATION

	INTRODUCTION	371
I	THE FIRST THREE DEGREES OF CONTEMPLATION	380
II	ERRORS OF FALSE MYSTICS IN REGARD TO THE PRAYER OF QUIET	398

CONTENTS

CHAPTER	PAGE
III. THE FOURTH, FIFTH, AND SIXTH DEGREES OF CONTEMPLATION	409
IV THE SEVENTH DEGREE OF CONTEMPLATION	427
V THE EIGHTH AND NINTH DEGREES OF CONTEMPLATION	444
VI THE TENTH DEGREE OF CONTEMPLATION	464
VII THE GRACES AND EFFECTS OF THE SPIRITUAL MARRIAGE	477

PART IV

MYSTICAL PHENOMENA DISTINCT FROM CONTEMPLATION

INTRODUCTION	493
I ON VISIONS AND APPARITIONS	498
II. CORPOREAL APPARITIONS OR VISIONS	512
III. THE APPARITIONS OF THE BLESSED VIRGIN AND THE SPIRITS	527
IV IMAGINATIVE AND INTELLECTUAL VISIONS	541
V DIVINE LOCUTIONS OR SUPERNATURAL WORDS	556
VI ON REVELATIONS	575
VII REVELATION OF THE SECRETS OF SOULS	595
VIII ON PROPHECIES	609
IX ON THE GIFT OF MIRACLES	624
CONCLUSION: SUMMARY OF ADMONITIONS AND DIRECTIONS	641
INDEX	657

PART I

MYSTICAL THEOLOGY AND CONTEMPLATION IN GENERAL

A MANUAL OF MYSTICAL THEOLOGY

CHAPTER I

MYSTICAL THEOLOGY ITS MEANING, OBJECT AND DIVISION

1. THE word 'mystical' signifies something obscure, occult or mysterious. A person initiated into mysteries may be called a mystic, and the science which treats of mysteries may be called mystical. We must not suppose, from this acceptation of the word, that, when 'mystical' is applied to sacred science, there is in the Church of Jesus Christ some occult science the secret of which is reserved to the initiated, but that there is a science of the mysterious called mystical theology. This science may be called secret, in the sense that the great things of God are secret. They are secret on account of their magnitude, according to our Saviour's words *He that can take, let him take it.*[1] And, again. *If I have spoken to you earthly things, and you believe not. how will you believe if I speak to you heavenly things?*[2] They are secret on account of their dignity, according to the words *Behold, to you it is given to know the mysteries of the kingdom of*

[side note: 1. Meaning and application of the word 'mystical']

---
[1] St Matt xix 12   [2] St John iii 12.

heaven: but to them it is not given.[1] They are secret on account of the unfitness or inability of men to receive them, according to the words: *Give not that which is holy to dogs,*[2] and those of St. Paul *My speech and my preaching was not in the persuasive words of human wisdom, but in showing of the spirit and power.*[3] This science may be called occult because it illumines the secret things of the mind and of the heart by its light, and because the actions of the mystical soul proceed from the Divine and mysterious power of God acting upon such souls in an extraordinary manner. It is not only a secret and occult science in the sense herein explained but it is a holy science because it is ordained to the higher sanctification of souls according to the three ways of perfection—the purgative, the illuminative and the unitive

We have an illustration of this use of the word in its application to the mystical sense of many passages of Sacred Scripture—that is, the sense not indicated by the words themselves, but by the things signified by the words This is expressed by St Gregory when he says: 'The book of the Scriptures is written within and without; it is written within by allegory, without by history—within by spiritual meaning, without by the simple literal sense'

2 The definition and subject matter of mystical theology

2 Some writers teach that, as there are three stages or ways of perfection—the purgative, illuminative, and unitive—and the three corresponding states of beginners, of those in progress, and of the perfect, it is necessary to give three definitions of mystical theology. This supposes that the mystical life may belong to each of these three ways or states, and I

---

[1] St Matt xiii 11 [2] St. Matt vii 6 [3] 1 Cor ii 4

see no reason why mystical phenomena, or the favours of the mystical life, may not appear to be manifested in the lives of those who are in one or the other of these ways, but the state of the favoured soul would not make the mystical life any different, and therefore we may conclude that one definition of mystical theology can be given, and will suffice, which may apply to every state in due proportion, principally, indeed, to the state of the perfect, and in a lesser degree to the state of beginners and to the state of those in progress.

Mysticism considered in its entirety forms a branch of theology, and understood in its general sense embraces all that part of the sacred science which expounds the principles and formulates the rules of Christian perfection, or the supernatural life of the soul and its union with God. Understood in this sense, mystical theology is confounded with ascetical theology, but as distinct from ascetical theology it has a special signification and characteristic, and limited to its own proper sphere it teaches one aspect, and that the highest of the spiritual life. According to Scaramelli, the direction of souls advancing in perfection by extraordinary ways belongs to mystical theology. Strictly speaking, ascetical theology is not included in mystical theology. Ascetical theology teaches the usual and beaten paths of perfection, but mystical theology shows a more unusual and extraordinary way, and it may be a more excellent way. It is the science which teaches how the evil passions of our nature are to be eradicated by the extraordinary operation of God, and how man as far as possible is to be by perfect charity transformed in God. It is the discipline which leads souls already arrived at the third degree of charity, by way of perfect conformity to God's will, to mystical union.[1]

In the third degree of perfection, in which the soul is in the unitive way, we can consider two forms of that spiritual state. In one of these, which is common and ordinary, the soul is more active than passive; it produces acts of virtue with full consciousness of what it is doing, and with its full energy, aided, of course, by supernatural grace. In the other the soul is said to be more passive than active; God brings it under an extraordinary action, which no human effort can realize; He purifies, enlightens, and inflames it, and permits often wonderful attestations of these interior operations to appear externally.

It is the second form or phase of the unitive way with which mystical theology is really concerned according to the general interpretation of doctors, whether they consider it in its own proper sphere, or whether they confine it to passive union or to infused contemplation, for it would seem that these expressions may be taken as signifying one and the same thing as mystical theology.[2]

Cardinal Bona ('Via Compendii ad Deum,' c. iii., m. 182, p. 109), speaking of the unitive way, says that this way of quiet, seclusion, and of abstraction leads to mystical theology, namely, to that untaught wisdom which is superior to all human wisdom, by which the mind without discussion acknowledges its God, and, as it were, touches Him, and without reasonings tastes Him. Mystical theology is the

[1] Voss 'Direct Myst Scaramelli Compend,' p 21
[2] Ribet. 'La Mystique Divine,' Introduction, pp 17, 18

most secret speaking of the soul with God, etc He tells us that, as the subject is abstruse and difficult, and altogether Divine, it cannot be confined within certain definite limits, nor subjected to the strict rules of dialectics.

When it is said that in mystical theology the contemplative soul is to be considered more passive than active, this has to be understood properly, and we must never suppose that the soul is entirely passive, because the soul in that state operates by its faculties, the intellect and the will, and for some end These faculties receive the Divine favours and gifts, though they can refuse them. By co-operating with these favours and ordaining the actions to the final end, the soul is always active, but in the mystical life the passive state predominates, as in that state God more abundantly infuses into the soul supernatural graces, supernatural virtues, and supernatural illuminations which are not common to all the just.

The Rev. F. V. Voss, in his Compendium of Scaramelli's 'Mystical Directory,' gives the following explanation of mystical theology 'Man consists of body and spirit; he holds a middle place between the world of matter and the world of spirits, and he belongs to both. He dwells here in the world of matter, and he tends to the world of spirits hereafter After dwelling for some time in the world of matter, he deposits his material substance at the gate of death, and, passing through it, he enters the world of spirits. The body which is his material part is to be dissolved before it is clothed with a certain spirituality; that happens when at the resurrection it becomes by the omnipotence of God an incorruptible body, in order that, united again to the soul, it may be received into the kingdom of spirits. This is the ordinary course of Divine providence in dealing with men and their salvation. By the extraordinary way of Providence man can, even whilst living here in the body, be introduced in some special way into the world of spirits, and this way, because it is obscure and full of hidden mysteries, is called mystical.'

Division of mystical theology into experimental and doctrinal

3. To obtain a full and correct notion of mystical theology, it is necessary to consider it as an experience and as a science, and hence it may be divided into *experimental* and *doctrinal*, and this distinction is to be remembered in order to save us from dangerous and erroneous conclusions regarding it. The supernatural work of God in the soul and the extraordinary effects of this work is the subject of *experimental* mystical theology. The teaching which collects and formulates into a system of doctrine the facts and laws which accompany and regard these supernatural communications is called *doctrinal* mystical theology, or the science of mystical theology. On this division some useful remarks are given by Scaramelli to the following effect. There are some who, reading what the holy Fathers and mystical doctors have written on this subject, namely, that it is a science which is taught directly by God, that it cannot be understood except by one who has had experience of it, wrongly conclude that this science cannot be understood or taught by other theologians than mystics, and that therefore the science is practically useless. If the real knowledge of the mystical life can be gained only by those who have been elevated to the heights of contemplation,

how, they ask, can those who have not been thus favoured understand or teach it? And, again, how can the science of theology benefit those souls whom God Himself directs and teaches and guides in the sublime paths of contemplation and mystical union to which He has raised them? The holy Fathers and doctors, when they say that mystical theology is a science taught by God Himself, and that it can be understood only by those who have experienced its gifts, speak of experimental mysticism, which consists in the clearer knowledge of God which the soul receives *in luminoso caligine*, the obscure light of high contemplation together with experimental love so intimate as to cause the soul to be lost to itself and transformed in God; but they do not speak of doctrinal mysticism. This is the science which considers the acts and phenomena of experimental mysticism in their essence, in their properties, and in their effects. It examines them according to the teaching of Holy Scripture and the interpretation of the Fathers; it indicates rules according to which souls not yet contemplative may be guided on their way towards that state, and according to which souls already contemplative may make further progress in that sublime and exalted state. Doctrinal mystical theology may therefore be learned by a man who is without the experimental knowledge. No one is so foolish as to imagine that a medical man cannot understand a disease unless he himself has experienced it. And as the doctor knows the disease better than the sick person, so an expert director may gain a better knowledge of the sublime contemplation and communications between the soul and God than the soul which enjoys the contemplation and experiences the communications. Therefore it is an error to suppose that the science of mystical theology is entirely hidden from all to whom God does not impart the experimental knowledge, and it is equally erroneous to consider the science of mystical theology useless, for the reason that God Himself directs contemplative souls

4 The same author further says 'To exempt souls elevated to contemplation from the rules of doctrinal theology would be to leave them to their own uncertain experience, and to their fallacious judgment, and thus expose them to great danger of perdition. For, as Gerson says, "it has been discovered that many have devotion, but not according to knowledge, who are more prone to error than even the indevout, if they do not regulate their affections according to the pattern of the law of Christ, especially if they adhere to their own understanding and prudence, and despise the advice of others. Experience has proved this in the case of the Beguards and the Turpulini. For whilst they followed their affections, without law and order, and overlooked the law of Christ, deceitful presumption ruined them."

'There is no soul, how favoured soever with visions, revelations, and such-like heavenly gifts, which is free entirely from the deceptions of the phantasy, and from the subtle deceits and illusions of the devil. Besides, in the order of the sanctification of souls which God has established, man is to be directed by man—that is, by the prelates and ministers of the Church in the way of salvation Thus Saul, terrified by a heavenly vision and by the

---

1 The necessity of the science of mystical theology

voice of God, is sent to Ananias to learn from him what he is to do.'

From this consideration this eminent authority on spiritual direction concludes the necessity of mystical knowledge and of the study of mystical theology for those charged with the care of souls From it they are to obtain light to understand the extraordinary works of God and of His Divine grace, and the rules to be observed in the good use of them, and in discerning the real from the imaginary, true visions and revelations, etc , from false , and in detecting the numerous counterfeit visions, revelations, and other phenomena, that can be the work of the evil spirit or the result of natural causes. He gives a very useful admonition in connection with the duty of directing souls in these matters by reminding directors that it will be very much to the prejudice of souls committed to their care, if they be too incredulous and reject in a blind manner all extraordinary works of grace ; or if, on the other hand, they be too credulous, and admit without sufficient grounds all extraordinary phenomena as the supernatural works of God. To these may be applied our Lord's words *They are blind, and leaders of the blind. And if the blind lead the blind, both fall into the pit.*[1] Hence he concludes · 'There is no doubt but that the directors of souls should know all the ways by which souls are led to God, especially souls dedicated to God and to a life of prayer, among whom extraordinary graces are more frequent.'

5. So far we have treated of true mysticism, but our explanation on this subject would not be complete without taking into account false mysticism or

5. Division of mystical theology into Divine and diabolical

[1] St. Matt xv 14

diabolical mysticism, which comes under the science of mystical theology. The Rev. F. V. Voss tells us that there is one mystical way which leads to the kingdom of light and of heavenly spirits; another which leads to the kingdom of darkness and of infernal spirits. The former ascends, the latter descends; the former is called Divine mysticism, the latter diabolical mysticism. Diabolical mysticism leads the soul by means of creatures and their abuse to a mystical union with the prince of darkness; Divine mysticism by the good use of creatures, and by their renunciation, leads to the mystical union of the soul with God. How this happens he explains in a few words. The principle of every mystical operation in man is the soul or spirit, which communicates with the spirits of heaven or of hell, just as the body communicates with material things. And as every material and sensitive operation passes from the body and the senses to the spirit, so every spiritual operation begins from the spirit and expands to the body. Wherefore, in the mystical life, when the spirit of a man becomes assimilated to the higher spirits, even his body experiences a great transformation. In Divine mysticism the body becomes assimilated in some sense to a glorified body; and in diabolical mysticism it becomes even here marked with the stigmas of perdition. There is, however, a difference to be noticed between the action of God on the soul, and the action of created spirits. The action of God is creative and life-giving, that of the spirits is not. Their action can only utilize the natural agents, and produce from their properties wonderful effects. It can open the germs of nature and develop them quickly. It can restore the equilibrium of the physical forces of the human body; but it cannot produce life, nor impart it, nor restore it by any real vital infusion. The action of God reaches the very depth of the soul to illuminate it, and to move it. The action of spirits is confined to the frontiers of the body and the soul, it can move only the imagination and the sensibility.

The Church teaches that there are good and bad spirits, angels and demons; and this teaching is in perfect harmony with the traditions of the whole human race. The action of the good angels is always subordinate to the action of God, who makes use of them as His instruments, and He invests their operations with a special characteristic authority. The action of the evil spirits, on the contrary, is produced without the beneficent will of God, and with irreconcilable opposition to it; therefore the marvels produced by it or resulting from such action have to be carefully distinguished from the Divine marvels, as we distinguish two terms which form an absolute contrast to each other.

It is also to be remarked that some of the mystical phenomena, and these few in number, relate to God alone; they are the most interior, and therefore the most difficult to know and to verify. Others, and these the greater number and the most apparent, relate to, or proceed from, the power of the spirits. When it pleases God to produce these latter, He employs the ministry of His angels. But, on the other hand, the demons seek to counterfeit or imitate them, and hence the necessity of some rules in order to be able to distinguish between angelical and demoniacal influence. These rules will be given, together with the necessary observations, when we shall have to deal in the course of this work with particular phenomena.[1]

6. Natural phenomena in relation to mystical theology

6. We have not yet covered the whole field of the subject-matter of mystical theology. Human nature itself has its freaks and its mysterious developments, some of which, without going beyond their own proper sphere, by their manifestations of the good and the beautiful, seem to be on the confines of the Divine world, and some, by their appearance of wickedness and boldness, seem to belong to the demoniacal regions. It will be necessary to notice these eccentricities of nature, so that they may not be confounded with genuine supernatural results.

Amongst some scientific writers of the present day there is a theory that by the aid of psychological and medical sciences they can prove that the most marvellous phenomena in the lives of the Saints are due to nervous diseases, and to nothing else. They argue that, if only science can be made to explain these so-called wonders by means of known pathological laws, the whole theological edifice sustained by the virtues of the Saints will come down with a run. As an instance of this, I may quote the following from the 'Psychology of the Saints,' by Henri Joly. 'Two doctors have been discussing the life of St. Vincent Ferrier in the *Revue Scientifique*. He was a very celebrated "thaumaturge," and one of those to whom tradition has ascribed the most miracles. Our two critics do not attempt to compare the degrees of authenticity of the different stories. They take them altogether in lump, and are evidently extremely delighted to come upon a sort of

[1] See Dom B. M. Marechaux, 'Le Marveilleux Divin et le Marveilleux Demoniaque,' pp. 12, 37.

retrospective verification of their theories. They do not deny the facts, but they class them all as instances of lucidity or second-sight, telepathy, hallucination, suggestion or fascination. We are left to discover for ourselves (this essay being of a psychological character) what place these phenomena may have occupied in the mental and moral life of the Saint.' The author on this point remarks: ' Not only is it a fact that these phenomena are by no means one and all the distinguishing characteristics of sanctity, but many of them are to be found both in saint and sinner.'[1] There are, of course, certain differences between the two cases which have to be examined and noticed by mystical science.

7. M. J Ribet makes some useful observations regarding the mystical life, and the order and dependence of the three states of perfection in regard to that life, to which our attention may be profitably drawn.

7. Some general observations on the mystical life.

According to the usual manner of advancement, the soul is gradually raised to the state of perfect union by passing through the state of purification and that of illumination But this rule is by no means absolute, and a miraculous intervention or a very special grace may bring the soul suddenly from the lowest depths of moral abjection to the most sublime heights of charity, as may be seen in the case of St Mary Magdalen and other celebrated penitent Saints.

The second remark, no less important, concerns the complete gratuitousness and the comparative rareness of the mystical favours which culminate in

[1] Joly, 'The Psychology of the Saints,' pp 66, 67

the climax of the unitive way. The grace of God is always gratuitous. Nevertheless, the progressive development of the spiritual life in its activity from the purgation of sin to the love of benevolence is the law of supernatural providence which applies to all those who enter upon and advance in the way of perfection. Those who commence and persevere, after passing through the tribulations and pangs of fear, will arrive at the illuminations of hope and obtain the pure fervour of charity.

This is not the case with respect to the mystical ways. Without a special vocation, which is neither due nor promised to anyone, no one will be raised up to those sublime communications; God must by an extraordinary action of His grace subjugate the soul so as to bring it into the state of sweet and fruitful passiveness which is understood as proper to the mystical state. We may say that there are many whom God would raise up to the highest degrees of sacred love who yet place some obstacle in the way, and through their own fault resist the first advances of His Divine bounty; and it is no less true that God refuses these favours to many faithful souls who have advanced generously in the degrees of the purgative and illuminative ways, and who grow and shine forth in that fervent charity which is the essence and crown of perfection.

3. The three states of the soul—purgative, illuminative and unitive—not entirely distinct and separate

8. A third observation reminds us that the three states of perfection are not so entirely distinct that there may not appear in any one of them, taken separately, something of the other two. In each and all of them there is to be found the effort and care to preserve and guard the soul from sin, that which is said to belong properly to the purgative

way; in each and all of them virtue has to be practised, and from its practice light and progress result. Then in each and all of them the soul gives itself to God, in order to live solely for Him and by the supernatural life which He imparts, and this may be said to be the commencement of the unitive way. The characteristic and distinctive feature of these states is determined from the form that is dominant in the soul in its efforts towards perfection. When strife and fear predominate, the soul is said to be still in the purgative way; when the desire and fervour to advance in virtue and the attraction of hope prevail above fear, then the soul is said to be in the illuminative way. If charity is dominant above all, the soul is in the unitive state; but so long as this mortal life lasts, for the strong and feeble there will always be the labour and activity of purgation, illumination, and of union in the work of supernatural perfection.

Suarez confirms this doctrine in very distinct terms. 'These three states,' he says, 'are never so distinct that any one of them may not participate of the other two. Each of them takes its name and character from that which predominates in it. For it is certain that no one can attain to such a state of perfection in this life that he may not and cannot make further progress' ('De Orat.,' l. 2, cap. 11, n. 4, p. 166).

In like manner, supernatural phenomena, which are the object of mysticism, generally appear in the most perfect state, and are, as it were, its crown. And one special favour which is called spiritual marriage manifestly supposes the unitive way, and cannot be ascribed to either of the inferior grades of perfection.

But many of the other Divine and mystical favours, such as ecstasies, visions, locutions, may be found by way of exception in the first or in the less advanced stages of the spiritual life. But when this happens they fall under the general laws, in the sense that they are bestowed by God as a sign that He wishes the souls thus favoured to advance to the highest degrees, and if they be faithful they will attain the highest degree of the unitive way.

Again, Suarez is quoted in proof of this teaching, when he says that contemplation in this life is the gift of those who are perfect in virtue and sanctity. Because contemplation either is the perfect union of the soul with God, or the most perfect intuition which it is possible to have of God in this life, and both these are proper to the perfect. Nevertheless, he adds that contemplation is not so proper to the perfect that it may not be sometimes tasted by the imperfect, and even by beginners (*ibid.*, n. 1, p. 165, and n. 10, p. 168).[1]

To these observations I may add one or two more which I find in the 'Compendium of Scaramelli's Mystical Directory,' by F. V. Voss. One of these refers to the remark above made about the special vocation of God required for the mystical state. It is to the effect that no one without the vocation of God may presume to move a step in Divine mysticism. The soul by the exercise of Christian asceticism can prepare itself for this intimate communication with its Divine Spouse, but it must await with humility the time and the moment in which it is to be introduced by the heavenly Spouse into the state of contemplation.

[1] Ribet, 'La Mystique Divine,' introduction, p. 18.

9. From the same author we learn the place to be assigned to contemplation in the mystical life. We are told that contemplation is the principal operation of that life; that it is that by which God introduces the soul into the mystical life, and enlightens and moves it to heroic perfection; that all other favours in that state may be reduced to this. For by contemplation God elevates the soul above the material world and above itself, and introduces it into the world of spirits; by contemplation He both prepares it for, and elevates it to, the mystical union. Contemplation itself is inseparable from what is known in this science as passive purification, just as meditation is inseparable from active purification. And in the mystical life, even more than is the case in the ascetical and in the moral life, the work of sanctification consists in extirpating vices and defects, and in building up or increasing virtue. In it the evil passions have not only to be subdued, but eradicated, and charity is to be increased, not only to ordinary but to extraordinary perfection.[1]

[1] Voss, 'Compend. Direct. Myst.,' p. 66.

CHAPTER II

THE THREE KINDS OR STATES OF THE SPIRITUAL LIFE

The three kinds or states of the spiritual life

BEFORE treating of contemplation, it may be useful to call attention to the three kinds of religious or spiritual life, namely, the *active*, the *contemplative*, and the *mixed*.

(1) The active life

(1) All agree that there are these three kinds of spiritual life, and I find them briefly and clearly described by Benedict XIV. He says 'Those among the faithful who give themselves up to the continual, or, at least, very frequent, practice of spiritual and corporal works of mercy, and to the constant exercise of virtue, both towards God and their neighbour, whether they are works of precept or of counsel, are said to live an active life. Hence an uncertain author, in a treatise "On the Way of Living Well," says "There is the greatest difference, beloved sister, between the active and the contemplative life. The active life is to give bread to the hungry, to teach thy neighbour the word of wisdom, to correct the wanderer, to bring back the proud into the path of humility, and those who are at enmity into the way of peace, to visit the sick, to bury the dead, to dispense to each that which is best for him, to provide for the necessities of all."

(2) 'Those who give themselves up to continual or very frequent consideration of God, and the things of God, and of everything that has been revealed to us, who are endowed with charity, together with a total renunciation of the world, with purity of heart, and complete subjugation of their passions, are said to live the life of contemplation, of which the same author goes on to speak as follows "The contemplative life is to keep warm in our heart the love of God and our neighbour, to rest from external action, and to desire the Creator alone, and this in such a manner that the soul is now no longer free to do anything, but, despising all the cares of the world, burns with the desire of seeing the face of her Creator, has learnt how to bear the burden of this corruptible flesh, with pain and grief, and to desire most earnestly to take part in the hymns of praise which the choirs of angels sing, to mingle among the citizens of heaven, and to rejoice in the gift of immortality in the presence of God"

(3) 'Lastly, those who go through all this, and who now exercise themselves in the active life, now in the contemplative, are said to live a mixed life Concerning those, the above writer speaks thus "Some holy men there are who come forth from secret contemplation into active life, and then return again from active life to the hidden life of inward contemplation, so that when they have received the grace to advance the glory of God abroad, they return to praise God in retirement at home And as God wills that contemplatives should sometimes come forth into active life that they may profit others, so He sometimes wills that no one should

disquiet them, but that they should rest in the secret joy of sweet contemplation This is what is said in Canticles viii. 4 (which we may paraphrase) *I adjure you, O daughter of Jerusalem, that you stir not up nor awake the soul that is given up to contemplation, that is occupied with prayers and devout lections."*'

2 The contemplative life more perfect than the active

2 The same author says, with all other theologians, that the contemplative life is preferable to the active, and that the mixed is more perfect than either, and in proof of this he gives the following reasons 'We learn that the contemplative life is more perfect than the active from St Gregory on Ezekiel,[1] where, with reference to those words of Christ, *Mary has chosen the best part, which shall not be taken away from her,*[2] he says. "These two women, Martha and Mary, are very well made to signify the two kinds of life, inasmuch as the former was busily engaged in much serving, while the latter sat at our Lord's feet and listened to the words that proceeded out of His mouth. And when Martha complained, our Lord answers her *Mary has chosen the best part, which shall not be taken away from her* Nor does He say, *Mary has chosen the good part*, but the *best part*, that the part of Martha might be pointed at as good likewise."' Many arguments are brought forward by St Thomas to prove that a life of contemplation is the more perfect. The value of both the active and contemplative and their relative excellence may be estimated by the following reference which Benedict XIV. makes to St. Peter and St John. 'It may, it would seem, be gathered from Holy Scripture that while St. Peter loved Christ

[1] lib ii, nom 2, n 2   [2] St Luke x 42

more than the rest, yet that St. John was more beloved by Him. Accordingly, St Augustine writes: " Who is there that is not moved to inquire respecting these two Apostles, Peter and John, why it is that our Lord loves John the more, when it was St Peter who loved Him the more. For wherever John makes any mention of himself, in order that it may be secretly understood who is spoken of, he adds, *Him whom Jesus loved*, as if He loved him alone, so that he might even be known by this sign from the rest, all of whom shared our Lord's love What is it that he intended to signify by this, but that he was more loved than the others?" St Augustine himself answers this question, we find his answer expressed by St Thomas in a few words "The active life, which is so signified by St. Peter, loves God more than the contemplative life, which is signified by John. And this because it feels the trials and pains of this life more, and more ardently desires to be delivered from them, and to enter into the presence of God. But God loves the contemplative life the most, because He preserves it the more, since it does not, as the active life, come to an end with the life of the body."

3. ' Lastly, it is easily proved that the *mixed* life of the active and contemplative together is more perfect than either. Since, if each kind of life is good and perfect by itself, that which is made up of both will be more perfect. Moreover, Christ, our Lord, who is our Master and Teacher, the Example and Prototype of all virtues, thought it meet to exercise Himself most perfectly in either kind of life. And the same thing was done by the

_{3 The mixed life more perfect than either the active or contemplative}

Apostles, and occasionally' (we might say very frequently) 'by other Saints.'[1]

What is said with regard to the three ways of perfection—the purgative, illuminative, and unitive—may be said to apply to the three kinds of religious or spiritual life—that is, that they are not so entirely distinct as to exclude each other. The mixed life is made up of the contemplative and the active: but even in the active we may discover something of the contemplative, and in the contemplative, as we learn from the lives of contemplative Saints, a great deal of the active. This is especially exemplified in the lives of St. Teresa, St. Catherine of Siena, St. John of the Cross, St. Francis de Sales, St. Vincent de Paul, and many others, who were active, organizing, and devoted to the corporal as well as the spiritual works of mercy, and yet had reached the heights of contemplation and of the unitive way.

4 *The active and contemplative life exemplified in St Teresa and St John of the Cross* Cardinal Wiseman calls attention to the active and useful character of the lives of our two most celebrated mystics, St Teresa and St John of the Cross.

Speaking of St Teresa, as represented by an authentic portrait of that Saint, he says 'While no mystical Saint has ever been more idealized by artists, or represented as living in a continual swoon than St Teresa, her true portraits all represent her with strong, firmly-set, and almost masculine features, with forms and lines that denoted vigour, resolution, and strong sense. Her handwriting perfectly suggests the same conclusion

[1] Benedict XIV, 'Treatise on Heroic Virtue, vol 1, p 256 *et seq*

'Still more does the successful activity of her life, in her many struggles, under every possible disadvantage, and her final and complete triumph, strengthen this idea of her. And then her almost superhuman prudence, by which she guided so many minds, and prosperously conducted so many complicated interests and affairs, and her wonderful influence over men of high education and position, and of great powers, are further evidences of her strong, commanding nature, such as, in the world, might have claimed an almost unexampled preeminence.'

Referring to the works of St. John of the Cross, and to the Saint himself, he says 'It is not improbable that some who take up these volumes, or dip into them here and there, may conceive that they were written by a dreamy ascetic who passed his life in hazy contemplation of things unreal and impracticable. Yet it was quite the contrary. Twin Saint, it may be said, to St. Teresa, sharer in her labours and in her sufferings, St. John of the Cross actively and unflinchingly pursued their joint objects—that of reforming and restoring to its primitive purity and observance the religious Order of Carmelites, and founding through Spain a severer branch, known as discalced or barefooted Carmelites, or more briefly as Teresians.' He also gives an outline of the Saint's labours and studies, to show that he was a man of an operative mind always at work and ever in movement [1]

5. We may therefore say that the character or distinctive feature of each kind of life determines its

[5. The character or distinct feature of each kind of life]

[1] Preface to the English translation of the 'Works of St John of the Cross,' by David Lewis

name. Thus, when external works of charity are the predominant object or feature of a life or an institute, then that life or institute is called active; and when prayer and contemplation, recollection, silence and solitude, are the prevailing characteristics of a life or institute, then that life, or institute, or society is known as contemplative, and the mixed, as we have said, is made up of both, as exemplified by those Orders in the Church whose members unite in their profession and in their lives both active and contemplative duties. St Thomas, referring to the various kinds of life, says that some men are principally devoted to external actions, and others are principally intent upon contemplation, and on this account the spiritual life of man is divided into the active and contemplative.

When the mixed life is said to be more perfect than either the active or the contemplative, this is to be understood of the state or kind of life considered in the abstract and *in specie*, for, with regard to individual perfection, a man may be far more perfect either as leading an active or a contemplative life than another man who combines these two in the mixed life.

Benedict XIV reminds us of the way in which the active and contemplative states are to be understood in regard to the perfection of individuals We know that many have been enrolled in the catalogue of the Saints and the blessed who never were contemplatives. He says 'Although, according to the words of our Saviour, the contemplative life is better and more perfect than the active life, yet it does not follow that perfection consists in it alone. For but very few have time for contemplation, as is notorious, especially for infused contemplation, but a great many have time for meditation. And yet we find a great many perfect persons canonized, although in their processes there is no mention made of infused contemplation, while proof is always required of their other virtues in an heroic degree, as well as of their miracles' The same author, speaking on this subject, directs our attention to the distinction given by St. Thomas between the expression to *contemplate* and to be a *contemplative*. 'Although all,' he says, 'may ordinarily be called religious who worship God, yet they are called so more especially who, keeping themselves always from all worldly business, give up their whole life to the service of God. And so they are called contemplatives, not merely who contemplate, but who dedicate their whole life to contemplation.'[1]

[1] 'Treatise on Heroic Virtue,' English translation, vol 1, pp 270, 271

CHAPTER III

ON CONTEMPLATION IN GENERAL

I HAVE said that contemplation is the chief operation of the mystical life, and that all other favours in that life may be reduced to this. I shall therefore, in this chapter, briefly explain what is meant by contemplation before proceeding to treat of it in detail.

1. Definition of contemplation

1. There are various definitions of contemplation given by mystical writers. According to St Augustine: 'Contemplation is an agreeable admiration of perspicuous truth' According to St Bernard 'Contemplation is a certain elevation of the mind dwelling or resting upon God and tasting the joys of eternal sweetness.' Richard of St Victor defines it as 'the free insight of the mind dwelling with admiration on the sights or scenes of wisdom.' St. Thomas tells us that contemplation is the simple intuition of Divine truth, and he adds that contemplation terminates in affection or love. From all these definitions it may be gathered that three things are required for contemplation. First, that there be the simple intuition of some Divine truth; secondly, that the intuition be of such clearness as to excite admiration in the mind; thirdly, that the intuition be united with a pleasing affection towards

those objects which the soul admires. Having given these conditions, the Rev. F. V. Voss formulates the following definition. 'Mystical contemplation is the elevation of the mind to God and to Divine things, joined with an admiring and loving intuition of the same Divine things.' I do not find the *admiration* given by many authors in the definition, and some hold that it is to be regarded as a property of contemplation rather than as something belonging to its essence. We cannot, however, very well conceive contemplation in its true sense without admiration, which arises from the unusual and extraordinary clearness with which the objects of contemplation are seen by the mind, as also from the manner in which these truths are perceived, not according to the usual manner of human knowledge, but in some way rather after the manner of the Angels

Omitting further notice of this quality, let us adopt the simpler and clearer definition given by Rev. F. C. Doyle in his 'Principles of Religious Life,' with its explanation founded on the teaching of that other eminent and learned Benedictine, the Rev. D. Schram in his standard work on mystical theology. Writing on contemplative prayer, this author tells us that ' this is the uplifting of the soul to God by a simple intuition full of affection.' ' It is,' he says, ' like all prayer, in that it is an uplifting of the mind and heart to God. It differs from meditation in that it is made without reasoning, without the use of sensible images, without the *perceptible* use of the internal senses, but by a pure, quiet, simple operation of the mind which we call *intuition*. It is the outcome of meditation.' In proof of its reality, we are referred to the following texts of Scripture *O taste and see that the Lord is sweet blessed is the man who hopeth in Him,*[1] and *Blessed are the clean of heart for they shall see God.*[2] 'These texts point to an experimental knowledge of God, and to a close union of will with Him, which, while they are compatible with our state here below, are such as it is impossible' (unusual, I should say) 'to have in the lower levels of the spiritual life. The way of intuition seems unsuitable to man, and compatible only with Divine and with angelic nature; but yet it is not so, for man by intuition can know first principles and revealed truths, and this method may, by the grace of God, become his ordinary way of looking upon the truths of faith."[3]

The contemplation of the faithful Catholic is distinct from that of the philosopher

2. The contemplation we here speak of is that of the faithful Catholic It is Divine, mystical, theological, and affective, which enlightens the intellect, and inflames the will in a special and sublime manner, and above the human way of acquiring knowledge by reasoning and inference, so that this contemplation itself is called by a special right mystical theology by pious writers It is different from philosophical contemplation—namely, that by which philosophers, guided by the light of Nature, contemplate God, of Whom St. Paul speaks when he says *When they knew God, they have not glorified Him as God, or given thanks; but became vain in their thoughts, and their foolish heart was darkened*[1] It is also different from purely speculative theology, that by

[1] Ps xxxiii 9   [2] St Matt v. 8
[3] 'Principles of Religious Life,' appendix, p 532
[4] Rom i 21.

which the theologian, helped by the light of faith, contemplates God, because in the theologian, as well as in the philosopher, the contemplation is vain if it only proceeds from curiosity, and rests in the intellect, and is satisfied with knowledge without moving the affections of the heart and will. It is true that contemplation itself is the act of the intellect, yet, in order that it be really fruitful and sanctifying, the will must concur with it in many ways. This it does first as the principle which moves the intellect to contemplate. For the contemplation we speak of proceeds from charity or the love of God, which belongs to the will and is its act. Then, again, charity, or the love of God, is the end of contemplation, and here we have the will concurring with the intellect, directing the contemplation to an increase of charity and union with God. Lastly, we are told by mystical writers that joy and delight are the result of contemplation, or are concomitant with it, and these reside in the will and are its acts.

3. Father Schram takes some trouble to explain the meaning of 'simple intuition' as applied to contemplation, with almost as much minuteness as Cardinal Newman observes in the 'Grammar of Assent' in explaining the nature of assent and certitude. He shows us in the first place that simple intuition is not at variance with man's rational mode of knowledge, because it is by that a man knows without reasoning first principles, and assents to revealed truths; that ratiocination is attributed to him because it is his more frequent, and, as it were, the congenial, mode of acquiring knowledge, distinguishing his mode from that of

the Angels. Secondly he replies to the objection that simple intuition is not a judgment of reason by saying that, without going into useless philosophical questions, it is quite sufficient for the mind by one act of intuition elicited through the light and strength of grace to come to a certain decision or knowledge. To the objection that meditation leads up to contemplation, and meditation is by reasoning and reflection, he replies that meditation is the ordinary preparation for contemplation, but that contemplation itself is one act, and that an intuition of the truth proposed to the mind. Finally there is the objection that intuition is inadequate to produce certitude, taking certitude in its strict sense as a deliberate assent given after reasoning. To this the answer is, as given by Rev F. C. Doyle. 'Reason is not the only instrument capable of giving certitude to our minds. A supernatural light accompanies contemplation, and makes the soul perfectly certain of the truths which it is contemplating. For, if the light of faith can make the soul adhere with full certainty to revealed truth, why should not that same light, intensified by the gifts of the Holy Ghost, enable it to have absolute certitude about a truth which it knows by simple intuition?'[1]

The force of this assent and its certitude may be illustrated by the example of the Martyrs, whose example is typical of all other heroic Christians, as expressed by Cardinal Newman. 'If we would see what the force of simple assent can be, viewed apart from its reflex confirmation, we have but to

[1] Schram, 'Theol. Myst.,' tomus primus, p. 371. Doyle, 'Principles of Religious Life,' appendix, p. 532.

look at the generous and uncalculating energy of faith as exemplified in the primitive Martyrs, in the youths who defied the pagan tyrant, or the maidens who were silent under his tortures. It is assent, pure and simple, which is the motive cause of great achievements ; it is a confidence, growing out of instincts rather than arguments, stayed upon a vivid apprehension, and animated by a transcendent logic, more concentrated in will and in deed for the very reason that it has not been subjected to any intellectual development.'[1]

This simple intuition of contemplation is not an intuitive vision such as the blessed in heaven enjoy, but is a vision such as St. Paul describes as *seeing through a glass in a dark manner* and by the aid of created species. Neither is it always a purely intellectual vision, like those which God bestows even in this life upon some few specially exalted and privileged souls. The intuition of which we speak is the assent of the intellect given to some Divine truth which appears in such a clear light as to hold the mind captive, fixed, and immovable, gazing upon its object. If the truth be an article of faith, as is usually the case, then the assent is a true act of faith, that faith being further strengthened and enlightened by the rays of the Spirit of wisdom, so that its object is not only clearly understood, but the mind adheres to it with admiration and delight. When the object of contemplation, as may sometimes happen, is not an article of faith, then the assent is not an act of faith, but a simple assent of the mind, clear and luminous, however, by reason of

[1] 'Grammar of Assent,' p 216

the gifts of the Holy Ghost with which the contemplative soul is adorned.

<small>4. Description of contemplation by Benedict XIV</small>

4. Benedict XIV, with his usual clearness and accuracy, gives us a description of contemplation which may elucidate what others have written on the subject. He says, speaking of infused and supernatural contemplation—and his words apply to the nature of contemplation in general—that contemplation is 'a simple intellectual gazing at, together with a delicious love of, Divine things and whatsoever is revealed, proceeding from God's moving the understanding in an especial manner to gaze at, and the will to love, the things revealed, and aiding such acts by the gifts of the Holy Spirit, understanding and wisdom, together with a greatly enlightened intellect and inflamed will' He then continues to explain : ' For the gifts of understanding and wisdom are gifts of the Holy Spirit, of which the first consists in a certain light by which the intellect, when endowed with faith, understands the things that are revealed by God so clearly as to gaze at them without obscurity ; while the other, that of wisdom, consists in a certain infused quality, by which the soul, beholding the revealed object, perceives a most sweet and delicious taste in the knowledge of that truth. Such is the doctrine of St. Thomas, who says of the gift of understanding "that it is the property of understanding to know the supernatural things that lie hid in what is revealed, as it is the property of the human understanding to know the nature of the substance by the accidents, the meaning by the words, and the truth which is shadowed forth by figures and similitudes " And, speaking of the gift of wisdom, he says · " It is

fitly called wisdom, as if it were the knowledge of the wise, according to what is written in Ecclesiasticus : *The wisdom of doctrine is according to her name.*"[1] Both of these, then, come into this contemplation, and cause the objects revealed by God to be more clearly known, and more sweetly and ardently loved '[2]

I have to note, however, that we have not to limit contemplation to the gifts of understanding and wisdom as its adequate principles, for we are told that the most perfect act of contemplation is elicited by some higher principle. Neither must we understand, from the reference made in this place to the gifts of the Holy Ghost, that such gifts are limited to extraordinary and heroic actions, because, as has been stated and proved in the 'Manual of Ascetical Theology,' these gifts are always infused with sanctifying grace, and are inseparable from it, and they are therefore common to all the just.'[3]

5. Richard of St Victor, as interpreted by the Most Rev. R. Bede Vaughan in his 'Life of St. Thomas Aquinas,' considers the faculties of the soul in relation to their object in a threefold light, which he calls imagination, reason, and the intelligence. The reason, he tells us, stands between the imagination and intelligence The office of the imagination is to seize and hold sensible impressions; the reason is the instrument of discursive thought, by which we advance by way of premises and conclusions towards the truth ; the intelligence is a still higher power which, as the senses seize, by immediate apprehension, their proper objects,

[5] Distinction between thought, meditation and contemplation

---

[1] Ecclus vi 23   [2] 'Treatise on Heroic Virtue,' vol 1, p 266
[3] 'Manual of Ascetical Theology,' p 241

grasps, in an immediate manner, its proper object The intelligence is pure, inasmuch as it excels the imagination; and simple, inasmuch as it excludes processes of reasoning. He then gives the following distinction between *thought, meditation,* and *contemplation* · 'Now, to these three powers of the soul correspond three methods of knowledge thought, meditation, and contemplation—*cogitatio, meditatio,* and *contemplatio* Thought comes from the imagination, meditation from the reason, and contemplation from the intelligence. Thought wanders about here and there, without direction, slowly, as at will; meditation, with great labour of the soul, strives, by hard and difficult ways, towards the given end; contemplation is carried with freedom and great facility, wherever the power bears it, to its proper object Contemplation is seeing truth pure and naked without any cloud or shade standing in the way.'[1]

Without accepting this teaching as psychologically accurate or in accord with scholastic philosophy, which excludes the imagination from the powers of the soul, and classes it as an organic faculty, we may take the description given of thought, meditation and contemplation as showing the operations of the mind with regard to these acts, and as throwing light on the nature of contemplation as understood in mystical theology

[1] 'Life of St Thomas Aquinas,' vol 1, p. 248

CHAPTER IV

VARIOUS SPECIES OF CONTEMPLATION

1. MYSTICAL writers distinguish two kinds of contemplation, one of which is called acquired, active, or ordinary, the other called infused, passive, and extraordinary. Although the names in each group differ among themselves, they are used, however, by these writers to signify the same thing.

<small>1. Ordinary and extraordinary contemplation</small>

Benedict XIV., following Cardinal de Lauræa, adopts the terms *acquired* and *infused* to signify this general division of contemplation. Schram, on the other hand, quoting P. Reguera, uses the words *ordinary* and *extraordinary* to designate the two species of contemplation, and he considers that the other terms used mean what is more aptly expressed by these; and it will be more in accordance with the tone and spirit of this work, and of the former work of the author, on 'Ascetical Theology,' to designate the two species by the words of Schram, and according to the explanation of them given by this author.

(1) Ordinary contemplation may be defined as the elevation of the soul to God by a simple intuition full of affection which does not exceed or depart from the laws of Divine providence in the supernatural order. It can be called *acquired* inasmuch as the soul can be prepared for it, not by its own

<small>(1) Ordinary contemplation</small>

natural gifts alone, but aided by grace, and even with the aid of grace and prayer, it cannot be said to be merited except in a *congruous* sense, so that it can never be said to be due to the soul. It may be called *active* by reason of the various acts that dispose the soul for its reception. Strictly speaking, it cannot be called *natural*, for essentially it is supernatural and infused, and this is a further reason for calling it *ordinary* rather than *acquired*, because it, as well as *extraordinary* contemplation, is really and of necessity infused. This species of contemplation is that which, by the help of grace and our own industry, especially by the long and faithful exercise of meditation, may be obtained, but is never due to our own exertions or efforts. It may be called the fruit of past meditations, the reward of pious labour and industry not merited *de condigno*, but at most *de congruo*.

(2) Extraordinary contemplation is the elevation of the mind to God by a simple intuition full of affection, and by special privilege outside the ordinary laws of Divine providence in the supernatural order. Fr. Louis de Ponte explains this extraordinary contemplation. Speaking of the divers ways by which the Spirit of God guides and moves us in prayer, he says: 'The *extraordinary* way comprehends other forms of prayer more supernatural and special, which we call prayer of *quiet* or silence, with suspension, ecstasy, or rapture, and with imaginary figures of truths which are discovered, or with only an intellectual light of them, together with revelations and interior locutions, and with other innumerable means that Almighty God has to communicate Himself to souls, of which no certain

rule can be given, because they have no other rule but the teaching and direction of the Sovereign Master, who teaches it to whom He wills and how He wills."[1]

This form of contemplation is called *infused*, not in the sense that ordinary contemplation is not also infused, but in the sense that it cannot be acquired by being prepared and disposed for it as in the case of ordinary contemplation. It is in this same sense called also *passive*, and it is called *supernatural* in a comparative sense, as being more supernatural than ordinary contemplation, although it must be borne in mind that both forms are supernatural.

2. Extraordinary contemplation is accompanied, we are told, by graces *gratuitously given*, such as prophecy and miracles; and on this point both Schram and Father Doyle propose and solve some objections that serve very much to elucidate this form of contemplation 'Objection Graces gratuitously given are not necessary for extraordinary contemplation, for they are given chiefly for the edification of others Answer They are not *absolutely* requisite' Or, as Schram says : 'They are not precisely required for extraordinary contemplation, but they are required for its complement and perfection, presupposing the virtues and gifts.' 'Their primary effect or utility is not for the person to whom they are given ; nevertheless, they infuse fresh life, strengthen graces, and make the soul pleasing to God' 'Moreover,' continues Father Doyle, 'although *graces gratuitously given* do not necessarily indicate the presence of sanctity in the possessor of them, yet this does not prove that they

2. Extraordinary contemplation and the graces gratuitously given

[1] 'Introduction to Mental Prayer,' chap xi.

are not necessary for contemplation; for when ecstasies and raptures, etc., are given to sinners, they do not flow from the sanctifying operations of the Holy Spirit—they are *gratuitously given graces*, however, the contemplation of which we speak presupposes that the soul which exercises it is perfect. Hence, the origin whence it springs is not simply a gratuitously given grace, but charity and the gifts of the Holy Ghost. Objection. *Graces gratuitously given* do not make extraordinary contemplative prayer more perfect than that which is ordinary, for this latter is accompanied by sanctifying grace, which is of a more sublime nature than grace gratuitously given. Answer. Graces gratuitously given, in a secondary way, dispose the soul to a closer union with God, which fact proves that such graces are not the essence of contemplation, but only accidentally assist and perfect it *directly* in its relations to others, *indirectly* with respect to him who is in possession of it.

'Objection. There are some who say that contemplation is a gratuitously given grace. If this be true, it will be found among those enumerated by the Apostle, but no mention is made of it by him; therefore it is not a grace gratuitously given. Answer. Extraordinary contemplative prayer is not mentioned by St. Paul among the graces gratuitously given—*i.e.*, it is not mentioned *explicitly*, we grant; it is not mentioned *implicitly*, we deny, for the grace to which it may be referred is mentioned.'[1] To this Schram adds the remark that we are not

---

[1] 'Principles of Religious Life,' appendix, pp. 533, 534. Schram, vol. i, pp. 337, 338. For the explanation of grace *gratum faciens* and grace *gratis data*, see 'Sacraments Explained,' chap. i.

bound to believe that the Apostle, in his enumeration, mentions all the graces gratuitously given, but only the principal ones, as Bellarmine proves.

3. It is commonly held that the gift of contemplation may be both unitive and sanctifying, and a grace gratuitously given (*gratis data*); that is, it may sanctify the person who receives it or increase his sanctity, and it may be destined for the instruction and sanctification of others. In principle, extraordinary contemplation is of the order of graces gratuitously given, and the exterior prodigies that accompany it are directed to the edification of others. For this reason these mystical phenomena, such as visions, locutions, and revelations do not necessarily suppose sanctifying grace and merit in the persons thus favoured At the same time the separation of these gifts from sanctifying grace is very rare, and constitutes an anomaly in the supernatural order.

As a general rule, supernatural illumination of this kind is united with grace and charity, and this, too, in a very high degree Let us, however, take to heart the wise admonition of St Gregory. He says. 'The grace of contemplation is not one which is given to the highest and not to the lower ones, but oftentimes those who are greatest and those who are the least receive it, oftener those who are in retirement, sometimes even those who are married. If, then, there is no rank or condition of the faithful from which the grace of contemplation is excluded, whosoever keeps his heart within him (pure) may also be enlightened with the light of contemplation.' And a little after he says. 'Let no one glory in this grace as if he possessed some singular privilege. Let no one think that he has a private gift of the

_{3. The gift of contemplation may be both sanctifying and a gift gratuitously given}

true light, for it is often the case that, in that which he thinks he has the chief share of, another is richer than he, and one, too, of whom he thought within himself that there was no good in.'[1]

4. Points in which ordinary and extraordinary contemplations agree and differ

4. Theologians teach that ordinary and extraordinary contemplation are alike in many respects, and that in many respects they differ.

First, they agree in this, that both are the simple intuition of some Divine truth joined with the love of God.

Secondly, they agree in their objects, although extraordinary contemplation may extend to other objects and circumstances which God reveals to some contemplative souls.

Thirdly, they agree in the means—that is, the material and intellectual species by which they gaze at and know their objects.

Fourthly, they agree in the dispositions of soul usually required for contemplation, although extraordinary contemplation requires, as a rule, more excellent dispositions, namely, greater purification and cleanliness of soul, and greater splendour of virtue.

Ordinary contemplation, however, differs from extraordinary—first, in the excitation or enlivening of the *species* through which the soul perceives its object. In the ordinary contemplation the species which the soul itself forms by meditating are enlightened or enlivened by God with infused light. In extraordinary contemplation God not only stirs up and enlightens these in the mind, but He sometimes infuses new *species*, so that the soul thus

[1] Benedict XIV., 'Treatise on Heroic Virtue,' appendix, vol. i, p. 269.

illumined by a peculiar light is raised up to more sublime contemplation. Hence, it happens that by degrees and imperceptibly the soul, only at the time of prayer, arrives at ordinary contemplation and is occupied with only the truths on which it has been meditating, whilst in extraordinary contemplation the soul is suddenly raised up to it by God, and even out of prayer, so that it contemplates new truths on which it has not meditated at all. Secondly, these two forms of contemplation differ in the degree of light received and in the fervour of the affections The affections are more fervent and sweet, and the lights of the intellect more clear and more resplendent, in extraordinary than in ordinary contemplation. On account of the abundance of light and the intensity of love the soul remains fixed on the Divine objects with such enchantment that it cannot withdraw itself from them, neither can it give attention to its other acts, so that after the prayer is over it cannot remember or give any account of it The phantasy is not disturbed in this contemplation by imagination, which often happens in ordinary contemplation. It is only in extraordinary contemplation that the mind undergoes alienation from itself and its surroundings and reaches the higher grades of union from which follow raptures and ecstasies, with the loss of the use of the senses [1]

5 Benedict XIV, following the teaching and quoting the work of Cardinal Lauræa on prayer, describes how these two forms of contemplation (for which he retains the words *acquired* and *infused*) are alike and how they differ, as follows 'They are alike in certain dispositions to be found in those who

[1] Voss, 'Compend Direct Myst Scaramelli,' p 91

possess them, inasmuch as contemplatives of both sorts must be persons well exercised in the moral virtues and in the purgative way. In both are required purity of heart, or a state of grace, impulses of charity and the help of God efficaciously calling and aiding them. They differ inasmuch as infused contemplation, properly speaking, requires many more dispositions in him who contemplates than that which is acquired. It requires not only that he should have passed through the way of purgation, but, moreover, have exercised himself a long time in it, and have subjected the senses to reason by the exercise of all the moral virtues. Whereas, too, in acquired contemplation, a man, after a good deal of labour and difficulty by previous reading, reflection, or contemplation, draws himself away from other things in meditation, in order that he may gaze upon and love that which is revealed. In infused contemplation, on the other hand, after reading, or thinking of, or meditating upon some object of revelation without any labour or trouble on his part, a man throws off all thought of other things, and is raised by God to the sight, love, and desire of the object revealed. Besides, by acquired contemplation other objects are not known beyond those which were before believed by faith; but by that which is infused God not only shows those things which were already believed, but either shows them with new circumstances and perfection, or reveals new objects, by infusing into the mind new forms and appearances (species). Further, also, while ecstasy or a perfect alienation of the senses seldom happens in acquired contemplation, it frequently takes place in infused, and after an act of acquired contemplation a man may remember the things which he contemplated, and give an account of them to others, but after an act of infused contemplation he who has had it seldom remembers what he has seen, as is borne witness to by the Blessed Angela de Fulgineo, St Teresa, St Peter of Alcantara, and St John of the Cross Lastly, the forementioned theologians teach that infused contemplation is granted sometimes to the perfect, sometimes to those who are not so perfect For it is granted occasionally to beginners, and to those who are making progress, who neither of them are as yet perfect"[1]

6. After explaining the general and principal divisions of contemplation, it may be well to indicate one or two other forms or divisions given by mystical writers.

6 Some other forms or divisions of contemplation as given by Richard of St Victor

Richard of St. Victor distinguishes three sorts of contemplation The first he calls enlargement (*dilatatio*), when the vision of the soul is wider and stronger, but this is confined to the natural efforts of the soul, and does not exceed the limits of human industry, the second is elevation (*sublevatio*), when, through the influence of Divine light, the soul is carried beyond its natural capacity, still without being lifted out of the general conditions of its empirical knowledge, as expressed by Archbishop Vaughan in his 'Life of St. Thomas Aquinas',[2] the third is alienation (*alienatio*) by ecstasy, in which, through the action of Divine grace, the soul is placed in such a position that all thought of present things, all consciousness of empirical knowledge, vanishes, and the soul is wholly absorbed in the

[1] 'Treatise on Heroic Virtue,' vol 1, pp 267-269.
[2] 'Life of St. Thomas,' vol 1., p 254

vision of things Divine. The first grade results from the action of human activity; the second from the action of human activity and grace combined; the third is solely dependent upon grace. Or we should rather say that the first is natural, and the second supernatural, and this takes two forms, in one of which there is the combination and accord of grace and human industry, and in the other the Divine action subjugates the soul, and brings it into a state of sweet and fruitful passiveness. The first of these is entirely outside the scope of this work, the second, in its twofold form, appears to be much the same as the two forms of contemplation already explained, namely, the *ordinary* and the *extraordinary*

7 Cherubic and seraphic contemplation

7. Contemplation, whether ordinary or extraordinary, is subdivided into *cherubic*, or intellective, and *seraphic*, or affective. These two terms are derived from the names given the first two choirs of the Angels—the Cherubim and the Seraphim. In the Seraphim the ardour of love exceeds the light of science, although this science is also eminent. The Cherubim, who are said to possess pre-eminent science, are more distinguished by their intellectual light than by the ardour of their love, although they possess both in a perfect degree. After the example of the Angels, in contemplation the same distinction has been used to signify the lively faith and the intense charity of contemplative souls, according as the one or the other predominates In a case where the intellectual light of a lively faith is greater than the ardour of charity, the contemplation is called *cherubic*, or intellective; but when the ardour of charity prevails, the contemplation is called *seraphic*, or affective. In the first the love does not

attain the proportions of the science, and in the second the science does not attain the proportions of the love, although science and love are found in both.

It is quite clear that a person may be known better than he is loved, and a person may be loved better than he is known, in the natural order of things and with regard to human beings, and this is true also with regard to God and Divine truth. It is not true, however, to say that an act of contemplation can exist by the sole adhesion of the will without any foreknowledge of the object, because, according to sound philosophy and sound reason, we can have no act of the will without the previous knowledge of the intellect. The object of the will is good as apprehended by the intellect, and it is for this reason that the will is called a rational appetite, and hence the common axiom *Nihil volitum quin præcognitum.*

Although the soul cannot naturally love what it does not know, it can, however, supernaturally love God intensely and with very great ardour, even though its knowledge of Him may not be great nor very distinct. A little knowledge acquired by the light of reason suffices for great love. This is proved from experience, because very many simple, ignorant people love God very much, and many learned and wise people love Him very little. Knowing God by faith, many give Him their whole heart, and dedicate themselves entirely to His service, without troubling themselves about speculative and curious questions concerning Him and His attributes. We shall have to consider this question again when we treat of the operations of the intellect and of the will in contemplation.

CHAPTER V

THE OBJECTS OF CONTEMPLATION

The primary object of contemplation. Its secondary objects enumerated

1. By the object of contemplation we are to understand the eternal truth which the soul, penetrated with the light from heaven, can contemplate with affections of admiration and love. The first and principal object of contemplation is God Himself, the Eternal Truth, and creatures, inasmuch as they lead us to the knowledge and the love of God, may be considered as the secondary object of contemplation. St. Thomas teaches that a thing may belong to the contemplative life in a twofold way, one principally, the other secondarily. The contemplation of Divine truth belongs principally to the contemplative life, because it is the kind of contemplation which is the end of all human life. But inasmuch as, according to the words of St Paul, *The invisible things of Him from the creation of the world are clearly seen, being understood by the things that are made*,[1] it so happens that the contemplation of the Divine effects belongs to the contemplative life, for they lead a man to the knowledge of their cause—God.[2] And Suarez in his treatise on religion teaches that theological contemplation is primarily and of itself occupied about God, and secondarily

[1] Rom i 20   [2] 'Sum Theol,' 2, 2, q. 180, a. 4

[48]

about Divine things or the works and benefits of God, or their effects in so far as they impart the knowledge of Him. Hence contemplation, whether ordinary or extraordinary, may be employed about the following objects, which, for the sake of clearness, I here enumerate before considering each in particular ·

(1) God Himself in Unity and Trinity; His attributes in general and in particular.

(2) The Mystery of the Incarnation and the Sacred Humanity of Christ.

(3) The Mystery of the Holy Eucharist.

(4) The Blessed Virgin, the Angels and Saints.

(5) All the supernatural works of God and all Christian truths.

(6) All creatures as viewed by the eyes of faith, so that by considering them we can contemplate God in His goodness and providence.

2. We must bear in mind that contemplation is the simple intuition or view of the object accompanied with affections of admiration and love. We have to examine in what manner, therefore, God is said to be the object of contemplation, or how God is seen and loved by contemplative souls. God is the object of the soul's natural knowledge and natural love He is also the object of our faith and of supernatural love or charity, according to all theologians. He is the primary object of contemplation. The very notion of God is sufficient to show us how He can be and is the object of contemplation. God, as known to all theists and to all Christians by the light of faith as well as by the light of reason, is a God Who is numerically One, Who is Personal; the Author, Sustainer, and Finisher of all things, the

God and His attributes as the objects of contemplation

Life of law and order, the Moral Governor; One Who is supreme and sole; like Himself, unlike all things besides Himself, which all are but His creatures, distinct from and independent of them all, One Who is self-existing, absolutely infinite, Who has ever been and ever will be, to Whom nothing is past or future; Who is all perfection and the fulness and archetype of every possible excellence, the Truth itself, Wisdom, Love, Justice, Holiness; One Who is All-powerful, All-knowing, Omnipresent, Incomprehensible. These are some of the distinctive prerogatives which we have to ascribe unconditionally and unreservedly to the great Being Whom we call our God, and it is to such a Being we give our notional as well as our real assent—that is, to Him as to the Eternal Truth. Cardinal Newman, after describing the notion of God in the manner given above, then asks: 'Can I attain to any more vivid assent to the Being of a God than that which is given merely to notions of intellect? Can I enter with a personal knowledge into the circle of truths which make up that great thought? Can I rise to what I have called an imaginative apprehension of it? Can I believe as if I saw? Since such a high assent requires a present experience or memory of the fact, at first sight it would seem as if the answer must be in the negative: for how can I assent as if I saw unless I have seen? But no one in this life can see God.' 'Yet I conceive,' he says, 'a real assent as possible.'[1] He speaks of real here according to his own philosophical distinction between real and notional assents, and he proceeds to show how

---

[1] 'Grammar of Assent,' pp. 101, 102

3. This same author, after developing the manner in which the real apprehension of a Divine Sovereign and Judge is derived from the special feeling of conscience which follows on the commission of what we call right and wrong, describes as follows the image of God as it exists in the soul of a religious child. 'Supposing he' (the child) 'has offended his parents, he will, all alone and without effort, as if it were the most natural of acts, place himself in the presence of God, and beg Him to set him right with them. Let us consider how much is contained in this simple act First, it involves the impression on the mind of an unseen Being with Whom he is in immediate relation, and that relation so familiar that he can address Him whenever he chooses; next, of One Whose goodwill towards him he is assured of, and can take for granted—nay, Who loves him better, and is nearer to him, than his parents; further, of One Who can hear him wherever he happens to be, and Who can read his thoughts, for his prayer need not be vocal; lastly, of One Who can effect a critical change in the state of feeling of others towards him. That is, we shall not be wrong in holding that this child has in his mind the image of an Invisible Being, Who exercises a particular providence among us, Who is present everywhere, Who is heart-reading, heart-changing, ever accessible, open to impetration. Moreover, this image brought before his mental vision is the image of One Who by implicit threat and promise commands certain things which he, the same child, coincidently, by the same act of his mind, approves; which receives the adhesion of his moral sense and judgment as right and good. It is the

The notion and image of God present in the soul described by Cardinal Newman

image of One Who is good, inasmuch as enjoining and enforcing what is right and good, and Who, in consequence, not only excites in the child hope and fear—nay (it may be added), gratitude towards Him, as giving a law and maintaining it by reward and punishment—but kindles in him love towards Him, as giving him a good law, and therefore as being good Himself, for it is the property of goodness to kindle love, or, rather, the very object of love is goodness, and all those distinct elements of the moral law which the typical child, whom I am supposing, more or less consciously loves and approves—truth, purity, justice, kindness, and the like—are but shapes and aspects of goodness. And having in his degree a sensibility towards them all, for the sake of them all he is moved to love the Lawgiver Who enjoins them upon him. And, as he can contemplate these qualities and their manifestations under the common name of goodness, he is prepared to think of them as indivisible, correlative, supplementary of each other in one and the same Personality, so that there is no aspect of goodness which God is not; and that the more because the notion of a perfection embracing all possible excellencies, both moral and intellectual, is especially congenial to the mind, and there are, in fact, intellectual attributes, as well as moral, included in the child's image of God as above represented. It is an image of the good God, good in Himself, good relatively to the child, with whatever incompleteness. It is certain, too, that, whether it grows brighter and stronger, or, on the other hand, is dimmed, disturbed, or obliterated, depends on each of us individually, and on our circumstances. Conscience is a connecting principle between the creature and his Creator, and the firmest hold of theological truths is gained by habits of personal religion. When men begin all their works with the thought of God, acting for His sake and to fulfil His will, when they ask His blessing on themselves and their life, pray to Him for the object they desire, and see Him in the event, whether it be according to their prayers or not, they will find everything that happens tend to confirm them in the truths about Him which live in their imagination, varied and unearthly as those truths may be Then they are brought into His presence as that of a Living Person, and are able to hold converse with Him, and that with a directness and simplicity, with a confidence and intimacy, *mutatis mutandis*, which we use towards no earthly superior ; so that it is doubtful whether we realize the company of our fellow-men with greater keenness than those favoured minds are able to contemplate and adore the unseen, incomprehensible Creator.'[1]

4. Although Cardinal Newman represents the image of God as it is viewed by the mind of a religious child, I think that image may also serve as representing the view of God before the mind of the contemplative soul advanced in perfection. It is necessary, however, to show further how this view of God may be adapted to contemplation. The intellect, which is the highest faculty of the soul, enlightened by faith, fixes its attention upon God. With the highest and the keenest vision of this intelligence adorned by faith, the soul contem-

[4. How this image may be adapted to contemplation]

[1] 'Grammar of Assent, p. 112 *et seq*.

plates God, not by parts or the particular forms of His attributes, but altogether and by a universal concept, for such is the capacity of the intellect, that it is not satisfied with the knowledge of one attribute, but seeks to know God as a whole, and, although it can know God only in a finite manner, it desires to know Him according to His entire Being. And, as the intellect is moved by its object, and especially by Him Who gave it the power of understanding, so the will is moved by its object—namely, that which is good or the *good*, and therefore by Him Who has given it the power of willing. The will can be moved as by its object by any good, but it cannot be sufficiently and efficaciously satisfied by any other good but God, because the passive power of the will extends to the universal good, as the passive power or capacity of the intellect has for its object Being in its universality. God alone is the universal Being and the universal Good, and therefore He alone can fill and satisfy the whole mind and heart of man. In the contemplation which is practised through the light of faith having God for its object, we find the three qualities required by human philosophy, as well as by theology, for perfect contemplation, namely, the act of the highest faculty of the soul, in the most noble habit or virtue, and having the most noble object. The intellect is the faculty employed in contemplation. Its act proceeds from the intelligence enlightened by faith, and it has for its object God, not as seen in creatures or in created images, but in Himself, through the medium of faith or the infused supernatural light. In this contemplation we find all the circumstances which our Lord assigned when He said: *But thou, when thou shalt pray, enter into thy chamber, and, having shut the door, pray to thy Father in secret, and thy Father Who seeth in secret will repay thee.*[1] By the words *enter into thy chamber* is meant the secret and hidden recess of the mind which is entered by the act of secret contemplation, because the mind should in prayer withdraw from external things; and *closing the door*—that is, excluding every worldly and earthly affection by shutting the exterior senses — *Pray to thy Father*—that is, as expressed elsewhere, *in spirit and in truth* Pray not for worldly things, because the soul taken up with such things is far from God Pray in the sense in which St. Jerome speaks when he says · *Aliud est narrare nescienti, aliud rogare scientem. Illi judicium, hic obsequium.* It is one thing to narrate to one who does not know, and another to ask one who knows. The former is opinion or judgment, the latter service. *Pray in secret*—that is, in the depths of the heart, not in a manner to be seen by men, or not necessarily by the sound of the voice, or the elevation of the hands, or the eyes, or other external signs *And thy Father*, etc.—here we have the promise. Our heavenly Father, Who sees in secret and even into the inmost soul, will repay—not merely give, but give as a reward of the act or exercise of prayer or contemplation

5. Contemplation has for its object not only God viewed as a whole, but also His various attributes through which He reveals Himself, such are His simplicity, His greatness, His wisdom, providence, immensity, justice, mercy, and beatitude He

_{5 The attributes of God the object of contemplation}

[1] St. Matt vi 6

appears to the contemplative soul especially as life, truth, beauty, goodness, sanctity, and as absolute perfection. Under this last aspect, as embracing all His attributes, it is that He is viewed, that He is gazed upon and enjoyed by the soul in contemplation. A passage from St. Bernard is often quoted to show the different ways in which God manifests Himself in contemplation 'Those who with Mary give themselves to God alone, considering what God is in the world, what He is in men, in Angels, in Himself, in the reprobate, comtemplate or perceive by the gift of contemplation that God is the Ruler and Providence of the world, the Liberator and Helper of men, the Joy and Splendour of the Angels, in Himself He is the beginning and end of all things, an object of terror and horror to the reprobate; admirable in creatures, amiable in men, desirable in the Angels, incomprehensible in Himself, and intolerable in the reprobate.'

According to mystical writers, the soul is raised up to this knowledge of God by a twofold process signified by the words *affirmation* and *negation*, or, as expressed by scholastics, *position* and *subtraction* (per *positionem* and *ablationem*). Although this particular point has reference to the manner in which the soul may form its notions of God, and cannot be understood as a twofold process of contemplation — for we have seen that contemplation proper consists in the simple intuition or view of God—nevertheless the twofold process here mentioned is referred to by St. Denis the Areopagite, and after him by Saints and Doctors generally who have written upon this subject, as bearing upon contemplation and as illustrating its operation, even whilst we admit that it is also common to ordinary theological science as well as to ordinary meditation. The first process, that by way of affirmation or position, consists in attributing to God all the perfections that we see in creatures, and that in an infinite degree. In the second process, considering in all creatures their finite and limited character, we conclude or come to form the idea of God by the negation of all limits and bounds, and consider the Divine Being in His essential attributes of infinitude or being of Himself. The Pseudo-Dionysius is mentioned as the first author who proposed and followed the way of negation as the most direct, the most efficacious, and most perfect of giving to the mind a true notion of God. I may, however, say that very many, like myself, may prefer the way of affirmation as somewhat more tangible and real, and I think no less efficacious, and in that case they may use it in their meditations and thoughts of God, but not necessarily to the exclusion of the way of negation ; both seem to me to go hand-in-hand and to be inseparable one from the other. Both ways are illustrated by the image of a king, which may be produced either by painting or by sculpture, either as a picture or as a statue. The painter produces the image by addition, the sculptor by subtraction. In this twofold way the concept of God may be formed in the mind. First, as it were, by painting, when we attribute to Him, as if they were so many colours, the perfections of creatures. Secondly, after the manner of a sculptor, when we remove from Him, as so many superfluous particles, all involving any imperfection that we have ascribed or attributed to Him.[1]

[1] Ribet, 'La Mystique Divine,' vol 1, chap ix

6 The mystery of the Blessed Trinity the object of contemplation

6. The contemplation of the Most Holy Trinity has for its foundation faith. Schram, in giving an outline of the practice of the contemplation of the Holy Trinity, first states the doctrine of our holy faith in regard to this mystery. Following his example, we may also state the doctrine, and this cannot be better expressed in English than in the words of Cardinal Newman : ' It is the belief of Catholics about the Supreme Being that this essential characteristic of His Nature (namely, that He is a Personal God) is reiterated in three distinct ways or modes, so that the Almighty God, instead of being One Person only, which is the teaching of natural religion, has three Personalities, and is at once, according as we view Him (and in reality) in the one or the other of them, the Father, the Son, and the Spirit—a Divine Three Who bear towards each Other the several relations which those names indicate, and are in that respect distinct from each Other, and in that alone

'This is the teaching of the Athanasian Creed viz, that the One Personal God, Who is not a logical or physical unity, but a living *Monas*, more really one even than an individual man, is One. He (*unus* not *unum*, because of the inseparability of His Nature and Personality)—He at once is Father, is Son, is Holy Ghost, each of Whom is that One Personal God in the fulness of His Being and attributes ; so that the Father is all that is meant by the word "God," as if we knew nothing of Son or of Spirit ; and in like manner the Son and the Spirit are each by Himself all that is meant by the word, as if the other Two were unknown ; moreover, that by the word "God" is meant nothing over and above what is meant by "the Father," or by "the Son," or by "the Holy Ghost", and that the Father is in no sense the Son, nor the Son the Holy Ghost, nor the Holy Ghost the Father. Such is the prerogative of the Divine Infinitude, that that One and Single Personal Being, the Almighty God, is really Three, while He is absolutely One.

'Indeed, the Catholic dogma may be summed up in this very formula, on which St Augustine lays so much stress, *Tres et Unus*, not merely *Unum*; hence, that formula is the keynote, as it may be called, of the Athanasian Creed In that Creed we testify to the *Unus Increatus*, to the *Unus Immensus, Omnipotens, Deus*, and *Dominus*, yet each of the Three also is by Himself *Increatus, Immensus, Omnipotens*, for each is that One God, though each is not the other, each as is intimated by *Unus Increatus*, is the One Personal God of natural religion."[1]

This author then goes on to show that the doctrine of the Trinity is not only of a notional character, but is the object of real apprehension, and that it belongs not only to theology, but to the real faith and devotion of the individual, and I may add, therefore, that the mystery forms the object of the soul's contemplation. Then, as Schram says, in contemplative souls, whilst they view this mystery under the shadow of faith, helped by the light of theology, there is sometimes granted to them a clear light, a light warm, resplendent, peace-giving, and pleasant, which represents this hidden mystery in a most lively manner; moreover, in it, as in a Divine mirror, are beheld many new truths, many Divine secrets, very many mysteries, and very many

[1] 'Grammar of Assent,' pp 124, 125

perfections, so that by one simple intuition or view the soul is suspended in admiration and delight ; it becomes inflamed, interiorly changed, and perfected.[1] This St. Teresa testifies of herself in her life. She says : 'As I was once reciting the Creed of St. Athanasius, *Quicumque Vult,* I was given to understand the manner in which there was only One God in Three Persons, and in so clear a way that I was both comforted and encouraged exceedingly. This did me a very great deal of good for increasing my knowledge concerning the greatness of God and His wonders. And now, when I think and speak of the Most Holy Trinity, it seems as if I knew something of the mystery, and this gives me great pleasure.'[2]

7. Cardinal Newman's estimate of the Athanasian Creed.

7. I may be excused for inserting in this place another quotation from Cardinal Newman, showing his estimate of the Athanasian Creed, that may be of some advantage both to contemplative souls and to others in their devotion to the Blessed Trinity : ' It must be recollected especially that the Athanasian Creed has sometimes been called the *Psalmus Quicumque.* It is not a mere collection of notions, however momentous. It is a psalm or hymn of praise, of confession, and of profound, self-prostrating homage, parallel to the canticles of the elect in the Apocalypse. It appeals to the imagination quite as much as to the intellect. It is the war-song of faith with which we warn ourselves, then each other, and then all those who are within its hearing, and the hearing of the Truth, Who our God is, and how we worship Him, and how vast our responsi-

---

[1] Schram, 'Theol. Myst.,' vol. i, p. 398.
[2] 'Life of St. Teresa,' chap. xxxix.

bility will be if we know what to believe and yet believe it not. It is

> '"The Psalm that gathers in one glorious lay
> All chants that e'er from heaven to earth found way,
> Creed of the Saints, and Anthem of the Blest,
> And calm-breathed warning of the kindliest love
> That ever heaved a wakeful mother's breast"

'For myself I have ever felt it as the most simple and sublime, the most devotional formulary to which Christianity has given birth, more so even than the *Veni Creator* and the *Te Deum*.'[1]

[1] 'Grammar of Assent,' p. 133

CHAPTER VI

THE OBJECTS OF CONTEMPLATION (*continued*)

WE have to continue in this chapter the explanation of other mysteries and truths that may be the object of contemplation; amongst these we have to consider in the first place the mystery of the Incarnation and the Sacred Humanity of Christ

[1] The mystery of the Incarnation and the Sacred Humanity of Christ the objects of contemplation

1 False mystics would exclude the Sacred Humanity of Christ from the field of contemplation as unworthy of the purity and sublimity of this Divine operation. Thus, according to the Beguards, the perfect should abstain from all sign of reverence towards the Body of our Saviour at the elevation of the host and of the chalice during the Holy Sacrifice of the Mass, and they considered it an imperfection to descend from the heights of contemplation in order to occupy the mind with the consideration of the Holy Eucharist and the mystery of the Passion These errors were condemned by Clement V. Then we have the following proposition of Molinos condemned by Innocent XI. in 1687 'We should not elicit acts of love towards the Blessed Virgin, the Saints, or the humanity of Christ, because, as these objects are sensible, so also is the love towards them.' This Michael Molinos, together with Francis Malavallus, may be regarded as the chief exponent

of the sect known as Quietists. By the Bull of Innocent XI., November 20, 1687, sixty-eight propositions of Michael Molinos were condemned ; and by a decree of the same Pontiff, April 1, 1688, a book of Francis Malavallus, entitled ' Pratique facile pour élever l'Âme à la Contemplation,' was condemned. Let us leave Quietism and its absurd and detestable errors for the present; it was necessary to refer to them in this place before treating of the sacred humanity of Christ, the Blessed Virgin, and the Saints as the objects of contemplation.

That it is right and profitable to contemplate the humanity of Christ, and especially His sacred Passion, we learn from the example and the words of St Paul Speaking of the visions and revelations made to him by Christ our Lord, as the result, it would seem, of contemplating Him in His Sacred Humanity, he says *If I must glory (it is not expedient indeed.) but I will come to the visions and the revelations of the Lord*, etc [1] And again *For I judged not myself to know anything among you, but Jesus Christ, and Him crucified.*[2]

We have also other texts of Scripture to show that in knowing God by contemplation we need not exclude the humanity of Christ. Christ as man, even is distinctly proposed for our consideration, according to the words of the Eternal Father. *This is My beloved Son, hear Him,*[3] and those other words of our Divine Saviour Himself *'Now this is eternal life: That they know Thee, the only true God, and Jesus Christ, Whom Thou hast sent.*[4]

Schram shows us the practice of contemplation on

[1] 2 Cor xii 1   [2] 1 Cor ii 2
[3] St Luke ix 35   [4] St John xvii 4

the mystery of the Incarnation. 'The contemplation of this mystery (1) has for its foundation faith, by which we are taught that the Son of God was made man in the womb of the Blessed Virgin Mary, hypostatically uniting the two natures, Divine and human, in the one Divine Person which supplies the place of the human personality and subsistence; that therefore in Christ there are two integral natures, but not two persons nor two sons The same faith teaches us that the actions of Christ are *Theandric*, that is, Divinely human; that He suffered as man and arose from the dead as God. (2) Theology confirms these truths, and explains and illustrates them in some way by various examples. (3) On these two fundamental truths meditation may be made effectively, with affection, and constantly. (4) To these truths, believed by faith, thought out by meditation with suitable reflections and affections, God suddenly imparts the light of contemplation, and diffuses it, bright and shining, into the understanding, through which it passes into the will, representing these truths in a new and admirable manner, and causes a knowledge so lively, quick, clear, and pleasing in the soul that the God-man draws and sustains the heart to Himself and in Himself, inflaming it with sweet contemplation and tender love. The soul thus superabounds with affections; it desires, loves, hears, and tastes in a Divine manner. Then faith is vivified, hope is strengthened, charity is inflamed, and all the moral virtues receive a fresh increase and renewed excellence. Very often Christ Jesus is represented as an infant, sometimes as preaching, at other times as crucified and dying upon the Cross, or in some other manner; so that within us may be excited affections of the moral virtues, such as compunction, patience, humility, sorrow, fear, confusion at the thought of His infancy, His life, His Passion and death; and thus souls are led to His imitation.'[1]

It is not necessary to give extracts from the Fathers in proof of our doctrine. Reason itself shows us that the humanity of Christ is a worthy object of contemplation. It is hypostatically or personally united to the Divine Word. It is sufficient to excite in the soul the highest admiration and love on that account. What can be more worthy of admiration than to see God clothed in our weak human nature, God descended into the very abyss of humiliation, God wounded, treated with the utmost opprobrium, and undergoing death amidst the scenes of Calvary? As expressed by St. Leo, of all the works of God which can attract the mind and affect it with admiration, there is none that can delight it more in human contemplation or be so profitable as the Passion of our Saviour. How can the flames of Divine love be better enkindled in the soul than by the contemplation of Him *Who for us men and for our salvation descended from heaven and became incarnate?*—than by contemplating Him Who was crucified for us under Pontius Pilate, suffered, and was buried? It was this thought that elicited the affectionate expression of St. Ignatius: 'My love is crucified . . . Believe me, that I love Jesus since He first loved me and delivered Himself for me.' 'In what,' says St. Bernard, 'is it more apparent than in Thy wounds that

---

[1] Schram, 'Theol. Myst.,' vol. 1, p. 398

Thou, O Lord, art sweet and and meek and most merciful.'[1]

The pious Blosius, speaking of meditating on the Passion, expresses what may serve also for the purpose of contemplation, and it seems to have been his own method of prayer. He advises persons of good will, without much discoursing, to represent to the mind any mystery to which the soul has an affection (as our Lord's agony, or *Ecce Homo*, or His dereliction on the Cross, etc.), and to regard Him in such a state with as much tenderness of affection as may be, exercising short acts of love, compassion, gratitude, etc. Moreover, he advises a person to endeavour (yet without much straining or force used) to preserve this object present to the mind all the day after, and to perform the daily employments as in our Lord's presence. By this means a soul will come well prepared with a tenderness of heart to her recollection, and so will have little need to spend time in employing the understanding.

[note: The Passion of Christ the object of contemplation]

2. I may be permitted to give an extract from Hilton's 'Scale of Perfection' that may further show how the sacred humanity of Christ, and especially the mysteries of His Passion as the subject of meditation, may bear upon and serve the soul in contemplation through the action of the Holy Ghost

'Sometimes after labour and exercise, and sometimes together with labour upon a man who has been defiled with sins, or upon another who, by the grace of God, hath been kept in innocency, our Lord bestoweth the gift of meditating on His sacred

[1] Voss, 'Compend Direct Myst Scaramelli,' append

humanity, His birth, His Passion, and on the compassion of our Lady, St. Mary. When this meditation is made by the help of the Holy Ghost, then is it right, and profitable, and grace-bestowing And the way to know that it is so made is this When thou art stirred up to a meditation in God, and thy thoughts are suddenly drawn off from all worldly and carnal things, and thou thinkest that thou seest in thy soul the Lord Jesus in a bodily form as He was on earth, and how He was taken by the Jews and bound as a thief, beaten and despised, scourged and condemned to death; and how humbly He bore the Cross upon His shoulders, and how cruelly He was nailed thereon; also when thou seest the crown of thorns upon His head, and the sharp spear which pierced Him to the heart, and in the spiritual sight feelest thy heart stirred up to such great compassion and pity for thy Lord Jesus that thou mournest, and weepest, and criest with all thy might of body and soul, wondering at the goodness, the love, the patience, and the meekness of thy Lord Jesus, that He would for so sinful a wretch as thou art suffer so much pain, and, nevertheless, thou feelest so much goodness and mercy to be in Him that thy heart riseth up into a love and joy and gladness in Him, with many sweet tears, having great trust for the forgiveness of thy sins and of the salvation of thy soul by the virtue of this precious Passion—when, I say, the meditation of Christ's Passion, or any other act of His humanity, is thus wrought in thy heart by such a spiritual sight, accompanied by devout affection answerable thereto, know well that it is not of thy own working, nor is it the will nor the work of an evil spirit, but it is done by grace of the Holy Ghost, for it is an opening of the spiritual eye upon the humanity of Christ . . . and it is right and a great help towards the destruction of great sins, and a good way to come to virtues, and so to the comtemplation of the Godhead. For a man cannot come to the spiritual light in contemplating Christ's Godhead unless he be first exercised in his imagination with bitterness and compassion, and in steadfast thought upon His humanity. Thus St Paul did, and therefore he saith *I judged not myself to know anything amongst you, but Jesus Christ, and Him crucified.*[1] As if he had said, My knowledge and my faith are only in the Passion of Christ, and therefore he saith also *God forbid that I should glory save in the Cross of our Lord Jesus Christ*[2] And, nevertheless, immediately after he says, *We preach Christ crucified*, and subjoins, *We preach unto them that are called Christ, the power of God and the wisdom of God*,[3] as if he had said, I first preached of the humanity and Passion of Christ, but now I preach to you of the Godhead, that Christ is the power of God and the endless wisdom of God.'[4]

Objections to this doctrine answered

3. One or two objections have been made to the doctrine which teaches that the humanity of Christ is the object of contemplation. One of these is that contemplation consists in the simple intuition of God ; therefore the humanity of Christ cannot be its object, but, rather, belongs to meditation which disposes a person for contemplation The short answer to this is that the contemplation of God is

[1] 1 Cor ii 2   [2] Gal vi 14   [3] 1 Cor i 23, 24
[4] 'The Scale of Perfection,' edited by Rev R Guy, O S B, p 54 *et seq*

the primary and principal object of contemplation, but this does not exclude a secondary object, to wit, the humanity of Christ. Another objection is that perfect contemplation abstracts from everything sensible, and therefore the humanity of Christ, being sensible, cannot be its object. This may be denied entirely, as things sensible can be, and are, the object of contemplation, inasmuch as by their consideration and through them we can contemplate.

4. Father Baker, in his admirable treatise on internal prayer, proposes the question—whether meditation on the Passion may be left off by a contemplative soul, and gives us some useful instruction that may serve to remove all misunderstanding on the matter, and which may also serve to show us in a clearer light the manner in which this meditation may come into all contemplation. He says: 'There are spiritual authors who, in persuading souls in due time to quit the exercises of the understanding for those of the will, always make an exception or reservation, to wit, the meditation on the Passion of our Lord.' This, say they, is never to be set aside, but will be a subject fit for the contemplation of the most perfect. What an ingratitude it would be to God, say they, and what a neglect of our soul's good, purposely to forbear a frequent meditation of this mystery, the ground of all our happiness, the root of all merit, the supremest testimony of Divine love towards us, the most inviting and winning object of love from us to God, the terror of all our spiritual enemies,' etc. 'This,' he tells us, 'is the position of many spiritual authors, and particularly of Father Benet Canfield.' A position, I hope, that may always be maintained by all devout souls.

⁴ Instruction of Father Baker upon this subject

Although Father Baker himself does not join in this position, nevertheless he explains his own position in a manner which does not exclude the Passion as the subject of contemplation, but, rather, excludes the necessity of discursive meditation upon it in the case of advanced souls. He explains himself as follows 'As for the mystery of the Passion, it does doubtless deserve all the titles given unto it, but yet souls are not to be discouraged if they find in themselves a disability to meditate on it, whether this disability proceed from the natural temper of the internal senses or from abundance of affections in the heart, that cannot expect, because they do not need, curiously to search motives from the understanding and discourse; neither is it to be supposed that such persons, exercising immediate acts of the will towards God without discoursing on the Passion, are therefore bereaved of the true (yea, only true) exercise of our Lord's Passion. On the contrary, in such exercises of the will is contained the virtue of all precedent meditations. Neither are the persons driven to the pains and expense of time in finding out reasons and motives to raise their affections to our Lord, but immediately, and without more ado, suffer the affections to flow; and they do far more truly, efficaciously, and profitably exercise, and, as it were, exemplify the Passion itself, and this in two manners, viz (1) in their internal prayer, wherein they produce the same affections and acts of love, humility, and patience of which our Lord gave them a pattern in His Passion, (2) in their external doings, on occasions really practising the same virtues (which are proper to the Passion) with far more perfection in virtue of such prayer than they could by meditation, and so do show themselves to be more true disciples of His.

'This Divine object, therefore, is far from being lost or forgotten by such proceeding in prayer—yea, it is in a far more noble manner both commemorated and imitated; and, surely, to tie the soul generally in recollections to a particular curious reflection on the circumstances belonging to our Lord's Passion would be as if one would oblige a person, that can read perfectly and with one glance of his eye join a whole sentence together, to make a distinct and express reflection on each letter, syllable, and word. Such a framing and multiplying of images would only serve to obscure the mind and cool the affections.'

With regard to sensible things being the objects of contemplation, the same author shows us well how this can be the case, and illustrates it by the example of the Saints in heaven. He says: 'When souls come to be perfect, they will be in such a state that the express consideration of this (namely, the humanity or the Passion of Christ) or any other good sensible object will be no impediment at all to their higher exercises; yea, it will very efficaciously advance the soul in them, and this is after perfect contemplation is attained to; for then the imagination is so rectified and so perfectly subjected to the superior soul that it will not only not obscure or distract, but, on the contrary, will with great readiness help to make contemplation more pure and clear. Then a view of the humanity of our Lord will drive the soul more deeply into the Divinity, as we see that the glorified Saints, without the least distraction to their vision of God—yea, surely, with an addition to the perfection of it—do in their thanksgiving reflect on the humanity and Passion of our Saviour, saying: *Dignus est Agnus qui occisus est*, etc.'[1]

5. The Holy Eucharist the object of contemplation

5. The same reasons that prove the humanity of Christ and His sacred Passion to be the objects of contemplation apply also to the Holy Eucharist. How in practice the Holy Eucharist is the object of contemplation is clearly explained by Schram, who quotes on this subject Godinez:

'The contemplation of the mystery of the Holy Eucharist (1) supposes for its foundation faith, that faith by which we believe that, when the words of consecration are pronounced by the priest in the Mass, the substance of bread and wine are changed into the Body and Blood of Christ, the species or accidents of bread and wine only remaining (2) Theology confirms and explains and defends these and other mysteries of the Holy Eucharist for those who make it their study. (3) Thereupon God enkindles in the souls of contemplatives the light of contemplation which represents the manner and design by which the Body of Christ exists under the Sacramental species, as a king on his throne with a curtain or veil intervening, as a glorious sun shaded by the passing clouds, as a fountain of Paradise hidden by the leaves of the Sacramental species, from which issue forth four rivers of grace, of mercy, of charity and piety, to irrigate, delight, and fructify the Church and the hearts of the faithful who drink of the waters Each contemplation represented after this manner may sometimes be of such force as to ravish the soul with admiration at the sight of these inventions and plans of Divine

---

[1] 'Holy Wisdom,' by the Ven Father Baker, p 422 *et seq*

love. Then the soul rejoices exceedingly, and, inflamed with the ardent fire of that Divine love, it is touched deeply and moved to affections of gratitude With how great facility does it not now believe that about which before it hesitated or in a way doubted ! With what great certitude does it not now embrace what it does not understand ! How clearly does it not understand truths impervious to human reason ! Faith implants its roots so deeply into the soul that it would elect to die a thousand times for any revealed truth; although men and Angels might rise up against it, these could not move it in the least from one jot or tittle of the truths it believes so firmly. In this perfection of the intellect the will does not remain idle, but burns with love and adores with veneration and with fear. It is terrified by the greatness of the Majesty which it adores, loves, admires, thanks, and magnifies with its utmost power and purity. The soul also humbles itself, and, as it were, astonished at the greatness of this gift by which God gives Himself incarnate, and in this Sacrament as the food of our souls it becomes unable to express itself either by internal or external speech, but endeavours, by its affections and its works, to render thanks for this great benefit and all the blessings that come to itself and to the world through the Blessed Sacrament By these and other secrets that cannot be expressed in words, the soul is employed and sustained in this kind of contemplation.'[1]

Our Divine Lord has graciously made known to the world how pleasing this contemplation of the Holy Eucharist is to Him by the marvellous

[1] Schram, 'Theol Myst,' vol 1, p 402

apparitions narrated in the lives of the Saints. We read that our Lord has appeared to them in one form or another in the Blessed Sacrament. He appeared in the guise of an Infant in the time of St. Louis of France, who refused to go into the chapel to see the vision because he said miracles were not needed by those who already believed. St. Veronica of Binasco saw Him with her bodily eyes, all environed with Angels. She saw at the same time, above the chalice, something which shone with a marvellous brightness, but she could not distinguish what it was. Vanhem, the Cistercian, saw in the Host the Infant Jesus, holding in His hand a crown of gold adorned with precious stones. He was whiter than snow, His countenance serene, and His eyes sparkling. Similar things are related of St Angela of Foligno, Domenica del Paradiso, and many others Our Lord often appeared in the Blessed Sacrament to St Catherine of Siena and under different forms. But she almost always saw Angels holding a veil of gold, the symbol of the mystery, and in the midst a Host with the semblance of an Infant. Sometimes she saw the Angels and Saints adoring our Lord on the altar Sometimes He appeared to be all on fire, and then she saw herself, the priest, and our Lord in the midst of flames. Sometimes a light shot from the altar and illuminated the whole church. Another time, when the priest was dividing the Host, she saw how the entire Body of our Lord was under each part. These and many other examples are given by Father Faber in his book on the Blessed Sacrament (pp. 534, 535), and I quote only a selected few of them in this place, for the purpose of showing that infused contemplation on the humanity of Christ, and especially of Christ in the Holy Eucharist, has been experienced by very many Saints, and our Saviour has approved of it by innumerable apparitions and visions. Of the nature of these apparitions and visions we shall have to treat later on in another part of this work.

CHAPTER VII

THE OBJECTS OF CONTEMPLATION (*continued*)

<small>1. The Blessed Virgin the object of contemplation</small>

1. THE Blessed Virgin may also be the object of contemplation. The thirty-sixth of the sixty-eight propositions of Michael Molinos, condemned by Innocent XI, is as follows. ' No creature, neither the Blessed Virgin nor the Saints, should have a seat in our heart, because God alone wishes to occupy and possess it.' This false principle of spirituality was most justly condemned by the Church, because its meaning is to remove the Blessed Mother of God as well as the Saints of God from the devotion of the faithful and from contemplative prayer. Strange aberration, we may well say, with Scaramelli, to imagine that devotion to the Queen and the Saints of heaven could interfere with contemplation. Whether we consider the act of contemplation in itself or in the conditions required for it, the intervention of the Blessed Virgin and of the Saints, who themselves continually contemplate the eternal splendours of heaven, far from being an obstacle, is, on the contrary, a means fully in accord with the very nature of this elevation of our souls to God.

2. St John the Evangelist, it cannot be denied, was in contemplation when he saw what he describes

in words which the holy Fathers interpret as applying in their literal and figurative sense to the Blessed Virgin *And a great sign appeared in heaven · a woman clothed with the sun, and the moon under her feet, and on her head a crown of twelve stars.*[1]

The heavenly spirits the object of contemplation & John's vision

He was also in a contemplative state when he saw the Almighty seated on His throne, in the splendour of His Majesty and with the marks of His supreme power, surrounded with the august choir of the Ancients, Saints, and Prophets. These Prophets, represented by the *four living creatures*, are constantly employed in offering their homage to Him and singing His praises. *They cry out day and night, Holy, Holy, Holy, Lord God Almighty*, etc , repeating *Holy* three times, probably in honour of the Blessed Trinity ; and for the same reason they give to God three different kinds of praise, *glory*, *honour*, and *benediction*, or thanksgiving. And whenever the *four living creatures* sing these praises the *four and twenty Ancients* are ready to join their homage, by *falling down before Him that sitteth on the throne, and adoring Him that liveth for ever and ever*, and in token of their acknowledging all their happiness and pre-eminence to be His gift, they *cast down their crowns before the throne*, and thus they conclude their homage *Thou art worthy, O Lord our God, to receive glory, honour, and power, because Thou hast created all things, and for Thy will they are, and have been, created*—that is, We acknowledge Thy *power*, O Lord, because by Thy omnipotence *Thou hast created all things ; honour* is due to Thee because by *Thy will* they *are* or

---
[1] Apocal xii 1.

continue to exist; *glory* is due to Thee because they *were created* to serve to Thy glory.[1]

Many other examples might be quoted from the Apocalypse to show, as the above extracts show, how the heavenly spirits may be the object of contemplation, and how that contemplation may be to the homage and glory of God, and promote in the soul lively sentiments of admiration, love, and joy

Besides, it is often advisable, according to the teaching of mystical writers, when the soul grows weary of introversions and addresses to the pure Divinity, that, instead thereof, it should exercise itself in acts or affections to the humanity of our Lord, to the Blessed Virgin, to Angels and Saints, yea, as Father Baker says, it may sometimes address its internal speech to itself or to some person or creature absent, yet all with reference to God, for otherwise it would not be an act of religion nor profitable to the soul And he furthermore states that, for attaining to contemplation, it is not necessary (speaking of precise and absolute necessity) that the acts whereof the exercises consist should immediately be directed to the pure Divinity.

To illustrate this practice, I may subjoin here some of those acts which he gives as an exercise for the contemplative soul of devotion to the Mother of God.

3 Acts of devotion of the contemplative soul to the Blessed Virgin

3. 'Hail, sweet Mary! hail, most sacred Virgin, whom God before all ages did choose for His most sacred Mother!

'Obtain for me, I beseech thee, perfect pardon of my sins and the perfect grace of the Holy Ghost,

[1] Apocal. iv. 8-11

'That I may diligently worship, chastily and fervently love, thy Son, my Saviour, and thee, the Mother of Mercy.

'O my Lady, receive me for thy poor servant; adopt me, O Mother, for thy son,

'Grant that I may be numbered among them whom thou dost love (whose names are written in thy virginal breast), and whom thou dost teach, direct, help, cherish.

'Hail, sweet Mary, whom God by a most honourable privilege did preserve from sin,

'And adorned with most singular graces and most excellent gifts.

'O glorious Virgin! O gracious Virgin! O most pure Virgin! O most pure Virgin chosen amongst thousands!

'Do not repel me, a wicked sinner; do not despise and reject me, defiled with the stains of sin;

'But hear me, a miserable wretch, crying unto thee; comfort me, desiring thee, and help me, trusting thee' Amen [1]

4. We are told that many spectacles are revealed or manifested to contemplative souls, especially views of the world of grace and the world of glory, or the supernatural works of God.

<small>4 All the supernatural works of God the objects of contemplation. The state of the blessed in heaven and their glory</small>

We can well understand, and that, too, without much difficulty, that perfect contemplation may be exercised about our heavenly home and those eternal goods which are prepared for the Saints hereafter, and which so many of them now enjoy. The soul can contemplate in its view of heaven the nature, grace, and glory of the Angels, the labours which the Saints underwent for God in their lives, as well as their

---

[1] 'Holy Wisdom,' pp 619, 620

graces and their present glory. It can behold the ever-blessed Mother of God and understand her mercies towards men, and something of the glory which she now enjoys as the Queen of Heaven, seated at the right hand of her Son, above all the choirs of Angels. It can admire with great love and joy even here on earth that city of peace and of everlasting brightness. By one glance of contemplation it can see more and greater things of that state of beatitude than can be known by a long time spent in meditation. In illustration of this, let us call to mind the vision which St. John received when in contemplation, as narrated by himself. *And I John saw the Holy City, the new Jerusalem, coming down out of heaven from God, prepared as a bride adorned for her husband. And I heard a great voice from the throne, saying Behold the tabernacle of God with men, and He will dwell with them. And they shall be His people. and God Himself with them shall be their God. And God shall wipe away all tears from their eyes and death shall be no more, nor mourning, nor crying, nor sorrow shall be any more, for the former things are passed away And He that sat on the throne said, Behold, I make all things new.*[1]

St. John here speaks of a new heaven and a new earth after the Day of Judgment, but we are not to understand from his words that the present heaven and earth are to vanish entirely, but only that they are to be changed for the better and glorified. We do not know exactly in what this renovation or glorification is to consist,[2] but the

[1] Apocal. xxi 2-5.
[2] See 'Manual of Ascetical Theology,' p 576

New Jerusalem which St. John saw, and of which the earthly city was an imperfect copy, is evidently the Jerusalem that is above, the heaven of heavens, our future home and resting-place. In the days here described by St. John it will be realized fully both there and here below—there by the glorified bodies of the blessed, here below by the qualities with which the earth will be perfected and beautified so that it may be called a *new earth*.

This general and brief reference to St. John's revelation concerning the kingdom of heaven will be sufficient to convey the meaning of the doctrine which teaches us that the world of glory may be the object of contemplation, but it must not be inferred that contemplative souls receive revelations of the kind granted to St John, which were revelations made to the Universal Church, and forming a part of the deposit of faith. Our doctrine, however, is that all revelations and revealed truths may be the object of contemplation, and therefore St. John's visions of the heavenly Jerusalem may be with advantage brought before the gaze of contemplatives, as they may form the subject of meditation for all devout souls.

5. To the soul in contemplation there is often imparted an unusual light showing the dignity and sanctity of our holy mother the Church. How ardently she is loved by her Divine Spouse! how powerfully He protects her from error and preserves her the pillar of truth! how faithfully He frees her from the trials and persecutions of tyrants and of heretics! how He constantly provides her with Saints and worthy examples of every virtue! how mercifully He sustains her in the midst of so many

5. The state of the militant Church on earth may also be the object of contemplation

unfaithful children—namely, sinners, and how faithfully He calls to their reward the predestined.[1] These are the ideas of Alvarez de Paz, who reminds us also that the appearance of the Church is one thing when viewed with carelessness, and quite another thing in beauty and perfection when seen by the light of contemplation.[1]

6 Graces, Sacraments, and other supernatural things, the objects of contemplation, as well as all creatures

6. We have said that all the supernatural works of God may be the object of contemplation, and under this head are included sanctifying grace, actual grace, the holy Sacraments, the grace of vocations, and all other graces both general and special. It may further be added that all creatures may be the object of contemplation, inasmuch as by their consideration we may be elevated to contemplate God, or we may be so enlightened by His Holy Spirit as to see God in all His works and creatures, and hear the voice of God speaking to us through them, after the example of St. Paul of the Cross, St Francis, and many other Saints. I may repeat, in conclusion, that all objects of faith are also objects of contemplation, because, as the Angelic Doctor has said: *Ex hoc manuducitur homo in Dei cognitione*[2] (From this, namely, faith, and by it man is led to the knowledge of God).

7 Laws according to which God distributes His extraordinary favours not understood by us These favours entirely and always are gratuitous

7. After recounting the objects of contemplation, the question is asked as to whether any order exists in their manifestation. To this we may answer, with Ribet, that God is not bound by any inflexible law in bestowing His favours. He dispenses and measures at will, according to the designs of His supernatural providence over souls.

[1] Alvarez de Paz, apud Ribet, vol 1, p. 97
[2] 22 qu 180, art 4

To suppress liberty in love is to suppress love itself.

Nevertheless, without supposing any necessity in the matter as to order and measure and time, it is thought God follows laws in His mystic dealings with souls; but by reason of the gratuity of the gifts bestowed, let us say at once that we do not understand how this is done according to our notions of a strict and rigorous law. He has a law of His own eternal wisdom for all His dealings with His creatures, and it is beyond human investigation.

We are, however, told by mystical writers that the normal scale of ordinary contemplation in principle corresponds to the order of meditation, and this order appears to be to consider at first the Christian virtues which enlighten the spirit and practically regulate the life, then to study the perfect model of all perfection in Jesus Christ, after that to raise up the mind to the admiration of the absolute and relative attributes of God, and finally to establish the soul in close communion with the Holy Trinity

Now, as ordinary contemplation succeeds to meditation only when this has reached its climax, it follows that God Himself is its most usual object. But, in reality, the operations and attractions of the Holy Ghost are so various, and the Divine intervention which causes the soul to pass from discourse and reasoning so mysterious, that it is morally impossible for us to prescribe or to know any general or constant laws according to which these things are done. There are some souls who pass their whole lives in meditating upon one subject, as, for example, the Passion of Christ, or the mystery of the Holy

Eucharist, or the goodness and the wisdom of God, or one or more virtues. Others begin by considerations of God and His attributes, of Nature, or of the speculative truths of religion, and come later on to meditate on the sufferings of Christ, and then become astonished that they had so little experienced before or earlier in life a devotion so suitable to increase faith and love.

The order or process of extraordinary contemplation is not less difficult to determine. It is commonly taught that imaginary visions, as being less perfect, usually precede intellectual visions, but in the one and the other the same objects may appear, but in a different manner. We find, however, the masters of the spiritual life in common accord in affirming that the manifestation of God as the Trinity is reserved for the climax of mystical elevation (ita Ribet, p. 98) Notwithstanding all the rules and methods laid down by these venerable writers for ordinary or extraordinary contemplation, we have constantly to hold with Father Baker 'That God, Who is the free Master and Disposer of His own graces, may bestow them upon whom and when He pleases, either miraculously increasing His grace in some, or conferring His supernatural favours before the time that they are ripe for them, as He did to St. Catherine of Siena (and some others), who in their younger days have been favoured with a passive union'

'Mystic authors, likewise, except from the ordinary course the case where God, upon the death of well-willed and well-disposed souls happening before perfection attained, supplieth after some extraordinary manner what was wanting, and effects that in a moment which would otherwise have required a long space of time, and this, say they, God frequently doth in regard of the serious and fervent wills that He seeth in such souls, which were resolved to prosecute the way of His love for all their lives, though they should have lasted never so long.'[1]

I may still further remark as to the order in which the objects of contemplation are to be considered, that I do not think any of these objects ought to be entirely overlooked or omitted even by the most exalted souls. The four last things—death, judgment, hell, and heaven—the mysteries of the life and sufferings of Christ, the virtues, the supernatural works of God in the world of grace and in the world of glory, God Himself and His attributes, the Blessed Trinity, may be the fruitful subjects or objects of the meditation and the contemplation of all souls, whether they be in the purgative, the illuminative, or the unitive way, and at any stage or period of their supernatural lives. But the manner in which these objects present themselves to the soul may be different in the various degrees and stages of the supernatural state. This may account for a kind of subjective order according to the six steps of contemplation given by Richard of St. Victor. These I may give here, although they may be better understood later on after treating of the causes or principles of contemplation.

8. Archbishop Vaughan in his 'Life of St. Thomas Aquinas' summarizes and gives us in his own language the system of Richard of St. Victor on this matter in the following extract.

8. The six styles of contemplation arranged according to its objects by Richard of St Victor

'God is the proper object of contemplation, but

[1] 'Holy Wisdom,' p. 50.

the soul can also fix upon other objects. According to the subject-matter, there are six steps of contemplation. The first is in and according to the imagination (*in imaginatione et secundum imaginationem*). This looks upon the beauty and variety of creation, and thus is drawn to wonder at and honour the wisdom and goodness of God. The second is in the imagination and according to reason (*in imaginatione et secundum rationem*) This marvels at and considers the causes of the world of sense " according to reason," because the conclusions of reason are necessary for proceeding from cause to effect The third is in reason and according to imagination (*in ratione et secundum imaginationem*). Here we conclude from the facts of sensible nature to the world of ideas, which are brought before the intelligence. " In reason," because the reason alone can move from sensation to the world of ideas; "according to imagination," because that faculty provides matter for the operation of reason. The fourth is in reason and according to reason (*in ratione et secundum rationem*). At this step the mind is fixed upon the unseen world of spirits, their nature and attributes It is done " in reason and according to reason " because the imagination is now dropped, and the spiritual element alone is the object of thought. The fifth step is above reason, but not beside reason (*supra rationem, non præter rationem*). It rests immediately on God, inasmuch as He can be known by our reason. To this step belongs those truths which we know by reason, but cannot comprehend They are *supra* because we cannot grasp them, they are not *præter* whilst they can be an object of the reason The sixth and highest step of contemplation is above reason and beside reason (*supra rationem et præter rationem*). Its object is the impenetrable mysteries of God, which transcend all reason. Its object is both *supra* and *præter rationem*, because the human reason of itself can neither comprehend nor arrive at it.'[1]

'There is,' says Archbishop Vaughan, 'something supernatural in all these steps of contemplation; for if a man would raise himself up in contemplation, he must do so through the illumination of grace. No mortal can look upon the mysteries of God unless he be lifted up by God Himself to the vision, all the more since sin has wrought a thick veil over the eyes of men, which can only be removed by the action of the grace of God.'[2]

NOTE

Some mystical writers, and amongst them Ribet, in this place call attention to the scholastic method of explaining our intellectual operations in the ascent or elevation of the soul to God as given by the Pseudo-Dionysius. He divides the operations of the intellect in ordinary or acquired contemplation into three motions—the circular, straight, and oblique. St Thomas gives his authority to this method, and I shall follow him as closely as I can in his explanation of these three motions. *[The method of the operations of the intellect in the elevation of the soul to God. Intellectual motions, circular, straight, and oblique.]*

The method spoken of is an ingenious adaptation of the theory of motion then in vogue to the intellectual operations, which are described also as motions. In bodies they say there are three motions—one circular, by which a thing moves in a uniform manner round the same centre; the second is straight, which moves from any one point to another; the third is oblique, or indirect, made up of the two former. By similitude, therefore, in intellectual operations, those that have uniformity are called circular motions; those that proceed from one to another are

---

[1] 'Life of St Thomas Aquinas,' vol 1, pp 252, 253
[2] *Ibid*, p. 254

called straight motions, and those that have some kind of uniformity, and yet proceed from one thing to another, are called oblique or indirect

In three ways, therefore, the soul is moved towards God. One way is when the invisible things of God are seen by those that are made visible, and in this way the soul moves in a straight line, when proceeding from itself, and from those external things around, as from so many varied and multiplied signs, it is raised up to simple and united contemplations. In a second way the soul is moved towards God through the illuminations granted by God, which it receives according to its own manner that is, as it were, veiled under sensible figures. Thus, Isaias saw *the Lord sitting upon a throne high and elevated*[1] This motion is called oblique or indirect, as it possesses something of uniformity on the part of the Divine illumination, and something of defection or difformity by reason of the sensible figures hence the soul is said to move obliquely, inasmuch as according to its nature or proper capacity, it is illumined by Divine thoughts not intellectually nor simply, but in a reasoning and discursive manner. The third way is that in which the soul, casting aside all sensible figures and helps, thinks of God above itself and everything else, and thus separates its vision from all difformity. This motion is called circular, because by it the soul is withdrawn from all external things. It centres in itself, and in it all the virtues become united in their force to raise it, above all things else, to God Himself. To make this clearer, we may regard God as the centre of a circle, and the soul at a point in the circumference, and behold the soul in direct, simple, and continuous relations with its centre.

This doctrine is more fully explained by a worthy disciple of St Thomas, Thomas à Vallgornera, in his 'Mystical Theology.' The circular motion in contemplation is when the soul views God, beautiful and good, either as divinely revealed by infused light or known from His creatures and through them, and then remains quiescent, as having found its centre, or moves pleasantly around that centre. Being withdrawn from the admiration and love of itself, it becomes, as it were, absorbed, and finds sweet repose in its God, its Creator, its Redeemer, and its Spouse This motion is especially to be found in the supernatural con-

[1] Isa. vi. 1

templation which is granted in what this author calls the state of intimate union

The motion of contemplation is straight when the soul, from the consideration of all the beautiful and good qualities which are to be seen in their limited forms in creatures, raises itself directly to the contemplation of the greatest beauty and the infinite good which is God. This motion, we are told, is to be found especially in acquired or ordinary contemplation in the ascent of the soul to God It is not uniform, like the circular motion, because many other acts interfere with it and distract it, or make the operations remiss, and on this account it suffers interruption and change

The oblique motion is when the soul, from the contemplation of God, descends to contemplate the effects of His Omnipotence, His promises, and all His other works in His creatures, and then returns to contemplate again God Himself This motion is to be found both in acquired or ordinary contemplation and in infused and extraordinary contemplation It has something of the circular and something of the straight motion in it, and has the qualities of both It agrees with the circular by reason of the uniformity with which it contemplates God as the Beginning and the End. From Him, as has been said, it proceeds to the consideration of others, and then it returns again to Him It is like the straight motion in the multiplicity and defection of the acts which are formed in its manner of operation or exercise [1]

---

[1] 'Theol Myst,' auctore R P. Thomas à Vallgornera, append N N., 249 *et seq*, vol. ii.

CHAPTER VIII

THE CAUSES AND PRINCIPLES OF CONTEMPLATION

As contemplation tends to the mystical union of God and the soul, and is already the beginning of that union, it follows that it cannot be effected without the operation both of God and man. God acts as primary Cause, and that, too, in an extraordinary manner, for contemplation is a singular and extraordinary grace, and man could never attain it without such a grace and without a special supernatural influence of God upon the soul. Man in a secondary manner, and, as it were, passively, as mystical writers say, has to co-operate with the action of God in order to receive the gift of contemplation and to exercise that gift, or, in other words, he is to correspond to the Divine motion or gift. Wherefore the causes and principles of contemplation are in general to be found in God and in man.

<small>1. The principles of contemplation on the part of man</small>

1. Mystical writers and spiritual writers in general, when teaching of sanctity and perfection, seem to attach great importance to the human faculties that are exercised in producing acts of virtue, and in prayer and contemplation. This may be accounted for in the words of the author of a work entitled 'The Psychology of the Saints.' 'The Saint,' he

says, 'is a man of God, and we must not be surprised, therefore, to find that his faculties are put to very hard work indeed in order that everything that impedes the service of God may be eliminated, and all that leads to and facilitates that service may be increased and strengthened. The Saints tell us so themselves over and over again. It is no exaggeration to say that their ideas on the nature of the soul and on the harmony between its faculties constitute a complete psychology of the Saints This theoretical psychology, of which their writings are full, throws a valuable light upon the practical psychology of their lives.' It is for this reason, and for the further reason that ordinary readers may be able to understand the nature, the force, and the meaning of the terms used, that an explanation of the sensitive and intellectual faculties of man is here subjoined.

2. Doctors of theology and of philosophy distinguish two parts in man—one sensitive, the other intellectual The sensitive part by its sensitive faculties produces sensitive acts. The other and higher part produces intellectual acts The faculties of the sensitive parts are the external senses, namely, *sight*, *hearing*, *taste*, *smell*, and *touch*, and the internal senses, which are chiefly two, or, at least, the two suffice for my present purpose, namely, the *sensus communis* (or common-sense) and the phantasy or imagination. They are termed senses, or organic powers, because they operate by means of a material organ, and have for their formal objects individual, concrete, sensible facts. The word *internal* marks their subjective character and the interior machinery of their operations

<small>The sensitive faculties of man</small>

Our external senses communicate with objects outside us, by whose presentation or presence they are moved, and they receive an impression which we call organic. This impression immediately produces sensation, which the nerves in a way unknown to us transfer to the brain, which is the seat of the *sensus communis*.

This *sensus communis*, styled also the *internal* sense and the *central* sense, receives the sensation of all the external senses, so that it knows what the eye sees, the ear hears, the palate tastes, the nose smells, and the touch feels. 'By this faculty,' says Father Maher, 'we are conscious of the operations of the external sensuous faculties, and we are made aware of differences between them, though we cannot by its means cognize them *as* different.'[1] In order that, when the organic impression ceases, the images produced by it in the *sensus communis* may not be lost immediately, they are by the phantasy conserved. The phantasy is the faculty of imagining, which in so far as it preserves images is called the sensitive memory. Its duty is not only to preserve sensations, but also to produce former sensations, and to form new ones from things known in other ways. This outline corresponds to the scholastic classification of four internal senses. This classification 'was grounded on the existence of generic differences in the *formal objects* of the several faculties. The *formal object* of the *sensus communis* consists of the actual operations of the external senses; that of the *imagination* (or phantasy) is the representation of what is absent. The function of the *vis æstimativa* is the apprehension of an object as

[1] 'Psychology,' p. 157

remotely suitable or noxious to the well-being of the animal, that of the *sensitive memory* is the cognition of past sensuous experiences. Some writers reduced these faculties to two, others augmented them to six. The nature of the distinction between these senses was also disputed. Suarez, after a careful examination of the various opinions on the point, decides against the existence of either a *real* or *formal* distinction, and contends that Aristotle is with him in looking on the internal senses as merely diverse aspects or phases of a single sensuous faculty.[1]

3. The sensations, since they are always either pleasant or disagreeable, beget what are known as the *passions*. The passions, which may also be called the emotions, are defined as intense excitations of the appetitive faculty. 'The term *appetite*,' Father Maher tells us, 'was used in a very wide sense by medieval writers to denote all forms of internal inclination, comprehending alike the natural tendencies or affinities (*appetitus naturalis*) of plants and inorganic substances which impel them towards what is suitable to their nature, and the feelings of conscious attraction (*appetitus elicitivus*) in sentient and rational beings. The formal object of the appetitive faculty in the broad signification is *the good*. Under *the good* is comprised not merely the *pleasant*, but everything in any fashion convenient to the nature of the being thus attracted. Continued existence, felicity, development, and perfection, together with whatever is apparently conducive to these ends, are all in so far good, and consequently a possible object of appetency, whilst whatever is

3. The emotions or passions.

[1] 'Psychology,' by M. Maher, S J., p 162

repugnant to them is a mode of evil, and therefore a ground for aversion or the negative activity of the same faculty.

'Of conscious appetite, the Schoolmen recognised two kinds as essentially distinct—*rational* and *sensitive*. The former has its source in intellectual, the latter in sensuous, apprehension. The two faculties, however, do not act in isolation. Desires and impulses in the main sensuous often embody intellectual elements.'

In dealing with the *passions* for our present purpose, we can adopt no other classification than that given by the Schoolmen, and this I find given in good modern English by Father Maher 'They (the Schoolmen) recognised eleven chief forms (of the passions or emotions), which they divided into two great classes, called the *passiones concupiscibiles* and the *passiones irascibiles*. In the former class the object of the mental state acts directly on the faculty as agreeable or repugnant in itself, whilst the object of the irascible appetite is apprehended subject to some condition of difficulty or danger. In scholastic phraseology the object of the *appetitus* or *passio concupiscibilis* is *bonum vel malum simpliciter*, and of the *appetitus irascibilis* is *bonum vel malum arduum*. Six *passiones concupiscibiles* were enumerated—joy or delight, and sadness, desire and aversion or abhorrence, love and hatred. These are the affections of the appetitive faculty viewed as present, future, and absolute, or without any reference to them The five *passiones irascibiles* are hope and despair, courage and fear, and anger. The first pair of emotions are the acts elicited by the appetitive side of the mind in presence of arduous good, according as the difficulty of attainment is apprehended as slight or insuperable. *Courage* and *fear* are the feelings awakened by threatening evil viewed as more or less avoidable, whilst anger is aroused by actually present evil.'

The author here remarks · 'Whatever view be taken with regard to this scheme as a scientific classification, but little reflection is required to see that the several emotions mentioned are really phenomena of the appetitive activity of the mind. Appetency embraces the conscious tendency *from evil* as well as towards *good*, for these two inclinations are only negative and positive phases of the same energy But this faculty must also be the root of the mental states arising in the actual presence of good or ill. The words *desire* and *appetite*, indeed, bring more prominently before us the notion of the absent good, since it is in striving after such an object this power most impressively manifests itself. Still, it cannot be maintained that it is by a different faculty we stretch after or yearn for a distant joy, and take complacency in its actual possession. It is not by three separate powers, but by one and the same, that we dislike evil in general, shrink from its approach, and are sad in its presence. *Hope* is similarly a desire to attain an arduous good, unsteadied by a cognitive element of doubt; whilst *despair* is a painful prostration resulting from a negative phase of the same activity. The affinity of *courage* and *fear* to the two former states, and their like derivation from the positive and negative forms of appetitive activity, are obvious. Both involve intellectual appreciation of the threatening danger ; but whilst in the one case the will is strong and determined, in the other it shrinks back in feeble resolution. *Anger* implies at once dislike and desire of revenge.'

Furthermore, Father Maher refers to certain feelings 'which,' he says, 'have chiefly attracted the attention of modern psychologists,' and amongst these he enumerates the following: First, those peculiarly related to self-love; second, those of an altruistic or unselfish character; third, the sense of power; fourth, emotions of change and of intellectual activity; fifth, the æsthetic emotions; sixth, the moral sentiment.[1]

These names may be useful when it will be necessary to refer to the nature or conditions of the phenomena of feeling in regard to spiritual and mystical operations. The word 'feeling' in this connection may be interpreted as synonymous with the emotions, or, as we may call them by their scholastic name, the passions.

<small>4. The relation of the sensitive faculties to contemplation.</small>

4. None of the faculties of the sensitive part except the phantasy can co-operate with contemplation in a direct or proximate way, but they may do so in a remote manner with regard to the contemplation of sensible things, or by procuring images for the phantasy or thoughts for the understanding. It is said that the way in which they can co-operate is remote because their operations are always exercised beforehand, and not in the act of contemplation itself. They have not, however, to be overlooked or neglected, because if unrestrained they will not only not help to contemplation, but prove the greatest obstacles in its way. If in the soul the superior part is not dominant, and the

[1] 'Psychology,' pp. 395-398.

inferior part is not submissive, there can be no contemplation.

It will be seen from the above outline of the senses and the sensitive feelings that everything must begin at the senses and at the imagination, which preserves, continues, renews, and diversifies the impressions conveyed by means of them. The author of the 'Psychology of the Saints' pertinently asks and answers an important question on the subject of the mortification or purification of the senses, which spiritual writers discuss very carefully and minutely: 'Is the Saint a man who despises imagination and endeavours to destroy it? Allowances must first be made for the natural temperament of the Saint, for his social surroundings and the kind of study by which he has developed his mind. It is not surprising to find that St. Jerome, St. Francis of Assisi, St. Teresa, and St. Francis of Sales, were by nature possessed of a far livelier imagination than St. Thomas Aquinas, St. Jane de Chantal, and M. Olier. When this much has been granted, there still remains the fact that the particular character of Catholic dogma and morality, the study of Scripture, the teaching of certain recognised spiritual works (for instance, "The Imitation"), meditation, solitude, community life, and finally tradition, must exercise a lasting influence upon the cast of mind of great mystics, a class to which, as we have seen, all Saints belong.'[1]

The same author further proceeds to show how the work of destruction and of building up is effected with regard to the reformation of the senses and the imagination. 'The mystic dies and is born again.

[1] 'Psychology of the Saints,' by H. Joly, p. 120.

He dies to a sensual, agitated, troubled world, liable to corruption and destined to perish, and is born again to a transformed world. To quote his own expression, he passes through the night of the senses, after which his purified eyes are opened to a more brilliant light. . . . What is of importance to notice is that the Saint will return later on to sensible objects, to enjoy them in his own way, of course, but far more intensely than other men. He will return with all the greater alacrity, as the senses to which these objects appeal, though formerly stained and disordered, were so, not through their own fault or that of the objects themselves, but through the fault of the mind. "It is in the mind," says St. John of the Cross, "that the disorders of the animal part of our nature take rise, and from it that they derive their strength."

'The purification of the senses is accomplished by means of the purification of the mind. When the mind is healed, the senses which are animated by it are deprived of their poison. St. Teresa taught that we ought to seek God in creatures. She also tells us that, when once we have advanced far enough in perfection, we shall be able to return to creatures through the Creator, and that we shall then find them pure and adorned with the beauty they possessed in days of primeval innocence.'[1] Let us ever remember the saying of St. John of the Cross: 'God certainly does not wish to destroy Nature; on the contrary, He wishes to perfect it.'

5. The emotions or feelings in relation to contemplation.

5. Speaking of the sensibility or feeling of the Saints, much light may be thrown on what has been said above concerning the passions by the following

[1] 'Psychology of the Saints,' by H. Joly, pp. 128, 129.

explanation given by the same writer: 'Christian philosophy teaches that *feeling*, or what St. Thomas, who uses the word in a very general sense, calls simply *passion*, belongs not to the soul alone, but to body and soul together (*passio per se convenit composito*); or, in other words, that the complex phenomena of joy and pain, passion and emotion, are determined by the joint influence of physical and mental states. To my mind, it is impossible to deny that a man's feelings are coloured to a great extent by his habits of mind, good or bad education, trained or untrained reasoning faculties; by the natural bent of his imagination, his ideas, and, above all, by his religious beliefs. At the same time, it is equally certain that these emotions are keen or languid, intense or calm, according to the sensations we experience of physical disturbances, of correlated and sympathetic movements, and of those many reflex operations caused by the modifications of one organ affecting all the others. The emotional sensibility of the Saints is subject to the ordinary laws, and is therefore determined in the first instance by natural temperament. After further developing this point, our author continues:

'We see, therefore, that, in judging of the sensibility of the Saints, we must take into account less of their capacity for joy or suffering than of their will to suffer in the interests of some one cause or idea. Faith controls love, and love controls those mental images which excite the emotions, and thereby reveal the interior feelings of the heart. The world readily believes that the mystic has lost all power of feeling because he is no longer moved by the things of earth; but the mystic himself considers that his feelings were, so to say, dead during the years which preceded his conversion, and that they have been recalled to life by the action of grace. "My heart was then so hard," says St. Teresa, "that I could read the whole Passion without shedding a single tear. This want of feeling greatly distressed me." She tells us, again, "that tears, which are, in a way, the result of our persevering efforts, helped by grace, are of immense value, and it would be worth all the labours in the world, to obtain even a single one of them."[1]

I have endeavoured to show how the senses, the imagination, and the feelings or passions, have to be reckoned with in the case of souls who are to be disposed for contemplation. The work of disposing these faculties and feelings is to be effected by the exercise of the moral virtues. If we remember the kind of life led by the majority of the Saints, we see at once that their temperance, continency, and austerity must have had the effect of greatly simplifying the movements of the physical and animal parts of their organization. The moral virtues moderate the vehemence of the passions and quiet the tumult of external occupation, and therefore they dispose the soul for the contemplative life.

[1] 'Psychology of the Saints,' pp. 148, 155.

CHAPTER IX

THE SUPERIOR FACULTIES OF THE SOUL AS THE CAUSES OR PRINCIPLES OF CONTEMPLATION

1. THE faculties of the superior part, or the intellectual part, of the soul are the intellect and the will.

<small>1. The two faculties of the soul—intellect and will.</small>

(1) 'Intellect may be broadly defined the *faculty of thought*. It is a faculty by which a man knows what is true and false, and what is good and bad. It belongs to it to perceive the images of the phantasy or imagination, to judge or doubt about them, to reason about them, and finally to preserve them. Inasmuch as it perceives, it is called *intellect*; inasmuch as it judges or doubts, it is called *judgment*; inasmuch as it goes through a process of reasoning and drawing conclusions from arguments, it is called *reason*; and inasmuch as it preserves or retains these things, it is called the *intellectual memory*, which should be carefully distinguished from the sensitive memory.

<small>(1) The intellect.</small>

'There is, according to Catholic philosophy, a difference in kind between *sense* and *intellect*. The intellect is a faculty specially distinct from that of sense, and it possesses the power of performing operations beyond the scope of sense. Many of its acts and products are distinct in kind from all modes of sensibility and all forms of the sensuous action, whether simple or complex; and no sensation, whatever stages of evolution or transformation it may pass through, can ever develop into thought. To the sentient life of the soul are allotted the five external senses, internal sensibility, imagination, sensuous memory, and sensitive appetite. To the intellect, and under the term thought, we attribute and include attention, judgment, reflection, self-consciousness, the formation of concepts and the process of reasoning. These modes of activity all exhibit a distinctly suprasensuous element.'[1]

(2) The will.

(2) The will, which is the queen or ruler of all the faculties, is the power of choosing between good and evil as known by the intellect. 'Will or rational appetite in general may be described as *the faculty of inclining towards or striving after some object intellectually apprehended as good;* but, viewed strictly as a free power, it may be defined as *the capability of self-determination.* A volition is an act of will. By *free* will or *moral freedom* is meant that endowment by which an agent, when all the conditions requisite to elicit a volition are present, is enabled either to put forth or abstain from that volition. Free will thus implies that volitions are freely exerted by the *ego* or *person*, and are not the necessary outcome of his nature and the attraction of the moment.'[2] It always follows the intellect, not in a blind manner, but with freedom. The good use of the will is called virtue, its bad use vice, although in this application we do not mean to signify virtue and vice according to their formal and more correct

[1] 'Psychology,' M. Maher, p. 234.   [2] *Ibid.*, p. 363.

definitions. Knowledge is the act of the intellect, and volition that of the will, and it is admitted by all that knowledge is naturally prior to volition.

We desire because we perceive or think the object of our desire to be good. We are drawn or repelled by the pleasurable or painful character of the cognitive act. It is true, however, that some desires manifest themselves in an obscure way without any antecedent cognitive representation that we can clearly realize. 'This is especially the case with the cravings of physical appetite, such as hunger and thirst. Purely organic states which give rise to yearnings of this kind, however, are rather of the nature of physiological needs than properly psychical desires; and in proportion as they emerge into the state of mental acts the cognitive element comes into clearer consciousness. We may, therefore, lay it down as a general truth that appetite (will) is subsequent to knowledge and dependent on it. These faculties are thus to be viewed, not so much in the light of two co-ordinate powers standing side by side, as in that of two properties of the soul, the exertion of one of which bears to that of the other the relation of antecedent to consequent.'[1]

The will, which should be guided by the law of God, is the mistress of all the faculties. This is apparent from the consideration of the manner in which the will exercises its power over them. All the members of the body obey the will: the feet walk, the hands work, etc.; and these, again, remain idle according to the wish of the individual. This is not the case, however, with the sensations, the imagination, and the passions. The will cannot

[1] 'Psychology,' M. Maher, p. 39.

prevent organic impressions from causing sensation; sensations and imaginations excite the emotions or passions; and these often, as experience proves, rebel against the will, and sometimes gain the victory over her or induce her to consent to their inclinations.

But if the will cannot directly control sensations, imaginations, and the passions, it can, and ought to, do so indirectly. Then, from the power it has over the members of the body, it can impede the evil impressions of the organs, it can overcome the phantasy by fixing the attention on some good object. It can control the passions by changing their object, or removing that which may be the occasion of evil. It is for this reason that all souls desirous of perfection or sanctity are so constantly and urgently recommended to keep the sensitive faculties well under the power of the will, that thus proper order may be observed. Guard must be kept over the external senses that they may not occasion evil feelings; the imagination is to be curbed that it may not incite the passions; and the will has to rule the intellect itself so as to prevent it from following the bent of the passions; finally, all have to endeavour so that the will itself may desire nothing but to conform itself to the eternal and all-holy will of God.[1]

2. The memory as well as intellect or understanding and will considered in relation to the spiritual life of the soul.

2. In reference to the three powers of the soul, the author of the 'Psychology of the Saints' explains how they are to be considered in their bearing upon our spiritual and supernatural state. He says: 'Of ecclesiastical teachers, St. Augustine was the first to divide the powers of the soul into three—the memory, the understanding, and the will; and this

[1] 'Comp. Theol. Myst. Scaramelli,' p. 104.

division has been a familiar one to all those who have come after him. It is referred to at every turn by St. Catherine of Siena, St. Teresa, St. John of the Cross, and St. Ignatius. "His life is well regulated," says St. Catherine of Siena, "because he has regulated the three powers of his soul; the memory retains the recollection of the benefits he has received from God, the understanding strives to know His will, and the will to love Him." " In this," she tells us elsewhere, "consists all well-regulated life, both of soul and body, in every place and circumstance in which we find ourselves. The powers of the soul must act in concert: the memory must recall the thought of God's benefits; the understanding must strive to know His will; and the will must love Him to such a degree that it is unable to love or desire anything apart from Him." In like manner St. Ignatius insists in his first " Exercise " that we should meditate on the first sin, the sin of the rebel Angels. This exercise he divides into three parts: the exercise of the memory to recall the sin, the exercise of the understanding to reflect upon it in greater detail, and the exercise of the will to excite the consequent affections of the soul.

'This threefold division is, of course, susceptible of further subdivision, and it is far from necessarily excluding those, for instance, which distinguish between the imagination and the memory, and so on.' Writing of the will and of love as its act, the writer thus well remarks: 'With the Saints sentiment is not a separate faculty, nor do they associate love with that passive and emotional sentiment, which gains in interest among our contemporaries in proportion as it shows itself the more ill-regulated and diseased. According to them, the will is no arbitrary and negative force, and, in placing it as they do in such intimate relation with love, they wish to point out that there is its mainstay and the source of all its strength—its mainstay, because, in their eyes, a will that does not love, or that does not love the object most worthy of love, is a dead force; the source of its strength, because the love by which it is upheld is stronger than death. In short, in their brief but precise theories, the most prominent place is given to the will, upheld by love and enlightened by an understanding which we must not be surprised to find cares more for fidelity than originality.'[1]

The intellect and will the source or principle of contemplation

3. As the intellect and will are the principle of all human actions, so they must be regarded as the principle of contemplation, which, we are told, is of all man's operations the most noble. The intellect beholds with admiration and delight the truth which is the object of contemplation, and the will embraces it with loving affection, and, as Scaramelli tells us, there is no degree of contemplation in which these two powers of the soul do not co-operate. He says that all mystical writers agree in this with regard to the inferior degrees of contemplation, but that in the more sublime degrees some authors question it. As some importance is attached to a question treated by such authorities as St. Bonaventure, Gerson and others on one side, and St. Augustine, St. Gregory, St. Anselm, St. Bernard, St. Thomas, on the other, I may be allowed to state the question itself, and then give or select the opinion which may commend itself as the

[1] 'Psychology of the Saints,' pp. 119, 120.

one to be adopted, though I cannot now see any practical utility in dealing explicitly with the question at all

The Rev. F. V Voss, in his compendium of Scaramelli's 'Directorium Mysticum' gives the following propositions, which contain the opinions of all mystical writers on this point

(1) God cannot be loved without being known, therefore there is no contemplation without the knowledge of God I think no one can contradict that statement, and, according to Voss, no author asserts the contrary, though St Bonaventure and Gerson are credited with the opinion that in the most sublime and most perfect contemplations God is loved without knowledge, but Voss tells us that the Seraphic Doctor does not say that God can be loved without knowledge, but without previous thought of Him (*non sine cognitione sed sine prævia cogitatione*)

(2) The knowledge of God ordinarily proceeds from the intellect.

(3) The knowledge of God need not necessarily proceed from the intellect, according to St Bonaventure and others, but can be acquired by the soul in a superintellectual manner by the touch of love

(4) It is controverted whether in the most exalted contemplations the amorous knowledge of God proceeds from the intellect so that there can be no contemplation in which the act of the intellect is not found, or whether, the acts of the intellect being suspended for the time, the knowledge proceeds from love alone Scaramelli holds and defends the first opinion, the second is attributed to St. Bonaventure and others With regard to any

decision between the opinions of these great and holy mystics, all I need say is that my own judgment goes with Scaramelli and the authors whom he quotes in favour of the opinion that in every contemplation, even the most exalted, both the intellect and the will form their acts of knowledge and of God, although the acts of knowledge may sometimes be so spiritual and delicate as that the contemplative soul may not be aware of them nor be able either to feel or declare them. For the rest, with regard to this and other delicate and sublime questions of the mystical life, I shall have to comfort myself and others with the wise counsel of Father Baker when he says 'I know that some mystic authors do constitute several distinct states following active contemplation Thus Barbanson makes mention of the state of the Divine Presence in the soul, and after that of the manifestation of God to the spirit, etc, and in all these great varieties of ascents and descents, etc, likewise Father Ben Canfield, in his last and most perfect state of the essential and supereminent will of God, makes mention of several distinct exercises, as denudation, an active and passive annihilation, etc. These authors, perhaps, spoke according to the experience of the Divine operations in their own souls, and with regard to the particular manner of prayer Therefore, I conceive that what they deliver need not be esteemed a common measure for all, neither will I deny but that there may be distinct states (some of which I will mention), as the great desolation, etc, but it will be to no purpose to search closely into them Those happy souls whom God shall so highly favour as to bring them to the mount of vision and contemplation will have no need of light from any but God to conduct them in those hidden Divine paths, and the inexperienced will reap but little profit from such curious inquiries.'[1]

4. The will in contemplation must always be supposed free, so that the acts of love elicited during that time may be meritorious. No matter how much the soul may be ravished by the object of contemplation, even to the extent of being so absorbed as not to perceive its own operations, it merits at the time. In bestowing the great grace of contemplation upon a soul, we cannot suppose that God intends it to be useless, or that the precious time should be spent in vain, which would be the case if the will were under necessity or not free in the sense that freedom is required for merit. Notwithstanding, therefore, the efficacy by which God draws the intellect to Himself, and the extraordinary necessity by which it is held fixed upon the object of contemplation, the will must remain mistress of its acts and its affections, so that, absolutely speaking, it is able all the time not to love. For the intuition or view of contemplation is not the beatific vision so that God is seen in Himself, but it is an abstract vision which sees God through the mirror of the intelligible species. Therefore the soul is never placed under such a necessity that free will is destroyed, or that it cannot suspend the act of the love of God.

St. Teresa well describes the force of will, speaking from her own experience in contemplation. The will, which in hysterical subjects is so paralyzed,

[1] 'Holy Wisdom,' p. 508.

in her case unites itself even more closely to God than the intelligence and the memory. 'It is not a spiritual sleep,' she tells us, 'but the will acts alone' While the other faculties yield to nature, the will secures for them a safe refuge in God, to which, as the Saint puts it so prettily, they can return 'like doves, which, misliking the food they seek first on one side, and then on the other, hasten, after a fruitless search, to return to the dove-cot Elsewhere she compares the firm, patient will to the prudent bee which remains in the hive in order to extract honey from the flowers which its companions bring it For if, instead of staying in the hive, all the bees went out after the others, how could the honey be made?'[1] These extracts seem to show the full force of the will in contemplation, and how it remains a free power capable of self-determination and endowed with all the conditions requisite to elicit its volition or act of the love of God, or to abstain from that volition. By the example of the bee she would signify the merits gained by the soul in contemplation St Gregory the Great has said *Magna sunt activæ vitæ merita, sed contemplativæ potiora* (Great are the merits of the active life, but those of the contemplative life are greater).

When considering the causes of contemplation on the part of man, it is necessary to treat of one more question, which is of great importance, namely, whether all should desire contemplation and pray and work for it.

5. Contemplation may be desired and prayed for

5. Schram gives a careful and a wise answer to this question He says that it is holy and ex-

[1] 'Psychology of the Saints,' p 113

pedient for all to aspire to supernatural contemplation. This he proves from many passages of Scripture which manifest aspirations towards contemplation *My heart hath said to Thee My face hath sought Thee Thy face O Lord, will I still seek* [1] *Send forth Thy light and Thy truth they have conducted me, and brought me unto Thy holy hill and into Thy tabernacles.* [2] *Who will give me wings like a dove, and I will fly and be at rest?* [3] *Shew me O Thou Whom my soul loveth, where Thou feedest, where Thou liest in the mid-day, lest I begin to wander after the flocks of Thy companions* [4] *Come to Me, all you that labour, and are burdened, and I will refresh you . . . and you shall find rest to your souls* [5] *Behold, I stand at the door, and knock. If any man shall hear My voice, and open to Me the door, I will come in to him, and will sup with him, and he with Me* [6] In these places all are invited to the intuition, the rest, the refection and feast of Divine contemplation; therefore it is a holy and expedient thing to aspire to it. This truth may easily be understood from all that has been said concerning contemplation. Contemplation is a good to be desired By it the soul adheres to God, contemplating Him by the act of the intellect and loving Him by the act of the will. It is a supernatural good, and therefore to be desired, as all have to desire their supernatural perfection It is the work of the Holy Ghost, Who infuses it with His Divine gifts It has for its objects, God considered in Himself, and as the Author of nature and of grace; the Blessed Trinity, according to all

[1] Psa. xxvi. 8 [2] Psa xlii 3 [3] Psa liv 7.
[4] Cant. i. 6 [5] St Matt xi. 28, 29 [6] Apocal. iii 20

the perfections and attributes of the Three Divine Persons. It proceeds, also, from the human intellect enlightened by the Holy Ghost and is its most perfect act, and is therefore in all respects a good to be desired. Besides, all are exhorted to aspire to the greatest humility, the greatest meekness, and to the other virtues in their most perfect degree. Why, then, should they not tend to the most perfect degree of prayer, which is contemplation? From this it follows that it is lawful and commendable to pray for, and ask of God, the gift of contemplation. The following Scriptural texts, in addition to those already quoted, are given in proof of the practice of praying for this gift *Wherefore I wished, and understanding was given me and I called upon God, and the spirit of wisdom came upon me,*[1] and, *Her have I loved, and have sought her out from my youth*[2] And, again, St. James says *If any of you want wisdom, let him ask it of God, Who giveth to all men abundantly and upbraideth not, and it shall be given him*[3] St Thomas assigns the reason why we should pray for this gift as follows It is right to pray for what we may lawfully desire, and we can desire lawfully contemplation, therefore we can pray for it. We have furthermore to add that, according to all mystical writers, to obtain contemplation without prayer is very rare or even miraculous.

Conditions to be observed in desiring and in praying for contemplation

6 Having established the truth of this teaching, we have now to qualify it by a few remarks suggested by prudence and founded on doctrinal teaching.

(1) We must remember that the Divine action granting contemplation is altogether gratuitous, and

---

[1] Wisd vii 7. [2] Wisd. viii 2 [3] Jas. i 5

that no effort of ours, even helped by the ordinary grace of God, can obtain it; and that it is a gift which cannot be strictly merited, but only congruously, so that the most ardent desire, the most fervent prayers, and life-long sanctity, cannot obtain for us the gift

(2) We must not expect our prayers and desires for contemplation to be immediately granted, or to be granted at any particular time, but we have to leave the matter with resignation to God's own time in the future, when the soul may be sufficiently prepared or disposed for this great favour. This grace depends entirely on the pure will of God, as we have already remarked in a former chapter and there is no particular fixed time in which souls can be said to receive it Some have received it early in life, some later on, some at the hour of death, and many holy and perfect souls never received it in this world

(3) Contemplation, whether ordinary or extraordinary, should be desired and prayed for only with the tacit or express condition, if it be expedient or profitable to the soul , for extraordinary contemplation is not always expedient, and ought not to be asked without a special Divine impulse. Likewise, ordinary contemplation is not always expedient, either on account of want of disposition on the part of the person asking, or for some other reason known to Divine providence , and it is not a grace necessary for the perfection to which we have all continually to aspire or to tend towards.

(4) Although all can aspire to supernatural contemplation, no one, generally speaking, should desire or pray for the external phenomena and miraculous

manifestations of the mystical state (at least, not without a special impulse of the Holy Ghost), such as ecstasies, raptures, apparitions corporeal or imaginary, visions, and things of this marvellous nature. It is not lawful to desire or to pray for them, and much less is it lawful to endeavour to obtain them, as this would be not only absurd, but evidence of great vanity and pride. And even when favours or wonders of this kind are granted, a holy and prudent person will shrink from them with humility, and beg God to lead them along the ordinary beaten path and safe way to heaven.

The Saints themselves warn us against desiring these extraordinary manifestations, because the devil and our own imagination are able by their means to trick us in a thousand different ways, and for this reason amongst others they are not to be sought or prayed for. More than anyone else St John of the Cross has laboured to impress upon men the real teaching of Catholic tradition, that phenomena of this kind do not constitute sanctity. We may go further, and say that in those countries which produce Saints, and where Saints are most honoured, these occurrences always, in the first instance, create distrust and suspicion. What is feared is that they are either caused by disease or that they will end by producing it, on account of the too great strain to which they subject the mental and physical organization of the person who experiences them. According to the teaching of St John of the Cross, the least unfavourable judgment that can be passed on them is that no one ought to show animus or ill-treat persons subject to these states. All that is necessary is to warn them of the dangers they run, and gently to turn their attention to other things. We read in the "Ascent of Mount Carmel" that "these souls should be led by the way of faith, and be taught by degrees to disregard these supernatural impressions They should learn to strip themselves of them for the sake of their own greater profit in the spiritual life. It should be explained to them that this way is the better one, and that one single action, one single movement of the will, proceeding from charity, is of more value, and is more precious in God's sight, than all the good put together which they may hope to derive from their revelations. What is more, many who have never received these gifts have become incomparably more holy than those who have received them, in abundance, from heaven " [1]

Benedict XIV tells us that 'when inquiry is instituted for the purpose of beatification or canonization, no examination is made of miracles until after the heroic virtues or the martyrdom of the servant of God have been proved These virtues are the first and most decisive witness to sanctity; visions, prophecies, and miracles are of only secondary importance, and they are absolutely ignored if proof of heroic virtues is not forthcoming.'

[1] See 'The Psychology of the Saints,' pp. 75, 76

CHAPTER X

THE PRINCIPLES AND CAUSES OF CONTEMPLATION ON THE PART OF GOD

As the act of contemplation, especially that of mystical union, which is the primary object of mystical science, exceeds the whole natural order, it follows that the human faculties alone, which are the principles, the causes and regulators of only natural actions, can neither begin nor perfect this act. We can know God by the light of natural reason, but we cannot by means of that light go beyond the bounds of nature, nor rise even to the lowest degree of supernatural contemplation. We need many graces of God to raise the soul to contemplation, and especially to that highest degree of it known as mystical union.

In treating of the principles and causes by which God leads the soul to contemplation, we have to consider three things in this chapter — namely, sanctifying grace, the habits of the virtues, and actual grace.

1. Sanctifying grace as the principle of contemplation

1. The first grace necessary for contemplation is sanctifying grace, that grace through which sins are forgiven, and which regenerates and sanctifies us, and makes us sons of God, heirs of the kingdom of heaven, members of Christ, and temples of the

Holy Ghost Without this grace we cannot be united to God by charity.

Formal sanctity consists in sanctifying or habitual grace by which we are made holy, and whose first infusion takes place either by the Sacraments or by an act of love or of perfect contrition, and which is increased afterwards by the meritorious acts of all the virtues, many of which contemplation exercises, with the addition of some accidental perfection derived from the gifts of the Holy Ghost or of some grace gratuitously given. Habitual or sanctifying grace, therefore, with a special force imparted to it, may be said to be the principle of contemplation. Not that all souls in grace have also the gift of contemplation, because in saying that sanctifying grace is the principle of contemplation we do not imply that contemplation is not a special and extraordinary grace, and it is to be understood that special and extraordinary graces may be habitual and sanctifying. We have said that contemplation is aided by some perfection of the gifts of the Spirit, or, speaking of the extraordinary contemplation, its act is usually assisted by one or other of the graces *gratuitously given* (*gratis data*). We have seen in a former chapter that contemplation itself may be regarded as a grace gratuitously given, and is contained implicitly in some of those graces explicitly mentioned by the Apostle,[1] in the supposition that the Apostle intended to enumerate all those graces, which Bellarmine denies It does not follow that the contemplative soul needs more grace or is holier than a soul not gifted in the same way. The more virtuous a person is, not the more contemplative, the holier

[1] 1 Cor xii.

he is, and if souls without contemplation are more virtuous, they are also holier than contemplative souls. It is an error, however, to suppose that one can reach to a high degree of contemplation without many virtues and without labours and difficulties, unless aided by a special privilege of God.

Habitual or sanctifying grace unites us to God meritoriously as to our final End, which we can merit and will obtain in due time if we persevere in it. Charity unites us to God as to its Object, to Whom, as a theological virtue, it ordains us, and its act, inasmuch as it is meritorious, is a disposition, which merits habitual grace, or, rather, an increase of it, as the seed of glory and of the final end. But contemplation supposes habitual grace and its union, and it includes intrinsically charity as its component, element, or part, and it therefore regards God as its Object, and unites the soul with God as its Principle. Contemplation, associated with grace and charity, unites the soul with God as its first Principle or Beginning, its Object, and its End, which are the three greatest unions the soul can have with God as long as it is a wayfarer in this world living by the light of faith.

Manner of God's presence in the contemplative soul

2. The manner of God's presence in the contemplative soul may also be considered in this place. God is present in all things substantially by His essence, His presence, and His power. He is present in a special and peculiar manner to the Saints in heaven by the light of glory, and to the just souls on earth by the light of faith and contemplation. By this hidden, substantial and vital presence to the just souls He communicates a certain power and vitality in a Divine manner, so

as to enable the powers of the will and of the intellect to produce sublime and contemplative acts. Then God may be said to be in the soul by way of mystical union, not as the *form informing* it, as scholastics say, but as the principle subjecting the soul entirely to Himself, and elevating it as a co-principle raised up to a new mode of operating supernaturally, after the example of the blessed in heaven, who by means of the light of glory are raised up to see God clearly in His essence.

By this union God does not sanctify the soul, but supposes it already sanctified by habitual grace, which is the *form informing* it, or making it holy. God is in the soul, not as such a form, but as the efficient and elevating cause of sanctification and perfection and by His special indwelling.

We have now to notice one more point—that is, the manner in which God and the soul itself are to be regarded as the joint causes or principles of contemplation. Since God in the mystical union is not the form informing, but the efficient cause, the soul is not the material cause, but a co-cause or principle efficient and elevated. God does not and cannot enter into any composition with the soul, but its entire subjection to Him under this influence suffices for the mystical union. This may also be called substantial contact, inasmuch as this name signifies the co-existence of the Divine substance as an elevating principle with the human substance as the elevated principle, in such a way, however, that God and the soul are not to be regarded as one adequate principle made up of two inadequate ones, but God is the first total principle, and the soul is also the principle or second total cause together with the graces given to it by God. The two do not coalesce or form any composition, but one is entirely subject and subordinate to the other.

3 Divine contemplation and the uncertainty of grace

3 The question arises in connection with grace and contemplation, as to whether Divine contemplation can make a person certain or secure of being in a state of grace. To this we can answer, with Scaramelli, it is certain that no one, without a special revelation from God, can be absolutely certain of his justification; but it is doubted whether the gift of contemplation may be regarded as a sufficient revelation in the matter. It is the common opinion of Doctors that the contemplative soul, during the time that it enjoys the mystical and transforming union of love, is certain of its justification. That sublime state seems to imply that God would reveal to His spouse His friendship for her, when in such intimate communion with Him St Teresa teaches that after this mystical union the soul knows with indelible certainty that it was with God and God with it, and if the soul is certain of being in communion with God by the union of love, it cannot doubt that it is pleasing to God and living in His grace 'With great but humble security,' says W Hilton in his work 'The Scale of Perfection,' 'and with great spiritual gladness, it [the soul] conceiveth a very great certainty of salvation by reason of this union For it heareth a secret witnessing of the Holy Ghost to the conscience, that it is the chosen child of a heavenly heritage. Thus saith St Paul *The Spirit Himself giveth testimony to our spirit, that we are the sons of God* And this witnessing of the conscience truly felt through grace is the very joy of the soul, as the

Apostle saith. *Our glory is this, the testimony of our conscience*—that is, when it witnesseth peace and accord, true love and friendship, betwixt Jesus and the soul.'[1]

I think it well here to say a word of warning on my own account, that no one would be justified in concluding with certainty the state of grace unless there be the special revelation to that effect, no matter how exalted soever the state of contemplation may be, with the one exception mentioned below, and the advice of Scaramelli, who quotes Alvarez de Paz to corroborate his opinion, may apply to all contemplatives in general, although he limits it to those only who enjoy contemplation of an inferior order. It is that these cannot be sure or secure as to the state of grace, because they cannot be sure that these contemplations do not proceed from some grace gratuitously given which is consistent with a state of mortal sin, for it can proceed from the gift of wisdom not in so far as this is a gift of the Holy Ghost, but in so far as it is a gift *gratuitously given*. The peace and happiness which accompany such contemplation may sometimes proceed from natural causes or from the artifices of the devil, and although the contemplation may be a simple and affectionate intuition of God, it cannot be infallibly held that it has its origin in sanctifying grace and in charity. Hence it happens that at all times (except, as Scaramelli says, the time of mystical union) God permits the soul to be in fear and doubt concerning its own experience and revelation, so that it may always *work out its salvation in fear and trembling*.[2]

[1] 'Scale of Perfection,' p 299
[2] 'Comp Direct Theol Myst,' p 118

4. The virtues as principles of contemplation

4. As man is composed of body and soul, so in like manner an act of contemplation is the product of a lively faith and ardent charity. The act made up of these two coalescing is more noble than each of its parts taken separately, and for this reason it may be said that the act of contemplation in which we find the virtues of faith and of charity united in one act is more noble and perfect than the act of faith alone, or of charity alone, just as the accumulation of virtues joined with the gifts of the Holy Ghost, and, it may be, with some of the *gifts gratuitously* given, make the soul more noble and perfect in its acts than when considered apart from these gifts, and constituted merely in a state of grace, with only the virtues that necessarily are united to grace or always accompany it.

Merit which is the result of a physically vital and supernatural act arises either from the greater or lesser habitual grace, or from actual elevating grace, or from free will elevated by grace, or from the greater or less difficulty with which grace prevails in a virtuous act, or from its greater or less intensity or extension. If an act of a moral virtue in all these circumstances abounds more than an act of contemplation, such act of moral virtue will be more meritorious.

Raptures, ecstasies, visions, are all regarded as holy things; but in so far as that which is apparent and external in them is beyond our power, and to the extent that they are devoid of liberty, they are not free or meritorious. But if these be present at the same time with our interior act, supernatural and free in the superior part of the soul, proceeding from a supernatural source, then the interior free acts are meritorious, but not the necessary external actions and passions [1]

Therefore it is to be understood that for contemplation the virtues of faith, hope, and charity, which with sanctifying grace are infused into the soul, are required. The virtue of faith is necessary because, generally speaking, contemplation is nothing else than an act of faith in some revealed truth, or suspended, as it were, in gazing upon some revealed object. I have said generally speaking for the reason that the object of contemplation may be sometimes only the result of some reasoning or a theological conclusion.

The virtue of hope is necessary for contemplation, because we find a proposition to the contrary condemned by Innocent XII, March 12, 1699 The condemned proposition states that in the state of the contemplative or unitive life every interested motive of hope and fear is lost. And the necessity of charity for contemplation is evident from the definition of contemplation. It seems, however, necessary to explain in this place more clearly contemplation in its relation to the virtue of faith, speaking as we do here of supernatural contemplation considered intrinsically and as to its substantial act, and not extrinsically only, or on the part of its object For every consideration of the mysteries of faith, namely, of the Holy Trinity, the Incarnation, or the Eucharist is not supernatural contemplation, though it be made by the light of faith. The question concerns that which is the immediate principle which elicits the act of contemplation, not the remote principle in the supernatural order.

[1] Ita Schram, vol. 1, pp 481, 482.

The virtues of faith and charity, as have been said, are united in their act, yet we may hold that the principle eliciting (*principium elicitivum*) is some gift of the Holy Ghost—either the gift of understanding, or of wisdom, or of knowledge, or some other light superior to these, or some infused knowledge. When the supernatural principle which elicits contemplation is habitual, or a habit, the special actual motion of the Holy Ghost concurs with it in the act of contemplation; when that principle is actual and transitory, it at one and the same time elevates the intellect, and applies it to elicit the act of supernatural contemplation.[1]

The necessity of actual graces for contemplation

5 This brings us to the consideration of the necessity of actual grace for contemplation. It is commonly held that for good and meritorious acts, and therefore for contemplation, sanctifying grace and the infused virtues do not suffice, but that in the case of everyone there is required also, on some occasions, actual grace, which, enlightening the intellect by supernatural lights and moving the will by interior affections, prevents, accompanies, and follows the good works which we perform.

In the 'Manual of Ascetical Theology' a full explanation is given as to the necessity of actual grace in connection with the good works of the just. The teaching therein given on the authority of Billuart is as follows. For a just man, besides habitual grace and the infused virtues annexed to it, the general motion of God, as the supernatural Author, is necessary for all acts of piety, and suffices for some. This motion may, in a certain

[1] 'Myst Theol Divi Thomæ' auctore Thoma à Vallgornera, N 589

sense, be said to be special and gratuitous; but, that a just man may persevere in such acts for a long time, it is necessary that a special grace be superadded. It does not require any proof to show that the general motion of God is required; for every creature, whether corporeal or spiritual, is dependent on God as its First Cause, and cannot move or act without that general motion of God. As the natural powers, namely, the intellect and will, even when possessed of the acquired virtues which give the power to do acts morally good, in order that they may actually do them, need to be applied and moved by the general motion of God as the natural Author, so the same powers, informed by grace and the infused virtues which give the *power* to do supernatural acts, in order *actually* to do them, always need a like general motion of God as the supernatural Author.[1]

Without holding the opinion that actual grace or special actual grace is necessary for every good work when the soul is in a state of grace, except in the sense that the general motion of God, as above explained, is required and may in the individual case be called special, we must, however, hold, with all theologians, that special actual grace is required to enable a man to persevere a long time in good works; that ordinary grace suffices for ordinary persons and ordinary works. But extraordinary grace is required for contemplatives and for contemplation, and we have, therefore, to speak of special actual graces as influencing the lives and actions of those who have received from God the extraordinary grace of contemplation.

[1] 'Manual of Ascetical Theology,' p. 312.

This particular point is well explained by Father Baker. 'As for contemplative livers,' he says, 'those, I mean, that have made a sufficient progress towards perfection, besides the common grace, light, or inspirations necessary for a due performance of essential duties, the which they enjoy in a far more sublime manner and degree, so as to purify their actions from a world of secret impurities and subtle mixture of the interests and ends of corrupt nature, invisible to all other souls—besides this light, I say (which is presupposed and prerequired), they walk in a continual supernatural light, and are guided by assiduous inspirations in regard to their most ordinary and, in themselves, indifferent actions and occurrences, in all of which they clearly see how they are to behave themselves so as to do the will of God, and by them also to improve themselves in the Divine love, the which extraordinary light is communicated unto them only by virtue of their almost continual recollectedness, introversions, and attention to God in the spirit.

'More particularly by this internal Divine light an internal liver is, or may be, directed 1. In the manner and circumstances, when, where, and how any virtues may most profitably and perfectly be exercised; for, as for the substantial act of such a virtue, and the necessary obliging circumstance in which it cannot without mortal sin be omitted, the light of common sanctifying grace will suffice to direct. 2. In the manner, frequency, length, change, and other circumstances of internal prayer. 3. In actions or omissions, which, absolutely considered, may seem in themselves indifferent, and at the present there may be, as to ordinary light, an uncertainty whether the doing or omission is the more perfect. This is discovered to the soul by these supernatural inspirations and light. Such actions and omissions are, for example, reading, study of such or such matters, walking, conversing, staying in or quitting solitude in one's cell, taking a journey, undertaking or refusing an employment, accepting or refusing invitations, etc., in all which things well-minded souls, by solitude and introversion disposing themselves, will not fail to have a supernatural light and impulse communicated to them, which will enable them to make choice of that side of the doubt which, if they correspond thereto, will most advance them in spirit, and suit with the Divine will; whereas, without such light, generally souls are directed by an obscure light and impulse of nature and carnal ends or interests, without the least benefit of their spirit—yea, to their greater distraction and dissipation."[1]

In all these particulars enumerated by Father Baker we are able to recognise actual graces, such as the illuminations of the intellect and the affections of the will, and how useful and practical the gift of contemplation may be in its influence on our every-day lives and actions. We are able also to understand the necessity of these actual graces for such an extraordinary and important spiritual work as that of contemplation.

[1] 'Holy Wisdom,' pp. 70, 71.

CHAPTER XI

THE PRINCIPLES AND CAUSES OF CONTEMPLATION ON THE PART OF GOD (*continued*)

1. The gifts of the Holy Ghost principles of contemplation

1. IN a former work I have treated at some length the gifts of the Holy Ghost considered in general and in particular,[1] and in this place it will only be necessary to consider the gifts in so far as they are the principles of and influence supernatural contemplation.

As contemplation is, of all the operations of man, the most perfect, and surpasses all human manner of operation, it requires the special influence of the gifts of the Holy Ghost. These gifts of the Holy Ghost, according to St Thomas, are 'certain habits that perfect the soul to obey the Holy Ghost with promptitude.' 'These habits,' says Bishop Ullathorne, 'attract the soul to follow the Divine inspirations with ease and freedom.' The Holy Spirit Himself is called *Altissimi donum Dei*, the gift by excellence of the Most High God. The seven gifts are called the seven spirits as well— that is to say, the seven radiations of Divine light, flowings of spiritual unction, breathings of power

---

[1] See 'A Manual of Ascetical Theology,' chaps. XVIII and XIX, part I.

that attract and draw the will to comply with the inspirations of the Holy Ghost.

In that former work I have followed the doctrine of those who teach that the gifts of the Holy Ghost are real habits or qualities of the soul, and not merely acts; that they are to be distinguished from the virtues; that they are inseparable from charity and necessary for salvation, and that they are infused into all in justification; finally, that the gifts are not to be confined in their operations to heroic acts of virtue. It belongs, indeed, to the gifts of the Holy Ghost to make heroes in virtue, but an equal share of influence must be assigned to the virtues themselves. If they were only given for heroic acts, these gifts would be found to be idle and inactive in most men, and no reason could be assigned for their infusion into all indiscriminately, or for their infusion at all, because for actions that are rare and singular, such as heroic actions, the actual help of the Holy Ghost would suffice. Therefore heroic acts of virtue are not entirely the acts of these habits called gifts, but they are explained by them, inasmuch as they signify to us the singular action of the Holy Ghost in our souls. At the same time, the Holy Ghost can, and does, move us in that singular manner to act in other matters of virtue that are of precept or of counsel, so that in the same matter in which a man acts by the virtue he may also act in a higher way by the gifts, and these habits of the gifts do not, therefore, remain idle and inactive in us, but are often exercised if a man remains long in a state of grace and is obedient to the movements of the Holy Spirit.[1]

[1] See 'Manual of Ascetical Theology,' part 1, chap. xviii.

In regard, however, to contemplation, whose acts are elevated so far above all human manner of operating, there is need of the gifts of the Holy Ghost for the extraordinary illumination of the mind and the special movement of the will. We need not hold, however, that all the gifts of the Holy Ghost concur necessarily or equally in the act of contemplation, but only those that serve to illumine and illustrate our faith in Divine truths and to inflame the will with sweet love of Divine objects. Some of them, as, for example, the gifts of wisdom, knowledge, understanding, and counsel, especially appertain to contemplation; and as contemplation is not confined alone to the intellect in which these gifts reside, but passes to the affections of the will, we may say that all the gifts concur in a certain way, and may be regarded as causes of the act of contemplation. For this reason we may briefly explain each of the gifts separately as to the manner in which each influences the soul in contemplation.

The prophet acknowledges in the person of Christ seven gifts, which he enumerates, beginning with the highest. *And the Spirit of the Lord shall rest upon Him the spirit of wisdom and of understanding, the spirit of counsel and of fortitude, the spirit of knowledge and of godliness. And He shall be filled with the spirit of the fear of the Lord*[1] As Christ is our Archetype, and as we by grace become members of His mystical Body, theologians and the masters of the spiritual life conclude from the prophetic text that we also ought to participate in these same privileges.

2. This gift is said to be sometimes the formal

---
[1] Isa. xi. 2 *et seq*

principle from which the act of contemplation is elicited, because it imparts to the intellect the highest and the simplest knowledge of God and of Divine and heavenly things, and of those things by which sanctity is promoted and increased, and that in a wonderful, sweet and pleasant manner. It gives clearness to the light of faith, which it perfects and elevates as far as this is possible in this life. If in a room there be at first only the light of a single candle, and then a strong electric light be introduced, this will throw a wonderful light on everything around. So in the light of this life, when wisdom is enkindled in addition to the light of faith already in the soul, the truths of faith are perceived with wonderful clearness and distinctness, and the sweetness and spiritual savour which belong to wisdom, united with charity, cause the soul to delight in God and unite it more closely with Him. St. Thomas, speaking of this gift, says that it advances to a species of Godlike contemplation and a certain explicit view of the articles which faith perceives in a dark manner, and as involved in a kind of mental mist. Wisdom is a gift which, when it knows God as good, views Him as good above every manner of goodness to be found in creatures, and in like manner does it enable the soul to behold God as just, merciful, and perfect with a perfection superexcelling and transcending every degree of imaginable or intelligible perfection. Both the imagination and intellect are corrected by wisdom as defective in the concepts with which they contemplate God.[1] To this gift and its influence we may apply the words of St. Paul *Let the word of Christ dwell in*

[1] 'Myst. Theol Divi Thomæ,' N 654 *et seq.*

you abundantly, in all wisdom teaching and admonishing one another in psalms, hymns, and spiritual canticles, singing in grace in your hearts to God.[1]

<small>3. The gift of understanding in relation to contemplation</small>

3. The gift of understanding may also be sometimes the formal principle from which the act of contemplation is elicited. The Holy Ghost imparts to the soul by this gift a luminous and immovable certainty. He makes us see clearly and feel in a lively manner in the secret depths of our soul the power of revealed truths, and He causes to originate in and emanate from the mind holy thoughts which inflame our hearts with love and fill them with pious affections and salutary desires. Faith is simple assent to the truths which one believes; the gift of understanding is a kind of Divine light, by virtue of which the soul enters in some manner, as it were by instinct, into the object of its faith to know its nature, its reason, its convenience or utility. Some such profound sense of sublime truths is sometimes discovered in simple children, in illiterate and uneducated people, and in contemplative souls. Without effort or labour they learn and know the things of God with astonishing accuracy and clearness, and although they may not know these things after the manner of reasoning, nor so as to be able to give an account of them or to translate their ideas into suitable words, the gift of understanding, which raises them and delivers to them the spirit of truth and light, is their teacher and master.[2] From this description of the gift it may be easily seen how it influences the act of contemplation, and how that act can emanate from it.

4. The gift of knowledge may also be regarded as

---

[1] Col. iii. 16.   [2] 'Manual of Ascetical Theology,' p. 257.

being sometimes the formal principle from which the act of contemplation emanates. It differs from wisdom in this, that, in reasoning about revealed doctrines, knowledge uses the light obtained from created things, although its formal object is the light Divinely infused. It may also be said to be a gift by which we know temporal things in so far as they conduct or help us towards our salvation, and the manner of using them properly. Wisdom does not reason according to temporal, but according to eternal maxims as they are in God, the principle and end of all things. We have already seen how created things may be the object of contemplation, and how we can see God in His creatures, and in this respect we can understand how the gift of knowledge is that by which the act of contemplation is exercised in regard to these objects. ' The gift of knowledge,' says Bishop Ullathorne, 'gives us light to distinguish what is true from what is false, what is of God from what is of the creature, what is solid from what is vain and imaginary, and what is truly great from what only appears to be great, although not so in reality.' For example, it enables us to see the perfect harmony that exists between humiliation, poverty, and suffering, and the real wants of the fallen man, and thus we learn to accept them as the sick man takes medicines to save him from death and restore him to health. It is a holy commerce, in which we exchange what is temporary and trivial for a wealth that is imperishable. St Paul understood the commerce well. *The things*, he says, *that were gain to me, the same I have accounted loss for Christ. Furthermore, I count all things to be but loss for the excellent knowledge of Jesus Christ*

<small>¹ The gift of knowledge in relation to contemplation</small>

my Lord, for whom I have suffered the loss of all things, and count them but as filth that I may gain Christ.[1]

<small>5. The gift of counsel in relation to contemplation</small>

5. From the description of this gift, we can see clearly how much it has to do with contemplation. Counsel is one of the intellectual gifts. As men give counsel to others when they direct them in the way they should go, so contemplative souls, like others who are not contemplatives, receive counsel from God as to what they are to do in order to advance rightly in the way of salvation. As the Holy Ghost is a far higher and better guide than human reason, it is evident that this gift is to be regarded as the most perfect, as well as the surest, rule of our actions. It is especially this gift which gives light and direction in singular and extraordinary actions, such as contemplation. It enlightens the soul to judge and determine in what circumstances and with what concurring qualities an act of virtue ought and may with the best advantage and perfection be exercised. It imparts spiritual discretion, without which even noble and heroic actions may be performed with little or no profit. To this gift we may apply what Father Baker has written concerning spiritual or supernatural discretion. He says: 'This permanent light of supernatural discretion informs the soul generally in all things efficacious to her advancement towards contemplation. It teaches her in religious observances culpably to neglect none, and to perform them with a pure intention for her spiritual good; in mortifications, to support the necessary ones willingly and profitably, and assume only such

[1] 'Christian Patience,' lect. ix.

voluntary ones as God directs her to, therein considering the infirmity of the body as well as the fervour of the will, lest by overburdening nature unnecessarily she be rendered unable to bear even those which are of obligation. In prayer it teaches the soul what degree is proper to her, and how long she is to continue in it without change till God invites her to a higher, and then readily to accept of His invitation. Likewise, what proportion of time is requisite to be spent in prayer, so as to make a discreet and sufficient progress therein. It teaches her to suspect sensible devotion, and not to glut herself with the honey of it, nor to follow it too fast to designs of seeming perfection and extraordinary tasks, which, when such devotion ends, would be burdensome and harmful; in a word, it teaches the soul that due moderation in all things which makes them laudable and meritorious'[1]

6. The necessity of the gift of fortitude for contemplation is also apparent. It is that gift which enables a man to bear adversities and trials, and even martyrdom, when God's glory or honour demands it. It has this in common with the virtue of fortitude—that it makes a man capable of overcoming the difficulties in the way of salvation. But it does this in another way. The virtue of fortitude proceeds from the motive of honesty, which it discerns in the difficulties that have to be courageously overcome. But according to the gift of fortitude a man resists the difficulties, relying upon the motion and assistance of the Holy Ghost; and as the power of the Holy Ghost is not to be measured by our strength, it may happen that a

6. The gift of fortitude in relation to contemplation.

[1] 'Holy Wisdom,' p 110

man under this motion can dare to do those things that are above his strength. It is this gift that made martyrs invincible in the midst of all their affronts, their tortures, and their sufferings, and enabled the Saints to endure poverty, sickness, and pains of every kind with a heroism untold and with supernatural courage; for such is the power of this gift that it strengthens the soul against temptations to pusillanimity, and makes it contemn all fears, all dangers, and all evils.

To attain the end of a contemplative life—namely, the vision of God in heaven—all assert that there is requisite an immovable resolution, through God's grace and assistance, to attempt and persevere in the prosecution of so glorious a design in spite of all opposition, through light and darkness, through consolations and desolations, etc., as esteeming it to be cheaply purchased, though with the loss of all comforts that nature can find or expect in creatures. Hence the necessity of this gift, to which we may further apply the words of Father Baker: 'The fixing of such a courageous resolution is of so main importance and necessity that, if it should happen to fail or yield to any, though the fiercest temptations, that may occur and are to be expected, so as not to be reassumed, the whole design will be ruined, and therefore devout souls are oftentimes to renew such a resolution, and especially when any difficulty presents itself.'[1]

7. The gift of godliness or piety in relation to contemplation

7. The virtue of piety means affection and observance of duties towards parents. God is in the highest sense our Father, especially in the supernatural order. Therefore the observance of duties

[1] 'Holy Wisdom,' p. 44.

towards Him, by whatever acts it is shown, is through the gift of piety, inasmuch as it proceeds from the Holy Ghost It is in this sense St Paul speaks when he says · *You have received the spirit of adoption of sons, whereby we cry Abba (Father).*[1] This gift is defined as that by which we venerate God as our supreme Parent, and adore Him with the greatest reverence, and by which we observe equity and benevolence towards others as our brethren. The author of the 'Theologia Mystica Divi Thomæ,' speaking of the offices which piety enables the soul to perform, thus concludes 'To it belongs to honour the Saints, not to contradict the Scripture, whether understood or not understood.'[2]

8 This author, writing on the manner in which the gift of the fear of the Lord helps contemplation, refers us to St. Thomas, where, speaking of this fear in the exposition of the words of the Psalm, *The fear of the Lord is holy, enduring for ever and ever,*[3] the holy Doctor says 'Concerning this fear, the prophet (or Psalmist) teaches two things · first, that fear is holy, secondly, that it is enduring But all fear is caused by love, because a man fears to lose that which he loves, and as love is twofold so also is fear Fear is holy that is caused by holy love. That love is holy by which God is loved, according to the words of St. Paul · *The charity of God is poured forth in our hearts by the Holy Ghost, who is given to us.*[4] This holy fear causes three things (1) Fear to offend God , (2) refusal to be separated from God ; (3) subjection of one's self with

8 The fear of the Lord in relation to contemplation

---

[1] Rom viii 15
[2] 'Theol Myst Divi Thomæ,' append , N 266
[3] Psa xviii 10
[4] Rom v 5

reverence to God; and this fear is called chaste and filial which is the gift, and as such it helps contemplation.'[1] In this respect, also, we may quote the words of St. Anselm: 'The fear of the Lord is the beginning of the Divine gifts, and the Holy Spirit gives His fear for a foundation on which to build other gifts.'

9 The graces gratis datæ in relation to contemplation

9 Having treated of the gifts of the Holy Ghost, a question arises which has claimed the attention of mystical writers, as to whether the gifts of understanding and of wisdom suffice for the most exalted kind of contemplation, or whether it is necessary that the graces *gratis datæ* concur with them in some cases. Scaramelli says that some maintain that the gifts of understanding and of wisdom suffice for every grade or degree of contemplation. Others make a distinction, and say, for the more sublime and extraordinary kinds of contemplation, such as are accompanied with ecstasies, raptures, visions, locutions, that the gifts of the Holy Ghost do not suffice, but that the graces *gratis datæ* are required.

Understanding by the graces *gratis datæ* those enumerated by St. Paul—*To one, indeed, is given the word of wisdom*, etc.,[2] and which the Angelical Doctor says are not given that a man may be justified himself, but rather that he co-operate towards the salvation of others—Scaramelli holds that the gifts of understanding and of wisdom suffice for every degree and kind of contemplation, and that the graces *gratis gratæ* are not required. He holds that they are not necessary, but he does not deny that these graces often influence and

[1] 'Theol. Myst.,' append., N. 267. [2] 1 Cor. xii 8

accompany contemplation, as we shall afterwards explain in its proper place. He gives his reason for his opinion as follows.

The gifts of understanding and of wisdom can be increased to the extent of all other supernatural lights, so that the higher the degree of contemplation, these gifts can be just as high and as perfect, and the more perfect these gifts, the more perfect the contemplation. He takes an example from the light of glory. The greater this light, the clearer do the blessed see God, and the greater their beatitude. So, in like manner with regard to contemplative souls, the more the light of understanding and of wisdom is increased in them, the clearer do they see God—always, however, in the obscurity of faith, and not intuitively, as the blessed in heaven, and the more fervently and happily are they united to Him by love. He then attributes to the lights of these two gifts the higher kinds of contemplation, which he mentions as the prayer of quiet, the intoxication of love, mystical union, ecstatic union, raptures, and spiritual matrimony. And he says the same with regard to locutions and visions, in so far as they are ordained for the good of the soul itself, but not in so far as they are ordained for the good of others.

Father Voss, in his compendium of Scaramelli's 'Directorium Mysticum,' remarks, in a note as to visions and locutions, that, whilst admitting these can be without the graces *gratis datæ*, he does not see how the gifts of understanding and of wisdom can suffice for them. In order that the soul may enjoy visions and locutions, it is necessary that God manifest Himself to it in some sensible manner and speak to it, and this cannot be solely by the light of understanding and of wisdom. A special grace seems to be necessary which cannot belong either to the gifts of the Holy Ghost or to the graces *gratis date* (according to the definitions of St Thomas)[1]

I may notice here that the graces of the Holy Ghost manifest themselves in two ways: One way, as dwelling in the Church, teaching and sanctifying her, as, for example, when some sinner in whom the Holy Ghost does not abide works miracles to show that the faith of the Church which he preaches is true. Hence the Apostle writes *God also bearing these witness by signs, and wonders, and divers miracles, and distributions of the Holy Ghost, according to His will*.[2] In another way, the manifestation is made by the graces of the Holy Ghost as dwelling in him to whom the graces are granted. Hence in the Acts it is said that St Stephen, *full of grace and fortitude, did great wonders and signs amongst the people*.[3] In this we have a distinction clearly drawn out as to the manner in which graces *gratis date* may be to the advantage of the person receiving them as well as to the utility of others, and how it is that through these graces persons without sanctifying grace, and consequently without the gifts of the Holy Ghost, may perform signs and wonders for the good of others. But these are rare and exceptional cases.

From the teaching contained in the two chapters on the principles or causes of contemplation considered on the part of God, a full answer may be given to those who object to ordinary contemplation

[1] 'Comp Direct Myst,' pp 127, 128
[2] Heb ii 4
[3] Acts vi 8

and look upon it as an unsafe method of prayer on the ground of the apparent absence of principles upon which it may rest. They say, as Father Doyle represents, that the habit of faith is not one of these principles, nor is theological science, nor the gift of understanding, nor science, nor wisdom. We have seen that some of these, taken even singly, may be a principle of contemplative prayer, and when all, or at least most of them, are found united in any person, we can conclude that they may have an influence upon him as principles which at least prepare and dispose him to contemplative prayer. Speaking of faith and theological science, Father Doyle asks 'Can it be denied that faith has such an influence as this, especially since contemplation itself is an act of faith, the obscurity of which is suddenly enlightened from on high? Does not theological science, when elevated by faith and elevated by God's gifts, aid the soul to contemplate at least by preparing and disposing it for that heavenly favour?'[1]

[1] 'Principles of Religious Life,' p. 218.

CHAPTER XII

THE EFFECTS AND FRUITS OF CONTEMPLATION

SCARAMELLI distinguishes between the effects and the fruits of contemplation. When the soul is in the act of contemplation it experiences certain results and feelings. These he calls the effects After the act of contemplation it experiences other results and feelings, and these he calls fruits. Other writers designate as properties of contemplation those which Scaramelli calls effects, and as effects those which he calls fruits. It will not matter much by which name they may be called so long as the things are properly understood By limiting effects to those things inseparable from the act of contemplation, we may well call them properties or qualities of contemplation, and we have some definite and common results to treat of The fruits are innumerable, but we shall select only some of the principal interior fruits for our consideration in this chapter. Other fruits and external results or manifestations will call for separate treatment in the course of the work.

1 The effects inseparable from contemplation

1. The effects inseparable from the act of contemplation, which may be called also its properties, are three (1) Elevation and suspension of the mind, (2) admiration, (3) joy or delight.

(1) All prayer is an elevation or a raising up of the mind and heart to God, but as to the manner of elevation there is a great difference between ordinary prayer and contemplation. In ordinary prayer the mind raises itself up to God with an effort and with labour, but in contemplation this is done with ease and sweetness. In the former the process is by steps and degrees of reasoning, like the manner of ascending a steep hill; in the latter the ascent is effected in a moment, in the twinkling of an eye. In the former the soul feels itself stationed here below with eyes raised up to heaven; in the latter it seems to be, as it were, admitted into heaven, and therein for the time being it takes up its abode.

(1) The elevation and suspension of the mind

On this elevation follows the suspension of the mind in contemplation, which is nothing else than the most perfect attention to the object contemplated. The causes of this suspension are the Divine light, which, representing the object with great clearness, not only fixes the mind upon it, but keeps it immovable in its operation; and love, which centres all the powers of the soul on the object loved in such a manner as to be totally immersed in it.[1]

That this suspension may not be misunderstood, and that none may think that contemplation means a state of idleness or a mere gazing into space and vacancy, some remarks of Bossuet and of St Teresa may be quoted to some purpose. Bossuet tells us that not only do 'spoken words,' which are the term of discursive operations and efforts, necessarily (I

[1] See Ribet, vol 1, p 128, notes, and Voss, 'Comp Scaramelli,' p 130

should say sometimes) precede this state of prayer, but that even while it lasts the state of passivity is by no means universal or continuous. The soul gives itself as the spouse to her lover. It gives itself to God as actively and freely as God gives Himself to it, for God raises its free election to its highest pitch on account of the desire He has to be chosen freely.

Such, then, are those operations which are higher than discursive operations. St. Teresa treats them beautifully when she speaks of souls who, without losing (far from it) their recollection and knowledge of mysteries, become capable of seizing them by a 'single look,' and only appear unable to speak about them because they enjoy in complete repose everything that has been engraved upon their memory and made present to their minds by previous meditations. But while they thus gather into one single action the operations which have gone before, they are not rendered incapable of further reflections. Bossuet, at least, did not think so when he wrote: 'It would seem that the extreme simplicity of this kind of prayer renders it less easy of recognition.'[1]

(2) Admiration

(2) As suspension follows elevation, so admiration follows suspension in the act of contemplation. It results from the knowledge or apprehension of something which exceeds our faculties, according to St. Thomas, and it is an act consequent on the contemplation of sublime truth. This admiration all experience, both those who are beginners and those who are more advanced in contemplation, because it of necessity is excited by the greatness of

[1] 'The Psychology of the Saints,' p. 146

the things which the soul sees and the perfection of the light with which it sees them. Heavenly things are so great that, even if they were perfectly known, they could not fail to be otherwise considered than with the most worthy and loving admiration. Even the Angels in heaven stand before God with the greatest and most reverent admiration, how much more souls on earth, even those gifted with the highest contemplation! We may not suppose that they get so accustomed to contemplation and know the things so well that admiration ceases in the case of the more advanced; for the things of God are inexhaustible, and the admiration is more likely to increase as step by step the soul becomes more enlightened and more inflamed with Divine love

(3) Mystical writers with one accord, after St. Thomas, teach that joy or delight in contemplative souls is the result of admiration, or, as St. Thomas explains it, admiration is delightful when it has united with it the hope of gaining the knowledge of that which the soul desires to know, and on that account all desirable things are delectable or delightful. Sometimes mystical writers tell us that delight proper to contemplation is confined to the superior part of the soul, and then, as the joy is more spiritual, it superabounds all the more or overflows into the will. Sometimes from the superior part it is transmitted to the inferior, and then the internal senses are filled with sweet emotions and moved to tears of joy. Sometimes this joyful feeling passes from the internal to the external senses, and is manifested or experienced as sweet fragrance or melodious harmonies, and in

(3) Joy or delight

other ways described and accounted for by Richard of St Victor.[1]

This is well described by Louis de Ponte writing of what he calls spiritual taste This is a manner in which God communicates Himself to the contemplative soul with such fervour and sweetness in spiritual things that those of the flesh become unsavoury to it. Commenting on the words, *Taste and see how sweet the Lord is*,[2] he says 'If you taste what God is and the works that He does within you, by taste you shall know how sweet He is, how good, how wise, how potent, how liberal and how merciful. And after this manner we may say, taste and see how sweet is His yoke and His law, how sweet His obedience and humility, etc .
To some God gives His sweetness meditating on His perfections, to some meditating on His benefits, and to others meditating on His holy law, which Daniel said was sweeter unto him *than honey and the honeycomb*. But this sweetness is hidden (reserved) for those that fear God and love Him, for *they* only taste it with most abundance ; but having once tasted it, they have (says Cassian) no tongue to declare it, for it surpasses all whatsoever our sense attains to. True it is that God gives part of this to beginners, and even to sinners, to wean them from the milk of their earthly consolations; but much more abundantly He gives it to those who, for His love, have mortified themselves in depriving themselves of them.'[3]

2. It would be almost impossible to recount all

---

[1] Voss, 'Comp. Scaramelli,' p. 131   [2] Ps xxxiii 9
[3] De Ponte, 'Introd on the Practice of Mental Prayer,' English translation, vol. 1, p. 63.

the fruits or good effects which come to pure and holy souls through contemplation. Scaramelli mentions the following as the principal fruits: humility, detachment from earthly things, purification of the soul from its defects, desire of mortification, fortitude and patience in trials and sufferings, renunciation of one's own will and judgment, charity towards our neighbour. Ribet adds to the above peace (which Scaramelli mentions as an effect inseparable from the act of contemplation), hunger and thirst after justice, and a great desire and impatience to be with God. The author of the 'Theologia Mystica Divi Thomæ' includes two or three others in his enumeration: such as the desire of eternal things, and liberty of spirit—that is, when the soul is raised through contemplation above all temporal things, it gains that true liberty of spirit or freedom from all earthly ties and cares. He mentions, also, perfect charity according to the condition or nature of contemplation itself. From all these fruits we may learn how the theological and moral virtues are increased in the souls of contemplatives, and how through the acts of these virtues their merits are continually increasing, and with them the grace of God in its degrees, and thus their beatitude, which begins here and is consummated in heaven.

I need not say that it is not necessary to write at length on the above fruits in particular, and to elucidate their connection with contemplation; but I wish to call attention to three of them, which seem to me especially characteristic of true contemplatives.

3. The first of these is *humility*. To illustrate how this gift belongs to those favoured souls, I may quote some passages from the 'Psychology of the

Saints' which the author applies to those favoured with the gift of miracles, but which equally apply to the gift of contemplation. 'First and foremost the Saint holds that the gift of miracles is absolutely worthless, that it is either an illusion or else the greatest possible danger to its possessor, if it is not completely under the control of two virtues which are of far greater value—charity and humility. No one will be surprised, I think, that I place these two virtues side by side, for there is nothing so inimical to the love of our neighbour as self-complacency and, still more, pride For this reason the Saint fears that the frequency of so great a gift may increase the frequency of the temptations likely to accompany it. And yet his humility is, in a way, safeguarded for . . . the very sublimity of his intercourse with God, and the very intensity of the love to which he strives to correspond, enable him to measure the depths of the misery of our fallen nature. If he has been raised so far above it, his ideals have also been proportionately raised, and therefore it is that consciousness of the gift of which he believes himself wholly unworthy is so frequent a source of anxiety to him, especially during the active portion of his life.

'The following story is told by the latest biographer of St. Bernard : "One dark thought tormented him, and that was the recollection of the miracles he had worked At last he spoke out to his travelling companions 'How can it be,' he said, 'that God should use such a man as I am to work these wonders? Generally speaking, real miracles are worked by great Saints, false miracles by hypocrites. It seems to me that I am neither one nor the other.' Nobody dared give him the answer that was in the minds of all, for fear of offending his modesty. All at once the answer to the riddle seemed to strike him. 'I see,' he said 'miracles are not a proof of sanctity; they are a means of gaining souls. God worked them, not to glorify me, but for the edification of my neighbour. Therefore miracles and I have nothing in common.'"

'No one is more on the watch than the Saint to detect false sanctity and to avoid contagion with it. When St. Teresa first began to receive Divine favours and to be led by "extraordinary ways," she was tormented by the thought that she was like a certain Poor Clare, who for thirty years excited the admiration of all Spain, but who in the end confessed that she had criminally deceived almost the whole of Christendom.

'St. Teresa, far from seeking these supernatural gifts, felt more and more anxious; her fears increased (the words are her own) in proportion as she felt that what was taking place within her was above the capacity of nature It was only after years of trial and struggle, and by comparing reiterated experiences, that, reassured on the score of her own good faith, and vanquished by love, she gave way without fear, and consequently without reserve She was sure of God's love and sure of herself, and from that time onward there was no gift that she did not accept and describe'

4 *Charity towards our neighbour* is the next fruit of contemplation to which I wish to direct particular attention Scaramelli calls this one of its principal fruits, and it is one that manifests itself in labours

1 Fraternal charity the fruit of contemplation

and sufferings for others. No one can be inflamed with the love of God without having at heart the good of others, since charity towards God and our neighbour are inseparable. Hence the zeal of the Apostles and of other Saints in working by their preaching and by their actions for the salvation of their neighbour; hence so many religious of both sexes who devote their lives and labours to the spiritual and corporal works of mercy. And those who cannot give themselves to external works benefit all others by their devout prayers, and it often happens that through their intercession and merits God converts many souls, and saves not only individuals and families, but even nations, from many evils and calamities that would otherwise befall them

Speaking of the Saints—and I may apply his remarks to contemplative Saints—Henri Joly says some very useful and practical things about their love of their neighbour. He tells us of a nun who on the day after her clothing wrote as follows 'In obedience to the rule of novitiate, I have dropped all my correspondence. Sacrifices of the heart and universal detachment are what God chiefly requires of us poor women, who have nothing left on this earth, without country, home, parents, or friends' Having got that far, she pulls herself up, and continues, without even beginning a new sentence : ' Or, rather, I ought to say, the whole world is ours, for, according to St. Vincent of Paul, our love embraces the whole world '

This writer then foresees an objection. ' I shall be told that loving the whole world really means loving no one, and that this universal love is precisely what kills the natural affection. But is it loving no one to do as the Saints did when they deprived themselves of food and clothing for the sake of the poor, when they nursed the sick, and even kissed their wounds, when they entertained pilgrims and strangers gratuitously, when they founded homes for orphans and children, and braved contagion of lepers and the plague-stricken with no other protection than faith and prayer, when they freed captives at the price of their own liberty and enfranchised slaves, when they defended negroes against the tyranny of their masters, and, like St Catherine of Siena, assisted convicts at the hour of death; when they founded refuges for young girls whose poverty exposed them to evil, and opened their arms to the afflicted and to sinners for whom they felt all Christ's compassionate pity and mercy? There is no priest, no Apostle, no Father, worthy of the name, who ought not to be able to cry out at every hour of the day with St. Paul *Who is weak, and I am not weak? who is scandalized, and I am not on fire?* Who suffers in any way and I do not suffer with him?'

Speaking of St. Teresa, he says. 'Souls like hers are convinced that not only "no one can have too much intelligence," but also that " no one can have too much heart, and that, if only the intention is pure, we should love every creature on this earth." The former assertion I find re-echoed by St. Catherine of Siena, and also by the stern founder of St. Sulpice, M. Olier. Writing to condole with the Marquis de Fénelon on the death of his wife, he writes· "My dear child, your Madeleine is loving you and waiting for you in the bosom of

God. She knows that you cannot love her too much." I venture, therefore, to affirm that, when two souls are united in God, they cannot love each other too much. This was M. Olier's opinion, and that of the Saints also.'[1]

<small>5. Perfect charity towards God the fruit of contemplation</small>

5 Perfect charity towards God is the third fruit that claims our attention. By it I mean the love of God as to its essence, which is not changed by the conditions of contemplation. The act of contemplation itself is, as we have seen an act of the love of God, but the love of God shows itself in a remarkable manner in the lives of contemplatives. It is that love which transforms all other love into itself —the love of God. This may be considered in two aspects, well demonstrated in that work to which I am so much indebted for so much clear exposition on the fruits of contemplation H Joly, speaking of the Saints' love of God, says 'I shall consider it in two aspects—in its relation to suffering and its relation to action, for it is under these two aspects that the love of the Saints differs, not only from profane love, which seeks its own enjoyment, but also from the "quietist" love of false mystics.

'"I have always recognised," writes M Olier to a holy woman, his confidante at the time being—Marie Rousseau—"that to suffer is the very essence of being a Christian." And yet he goes on to tell her of his many troubles and of his dread of the trials of life. He bore them, nevertheless, with heroic courage, and in another letter, written shortly afterwards to his director, he explains why he was able to do so. "How easy it is," he says, "to love in the midst of enjoyment¹ But to love in the

[1] 'Psychology of the Saints,' pp 159, 160, and 164

midst of suffering is hard, and in my opinion that is the test of true love."

'(1) There are two ways of loving in the midst of suffering. A person may accept sufferings with resignation for the sake of obtaining future happiness. This is the first degree to which the Saints soon attained, and none sooner than the writer whose words we have been quoting But from this acceptance of suffering, which is within the reach of many philosophers and men of heroic character, he rose to a desire of suffering Why did he desire to suffer? (1) Love shown in suffering

'There are degrees even of this latter state. Suffering may be desired, not as the reward of a kind of self-interested devotion, but as a condition in which we are brought nearer to the attainment of an object which is in itself worth all the sacrifices of which man is capable. "Because like to the meek Jesus your Chief," writes St Catherine of Siena to Urban VI, "whose will it is that from the beginning of the world until the end nothing great shall ever be accomplished without much suffering..." St. Teresa used to say "Suffering alone makes life tolerable to me My greatest desire is to suffer Often and often I cry out to God from the depths of my soul, 'Lord, either to suffer or die is all that I ask of Thee....'" In what way does the ascetic exercise himself in sufferings? In bearing them patiently, then in seeking them in spite of his natural dislike of them, and finally in acquiring a love of them. Quite so, and this is the gradual advance we described above. But when he suffers voluntarily the Saint exercises himself in yet another way. He exercises himself in willing and acting, and this brings us back to the consideration that, according to the theoretical psychology of the Saints, love and the will are one and the same thing.'[1]

(2) The active love of the saints

(2) With regard to the active love of the Saints or the active aspect of their love, the same author writes as follows 'I am not asserting a paradox when I say that the activity of the Saints is nourished by contemplation, although Renan has contrasted Saints and men of action with the intention of showing that the former were idealists, and men of prayer and contemplation only His mistake is shared by a good many people, but it is none the less amazing on that account

'There is, as we have seen, one faculty which remains not only unfettered, but strong and active, while the Saint is wrapt in the highest kind of contemplation, and that is the intellectual will. The senses, memory, imagination, reasoning power, and the effective will, may be for a time paralyzed, but the simple action of the will which consists in the free gift of one's self is never suspended All true mystics agree on this point. And, again, psychological facts must be judged of by their development and effects Contemplation is, as we have seen, closely connected with love, and, what is more, with active love It is the fruit of an already intense and active love, and it inspires and directs a love that is still more ardent In the midst of a life of action St. Gregory the Great writes " If we wish to reach the citadel of contemplation, we must begin by exercising ourselves in the field of labour Whoever wishes to give himself to contemplation must first examine what degree of love he is capable of, for

[1] 'The Psychology of the Saints,' p 167, et seq

love is the lever of the soul. It alone is able to raise the soul, to detach it from the world and give it wings." Here work is made to precede contemplation, and contemplation in its turn produces work and makes it efficacious. It is impossible for the purified soul to contemplate the Passion of Christ without feeling called to suffer with Him in the same spirit and with the same end in view—the redemption of mankind'[1]

[1] 'The Psychology of the Saints,' p. 174

CHAPTER XIII

THE DURATION OF CONTEMPLATION AND ITS CESSATION

1. Contemplation not a permanent habit

1. THE following proposition of the pious and learned Archbishop of Cambrai was condemned by Innocent XII. It is the sixteenth of the condemned propositions, all of which Fénelon himself reprobated after they were condemned as erroneous by the Sovereign Pontiff 'There is a state of contemplation so sublime and so perfect as to be habitual, so that whenever the soul actually prays its prayer is contemplative, not discursive Then there is no further need to return to meditation and its methodical acts.'

As this proposition is condemned as erroneous, we are to conclude that contemplation is not a specific habit or quality of the soul, whose act can be elicited at will It is true the gifts of the Holy Ghost, which are the principles from which acts of contemplation proceed, are permanent supernatural qualities, like the infused virtues, but these require a special actual grace or Divine motion for the act of contemplation. We are to conclude also that contemplation does not differ logically from meditation, but only morally, in the sense that it is higher and simpler in its intuition, so that meditation can often participate in something of imperfect contemplation, and some meditation or meditation of some kind is mixed up with contemplation, and often alternates with it.

2. Keeping in mind these conclusions, let us examine what mystical writers teach us concerning the duration of contemplation. Speaking of contemplation in itself, or as taking into consideration all its operations together, they tell us that contemplation lasts a long time. This may be proved from the arguments given by St. Thomas. He says that a thing may be long-lasting in a twofold way: one way according to its own nature, another according as it affects us—or, in other words, on the part of the object or on the part of the subject. Considered in itself, it is manifest that the contemplative life is long-lasting in a twofold manner: first, because it is employed about things incorruptible and immovable; secondly, because it has not a contrary; for to the delight which there is to be found in considering these things is nothing contrary. Also, as regards us, the contemplative life is long-lasting, because in us it is the action of the incorruptible faculties of the soul, and because in the operations of the contemplative life we do not labour bodily, and therefore we can continue longer in works of that kind. The meaning of the holy Doctor's words is to be understood, as I have already expressed, of contemplation considered in itself, and, I may add, in the abstract. Its object is Divine, immutable, and eternal. The object can never fail to supply food for contemplation, and it is inexhaustible in the multiplicity and the profundity of its aspects. The subject or recipient in its turn, namely, the soul, can be for a

² The duration of contemplation.

long time maintained in contemplation, as it is immortal and incorruptible, and it has a connatural affinity to intellectual vision of every kind in which it finds pleasure and rest, and that which is, as it were, natural can easily be prolonged Furthermore, contemplative operations, considered in themselves, do not imply any corporal intervention or fatigue, inasmuch as they cannot be subject to the rest and cessations which organic life requires. We shall see, however, that contemplation causes a reaction on the body which impedes its duration.

It is one thing to speak of the contemplative life in general as embracing all the actions of the mind which it includes, and as it may exist in individual souls in heaven; it is another thing to speak of contemplation taken in its strict and proper sense, in one simple and uniform intuition which souls enjoy in this life In the first way of speaking we can say that contemplation may be long-lasting and in heaven everlasting, in the second way we have to assert that in this life it is not possible for a man to remain a long time in the act of contemplation.

'Mental prayer, whether of meditation or contemplation, cannot continue long, considering the weakness of the present life. Hence we read in the Apocalypse that "there was silence in heaven, as it were, for half an hour"; and St. Gregory on the passage says "By heaven is meant the soul of the just, as the Lord says by the prophet · *Heaven is my rest;* and again *The heavens show forth the glory of God.*" When, therefore, there is the quiet of the contemplative life in the soul, there is said to be silence in heaven, because the tumult of earthly acts ceases in the thoughts, so that the mind applies her ear to interior secrets. But because this rest of the mind cannot be perfect in this life, it is not said that there was silence in heaven for a whole hour, but, as it were, for half an hour; and this expression, "as it were," shows that not even that time was fully obtained, because by-and-by, when the mind begins to raise itself and to be surrounded with the light of inward repose, the tumult of thoughts rushes in upon it, and it becomes first confounded and then blinded by the confusion.' This, however, and similar passages, if taken in their proper sense, ought to be understood of acquired (or ordinary) meditation or contemplation, which cannot be protracted except by the special favour of God. But infused (or extraordinary) contemplation, not being liable to the impediments of earthly thoughts, remains as long as it is preserved by God, as Cardinal de Laurea explains (ita Benedict XIV.) [1]

On the authority of Suarez, we may say even of the most exalted contemplation that it is necessary to interrupt it on account of the infirmity and heaviness of the body, and to divert the soul to some other good action, lest we be deceived into a state of useless idleness and neglect. On the same authority we may say that, inasmuch as for sublime contemplation it is necessary to abandon the senses and all things that fall under the senses, and to suspend the reasoning or discourse of the mind, and to occupy it solely in the simple intuition or view of the highest and most spiritual object, it follows that this cannot be without great violence to the body and to all the senses, on account of the union of the body and soul and their necessary dependence on

[1] 'Treatise on Heroic Virtue,' vol. 1, p. 274

each other in this life in regard to all our actions; and therefore it must be very difficult to remain a long time in the act of contemplation.

We have to remember the statement of Cardinal de Laurea quoted by Benedict XIV.: 'Infused contemplation, not being liable to the impediments of earthly thoughts, remains as long as it is preserved by God,' and to this we may add the statement of Suarez, that all this work depends entirely on the Divine grace, to which nothing is impossible, and we have only one final way of knowing how the liberality of God is manifested in contemplation, namely, the experience of contemplative souls.

Experience of St Teresa and other Saints

3. St. Teresa, speaking of the exaltation of the mind in contemplation, and the suspension of the senses experienced in the first years of her religious life, tells us that the union was of very short duration, only for the space of an *Ave Maria*. She says that the suspension of all our natural faculties never lasts a long time; that it may sometimes last for half an hour, and she believed it never exceeded that length of time. St. Augustine, St. Gregory, St. Bernard, and St Thomas are all referred to as authorities for the opinion which holds that the time of the extraordinary Divine operation on the soul in contemplation is very short. A mystical writer named Philip of the Most Holy Trinity assigns, not half an hour, but an hour, as the limit of contemplation, and this is seldom exceeded. In this matter no one can assign exact limits to an operation which depends on the will of God, and His superabundant grace may always effect what is beyond all the strength of human nature and all the conditions of ordinary

grace. We must not, therefore, be surprised to read of Saints who spent several hours in contemplation, or even whole nights in prayer of this kind.

4. The explanation of the length of time which the Saints and servants of God spent in prayer and contemplation, which amounted to several hours, and often whole nights and days, claims special attention, as it presents to the minds of ordinary Christians some difficulty. From their own experience they must feel that it is no easy matter to spend half an hour in prayer without many distractions, and one in ten cannot fix the mind on any subject or object of meditation for an hour without the aid of a book or some kind of study, and therefore they naturally wonder when they read in the Lives of the Saints of so many examples of prolonged prayer and contemplation. We read that St. Lewis Bertrand spent four hours daily in mental prayer, calling to mind with great fervour and joy of heart the mysteries of our Lord's Passion. St. Paschal Baylon, we are told, worshipped the whole night without sleep, and, though wearied and wellnigh broken down by continual labours and afflictions, he returned not to his cell till daybreak, having spent the whole time in choir or in the church in the joys of meditation. St. Francis Xavier sometimes would pass whole nights in prayer, or the greater part of them, and when he was able he betook himself to a church for the purpose; and St. Aloysius Gonzaga, as narrated in the processes of his canonization, used to continue whole nights in prayer. Without doubting the extraordinary grace and favour by which Saints could spend so long in prayer, either in mental prayer or in contemplation, we may account for

<small>4 Meditation and contemplation alternate</small>

their power and capacity by supposing that they alternated meditation and contemplation, that the union and act of contemplation may have been frequently interrupted and renewed, whilst during the whole time those favoured souls may have experienced without any interruption whatever the sweet and pleasant effects of contemplation, its joy and delight. Thus we may be able to understand to some extent how by repeated awakenings and relapses into the suspension and exaltation of contemplation, the saints were able to spend hours, and even days and nights, in prayer, after the manner of a person awakened from sleep by external noises, and who again relapses into the state of sleep.

Suarez accounts for prolonged contemplation in the following manner That the operation may continue for a long time, it is necessary that love correspond in intention with it. He thinks that it very seldom happens that the mind rests in a simple act of love continued without variation, and that it would not delight the soul were it so continued. Therefore, he says, either the love is rekindled or renewed or exercised by new acts. These acts may be varied, though the intellect remain fixed by the same intuition or view of the object, which in various ways excites the affections of the will. It often happens that the gifts of the Holy Ghost are occupied with the same truth which the mind contemplates, illustrating it more, confirming it and rendering it lovable. The experience of these affections which are felt in contemplation also greatly assists the process. In this way, according to that eminent theologian, contemplation may last a long time, but duration for a long time in one simple act is very rare.

5. Souls favoured by the gift of contemplation may sometimes be deprived of it. This is apparent from the nature of the gift itself, because it is not a permanent habit, but an act, as I have said repeatedly. Many souls arrive at the contemplative state, that state of perfection and of prayer in which they are usually favoured by God by the gift of contemplation. Yet it often happens that this gift is withdrawn from them partly by reason of their own frailty and imperfection, and when it is withdrawn the soul falls back into the ordinary manner of prayer and into a state of suffering and trial It becomes weak, and feels itself blind and void of spiritual relish. It may seek and desire the return of that gift, but it cannot find it, according to the words of Sacred Scripture. *When He, our Lord, hideth His countenance, who is there that can behold Him?*[1] It is said of the Spouse in the Canticles: *I sought Him Whom my soul loveth, I sought Him, and found Him not.*[2] 'At last, when He pleaseth, He cometh again full of grace and truth, and visiteth the soul that languisheth with desire, sighing after His presence, and toucheth it, and anointeth it with the oil of gladness, and maketh it suddenly free from all pain.'[3] Sometimes this gift is withdrawn for the greater perfection and purity of the soul, and, it may be, without any fault of its own, and this withdrawal is but a trying of the soul, as we shall see later on when treating of the state of spiritual darkness through which contemplative souls

[1] Job xxxiv. 29. [2] Cant. iii. 1.
[3] 'The Scale of Perfection,' p. 306

have to pass. 'Happy is the soul,' says the author of 'The Scale of Perfection,' 'that is ever fed with the feeling of love in the presence of Jesus, or is borne up by desire in His absence. A wise lover is he, and a well-taught one, who conducteth himself soberly and reverently in His presence, and lovingly beholdeth Him without fitful levity, and yet calmly and patiently beareth His absence without gloomy despair or overpainful bitterness. . . . And,' he continues, 'this changeableness of absence and presence occurreth as well in the state of perfection as in the state of beginning. For even as there is diversity of feeling betwixt these two states as regards the presence of grace, just so is there in the absence of grace.' (By grace this author means here the extraordinary grace or gift of contemplation, as he explains himself in the same chapter.) 'And therefore he that understandeth not the absence of grace is apt to be deceived; whilst he that makes not much of the presence of grace is unthankful for the visitation thereof, whether he be in the state of beginning or of perfection.'[1] The same author concludes his chapter upon this subject in the following sentences. 'But the special grace felt through the invisible presence of Jesus, which maketh the soul a perfect lover, lasteth not ever the same as regards height and feeling, but changeably cometh and goeth. Thus saith our Lord: *The Spirit breatheth where He will, and thou hearest His voice, but thou knowest not whence He cometh and whither He goeth.*[2] He cometh sometimes secretly when thou art least aware of Him. But thou wilt

---

[1] 'The Scale of Perfection,' pp. 306, 307.
[2] St. John iii 8

always know Him full well ere He go; for He wonderfully stirreth and mightily turneth thy heart towards the beholding of His goodness. And then doth thy heart delightfully melt, as wax before the fire, in the joy of His love. And it is this that is meant by His voice. But then He goeth ere thou perceivest it; for He withdraweth Himself gradually, not wholly altogether at once, but from superabundance to sufficiency. The height of feeling passeth, but the substance of this effect of grace (or contemplation) dwelleth still in the soul. And this state remains as long as the soul of a lover of Jesus keepeth itself pure, and falleth not wilfully into the misery or apathy of sensuality, nor into outward vanity, as sometimes out of frailty it doth, though it have no delight therein This is the changeableness of grace (contemplation) which I meant and spoke of.'[1]

The reasons for which God sometimes withdraws from the soul the gift of contemplation are summarized as follows First, that He may purify the soul and dispose it for more sublime contemplation; secondly, that He may punish it on account of some slight defect, thirdly, that He may prove its constancy and fidelity; fourthly, that He may keep it humble and submissive, fifthly, that the health of the body may not be impaired by the endurance of very frequent contemplations of the soul; sixthly, that the soul may be fit to devote itself to works of charity, seventhly, that contemplation may be dearer and more precious to the soul.[2]

[1] 'The Scale of Perfection,' p. 310.
[2] Voss, 'Comp Scaramelli,' p. 160.

PART II

ON PREPARATION FOR CONTEMPLATION

CHAPTER I

THE DISPOSITIONS OF SOUL REQUIRED FOR CONTEMPLATION   SOLITUDE REQUIRED FOR CONTEMPLATION

ALTHOUGH, as we have said more than once, contemplation is a free and gratuitous gift of God which we cannot merit *de condigno*, it is also certain that God grants this gift to persons who are disposed to receive it, and who prepare themselves for its reception, rather than to those who are indisposed and unprepared.

We have, therefore, to consider the dispositions required for contemplation, and the preparations to be made for this heavenly gift.

1. According to Scaramelli, the dispositions required for contemplation are both natural and moral, and he remarks that he speaks of the remote dispositions, and not of those that proximately dispose the soul for contemplation. When he mentions natural dispositions, he does not mean that these can positively dispose a person either for grace or for contemplation, but he means that a person of a good natural disposition has not so many nor so great obstacles in the way

The reason why natural gifts or dispositions are to be taken into consideration is well stated by the

[169]

_{1. Natural dispositions in relation to contemplation}

author of 'The Psychology of the Saints': 'Those who have really made a study of the lives of the Saints, and whose duty it is to comment upon them, always take largely into account that foundation of natural character which sanctity transforms, but does not destroy.' This he proves as follows: 'No prudent ecclesiastical superior would admit to the priesthood or the religious state one whose mental organization was defective. St. John Chrysostom, in his magnificent treatise on the priesthood, long ago told us that, in order to exercise the sacred ministry, "a man must not only be pure, but he must also possess learning and experience." In like manner, solitude has great dangers in the way of unwholesome dreaming in store for weak, excitable souls and those who find meditation a difficulty. A priest one day brought a penitent of his, of whose angelic piety he had a great opinion, to St. Teresa The Saint was, all the same, very reluctant to admit her into the monastery. "You see, Father," she said, "even though our Lord should give this young girl devotion, and teach her contemplation while with us, nevertheless, if she has no sense, she will never come to have any, and then, instead of being of use to the community, she will always be a burden." "An intelligent mind," she says again, "is simple and submissive. It sees its faults, and allows itself to be guided. A mind that is deficient and narrow never sees its faults, even when shown them. It is always pleased with itself, and never learns to do right."[1] Then we are reminded that, 'when God has some extraordinary mission in store for one of His creatures, He nearly always bestows

[1] 'Psychology of the Saints,' p. 42

natural gifts upon him which create in him a great aptitude for the work.' And again : ' It is difficult to tell exactly how far the natural character of the Saints influences and determines their work.' As Bossuet says, ' When God wishes to make use of Saints for His glory, He exercises them in various ways, so that He may mould them according to His own mind. He takes account of their natural dispositions only just so far as to avoid doing violence to them.'[1] We may, therefore, understand that account must be taken of natural dispositions in respect of persons who are to be favoured by God with the extraordinary gift of contemplation, or who may wish to enter a contemplative state of life. If, therefore, according to the advice of Scaramelli, men of a restless and overactive disposition are not called by their state or by a special vocation of God to contemplation, they should occupy themselves in vocal prayer, in meditation, and in external works of charity, which are suitable for every kind of person Yet it may happen that those who are neither disposed nor enabled to make meditation, by reason of want of wit or judgment required for discursive prayer, may be very fit for the more perfect exercise of the will in aspirations and affections, and therefore not naturally disqualified or unfit for contemplation. Considering the great and inexpressible variety in the internal natural dispositions of persons, it is not possible to lay down rules in this matter, and yet it is a matter that demands serious consideration in the direction of souls, according to the wise and practical warning of Father Baker · ' To conclude, the great and

[1] 'Psychology of the Saints,' p 52.

inexplicable variety to be found in the dispositions of souls being considered, and likewise the great inconvenience that necessarily follows a misapplication of spirits to exercises improper for them, the sad condition of those good souls cannot be sufficiently deplored who, by their profession being, as it were, imprisoned in a solitary religious life, and being naturally inapt for discourse, are kept all their lives in meditation, repeating over and over again the same toilsome method, without any progress in spirit, to their great anguish and disquietness. And this misery is much greater in religious women, who, having no diversions of studies or employments, cannot possibly find exercise for their imagination, and therefore, seeing great defects and unsatisfactions in themselves, and not knowing the only cure of them (which is by ascending to the internal exercises of the will), their imperfections increase, and their anguishes proportionately, without any known means to amend them.'[1]

2 Moral dispositions in relation to contemplation

2. The moral dispositions of the soul are the virtues which can be raised to greater perfection by contemplation. The theological virtues are essential, and their exercise in contemplation increases their perfection. Without these there can be no sanctity, much less exalted sanctity. The moral virtues dispose the soul for contemplation, inasmuch as they serve to overcome our passions and evil inclinations, and to subject them to obedience to the law of God. They quiet the tumults of the inferior part of our nature, and enable the soul to gain that peace and rest which contemplation requires.

A great part of ascetical theology is devoted to

[1] 'Holy Wisdom,' p 409

the explanation of the virtues and the manner of increasing them in the soul, and of the merits of the good works performed through the virtues. To that branch of sacred science I have to refer my readers for all the necessary information and guidance regarding the ordinary manner in which souls have to be disposed for the higher paths of the spiritual life. It is when souls are well established in virtue, and adorned with the ordinary graces and virtues, that they may be said to be disposed for the extraordinary supernatural gifts, such as contemplation and the favours which accompany it.[1] It is not necessary to possess the virtues that dispose the soul for contemplation in a perfect degree, because it belongs to contemplation to perfect them. It suffices that the soul endeavour with all its strength to practise them, and that it make progress in them by their repeated acts and by the earnest intention of attaining the perfection of its state of life.

3. Besides the virtues, mystical writers require many other means and observances that a soul be disposed for contemplation. Amongst them we may mention in particular the retirement of the soul from all earthly and superfluous affairs, and the observance of solitude.

3. Retirement and solitude in relation to contemplation

Father Baker tells us that 'By the unanimous acknowledgment of all mystical writers, the only proper school of contemplation is solitude—that is, a condition of life both externally freed from the distracting encumbrances, tempting flatteries, and disquieting solicitudes of the world—and likewise wherein the mind internally is in a good measure, at

[1] See 'Manual of Ascetical Theology'

least, in serious desire—freed also from inordinate affection to all worldly and carnal objects, that so the soul may be at leisure to attend unto God, Who deserves all our thoughts and affections, and to practise such duties of mortification and prayer as dispose her for an immediate perfect union with Him.' Lest it might be imagined that contemplation is confined to the cloister and religious houses, the same author goes on to say: 'Nor though this so necessary solitude be found both more perfectly and more permanently in a well-ordered religious state, which affords likewise many other advantages (scarce to be found elsewhere) for the better practising the exercises disposing to contemplation, yet it is not so confined to that state, but that in the world also, and in a secular course of life, God hath often raised and guided many souls in these perfect ways, affording them even there as much solitude and as much internal freedom of spirit as He saw was necessary to bring them to a higher degree of perfection.'[1]

Solitude may be said to include retirement, custody of the senses, and the moderation of external occupation. In solitude God speaks to the heart, and by retirement, custody of the senses, and the moderation of external occupations, thousands of sensations and imaginations are prevented which would interfere with the recollection of the soul and its elevation to God. By solitude, however, we are not to understand that a person, through the desire of contemplation, should seek a solitude inconvenient and unbecoming his state, or that he should omit or neglect his official duties, or the external works which are necessary and proper to his state. Were

[1] 'Holy Wisdom,' p. 135.

he to do so in order to obtain the gift of contemplation, he would thereby lose the perfection of his ordinary actions, and never gain contemplation. The duties of one's state of life, since they are conformable to the will of God, are no obstacle to perfection or to progress in prayer and contemplation.

Holy solitude is twofold. First, it consists in this, that a man, having fulfilled all the obligations of his state, wastes not time in useless talking, that he indulge not in relaxations that are calculated to gratify curiosity and the cravings of nature rather than to bring repose to the wearied mind, but, rather, that he endeavour to be alone with God, either by vocal prayers, or by spiritual reading, or by holy meditation. Secondly, solitude consists or may be observed in the manner in which a man performs his duties or external works. If at the time of conversation or external works a man thinks of God, directs his work with a pure intention of pleasing Him and of doing all for His greater glory, and thus, as far as possible, keeps himself in the presence of God, then external works and conversation will not interfere with the solitude that is necessary for contemplation. This is what spiritual writers mean, I think, by the habitual remembrance of the presence of God, on which Father Baker gives us a profitable admonition in the following sentences.
' Moreover, if in practice, according to these points, a well-minded soul will be careful to have at least a virtual intention to the love and glory of God (that is, such an intention as follows in virtue of a precedent, actual intention made in prayer, etc), in so doing she shall perform after the best and surest manner the exercise of the continual presence of

God (so much commended by spiritual authors). . . . By the which exercise, surely, it cannot be intended that a soul should be obliged to have continually an actual remembrance of God; for this, being the same with actual internal prayer, would so much endanger the heads of imperfect souls especially, that they would quickly be disabled from making any progress in spirit.'[1]

In recommending solitude as a means of disposing the soul for contemplation, we do not mean, as Father Baker expresses it, to signify that this great gift of God is to be confined only in 'caverns, rocks, or deserts, or fixed to solitary religious communities.' And with him we can say 'that the poorest and simplest soul living in the world, and following the common life of good Christians there, if she will faithfully correspond to the internal light and track afforded her by God's Spirit, may as surely—yea, and sometimes more speedily—arrive to the top of the mountain of vision than the most learned doctors, the most profound wise men—yea, the most abstracted confined hermits.[2]

To show the true spirit of solitude in its relation to external duties of charity, and especially in its relation to charitable intercourse with our neighbour, I think the following valuable extract from W. Hilton's 'Scale of Perfection' may be appropriately quoted in this place.

Solitude considered in relation to charitable intercourse with our neighbours

4. The extract applies to religious or those who have retired from the world to devote themselves to prayer and contemplation, and Hilton advises them with regard to the visits of seculars and conversation with them.

[1] 'Holy Wisdom,' p. 213. [2] *Ibid*, p. 136.

'Thy communing with thy neighbour will not be of much mischief to thee, but will sometimes be of assistance, if thou managest the matter wisely, inasmuch as thou mayest try to find out thereby the measure of thy charity towards thy neighbour, whether it be much or little. Thou art bound, as all other men and women are, to love thy neighbour in thy heart principally, but also to show him tokens of charity by deeds as reason demandeth, according to thy might and knowledge. And since it is the case that thou, being enclosed, oughtest not to go out of thy house to seek occasions of profiting thy neighbour by deeds of charity, nevertheless thou art bound to love all men in thy heart, and to show some tokens of true love to them that come to thee. And, therefore, whoever wisheth to speak with thee, whatsoever he be or of whatsoever degree, though thou knowest not what he is or why he cometh, yet be thou soon ready with a good will to ask what his will is. Be not haughty nor suffer him to wait long for thee, but consider how ready and how glad thou wouldst be if an Angel from heaven should come and speak with thee, and be just as ready and as eager in thy will to speak with thy neighbour when he cometh to thee; for thou knowest not what he is nor why he cometh, nor what need he hath of thee or thee of him, until thou hast tried him. And though thou be at prayer or at thy devotions, and feelest loath to break off, inasmuch as thou thinkest that thou oughtest not to leave God to speak to anyone, I do not agree with thee; for if thou be wise thou wilt not leave God, but thou wilt find Him, and have Him, and see Him in thy neighbour as well as in prayer, only in another manner.

'If thou canst love thy neighbour properly, to speak to him with discretion will be no hindrance to thee. And methinks thou wilt have discretion if thou actest in this manner Whosoever cometh to thee, ask him meekly what he would have; and if he comes to tell thee the disease or trouble of his mind and to be comforted by thy speech, hear him gladly, and suffer him to say what he will for the ease of his own heart; and when he hath done, comfort him if thou canst, gladly, gently, and charitably, and soon break off thy discourse with him. And if that he has a mind to take to idle tales, or the vanities of the world, or other men's actions, answer him but little, and encourage not his conversation, and he will soon be weary and quickly take his leave.

'If it be another kind of man that cometh to thee, as, for example, an ecclesiastic, to instruct thee, hear him humbly, and with reverence for his holy order; and if his discourse comforts thee, ask more of him, according to thy need, and take it not upon thee to teach him, for it falleth not to thy lot to teach a priest, save in case of necessity. If his discourse comfort or profit thee not, answer little, and he will soon take his leave

'If it be another kind of man that cometh to thee, as, for example, one to give thee alms, or else to hear thee speak, or to be taught by thee, speak gently and humbly to each. Reprove no man for his faults, for this belongeth not to thee, unless he be so friendly and familiar with thee that thou knowest that he will take it well from thee. And, to be short in this matter of thy telling another of his faults, I say that, when thou conceivest that it will do him good in his soul, thou mayest tell him thy mind if thou hast the opportunity, and if he is likely to take it well. And, above all other things in this matter of conversing with thy neighbour, keep silence as much as thou canst, and then wilt thou see that by so doing thou in a short time wilt be troubled with little, through company coming to hinder thy devotions. This is my opinion in the matter, give a better if thou canst.'[1]

The editor of the English edition (1869) says of the concluding remark that it is the plain English for

'Si quid novisti rectius istis
candidus imperti, si non, his utere mecum.'

This author's advice is good and wise, but it has to be applied with discretion, according to different times, and places, and people. As I cannot give any better opinion, I have quoted his for the purpose of showing the sense in which we may observe retirement and solitude, and yet not neglect duties of charity towards our neighbour.

[1] 'The Scale of Perfection,' p. 132 *et seq*

CHAPTER II

PRAYER CONSIDERED AS A PREPARATION FOR CONTEMPLATION

ACCORDING to Father Baker, the whole employment of an internal contemplative life may be comprehended under two duties—to wit, mortification and prayer. Of these two duties, it may be said that they comprehend under them all that the soul has to do in order to prepare itself for contemplation. Contemplation itself is prayer of the highest order, and souls, therefore, must accustom themselves first to prayer in the lower degrees before they are ordinarily raised up by God to the higher degrees of contemplation. We shall therefore treat in the first place of prayer, which is the most noble and Divine instrument of perfection, and by which we can securely attain to the reward of all our endeavours, the end of our creation and redemption—namely, union with God, in which alone consist our happiness and perfection.

1. The meaning of prayer in general.

1. It is necessary at the outset to form a correct notion of the meaning of prayer. I say this because prayer is taken and used by Saints, theologians, and mystical writers in many senses. This may be fully accounted for by giving the explanation of St. Thomas, who takes prayer in a fourfold sense, according to the

four conditions contained in prayer, each one of which has its own definition, but almost all the definitions can be brought under the four considerations which he gives. His explanation is as follows: First, prayer is nothing else but the act of the practical intellect by which it intends to move the will to the external works of some virtue, so that prayer under this consideration means some good thoughts by which a man excites his will to perform a good work of any virtue—as, for example, when a man thinks to himself the way in which he can become humble, obedient, chaste, or how he can love his neighbour, or how he ought to believe the truths of faith, or how he should serve God and patiently conduct himself in all things. And under this consideration prayer is defined 'The raising up of the mind and heart to God.'

Secondly, prayer may be taken for the acts of the practical intellect by which a man moves himself to ask of God something lawful, honest, useful, and suitable for His service, or, in other words, prayer under this head is nothing else than to ask of God whatever is just, useful, and necessary for His service, for the salvation of our souls—namely, that He may pardon our sins and grant us the grace to love Him. In this sense St. Augustine defines prayer *Oratio petitio quædam est* (Prayer is a certain petition); and St. John Damascene: 'Prayer is the elevation of the mind to God, or a petition of gifts from God.'

Thirdly, prayer may be taken for the acts of the intellect by which we incite the will to love God, and in this sense it means a holy thought which moves us to love, for example, a man thinks of the

Passion of Christ and the benefits conferred on us through Christ's sufferings, or of the sins which have been pardoned through it, and a thought of this kind incites to the love of God. Prayer taken in this sense is said to be better, more elevated, and more perfect, because it is the same as contemplation. The difference between this and prayer taken under other considerations is that in this we do not ask anything of God, and in it the acts of the intellect and holy thoughts are ordained solely to the love of God. In the other considerations or senses in which prayer is taken, the acts of the intellect, the holy thoughts and petitions, are not only ordained to the love of God, but to the good works of the other virtues, such as of humility, patience, etc In this sense it is defined by St. Augustine ' Prayer is the pure affection of the mind directed to God '

Fourthly, prayer may be taken for every good desire and for every good work of any virtue which the will exercises within itself. And prayer is often taken in this sense in Holy Scripture and by the holy Fathers. For if the will elicits acts of love, hope, humility, sorrow for sins, or commands acts of faith, all these interior acts are called prayer Under this consideration prayer differs from the others, and the difference principally consists in this, that under the other considerations prayer is understood as the operation of the intellect, either as the thoughts by which we ask of God a good work, by which the will is incited to love God, or to perform some good work of any of the virtues ; and in a secondary sense it differs inasmuch as the acts of the will are considered in the three foregoing considerations as the effects and terms of the work of the intellect ; but in this the acts of the will, and the virtuous actions in which the will exercises itself, are principal and hold the first place, and the operations of the intellect hold a less principal or a secondary place. In this sense St Augustine defines prayer *Ascensio animæ de terrestribus ad cælestia, inquisitio supernorum, invisibilium desiderium* (The raising up of the soul from earthly to heavenly things, the investigation of things above, the desire of things invisible). And by St. Thomas it is defined *Desiderii coram Deo explicatio, ut aliquid ab ipso impetremus* (The manifestation of our desire before God, that we may impetrate something from Him).[1]

From this doctrine it may be gathered that we have not a comprehensive or complete definition of prayer in general. Every exercise of the mind towards God by which we think of His visible works, or meditate on His invisible mysteries, or contemplate His infinite perfections, and every thought by which we are moved to desire, to fear, and to love Him, receives the name of prayer, and hence the difficulty of giving any one comprehensive definition of this exercise. It is, as we have seen, an act of the intellect and an act of the will, and it belongs to philosophy rather than to the science of the Saints to explain how this order of things is observed. Mystical writers, I know, attach the chief importance to the prayer of the will, although it may be said philosophically that prayer is chiefly the act of the intellect.

2 From the explanation set forth we are enabled to understand some mystical writers in their treatment of prayer and in the meaning they attach to it,

Prayer as described by Father Baker

[1] 'Mystica Theologia Divi Thomæ,' vol. 1, p 167

without any suspicion of their differing from the commonly received definition and meaning of prayer as given in our Catechism and books of instruction. Amongst these, Father Baker gives us a beautiful definition and explanation of prayer as follows: 'By prayer, in this place, I do not understand petition or supplication, which, according to the doctrine of the schools, is exercised principally in the understanding, being a signification of what the person desires to receive from God. But prayer here especially meant is rather an offering or giving to God whatsoever He may justly require of us—that is, all duty, love, obedience, etc.; and it is principally, yea, almost only, exercised by the affective part of the soul.

'Now, prayer in this general notion may be defined to be an elevation of the mind to God, or more largely and expressly thus: Prayer is an affectuous actuation of an intellective soul towards God, expressing, or at least implying, an entire dependence on Him as the Author and Fountain of all good, a will and a readiness to give Him His due, which is no less than all love, obedience, adoration, glory, and worship, by humbling and annihilating of herself and all creatures in His presence; and, lastly, a desire and intention to aspire to a union of spirit with Him.

'This is the nature and these the necessary qualities which are all, at least virtually, involved in all prayer, whether it be made interiorly in the soul only, or withal expressed by words or outward signs.

'Hence it appears that prayer is the most perfect and Divine action that a rational soul is capable of;

yea, it is the only principal action for the exercising of which the soul was created, since in prayer alone the soul is united to God. And by consequence it is of all other actions and duties the most indispensably necessary.'[1]

As I have in former works treated of prayer,[2] its necessity and the conditions necessary that our prayers may be efficacious, and as there are already so many treatises and books which give full instructions on these subjects, it is not necessary to prolong my work and to enter upon the repetition of former instructions and explanations. It is fitting that I confine myself to the subject in hand as carefully as possible, and therefore to treat of prayer, and of the various kinds of prayer, in so far as they lead to and prepare the soul for contemplation and the higher forms of prayer which belong to it, and with which so many of God's servants and Saints were favoured.

I may, however, with advantage call attention to the necessity and importance of prayer in relation to Christian perfection, and in its relation to the higher spiritual life of the soul.

3. Cardinal Bona, in a treatise on the principles of Christian life, has the following passage on prayer: 'In it all the virtues are put in practice First of all comes faith; for no one would pray unless he believed that God was present and heard the prayers of those who called on Him, and was both willing and able, if we ask what is right, to grant our requests. Hope, too, is called into exercise, since we must needs have the greatest

Prayer relation to Christian perfection

---

[1] 'Holy Wisdom,' p 34
[2] 'Convent Life' 'The Commandments Explained'

confidence in the power and mercy of God. Charity is excited by the consideration of the goodness of God, which urges us to love Him above all things. By prayer we learn to fulfil all justice, and to weigh all things with the prudence of the just. Fortitude is exercised, because he who prays has firmly determined to serve God and to endure all adversities and trials for the sake of His love. Acts of temperance are also made, inasmuch as the mind of him who prays is drawn into a distaste for all earthly and corporeal things, and tastes the delights of heaven, and so of the rest. He, then, who applies himself to prayer is adorned with many virtues.'[1]

4. The division of prayer

4. Prayer is formally divided into vocal and mental, into meditative and contemplative, into public and private, and, lastly, into prayer of praise, prayer of thanksgiving, and prayer of petition. Father Baker finds fault with the division of prayer into vocal and mental, because the parts of the division are coincident; for vocal prayer, as distinguished from (and much more as opposed to) mental prayer, is indeed no prayer at all, he reminds us, and he adds: 'Whatever it is, what esteem God makes of it, He shows by His prophet, saying: *This people honour Me with their lips, but their heart is far from Me. In vain do they honour Me*, etc.'[2] However, he accepts the division, as do all other writers according to its proper sense and explanation.

Vocal prayer is that which is expressed by the voice, yet so that the act of the mind is united to that of

[1] Benedict XIV, 'Treatise on Heroic Virtue,' vol 1, p 232
[2] 'Holy Wisdom,' p 235 (St. Matt xv 8).

the voice. For otherwise, if it were done without either attention or intention, it would only deserve the Divine displeasure. It is prayer expressed in words, the soul attending to the sense of the words pronounced, or at least intending to do so. Mental prayer is made without external utterance. It is to say inwardly whatever a person is accustomed to say aloud in prayer, or there may be such pure and perfect elevations of the will that there are not any corresponding internal words or any explicable thoughts of the soul itself.

5. Mental prayer is divided into meditative and contemplative. Here we may give only a general description of meditative prayer and contemplative prayer in the words of Benedict XIV., as we shall later be obliged to consider the one as a preparation for the other, and the transition from meditative to contemplative prayer which takes place in privileged souls.

The division of mental prayer into meditative and contemplative

'Meditative prayer,' says Benedict XIV., 'is nothing more than an attentive consideration of any mystery of faith or anything revealed, and this is done by reasoning on it and proceeding from one part of it to another. Suppose, for instance, one should meditate on the Nativity of Christ: he turns over in his mind who it is that is born, and considers that it is God, Who became man, and he thinks on this with wonder. He considers the place, a stable, and is amazed at this; he considers the time also, the depth of a severe winter, and wonders at this; he considers the poverty of Him Who was born—He was wrapped in swaddling clothes and lay in a manger—and this excites his wonder; he considers next that He came forth from His mother's womb without offence to her virginal chastity and without pain, and at all this he wonders ; and so he considers the other circumstances connected with the Nativity, and from the consideration of all these things he draws forth an act of love towards Christ, Who was born, and towards God, Who accomplished all these wonders.

'Contemplative prayer, or contemplation, is defined by St. Thomas to be a gazing upon Divine truth. In order to explain this clearly, let us suppose that someone reads, or hears another read, this article of faith "The Son of God became incarnate." By the assistance of the Divine grace he believes it to be true. He turns over in His mind the Incarnation and the manner of it, and having made an act of believing, he meditates on, and carefully considers, that truth—viz., that the Son of God became incarnate—fixing on it the eye of his mind by simply gazing on it. He then adds to this act of the intellect one of the will—that is to say, an act of love and affection respecting this mystery. Hence St. Thomas, in answer to the first argument, in which it was contended that contemplation was an act of the intellect alone, says "Inasmuch as truth is the end of contemplation, it has from this cause the character of a good that is desirable and amiable and that causes delight, and in this respect it belongs to the appetitive faculty."

6. Public and private prayers. Prayer of praise, of thanksgiving, and of petition.

6 'Lastly, public prayer is that which is made by the Church in her name; private, that which is made by any private person, either for himself or for others. It is plain from the very terms what is meant by the prayer of praise, what by that of thanksgiving, and what by that of petition. Some

Psalms, for instance, belong to the prayer of praise, as the psalms *Confitebor tibi Domine*, *Benedictus Dominus Deus meus* Others have reference to the prayer of thanksgiving, as *Laudate pueri*, *Laudate Dominum de Cœlis*, *Laudate Dominum omnes gentes*, and *Confitemini Domino*. Of the prayer of petition Christ speaks in the Gospel of St. Matthew. *Ask, and it shall be given you, seek, and ye shall find; knock, and it shall be opened to you* And again *Your Father Who is in heaven will give good things to them that ask Him*.[1]

[1] St. Matt vii 7, 11. 'Treatise on Heroic Virtue,' vol 1, p 234 *et seq*

CHAPTER III

VOCAL PRAYER A PREPARATION FOR CONTEMPLATION

1. The necessity and utility of vocal prayer

1. It would be a great mistake in the spiritual life to undervalue or to neglect the practice of vocal prayer. Benedict XIV. reminds us that we are not allowed to doubt of the utility of vocal prayer, and he quotes the eminent Cardinal de Lauræa, who teaches that vocal prayer is useful—first, in order to excite interior devotion, secondly, in order that man may serve God with the whole being which God has given him; and thirdly, from a sort of overflowing that there is of the soul into the body, as it is said in the Psalms. *Therefore my heart hath been glad, and my tongue hath rejoiced*[1]

(1) Vocal prayer necessary for beginners

(1) For beginners this kind of prayer is most profitable, and therefore all beginners in the spiritual life are strongly recommended to say, and to keep saying, Our Fathers, Hail Marys, the Creeds, the acts of faith, hope, charity, and contrition, and to read the Psalter and suchlike. The author of 'The Scale of Perfection' assigns a good reason for this. He says. 'For he who cannot run easily and lightly by spiritual prayer needs a firm staff to hold by, because his feet of knowledge and love are feeble and diseased by reason of sin This staff is made up of

---

[1] Ps xv 9.

set forms of vocal prayer, ordained by God and Holy Church for the help of men's souls. By its means the soul of a fleshly man that is always falling downwards into worldly thoughts and sensual affections is lifted up above them, and held up as by a prop, and it is fed by the sweet words of those prayers as a child with milk, and guided and supported by them that he may not fall into errors or fancies through his vain imaginations, for in this kind of prayer no deceit or error can happen to him who diligently and humbly exercises himself therein.'[1]

(2) For religious persons this kind of prayer is not only useful, but necessary by reason of the precept of the Church and the prescriptions of their rules. They have set vocal prayers to be recited every day, and if only this one duty be performed in the proper manner, sanctity and observance will be found in any religious community. Take, for example, the Breviary and the manner of saying it The author just quoted, speaking of the Breviary, says : ' In saying it, thou sayest the Our Father and other prayers also And to stir thee up to greater devotion, there are in it, and ordered to be said, Psalms and hymns and other such prayers, which were made by the Holy Ghost even as the Our Father was. And therefore thou must not say these hastily nor carelessly, as if thou wert troubled or discontented at being bound to the recital of them, but thou must recollect thy thoughts so as to say them more seriously and more devoutly than any other prayers of voluntary devotion, deeming it a certain truth that, inasmuch as they are the prayers

[1] 'Scale of Perfection,' p 40

of Holy Church, there are no vocal prayers so profitably to be used by thee as these. And so thou must put away all slothfulness, and by God's grace turn thy necessity into a good will, and thy obligation into great freedom, thus making them no hindrance to thy other spiritual exercises. After them thou mayest use others if thou wilt, such as the Our Father or any other, and stick to those in which thou feelest most relish and spiritual comfort.[1]

(3) Utility of short prayers, ejaculatory for all

(3) Another kind of vocal prayer deserves mention, which may be used by all at stated times and under certain circumstances. It takes the form of pious aspirations, ejaculations, and affections of the will expressed in words. 'It consists,' as Hilton tells us, 'not in any set common form of words, but is that by which a man, through the gift of God and the feeling of devotion, speaketh to God as if He were bodily in his presence, with such words as best suit his inward emotions at the time, or as come into his mind and seem adapted to the feelings of his heart, making reference either to his past sins and wretchedness, or to the malice and wiles of the enemy, or to the mercies and goodness of God. And hereby he crieth with desire of heart and speech of mouth to our Lord for succour and for help, as a man that is in peril among his enemies, saying with holy David *Deliver me from my enemies, O Lord,*[2] or as a man that is in sickness, showing his sores to God as to a physician, and crying out *Heal me, O Lord, for my bones are troubled,*[3] or other suchlike words as

---

[1] 'Scale of Perfection,' p. 41   [2] Ps. cxlii. 9
[3] Ps. vi. 3

they come into his mind. And at other times there appears to him to be so much goodness, grace, and mercy in God that it delighteth him to love Him with great affection of heart, and to thank Him in such words and passages of the Psalms as do best suit the occasion, as when David saith. *Confess ye to the Lord, because He is good, because His mercy endureth for ever*[1]

2 According to Father Baker, by vocal prayer the ancients attained to perfect contemplation. 'It cannot be denied,' he says, 'but that in ancient times many holy souls did attain to perfect contemplation by the mere use of vocal prayer, the which likewise would have the same effect upon us if we would or could imitate them both in such wonderful solitude or abstraction, rigorous abstinences, and incredible assiduity in praying. But for a supply of such wants, and inability to support such undistracted long attention to God, we are driven to help ourselves by daily set exercises of internal prayer to procure an habitual constant state of recollectedness, by such exercises repairing and making amends for the distractions that we live in all the rest of the day' He adds, however, to this that the hand of God is not shortened, and that if He please He may now, as He did formerly, call souls to contemplation by the way of vocal prayer in the case of those who make it their general and ordinary exercise. He prescribes some rules which those who are called to contemplation by this way are recommended to observe. He tells them that they must use a greater measure of abstraction and mortification than is necessary for those who exercise mental

2 Vocal prayer as a means of contemplation in ancient times

[1] Ps cxxxv. 1

prayer; that they must spend a greater time at their daily exercises than is necessary for the others, to the end thereby to supply for the less efficacy that is in vocal prayer; that if during the vocal prayer they find themselves invited by God internally to a pure internal prayer (which is like to be of the nature of aspiration), they must yield to the invitation, and for the time interrupt or cease their voluntary vocal exercises for as long as they find themselves enabled to exercise internally. Then, after giving these rules, he continues 'If any such souls there be to whom vocal prayer (joined with the exercise of virtues) is sufficient to promote them to contemplation, certain it is that there is no way more secure than it, none less subject to indiscretion or illusions, and none less perilous to the head or health And in time (but it will be long first) their vocal prayers will prove aspirations, spiritual and contemplative, by their light and virtue illustrating and piercing to the very depth of the spirit.'[1]

Attention required for vocal prayers

3. That vocal prayer may be beneficial to the full extent, and that it may have the effect of leading the soul to perfection and preparing it for contemplation, there is one condition necessary, and one that, above all others, must be attended to, and that is attention St Thomas, and after him all spiritual writers, give a threefold attention—attention to the words, attention to the sense of the words, and attention to the end, both to God and to the thing for which we pray The attention must be internal, although theologians designate as external attention that to the words which consists in articulating them carefully and reverently. Founding his teaching on

[1] 'Holy Wisdom,' p 344 *et seq*

this division, though changing or varying it a little in his development, Father Baker describes the kinds of attention in prayer in a manner that may be of great assistance to many souls.

He says: 'There is an attention or express reflection on the words and sense of the sentence pronounced by the tongue or revolved in the mind. Now, this attention being, in vocal prayer, necessarily to vary according as sentences in Psalms, etc., do succeed one another, cannot so powerfully and efficaciously fix the mind or affections on God, because they are presently to be recalled to new considerations or succeeding affections. This is the lowest and most imperfect degree of attention, of which all souls are in some measure capable, and the more imperfect they are, the less difficulty there is in yielding to it; for souls that have good and established affections to God can hardly quit a good affection by which they are united to God, and which they find grateful and profitable to them, to exchange it for a new one succeeding in the office; and if they should, it would be to their prejudice. *[First degree—to the words and sense]*

'The second degree is that of souls indifferently well practised in internal prayer, who, coming to the recital of the office, and either bringing with them or by occasion of such recital raising in themselves an efficacious affection to God, do desire without variation to continue it with as profound a recollectedness as they may, not at all heeding whether it be suitable to the sense of the present passage which they pronounce: this is an attention to God, though not to the words, and is far more beneficial than the former. For since all vocal prayers in *[Second degree—to God]*

Scripture or otherwise were ordained only to this end, to supply and furnish the soul that needs with good matter of affection, by which it may be united to God, a soul that hath already attained to that end, which is union as long as it lasts, ought not to be separated therefrom, and be obliged to seek a new means till the virtue of the former be spent.

Third degree—to the sense and to God

'A third and most sublime degree of attention to the Divine office is that whereby vocal prayers do become mental—that is, whereby souls most profoundly and with a perfect simplicity united to God can yet, without any prejudice to such union, attend also to the sense and spirit of each passage that they pronounce; yea, thereby find their affection, adhesion, and union increased and simplified This attention comes not till a soul be arrived to perfect contemplation, by means of which the spirit is so habitually united to God, and, besides, the imagination so subdued to the spirit that it cannot rest on anything that will distract it'

The author, having explained these three degrees, adds . ' Happy are the souls (of which God knows the number is very small) that have attained to this third degree, the which must be ascended to by a careful practice of the two former, especially of the second degree. And therefore, in reciting of the office, even the more imperfect souls may do well, whensoever they find themselves in a good measure recollected, to continue so long as they can, preserving so much stability in their imagination as may be '[1]

[1] 'Holy Wisdom,' p 347

4. It seems to me that no soul, however holy or perfect, apart from the prayers that are of obligation, should neglect voluntary vocal prayers. It is most edifying to behold old ecclesiastics as well as religious and lay persons reading well-used prayer-books, and reciting the rosary, and performing the exercise of the Stations of the Cross with the aid of a Station Book. That the Saints never omitted this practice is abundantly proved by the histories of their lives, and Benedict XIV. asserts that the question should not be entertained of beatifying or canonizing any servant of God who did not in his lifetime use vocal prayer. He reminds us, however, that, as the value of vocal prayer is internal, it cannot be known to the Church directly; yet indirectly the perfection of vocal prayer must be collected from external acts—as, for instance, from tears, from the position and gestures of the body, from the place, from the time in which prayer is made, from the frequency of it. He does not mean that tears and the other external signs are to be taken as infallible proof of the excellence of prayer, but all taken together may amount to a strong proof in favour of the sincere devotion and piety of the servant of God. As to the length of time spent in prayer, he says 'The continuance in prayer ought not, however, to be measured by any set space of time, since, as regards private vocal prayer, it ought to be persevered in as long as is required to excite interior fervour. So St. Augustine says "There may not be much speaking, but there will not fail to be much praying, if only there is a perseverance in the intention." [1]

Voluntary vocal prayers recommended

[1] 'Treatise on Heroic Virtue,' vol 1, p 240.

5 The necessity and utility of vocal prayer illustrated by the example of St Pius V Pope

5. As an example in proof of the necessity and utility of vocal prayer, even for the Saints and contemplatives, and of the manner in which they should frequently return to this exercise, the same eminent Pontiff gives us some extracts from the life of Pius V. as given in the Bollandists. It is said of this saintly Pontiff. 'He was extremely assiduous in the practice of holy prayer, of which he used to say, that as it was an aid and protection to all others, so it was in an especial manner to Pontiffs. Accordingly, he was accustomed to rise before daybreak, and to remain so fixed in that exercise reciting certain prayers for priests that he sometimes scarcely heard those who approached to interrupt him unless he were restored to himself by having his clothes pulled, and when he retired from prayer he was often wrapped in Divine contemplation, and did not fully answer those who asked him about anything—a certain mark of a burning charity towards God of a soul filled with Divine influence In another place we find 'that while he was engaged in any more weighty or important affairs Pius always kept to this method of prayer. He also provided that the Litanies and other stated prayers should be recited every day at even in the Apostolical Palace, and that in his own presence, unless he was particularly hindered, and that of his whole household. In the meantime, however, he overlooked nothing that belonged to his own particular office. For he considered that the duty of a Pontiff lay chiefly in making intercession before God for the faults and necessities of his people, and that he ought, therefore, to be intimate with, as well as acceptable to, Him with Whom he was appointed to intercede.

PREPARATION FOR CONTEMPLATION

After the example, therefore, of Moses, who frequently went in and out of the tabernacle, he retired from business from time to time in order to discourse with God, that he might learn from God within what he should teach to the people without, and that, having been wrapped up in contemplation of God within, he might be able, on coming out, to bear the burthens of all, and provide for their salvation. He used to say that, in order to sustain properly the burden that had been laid on him, he stood in great need of the prayers of holy persons, and he took great care, therefore, that supplications should be continually offered, both in public and by holy communities, as well as by private persons, to God for himself and for the whole of Christendom He was so devoted to the Most Blessed Virgin Mother of God, that even when he was Supreme Pontiff, and occupied with such weighty affairs, he would never let a day pass in which he did not recite the devotion of what is called the Holy Rosary, and he granted many additional indulgences to this method of prayer And, further, he was accustomed to pray devoutly and carefully for the dead every day, and bears witness that this was of great service to him in many dangers.'[1]

From this example all holy souls may learn—Bishops and priests, religious and persons consecrated to the service of God, householders and others—how they should attend to the duty of prayer, and not neglect the practice of vocal prayer, and pay especial attention to family prayers, to prayers in order to know the will of God in matters of importance, prayers in times of danger, prayers

[1] 'Treatise on Heroic Virtue,' vol. i., p 241 *et seq*

for others, both for the living and the dead. The Litanies and Holy Rosary are expressly mentioned in the life of the holy Pontiff, and they may be especially recommended on all occasions and for all our needs. Such prayers when properly said cannot fail to prepare the soul for contemplation and advance it in perfection, and contemplation in itself will have the effect of making our vocal prayers more fruitful and efficacious.

CHAPTER IV

MEDITATION OR MENTAL PRAYER AS A PREPARATION FOR CONTEMPLATION

I KNOW of no better introduction to my chapters on mental prayer than that given by Benedict XIV. in his 'Treatise on Heroic Virtue,' especially as he confirms his doctrine by many appropriate texts of Holy Scripture.

1. 'Mental prayer is more excellent than vocal prayer. Hence St. Thomas says: "The more closely a man unites his own soul or that of another to God, so much the more pleasing is his sacrifice to God. From this cause it is that it is more acceptable to God that a man should apply himself to contemplation than to action." And so David teaches us: *Give me understanding, and I will search Thy law; and I will keep it with my whole heart*, and *Open Thou my eyes and I will consider the wondrous things of Thy law.*[1] *I will meditate on Thee in the morning.*[2] *I will meditate on all Thy works.*[3] *I will meditate always on Thy justification.*[4] It has been said above that it is necessary for all to pray to God, and this is confirmed by the words of Holy Scripture. In Ecclesiasticus we

[1] Excellence of mental prayer

---

[1] Ps cxviii. 34, 18 [2] Ps lxii 7.
[3] Ps. lxxvi 13 [4] Ps cxviii 117

read *Let nothing hinder thee from praying always*,[1] and in St. Luke *We ought always to pray, and not to faint*.[2]

2. Necessity of mental prayer

2. 'Respecting this necessity of praying, St. John Chrysostom speaks thus "He who does not pray to God, and desire continually to enjoy discourse with God, is dead, and wants life and sense." And further on he adds thus "It must, I think, be plain to all that it is altogether impossible to lead a life of virtue without prayer." It was also mentioned above [in his treatise] that theologians differed in their opinions as to whether there is any precept of private vocal prayer. There is a similar question among them as to mental prayer—that is to say, meditation or contemplation. To suggest something on which question I should say that contemplation and meditation are not necessary to eternal salvation, simply speaking, for our Saviour being asked, *What must I do to possess eternal life?* answered, *Keep the commandments*. And when the speaker asked Him again, He replied to him by enumerating the commandments of the second table only; for He was speaking to a Jew, who already believed in one God and kept holy the Sabbath. Our Saviour again being questioned by the lawyer, which was the great commandment of the law, said *Thou shalt love the Lord thy God with thy whole heart . . . and thou shalt love thy neighbour as thyself. On these two commandments dependeth the whole law and the prophets*. And upon his replying, *All these have I kept from my youth; what is yet wanting to me?* our Lord added, *If thou wilt be perfect, go sell what thou hast, and give to the poor*. This is explained at length by Suarez and Theo-

[1] Ecclus. xviii. 22 [2] St. Luke xviii. 1

philus Raymond also And so we find in Hurtado that the note of temerity is affixed to the proposition, that no one can be saved who does not give up some time every day to mental prayer.'

Whilst denying the absolute necessity of mental prayer, the same learned theologian and holy Pontiff directs our attention to another kind of necessity, which he calls necessity *secundum quid*—that is, when a thing is not absolutely requisite in order to obtaining a certain effect, but by way of obtaining it better and more easily, and he continues ' If we speak of this kind of necessity, we shall have to confess that contemplation and meditation are necessary, and are contained implicitly under what is, to say the best of it, of counsel It is quite certain that a counsel is given us to acquire perfection . *Be ye therefore perfect*, says our Lord, *as your heavenly Father is perfect.* And St Paul, in his Epistle to the Corinthians, says *Be zealous for the better gifts.*[1] And in the Apocalypse we read : *He that is just, let him be justified still ; and he that is holy, let him be sanctified still*[2] Now, if a counsel of acquiring perfection is given us, a counsel of meditating and contemplating is by consequence given us implicitly, though it is one which chiefly regards religious, as Hurtado also confesses. " It is true," he says, " that religious, although there is no Divine precept of mental prayer or meditation with respect to them, are bound to it by greater obligations by reason of their state, inasmuch as it is one of perfect charity, and fervour, and spiritual sweetness, and readiness for all good works, and especially for such as belong to the Divine worship and to piety."[3]

[1] 1 Cor. xii. 31.   [2] Apocal xxii 11
[3] 'Treatise on Heroic Virtue,' vol 1, p 253 *et seq*

It may be observed that Benedict XIV. in the above passages speaks of contemplation in a wide sense, and not inasmuch as it is an extraordinary gift of God, and not necessary even by the necessity of counsel for all who tend towards perfection or enter upon the state of perfection, as many holy religious and Saints have lived and died without being mystics or contemplatives in the strict sense of the words

As our purpose is to treat of meditation principally, in so far as it is a preparation for contemplation, it is necessary to distinguish it from contemplation proper, and to give some instructions regarding the various methods of mental prayer.

<small>3 True notion of mental prayer or meditation</small>

3. A definition of meditation, as distinct from contemplation, has already been given in the words of Benedict XIV. in the chapter on prayer in general Father Baker defines, or rather explains, meditation as follows : ' Meditation is an internal prayer in which a devout soul doth, in the first place, take in hand the consideration of some particular mystery of faith, to the end that, by a serious and exact search into the several points and circumstances in it with the understanding or imagination, she may extract motives of good affections to God, and consequently produce suitable affections in virtue of the said motives as long as such virtue will last.'[1]

Father Faber says . ' Mental prayer means the occupation of our faculties upon God, not in the way of thinking or speculating about Him, but stirring up the will to conform itself to Him, and the affections to love Him The subjects on which it is engaged are all the works of God, as well as

[1] 'Holy Wisdom,' p. 407

His own perfections—but above all, the sacred humanity of our blessed Lord.'[1]

Schram defines and describes mental prayer or meditation as follows · 'It is the exercise of the three powers of the soul—the memory, the intellect, and the will—by which exercise a man by means of the memory recalls some mystery, or history, or supernatural truth, by means of the intellect he reasons or discourses upon it, and considers seriously and minutely, and examines and thinks on its circumstances, its object, and its end, and then by means of the will he elicits pious affections and the resolution of amendment of life, and he concludes by colloquies with God, with the Blessed Virgin, and with the Saints, begging pardon for his sins, giving thanks for the graces received, asking help to keep his good resolutions, and then saying the Our Father or some other vocal prayer. This manner of meditating as to substance, though more or less varied in method, was that universally observed by the ancients, with whom it was held as a dogma that they should propose to all mental prayer acquired by discourse, as better and more efficacious for attaining perfection than vocal prayer.' He then quotes the text of the Psalm in approbation and confirmation of their practice and teaching *Blessed is the man whose help is from the Lord in his heart he hath disposed to ascend by steps, in the vale of tears, in the place which he hath set*[2] And he comments on it thus ' *Blessed is the man whose help is from the Lord*, who ascends by prayer, not of words, but of the heart, and ascends to beatitude, not by flying without discourse or reasoning, but by

[1] 'Growth in Holiness,' p. 246 [2] Ps lxxxiii. 6, 7.

these means disposing his heart and ascending, as it were, by steps'[1]

All these definitions and explanations are in accordance with the definition given by St. Thomas and by philosophers and theologians in general: 'Meditation is the discourse of the mind, by which the intellect engaged upon any truth passes from one consideration to another. This discourse is twofold: one direct and properly so called, when it draws our consideration from another; the other indirect and improperly so called, when it forms one after another. Meditation may be compared to the eyes of the body. They are movable members, and seldom remain long in the same position. Nature placed them in the head, and one at the right and one at the left side, that thus they may protect the body from danger and provide what is profitable for it. The same may be said of the eye of the mind. It ought to be watchful and mobile, because by meditation it has to ascend up on high to regard God and eternal goods; it has to descend down below to consider death and hell. Sometimes it has to look to the right, to attend to those things which have to be done; and sometimes it has to turn to the left, to guard against dangers and to shun the evils that are to be avoided.' In this sense St. Thomas, commenting on the thirty-first chapter of Isaias, says that the eye of the mind ought by means of meditation to open three doors—one of everlasting misery, another of a just life, and the third of heavenly glory. And on Psalm xxxvi. he says in his commentary that the eye of the mind by meditation knows wisdom in a fourfold way—viz., *credendo Christo, acquiescendo sapientibus, psallendo*

[1] 'Instit Theol Myst,' tom. 1, p. 87.

Deo, et docendo ut justi (by believing in Christ, agreeing or being in conformity with the wise, by chanting to God, and by teaching as the just).

This, then, is what is meant by meditation in contrast to contemplation and considered as distinct from it. It is the first of the two sorts of mental prayer spoken of by Rodriguez, which, he says, also is common and easy in contrast to the other, which is extraordinary and sublime.

4. It ought to be a matter of concern to all to know how to meditate well, and it is especially important for religious and other pious persons. It is for this reason that set forms or methods of meditation are prescribed, and it is the duty of each person to make use of that method which suits his disposition, in which he can best succeed, and which he may find the most profitable to his soul; it is for these reasons that I think it well to propose two or three methods well established and approved that may serve as a guidance to devout souls, so many of whom are often delayed in the way of perfection, and fail in mental prayer because they have adopted an unsuitable method and know no other.

Father Faber, speaking of the methods of mental prayer which approved writers have given us, says that they may be resolved into two—the Ignatian and the Sulpician. 'The advantages of the Ignatian method,' he tells us, 'are that it is more adapted to modern habits of mind, that it suits the greater number of persons, that it can be taught as an art, and that most meditation books are framed upon it. The advantages of the Sulpician method are,' he says, 'that it is a more faithful transcript of the tradition of the old Fathers and Saints of the desert, that it supplies a want for those who on the one

[4. The importance of. proper method of meditation]

hand can make no way with the Ignatian method, and on the other have no aptitude for what is called "affective prayer"; and that it is in some respects more suitable for those who are often interrupted at meditation, inasmuch as it is a perfect work whenever it is broken off, whereas the power of the Ignatian method is in its conclusion.' These, he says, are the characteristics of the two methods. He then proceeds to explain each method with his usual clearness and accuracy. Without following him and other authors in the lengthy explanations which they give, I must be indebted to Father Doyle, O.S.B., for the schemes or outlines which he gives of each of these methods, and which better than any detailed description imparts to us a true notion of their parts and their arrangements.

The Ignatian Method of Meditation.

Preparatory Prayer.

<small>5. A method of meditation according to the plan of St Ignatius</small>

5. *Faith:* O my God, I firmly believe that Thou art here present.

Adoration. I adore Thee from the abyss of my nothingness

Humility Lord, I ought now to be in hell on account of my sins.

Sorrow. I am grieved for having offended Thee.

Petition.

Eternal Father, through the merits of Jesus and the prayers of Mary, give me grace to draw fruit from this meditation.

Offering

To God the Father I give my memory; to God the Son my understanding; to God the Holy Ghost my will To thee, my most sweet and loving Mother Mary, I give my imagination. (Ask the prayers of Guardian Angels and Patron Saints.)

Body of the Meditation.

Upon each point of the meditation the three powers of the soul must be exercised. The understanding should be exercised to know what hindrances have to be removed, and what means are to be used in order to insure success for the future. If by the consideration of the first point the soul is moved to make acts of faith, hope, love of God, etc., it must continue to dwell upon them and to entertain the Holy Spirit. It must not proceed to the consideration of the second point so long as the impulse of the Holy Spirit lasts.

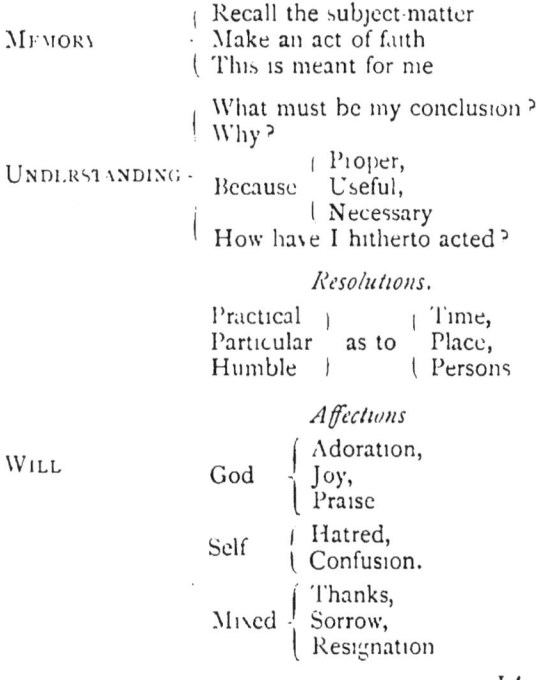

MEMORY — { Recall the subject-matter / Make an act of faith / This is meant for me

UNDERSTANDING — { What must be my conclusion? Why? / Because { Proper, Useful, Necessary } / How have I hitherto acted?

Resolutions.

Practical, Particular, Humble — as to — Time, Place, Persons

Affections

WILL

God — { Adoration, Joy, Praise

Self — { Hatred, Confusion.

Mixed — { Thanks, Sorrow, Resignation

Conclusion.

EXAMINATION
- Examination of parts,
- Sorrow for what is ill done,
- Thanks for what is well done

CONCLUSION
- Colloquy with God,
- Choice of ejaculation,
- Resolution.

PETITIONS
- For self
  - Perseverance,
  - Love of God,
  - Particular grace
- For others
  - Confessor,
  - Parents,
  - Friends,
  - Superiors
- For Church
  - Sinners.
  - Dying,
  - Souls in Purgatory

THE SULPICIAN METHOD OF MEDITATION.

6. This method, approved of by Père Olier, is founded on the method of prayer used by the Fathers in the desert.

Preparation.

REMOTE (removing)
- Sin
- The passions,
- The thought of creatures

LESS REMOTE
- Preparing subject overnight,
- Reviewing the next morning,
- Eliciting affections

PROXIMATE
- Putting ourselves in God's presence,
- Acknowledging our unworthiness and the necessity of God's grace

Body of the Prayer.

1 Adoration, or Jesus in our mouth—thus expressed by our Lord · 'Hallowed be Thy name'

2 Communion, or Jesus in our heart—thus expressed by our Lord · 'Thy kingdom come'

3 Co-operation, or Jesus in our hand—thus expressed by our Lord · 'Thy will be done.'[1]

---

[1] St Ambrose expresses these three parts thus (1) *Signa-*

In the first part, adore, praise, thank, love.

In the second part, transfer to the heart that which has been adored, praised, loved.

In the third part, co-operate with the grace received by fervent colloquies and by generous resolutions.

(*a*) ' If we experience any secret operations of the Holy Spirit in our soul during the second part, we ought to keep ourselves in perfect silence and repose, in order that we may receive the full effect of such spiritual communications, and we ought not to go on while these operations last.

(*b*) ' The first part—*adoration*—is extremely important—(1) because it leads us to contemplate our Lord as the Source of virtues, (2) because it makes us regard Him as our original Model; (3) because our adoration of God is a more perfect act of religion than our petitioning Him for grace; (4) because it is the shortest, surest, and most efficacious way to perfection.

(*c*) ' In the second part—*communion*—we must (1) convince ourselves, chiefly by motives of faith, that the grace which we ask for is most important for us; (2) we must strive to see how greatly we are at present in need of that grace, and how many opportunities of acquiring it we have lost; (3) we must pray for it with simplicity, through the merits of our Lord and the graces of our Lady, by thanksgiving for past graces, by insinuation like the sister of Lazarus · *Lord, he whom Thou lovest is sick*.

(*d*) ' In the third part—*co-operation*—we make our resolutions, which must be—(1) particular, or, if general, united with particular ones; (2) present, or

---

ulum in ore ut semper confiteamur, (2) *signaculum in corde ut semper diligamus*, (3) *signaculum in brachio ut semper operemur*

likely to be tested that very day; (3) efficacious—that is, such as will be carried out with fidelity, and such as we explicitly intend to carry out with fidelity.

'*Conclusion.*

'This consists in three acts—(1) in thanksgiving for the graces which God has given us in prayer, for having endured us in His presence, and for having enabled us to pray; (2) we must beg pardon for the faults which we have committed in our prayer through negligence, lukewarmness, distraction, inattention, and restlessness; (3) we must put it into the hands of our Blessed Lady to offer it to God, in order to supply our defects and to obtain all blessings. Then we should, according to St. Francis de Sales, form for ourselves a "spiritual nosegay"—that is, resolve frequently to call to mind some thought which has moved us during the meditation. We should never depart from prayer without begging God's grace for parents, for confessors, for brethren, for sinners, and for the souls in purgatory.'[1]

Father Alphonsus Rodriguez tells us that the Ignatian method or form of prayer has been confirmed by the Holy Father, as may be seen by the Bull in the beginning of the spiritual exercises of St. Ignatius. In that Bull of Paul III. it is mentioned that the Pope, after having with great attention very strictly examined these exercises, does not only approve and confirm them, but exhorts the faithful to make use of them as very profitable. The pious author adds: 'It was by this form of

[1] 'Principles of Religious Life,' append., p. 527 *et seq.*

prayer that Christ drew to Himself our blessed founder and his companions, it was in the practice of this holy method that He made him conceive the design, and form the model, of the Society (of Jesus); and this is the medium or means whereby he has gained so many other souls to Christ.'[1]

7. We have already seen what Father Faber says of the advantages and characteristics of this method. After describing all its parts, he speaks of it as follows 'The first perusal of the Ignatian plan is like a cleric's first look into a Breviary It seems as if we should never find our way about in it. But the processes are in reality so natural that they soon become easy to us, and follow each other in legitimate succession almost without effort or reflection It is much more easy than it seems. The method of St Francis de Sales is substantially the same, with some of the peculiarities of his own character thrown in The same may be said of the method of St Alphonsus, which is that of St. Ignatius, with somewhat more freedom, such as we would expect from the character of that glorious Saint, who to his many other titles to the gratitude of the modern Church might add that of the Apostle of Prayer Beginners are always inclined to dispense themselves from the mechanical parts of the system. But it is well worth our while to be patient for a few weeks. We shall never be sorry for it, whereas we shall regret the contrary line of conduct as long as we live. We must beware also of kneeling vacantly and doing nothing, which adds the fault of irreverence to that of idleness. We must not look out for interior voices, or marked experiences, or

7 Father Faber's estimate of the Ignatian method

[1] 'Christian and Religious Perfection,' vol 1, p 249

decided impressions of the Divine will upon our minds, nor give in to the temptation of leaving the plain road of painstaking meditation in order to reach God by some shorter way.'[1]

<small>8 His estimate of the Sulpician method</small>

8. Father Faber further tells us that much of what has been said of the Ignatian method is applicable to all methods in the way of direction and guidance. In speaking of the Sulpician method, he confines himself to those things which distinguish it from others, and he says that it is in the body of the prayer its chief characteristics are to be found. 'It consists, as the Ignatian does, of three points: the first is called adoration, the second communion, and the third co-operation. In the first we adore, praise, love, and thank God. In the second we try to convey to our own hearts what we have been praising and loving in God, and to participate in its virtues according to our measure. In the third we co-operate with the grace we are receiving by fervent colloquies and generous resolutions. The ancient fathers have handed down to us this method of prayer as in itself a perfect compendium of Christian perfection. They call it having Jesus before their eyes, which is the adoration; Jesus in their hearts, which is the communion; and Jesus in their hands, which is the co-operation; and in these three things all the Christian life consists. After their accustomed fashion, they deduce it from the precepts of God to the children of Israel, that the words of the law were to be before their eyes, in their hearts, and bound upon their hands. Thus St Ambrose calls these three points the three seals. The adoration he calls *signaculum in fronte ut semper confiteamur*,

[1] 'Growth in Holiness,' p. 255.

the communion, *signaculum in corde ut semper diligamus;* and the co-operation, *signaculum in brachio, ut semper operemur.* Others, again, declare that this method of prayer is according to the model which our Lord has given us. Thus, the adoration answers to " Hallowed be Thy name," the communion to " Thy kingdom come," and the co-operation to " Thy will be done." It seems that this method of prayer is, as far as we can judge, the same which prevailed among the Fathers of the desert, and it is astonishing how many scraps of ancient tradition there are regarding it. Its patristic character is quite the distinguishing feature of the Sulpician method of prayer. It is a piece of the older spirituality of the Church.'

His remark concerning the two methods after he has described them sums up his estimate of their relative value. 'These two methods of prayer are both of them most holy, even though they are so different. There is a different spirit in them, and they tend to form different characters. But they cannot be set one against the other. They are both from one Spirit, even the Holy Ghost, and each will find the hearts to which it is sent. Happy is the man who is a faithful disciple of either.'[1]

[1] 'Growth in Holiness,' pp. 258, 262.

CHAPTER V

INTERNAL AFFECTIVE PRAYER

SCHRAM tells us that meditation, to dispose the soul for contemplation, should be affective rather than intellective or discursive, and that it should be inflamed by aspirations and ejaculations, and in this way continued day and night. It is of this species of mental prayer that Father Baker treats so fully, and to which he attaches very great importance. He seems to have been a man endowed with a wonderful gift of prayer himself, and therefore most capable of enlightening others on the subject; and it is for this reason that attention should be directed to his teaching on what he calls 'affective prayer,' and to some of his remarks concerning the methods of meditation.

[margin: 1 Remarks on Father Baker's distinction between affective prayer and meditation]

1. He seems to distinguish affective prayer from meditation in the ordinary way, although according to the above methods affective prayer appears to form the most important part of the meditation, and the exercises of the memory and of the intellect are ordained solely to the moving of the will to pious affections, which is the same as affective prayer such as Father Faber describes it. He does not treat professedly of discursive prayer or meditation. Of this he says: 'The world is even burdened with

books, which with more than sufficient niceness prescribe rules and methods for the practice of it, and with too partial an affection magnify it, the authors of such books neglecting in the meantime, or perhaps scarce knowing what true internal affective prayer is, which, notwithstanding, is the only efficacious instrument that immediately brings souls to contemplation and perfect union in spirit with God.' After this statement we naturally expect an explanation of affective prayer as distinct from meditation, but that explanation we have to gather from what he writes about the excellence and necessity of affective prayer, the five admirable virtues of internal affective prayer, the conditions required for affective prayer, namely, that it may be continual in the sense of our Lord's words, *Oportet semper orare, et non deficere—We ought always to pray, and not to cease (or faint in it)*—and that it be fervent and devout. What he attributes to internal affective prayer in the treatment of all these matters seems to me to be attributed by others to meditation well made, and to be required as conditions for it. After reading carefully his chapters on this subject, all I can conclude with regard to the distinction between this affective prayer and the methods of meditation with which we are familiar is that it is not and need not be discursive, and that it is the immediate forerunner or preparation for contemplation. This I gather especially from one paragraph, where, speaking of imperfect religious, and after asserting that by their profession they ought to aspire to contemplation, he complains that, being mistaken in the true way thereto, they rest in such active exercises as the exact performance of outward observances and the solemn saying of the office and the practice of internal discursive prayer, and do not from them 'proceed to the truly enlightening exercises of internal affective prayer (which is a prayer of the heart or will by good affections quietly and calmly produced, and not with the understanding)—a prayer made without those distracting methods or that busying of the imagination and wearing of the soul by laborious discourses, which are only inferior and imperfect preparation to true prayer.'[1] It may be noticed that in the methods of prayer above proposed that souls do not rest in discursive exercise, but proceed from it to the internal affective prayer here mentioned, and that all exercise of the intellect and memory is ordained to the moving of the will to pious affections, etc.

Affective prayer as a preparation for contemplation. Example of Father Baltazar Alvarez

2. From the illustrious example which he gives us in the person of Father Baltazar Alvarez, and from the account given us in the words of that holy man of his system of prayer, we may learn more of the nature of affective prayer of the will and of its peculiar excellence as a preparation for contemplation. Of this venerable priest Father Baker tells us that, 'after he had spent with great diligence about fifteen years in meditation and the spiritual exercises (peculiar to his Order), and yet received but little profit to his spirit by them, being, on the contrary, tormented with extreme doubtfulness and unsatisfaction, he was at last guided powerfully, by God's Holy Spirit, to quit meditation, and to betake himself to a serious practice of meditation immediately in the will, by corresponding to which Divine motion he presently received abundance of light and

[1] 'Holy Wisdom,' p 352.

a perfect remedy against all his anguishes and perplexities.'

In the 'Apology' which Father Alvarez wrote at the command of his Father-General to justify his departure from the form of the 'Exercises,' he finds a full account of the order and manner of his prayer. From this 'Apology' and the following few extracts taken from Father Baker's 'Holy Wisdom' we may learn what that was in substance.

3. 'His prayer now was to place himself in God's presence, both inwardly and outwardly presented to him, and to rejoice with Him permanently and abundantly. Now he understood the difference between imperfect and perfect souls on the point of enjoying the Divine presence expressed by St. Thomas, and he perceived that those were blind that seek God with anxiety of mind and call upon Him as if He were absent; whereas, being already His temples in which His Divine Majesty rests, they ought to enjoy Him actually and internally present in them. Sometimes in his prayer he pondered awhile on some text of Scripture, according to the inspirations and lights then given him, sometimes he remained in cessation and silence before God, which manner of prayer he accounted a great treasure, for then his heart, his desires, his secret intuitions, his knowledge, and all his powers, spake, and God understood their mute language, and with one aspect could expel his defects, kindle his desires, and give him wings to mount spiritually unto Him Now he took comfort in nothing but in suffering contentedly, and desired the will of God to be performed in all things, which was as welcome to him in aridities as consolations, being unwilling to know

3. Method of prayer of Father Baltazar Alvarez

more than God freely discovered unto him, or to make a more speedy progress or by any other ways than such as God Himself prescribed unto him. If his heart, out of its natural infirmity, did at any time groan under his present burden, his answer thereto would be: "Is not that good which God wills to be, and will it not always incessantly remain so?" or, "Will God cease to perform His own will because thou dost not judge it to be for thy good?" In conclusion, his present established comfort was to see himself in God's presence to be a sufferer, and to be treated according to His Divine pleasure

'If sometimes, leaving this quiet prayer to which God had brought him, he offered to apply himself to his former exercises of devotion, he found that God gave him an internal reprehension and restraint. For his greater assurance, therefore, he searched mystic authors—St. Denis the Areopagite, St Augustine, St Bernard—out of which he satisfied himself that as rest is the end of motion, and a quiet habitation the end of a laborious building, so this peaceful prayer and quiet enjoying of God in spirit was the end of the imperfect, busy prayer of meditation, and therefore that all internal discoursing with the understanding was to cease whensoever God enabled souls to actuate purely by the will, and to do otherwise would be as if one should be always preparing somewhat to eat, and yet refusing to taste that which is prepared By this Divine prayer of the will, the Holy Spirit of wisdom, with all the excellencies of it described in the Book of Wisdom (chap. viii.), is obtained, and with it perfect liberty

'In consequence hereto he proceeds by reasons to demonstrate the supereminent excellency of this reposeful prayer of the will, as—(1) that though in it there is no reasoning of the mind, yet the soul, silently presenting herself before God with a firm faith that her desires are manifest to Him, doth more than equivalently tell God her desires, and withal exercises all virtue, humbling herself before Him, loving Him only, and believing that, leaving her own ways and constantly holding to God's, all good will proceed from thence to her; (2) that in this prayer a soul hath a far more sublime and worthy notion of God; (3) that this still and quiet prayer may be far more prolixly and perseveringly practised than the tiring prayer of meditation (yea, it may come to be continual and without interruption), (4) that all the good effects of meditation—as humility, obedience, etc—are far more efficaciously and perfectly produced by this prayer than by that which is joined with inward reasoning, (5) true indeed it is that the exercises instituted by St. Ignatius were more proper generally for souls than this, yet this ought to be esteemed proper for those whom God had called and prepared to it, and this was St Ignatius's own practice, who though in his less perfect state he practised the imperfect exercises instituted by him, yet afterwards he was exalted to the sublime prayer by which he came to suffer Divine things. That, therefore, as none ought to intrude into the exercise of this pure prayer till God has called and fitted them for it, so, being called, none ought to be forbidden it.'

'This is the sum of the account which the most venerable Father Baltazar Alvarez, after a retirement of fifteen days, with a most humble confession of his own defects and misery and a magnifying of

God's liberal goodness extended towards him, gave unto his General.'[1]

[*An outline of the immediate acts of the will in prayer by Father Baker*]

4. The same author later on in his work gives us an outline of the practice of the exercises of the immediate acts of the will as follows :

'The soul's aim is to recollect herself by that general notion that faith gives her of God; but being not able to do this presently, she doth in her mind and by the help of the imagination represent unto herself some Divine object, as some one or more perfections of God, or some mystery of faith, as the Incarnation, Transfiguration, Passion, Agony, or Dereliction of our Lord, etc ; and thereupon, without such discoursing as is used in meditation, she doth immediately, without more ado, produce acts or affections one after another towards God, adoring, giving thanks, humbling herself in His presence, resigning herself to His will, etc

'This exercise is more easy to learn and comprehend than meditation, because so many rules are not necessary to it, neither is there in it such study or exercising the abilities of the understanding or imagination It is, indeed, a very plain, downright, and simple exercise, consisting merely in the efficacy of the will, but notwithstanding such plain simplicity, it is a far more noble exercise than that of meditation, as being the fruit and result of it, for whatsoever the understanding operates with reference to God can produce no good effect upon the soul further than it hath relation to and influence on the will by disposing it to submit and resign itself to God, or to tend towards Him by acts of love, adoration, etc.'[2]

[1] 'Holy Wisdom,' p 384 *et seq*   [2] *Ibid*, p 434.

Elsewhere he says, by way of answering an objection to this kind of prayer.

'It is a great mistake in some writers who think the exercise of the will to be mean and base in comparison of inventive meditation and curious speculation of Divine mysteries, inasmuch as none but elevated spirits can perform this, whereas the most ignorant and simple persons can exercise acts or affections of the will. On the contrary, it is most certain that no acts of the understanding (as speculation, consideration, deduction of conclusions, etc.) in matters pertaining to God are of themselves of any virtue to give true perfection to the soul, further than as they do excite the will to love Him, and by love to be united to Him. And this union by exercise may be obtained in perfection by souls that are not at all capable of discourse, and that have no more knowledge of God than what is afforded from a belief of the fundamental verities of Christian faith, so that it is evident that the end of all meditation, etc., is the producing acts of the will. Therefore let no man neglect or scorn the exercise proper for him out of a conceit that it is too mean; but let him first try the profit of it, and not till then make a judgment.'[1]

No one, I think, can fail to see the wisdom and usefulness of Father Baker's instruction on the affective prayer of the will. The few extracts I have selected from his excellent work 'Holy Wisdom' may be the means of leading some to read the chapters in their entirety in that book, and they may well serve my purpose in this place, which is to show that this is a profitable method of mental

[1] 'Holy Wisdom,' p. 422.

prayer and easier than the other prescribed methods for those called to it, and that no one is bound to stick to hard-and-fast rules or methods, in prayer especially, when they know by experience that they cannot succeed according to them.

<small>5 When a soul can pass from meditation to contemplation</small>

5 There remains only one more question to which attention must be directed before concluding the subject of prayer—that is, when the soul can pass from meditation to contemplation.

When the soul has been sufficiently disposed in the manner explained by meditation, it is expedient and right, supposing a special inspiration of God calling it to contemplation, that it be obedient, and humbly conform itself to the Divine call, and then lay aside for the time being meditation. This may be proved from those texts of Scripture which invite souls to contemplation, and the reasons for this are taken from St Thomas, who states (1) Contemplation is the end of all human life, namely, beatitude, imperfect here and perfect hereafter, which everyone should accept when it is offered (2) Meditation is a laborious exercise by discourse or reasoning in quest of truth when it cannot be had by simple intuition as obtained by contemplation; therefore it would be vain to seek what God now offers. (3) We travel by the road of meditation towards contemplation, and it would be unreasonable to adhere to meditation when the Spouse of our soul meets us and comes to us through contemplation.

We must not force ourselves to contemplation or give up meditation rashly or too soon, because it is a fundamental rule that for passing from meditation to contemplation a special vocation and inspiration of God is required. According to all authorities, it would be rash and very injurious to the soul to attempt contemplation ; and without such a vocation and inspiration we should continue in vocal prayer and meditation ; but when the vocation comes, then it would be rash and injurious to our spiritual state not to accept it. Because contemplation is much more perfect than meditation when God moves the soul to it, and to reject that motion is not humility, but weakness or laziness, resulting in great detriment to the soul. Therefore St. John of the Cross censures those confessors and directors who, through want of experience or knowledge, place an obstacle in the way of souls thus favoured

6 To know the Divine vocation Schram gives two general rules. After stating that, in order to know this special vocation, the gift of the *discernment of spirits* is required, he gives a general rule laid down by Alvarez 'A person can embrace this kind of prayer when the spiritual director, after sufficient knowledge of the conscience, judges that he ought to do so ; when by interior inspirations and by a certain satisfaction of the mind a person is moved to it ; when he has been a long time suffering from aridity in meditation, and he finds that he profits much by simply gazing upon God and adhering to His love, and that thus he becomes dead to the world and to himself, and advances in every virtue' The other general rule or sign by which the Divine vocation may be known is that of the mortification and purification of the soul. Schram says unless a soul be purified by exterior mortification and by undergoing probations sent by God, unless it have made satisfaction for its sins and

7 General rules for knowing the Divine call to contemplation

removed their habits and subjugated its passions, unless it have ceased to sin deliberately, and unless it be well formed in the virtues, and especially in humility, we can scarcely suppose a Divine inspiration to contemplation except in very rare and extraordinary cases

In his exhortation this same pious author says that the best way of aspiring to contemplation, or, rather, of preparing and disposing one's self for this gift, is fervently to tend to perfection. He who in all things endeavours to act perfectly, who tries to love God above all things, and, in order to love Him more and more, begs that he may be more enlightened and inflamed and that this may be obtained, devotes himself with assiduity to vocal and mental prayer, to aspirations, and to the constant remembrance of the presence of God, and who does all this not through curiosity or for the sake of change or novelty, but with affection and with effect through the aid of Divine grace, who moreover, in the spirit of mortification and penance avoids all sins, even the least deliberate ones, who eradicates the vices of the heart, banishes distractions, despises earthly things, and does not desire inordinately sensible devotions or even spiritual pleasures and delights here, but with a humble heart resigns himself entirely to the Divine will, which is the best disposition for contemplation, this is the man to whom contemplation is granted. And whether it be granted or not, he will not desist from seeking perfection, as he knows that perfection does not consist in contemplation, and God may deny it even to a great Saint of this description, and supply its want by love securely preserved in humility, although it is to a soul thus disposed that the gift is given St. Theresa says. 'In humility, mortification, abdication, and in the virtues there is security, there is nothing to be feared, and no danger of not arriving at perfection in these things as well as, and sometimes even better than, by contemplation Rest secure,' she says, 'and do all you can according to what you have received, and prepare yourselves for contemplation with the said perfection, even if God denies it here (and I do not think He will refuse it, if there be true renunciation and humility), it is reserved for you hereafter, and you will certainly soon obtain it in heaven.'[1]

[1] Schram, Tomus Primus, ccclx *et seq*, p 391 *et seq*

CHAPTER VI

ON MORTIFICATION IN GENERAL

As precious ointment is not poured into an unclean vessel, so the heavenly balm of contemplation is not ordinarily infused into a soul stained by vices and subject to many defects, and not properly prepared to receive it. We can well conceive the purity and cleanness of soul required in those who desire to be with God in contemplation, and the sanctity that this union with God demands. Everything displeasing to the Divine Spouse of our souls should be removed, in order to receive and entertain Him in a worthy and becoming manner, and every ornament of virtue should be employed in adorning our souls, so that they may be pleasing in His sight. This adornment is effected by means of prayer and meditation; but as to the removal of vices and imperfections, we have to turn our thoughts to the consideration of another means to which great importance is attached by spiritual and mystical writers— that is, mortification and purification.

To prepare the way for our treatment of purification, both active and passive, which are the means to be dealt with chiefly in connection with contemplation, it will be necessary to give some explanation of mortification in general, and to give some instructions with regard to voluntary mortifications, especially with regard to corporal austerities.

1. Mortification, according to the etymology of the word, signifies a certain kind of death; it is composed of the two words *mortuus* and *facio.* It is in this sense St. Paul speaks when he says: *Always bearing about in our body the mortification of Jesus, that the life also of Jesus may be made manifest in our bodies. For we who live are always delivered unto death for Jesus' sake, that the life also of Jesus may be made manifest in our mortal flesh*.[1] According to its nature and essence it is defined: 'A spontaneous and free separation of the soul from a carnal life, and a liberation of its powers, internal as well as external, from unlawful deeds.' That we may know in what consists this separation and liberation, we have to remember that there are two parts in man, distinct in substance and in their office, the flesh and the spirit, as designated by St. Paul. *For the flesh lusteth against the spirit, and the spirit against the flesh; for these are contrary one to another, so that you do not the things you would*.[2] These two parts are at variance with each other in inclinations and desires. To establish and preserve harmony in the individual, it is necessary that the superior part rule, and that the inferior part, the flesh, be made obedient to the spirit. The spirit must set itself free from the tyranny of the passions of the flesh. It must free and separate itself by the renunciation of all those unlawful things which our lower nature craves, that thus order may be restored and preserved in the relations of the two parts of our nature. There must be a hierarchy of order in a

1. Mortification—its definition and explanation

[1] 2 Cor. iv. 10, 11   [2] Gal. v. 17

human being, and either the spirit or the flesh must rule: one must be subordinate to the other. The flesh and its appetites will throw everything into confusion and vitiate our whole nature by sin and its consequences. It is therefore man's duty to control and regulate it by reason and by a strong will aided by God's grace. For this purpose mortification is necessary to purify the soul from vices and defects, and to control the evil tendencies of our nature, to separate itself from the world and the spirit of the world, to liberate itself from self-love and selfishness, that it may be free with the liberty by which *Christ hath made us free.*

These two parts of man's nature are also signified by St. Paul when he speaks of the old man and the new in his Epistle. *Stripping yourself of the old man with his deeds, and putting on the new, him who is renewed unto knowledge according to the image of Him Who created him.*[1] By the *old man* is understood the man on the way to dissolution by sin and the vices, because sin causes ruin and corruption. By sin virtue and the spiritual life are lost, and through it death entered into the world; and therefore St. Paul says that it is our duty to crucify the old man, that the body of sin may be destroyed.[2] By the *new man* is understood a man renovated in the interior of his soul; a man before he receives sanctifying grace is subject to sin and stained with it, and when he is sanctified by grace he is renewed. He is made a new man by grace, but the old spirit remains in the flesh. When, therefore, he follows the judgment of the new man or the impulse of grace he puts on the new man, and when he desires

---

[1] Col. iii. 9, 10. [2] Rom. vi. 6.

again the things of the flesh he puts on the old man. It is in this sense that we are exhorted by St. Paul to put on the new man · *Put off, according to former conversation, the old man, who is corrupted according to the desire of error, and be renewed in the spirit of your mind and put on the new man, who, according to God, is created in justice, and holiness of truth.*[1]

'Mortification tends to subject the body to the spirit, and the spirit to God. And this it does by crossing the inclinations of sense, which are quite contrary to those of the Divine Spirit, which ought to be our chief and only principle; for by such crossing and afflicting of the body self-love and self-will (the poison of our spirits) are abated, and in time in a sort destroyed; and instead of them there enter into the soul the Divine love and the Divine will, and take possession thereof, and therein consist our perfection and happiness.'[2] It is by mortification that self-love and all other natural deordinations which hinder our union with God are removed, and it is by means of it that we exercise all duties and practise all the virtues through which our inordinate passions and affections are suppressed, as humility against pride, patience against anger, temperance against sensual desires, etc. Hence mortification is called by various names in Sacred Scripture, such as self-denial, self-hatred, the cross, death, and the like.

According to Schram, mortification is a virtue appertaining as a potential part to the virtue of temperance, taken in a general sense as restraining all inordinate desires of the sensitive appetite, inasmuch as mortification is ordained to overcome these

[1] Eph. iv. 22-24. [2] 'Holy Wisdom,' p. 208.

deordinations; and he says also that it appertains to the virtue of fortitude, inasmuch as this virtue enables us to endure pain and to encounter dangers. Mortification enables us willingly to endure penances contrary to our feelings, and to undertake penances in order that our souls may be purified and perfected after the image of our Divine Saviour, who tells us that if we wish to be His disciples it is necessary to take up our cross and follow Him in the road of suffering—the road to Calvary.

2. Division of mortification, or its various kinds

2. The division of mortification is given briefly and clearly by the Rev. F. C. Doyle in the following words 'When we refrain from actions which are forbidden by the law of God' (or the law of the Church), 'it is called *necessary* mortification; when we withhold ourselves from that which we may lawfully enjoy, it is called *free*. If we choose some privations and inconveniences for ourselves, it is considered to be *active* mortification; if we accept those which befall us by no wish of our own, it is termed *passive*. When these various acts of mortification affect the powers of the soul, it is called *internal* mortification; and when they touch the senses of the body, *external*.'

3. Necessity of mortification

3. Mortification in some degree is necessary, not only for a perfect life, but even for a Christian life, according to the words of our Divine Saviour: *If any man will come after Me, let him deny himself, and take up his cross daily and follow Me.*[1] Then, the Council of Trent teaches what is also certain from common experience, that there remains in the baptized evil concupiscence and the incentives (*fomites*) to sin with which they have to contend.

[1] St Luke ix. 23.

They cannot, indeed, injure those who consent not to them, but through the grace of Christ they may benefit those who fight against them *He that striveth for the mastery is not crowned except he strive lawfully*[1] Therefore, that through the grace received in Baptism we may ultimately be crowned, it is necessary that through the whole course of our lives we wage continual war against concupiscence and the evil effects of, and incentives to, sin which constitute our internal or domestic enemy, that we may not give way to this enemy nor yield to its attacks, but that we resist with fortitude, and this is what is meant by the self-denial and mortification prescribed by our Saviour Furthermore, the satisfaction which we have to make to God for our personal sins proves the necessity of mortification. Mortification is not only for the preservation of our new life as the cure for our infirmities, but is also ordained as punishment and chastisement for our past sins, without which the inferior and external man, always fighting against the interior and superior man, cannot be overcome. Finally, the necessity of mortification is proved from the existence of vices, passions, senses, and faculties, and temptations both from within and without, from the body and from the soul, which cannot be regulated or overcome without mortification.

Reason itself and common-sense dictate the necessity of mortification in order to live any kind of a good, decent life It is certain that discord exists in the different tendencies of our nature, and one part of our being must be in charge of the government of the other, and be invested with authority.

[1] 2 Tim ii. 5

This is demanded by the very necessity of things, even without taking into consideration either the religious or moral necessity. Between two powers which are at variance and yet indissolubly united the principle of respective independence is absolutely inapplicable; of necessity, one must command and the other must obey. Thus, if my senses or sensitive nature impel me to do one thing and my reason another, my reason must give way or my sensitive appetite must submit, the spirit must restrain the flesh or the flesh must subdue the spirit; and no one can deny that reason must guide and command, and that authority belongs to the superior rather than to the inferior nature. It is therefore clear that the spirit, with all its imperfections since the fall of man, is that power in man which has to direct and to determine the actions of the body, and that it is also called upon to govern and control itself and its own acts; and in all this it needs, according to Catholic teaching, the practice of mortification, and the guidance of the Spirit of God, and the aid of His grace.

To what extent necessary

4. When it is said that mortification is necessary for all who wish to live a Christian life in some degree, it must be understood that in the case of individuals it is not easy to determine the extent of this obligation. In general, it is that mortification by which one is disposed to observe the first and the greatest precept of the love of God, and to fulfil the other commandments when they become obligatory. To this observance nothing is more opposed than self-love, vices, passions, and temptations, and all these have to be kept within bounds by mortification, so that it may be said with certainty that morti-

fication is necessary for all to the extent of overcoming all those difficulties which would interfere with the observance of the law of God.

Besides the mortification that is of obligation and necessary for all, we have to hold that the more one tends to perfection, and accordingly to the greater perfection, the more he should exercise himself in mortification, and begin in the measure that is required from ordinary Christians. The following Scriptural texts are quoted in proof of this: *If any man will come after Me, let him deny himself,* etc. *Always bearing about in our body the mortification of Jesus, that the life also of Jesus may be made manifest in our bodies.*[1] *For you are dead, and your life is hid with Christ in God.*[2] And the words of St. Paul: *God forbid that I should glory, save in the cross of our Lord Jesus Christ, by Whom the world is crucified to me, and I to the world.*[3]

Christian perfection cannot be acquired in any state of life without indefatigable mortification, and this Schram applies to the various states of life, whether secular or religious, and to the various grades of the Christian life. The Apostle inculcates the duty of mortification on secular and married people by the words: *This therefore I say, brethren the time is short it remaineth, that they also who have wives, be as if they had none ; and they that weep, as though they wept not ; and they that rejoice, as if they rejoiced not ; and they that buy, as though they possessed not ; and they that use this world, as if they used it not for the fashion of this world passeth away.*[4] Herein the Apostle signifies that renuncia-

---

[1] 2 Cor. iv. 10. [2] Col. iii. 3.
[3] Gal. vi. 14. [4] 1 Cor. vii. 29-31.

tion which all make in Baptism, and the self-abnegation or mortification which cuts off all superfluities and meets contradictions and trials with equanimity. With regard to religious, it may be said that mortification is necessary in order to fulfil their obligation of tending towards perfection. It is not enough that they renounce the world and its pleasures, they must renounce themselves by self-denial and by the special practices of mortification prescribed by their rule and by their states, especially by the faithful observance of the evangelical counsels which they have professed by vow.

As regards the states or grades of the Christian life, whether of beginners, of those making progress, or of the perfect, mortification is necessary in order that they may be purified from their sins and vices, that they may be illuminated in acquiring and in practising the virtues, and that they may be united to God and keep themselves in the state of union with Him. As all perfection, in whatever grade, consists in a corresponding grade of charity, and charity increases in the same degree as cupidity or self-love is diminished, so this diminution is effected by means of mortification. Not even under the title of 'acquired perfection' is anyone exempt from mortification. Those who are most perfect are not to be excused from the labour of diminishing self-love and of purifying themselves still more both actively and passively, because our Lord, after saying that He is the vine, the Father the husbandman, and the just the branches, then adds *Everyone that beareth fruit, He will purge it, that it may bring forth more fruit*.[1] And from this St. Thomas con-

[1] St John xv 2

cludes that no one can be so pure in this life that he may not be more purified still.[1]

5. The benefits and advantages of mortification are well summarized by Father Baker. After telling us that in general mortification includes the exercise of all virtues, for in every act of virtue we mortify some inordinate passion and inclination of nature or other, he continues 'The benefit and blessings that come to our souls by exercising of mortification are many and most precious, as—(1) There is thereby avoided that sin which would otherwise have been committed (2) It causes a degree of purity to the soul (3) It procures greater grace and spiritual strength (4) One act of mortification enableth to another, as, on the contrary, by yielding any time to our corrupt nature, we are enfeebled and less able to resist another time (5) It diminisheth our suffering in purgatory, because so much of suffering is past, and a little pain for the present will countervail and prevent sharp and long pains for the future. (6) It procures internal light by dispelling and calming the unruliness of passions (7) It produces great peace to the soul, the which is disturbed only by unquiet passions. (8) It helpeth the soul much in her advancement in spiritual prayer and contemplation, the end of all our religious and spiritual exercises (9) It is of great edification to our brethren and neighbours (10) It increaseth all these ways our future happiness and glory.'[2]

The utility of mortification

[1] 'Schram, tom 1, p 148   [2] 'Holy Wisdom,' p 209

CHAPTER VII

BODILY MORTIFICATION OR CORPORAL AUSTERITIES

<small>1. Bodily mortification a preparation for contemplation</small>

1. THAT bodily mortification is a necessary preparation for contemplation may be shown from the following extract taken from the 'Treatise on Heroic Virtue' of Benedict XIV. 'We have already seen,' he says, 'of how much service prayer and contemplation are to sanctity. Now, if mortification of the flesh is wanting, it is very difficult to open the way to contemplation. This we are shown by Gerson "Bodily afflictions," he says, "exalt the mind to what is high and great, while they nerve and brace it against falling lower. It is in this way that the soul, not finding anything whereon the foot of its affections may rest, because the waters of tribulation have overflowed the world of sensuality, is compelled to return with the dove into the ark of interior peace. It will, however, astonish me if he who makes a practice of drawing back from the hardships of fasting and other mortifications is not found to be far off from exalted contemplation, and his soul to creep continually along the ground, content with the common thoughts of ordinary Christians, just as he is with their way of life, from which he does not, even for a time, withdraw himself. You see, then, of how much service hardness

[238]

of life is to the virtue of contemplation, in which the philosophers placed the perfection of happiness Without this, too, what will become of the virtue of fortitude and of zeal for gaining souls? What will become of faith, hope, and charity, either that they may be kindled in the breasts of men, or, when kindled, may be preserved, increased, and strengthened? In truth, they value not, as I believe, the loss of the body, so only that they obtain the end they have had in view. But consider well what thou owest to the health of the soul and the cure of vicious habits, when, as the poet Ovid says, 'You will bear cold steel and fire in order to save your body.'"[1]

2. By the same eminent author we are informed that the mortification of the body belongs to the virtue of temperance; but in order to explain the due measure of bodily mortification he premises that bodily austerities are not virtues, but instruments of virtue, and ought therefore to be exercised with due moderation: and he further states that they should not be equal in all persons, and that those are praiseworthy which are applied according to the prudent counsel of a spiritual director. He gives us the meaning and enumerates the various kinds of corporal austerities as follows Mortification of the flesh consists in abstinence, fasting, the use of the hair shirt, in watching, lying on the ground, voluntary scourging, called disciplines, and other like practices which afflict the flesh. He gives then the following reasons in proof of the need and value of this kind of mortification 'The Apostle St Paul, in his First Epistle to the Corinthians, says *I*

The due measure of bodily mortification

[1] 'Treatise on Heroic Virtue,' vol 1, p 351

chastise my body, and bring it into subjection lest perhaps when I have preached to others I myself should become a castaway.[1] And in the Second Epistle, speaking of the manner of doing this, he says: *In labours, in watchings, in fastings*.[2] Accordingly, St Jerome, in his commentary on the first of these passages, explains it thus "I chastise my body, and bring it into subjection by abstinence, by afflictions, by labours, as he says elsewhere, in many fastings, in hunger and thirst, in cold and nakedness, in labours and in prisons" In like manner, the author of the commentary on the Epistle of St. Paul, ascribed to St Ambrose, says: "To chastise the body is to afflict it with fastings, and to give it those things that are profitable for life, not for luxury" And St Augustine says "Behold that governor and traveller the Apostle Paul— behold him subduing his own beast *In hunger and thirst,* he says, *in fastings, often I chastise my body, and bring it into subjection*" So, then, do thou who desirest to walk tame thy flesh and walk, for thou dost walk if thou lovest; for we do not run to God by steps, but by afflictions."[3]

In theory all that has been said of bodily mortification is admitted, and pious souls are edified by the many examples of mortification of which they read in the lives of the Saints. But it is admitted that in extraordinary mortifications their examples are to be admired rather than imitated There is the danger, however, of confining ourselves entirely to their admiration, and of neglecting entirely their imitation. It may be said that our constitutions are

---

[1] 1 Cor ix 27 [2] 2 Cor vi 5
[3] 'Treatise on Heroic Virtue,' vol 1, pp 326, 327

now weaker, and nervousness as well as other physical ailments more common than in the days of St. Theresa, not to go further back, and therefore bodily mortification is unsuitable to our temperaments and dangerous to health. To this one might reply that some wise medical men of the present day would recommend a return to the simplicity of former ages in the matter of food and drink and clothing. A greater abstinence from modern luxuries would be the best prescription for the public health, as well as for the health of individuals.

3. For those, however, who devote themselves to religion and to the spiritual life, and who may be tempted to indulge ease and sloth in small things for the sake of their bodily comfort, the directions which St. Theresa gave to the Sisters of her convent may be useful. 'Now, the first thing we are to endeavour after is the banishing from ourselves the love of this body; for some of us are so delicate by our complexion that there is not a little pains to be taken herein, and such lovers of our health that it is a wonder to see the war these two things raise, especially among nuns, as also among such as are not. But some nuns among us seem to come to the monastery for nothing else but to contrive not to die. . . . Make account, Sisters, ye come hither to die for Christ, and not to feed yourselves for Christ; for this, the devil suggests, is needful the better to endure and observe the rule, and they so exceedingly desire, forsooth, to keep the rule by taking care of their health for the observing and keeping of it, that they even die without entirely practising it for a month, or perhaps a day. . . . Sometimes a frenzy takes them of doing penances

St. Theresa's remarks on bodily mortification

without moderation or discretion, which lasts two days, as I may say, afterwards the devil suggests to their imagination that these do them hurt, so that they never do penance more—no, not which the Order enjoins, having already found it hurtful to them. Nay, then, we observe not the meanest injunctions of the rule, such as silence, which can do us no harm; and no sooner have we a conceit that our head aches, but we forbear going to the choir, which is not likely to kill us, either—one day because our head aches, the next day because it did ache, and three more lest it should ache; and we love to invent penances of our own heads that we may be able to do neither the one nor the other, and at times when our evil abates, yet we conceive ourselves obliged to do nothing, but that by asking leave we satisfy all.'[1]

Bodily mortification considered in order to the canonization of Saints

4. What Benedict XIV. says of the mortification of the flesh and the body in order to the canonization of a servant of God may serve as a guide and direction to all pious souls who desire to be perfect and to keep their souls perfectly united to God in this life.

'Now, if the question is concerning those who have abstained from mortification of the body from an overlove of and care for it, and have nourished it with meat and drink and other sensible pleasures beyond what was necessary for its support, no one can fail to see that this is an insuperable barrier to proceeding further with the cause, although it may abound with other noble and meritorious actions. For, as St. Gregory Nazianzen says "Sufficient for the body is its own malice. What need of a

[1] 'Way of Perfection,' chap. x

great supply of fuel to the flame, or of feeding the wild beast more plentifully that it may become still more untamable?" And St. Basil has these excellent remarks on the same subject "Neither should we pay more attention to the body than that it may be subservient to the soul. For to spend all our labour in taking care that the body may be in as good condition as possible is not the part of a man who knows anything of his own nature. . . " And St. Paul says very much the same thing when he admonishes us that no care is to be taken of the body to afford matter for lust. Quite on the contrary, then, the body ought to be mortified and restrained and treated just as we should treat some great beast that was ever ready to attack us. The tumultuous passions which are excited by it in the soul are to be subjected, as it were, by a scourge to reason; nor is too much rein to be given to pleasures, lest the mind should love its power, and be carried off like a charioteer who is hurried along by uncurbed and high-spirited horses

'The same judgment,' he tells us, 'should be come to respecting those servants of God who, though they have not given the like signs, and have kept from a too excessive love of the body, have yet given no attention to mortification of the flesh during their lifetime. For although it is certain, as we have shown above, that mortification in the way of long and voluntary fasts, extraordinary watchings, lying on the ground, and voluntary disciplines, is not absolutely necessary in order that one may save his soul, yet, since it is necessary, in order to reach the summit of Christian perfection—and in the Church militant it is not all who die piously in the Lord who are enrolled among the Saints, but those only with regard to whom it can be shown by clear proofs that they have reached to perfection—we cannot doubt of the correctness of what Scacchus lays down when he teaches that a stop should be put to the cause of a servant of God who is a confessor, if proof is wanting of a due and fitting amount of bodily austerities during his life.'[1]

General rules for the practice of bodily mortification

5 The question is as to what may be reckoned a due and fitting amount, and although no rules can be laid down that would apply to each individual person, there are some general rules given for the guidance of all. The following, which are taken from the work of Benedict XIV. already quoted, are both practical and discreet

(1) Age and health should be considered

(1) Bodily mortifications are not to be equal in all the servants of God. Some are too old to practise severe austerities. Some are under age and too young, and the Church takes this into consideration in enjoining the law of fasting. Many are delicate and too weak in health, like St. Gregory when he wrote to Eulogius, the Patriarch of Alexandria: 'It is now nearly two years that I am confined to my bed.' And again, in his letter to Marianus 'It is now a long time that I am not able to rise from my bed. For sometimes I am tortured by the pain of the gout, sometimes it is as if a fire spread itself throughout my whole body, causing great agony, and it generally happens that this burning comes on together with the pain, so that my mind and body sink under it.' 'Who,' asks the learned Pontiff, 'would require in a servant of God who was worn out with old age the practice of

---

[1] 'Treatise on Heroic Virtue,' p. 349 *et seq*

all the bodily afflictions which he used in his youth and strength?' According to the opinion of St. Basil, our self-denial ought to be proportioned to our strength.

(2) In bodily austerities and mortifications singularity should be avoided, which happens chiefly in those things that are done openly, and in the case of servants of God who lead their life in some religious community. St. Bernard thus addresses his monks 'Avoid obstinacy and the most wicked vice of singularity.' And, again, after describing a monk infected with the vice of singularity, he goes on thus 'It is a disgraceful thing for a man to boast of himself as superior to others who does not do anything to make him appear superior to the rest Such an one is not satisfied with the common rule of the monastery, or with the examples of those who have gone before him And yet it is not that he studies to be better, but to seem so ; he is eager not to live more strictly, but to seem to do so, so that he may have it in his power to say, *I am not as other men.* He has greater self-complacency over one fast which he makes while others dine than if he were to fast seven days with the rest'

(3) There should be no place for such fasts, abstinences, disciplines, and other bodily austerities, as are likely to offer an obstacle to fulfilling the duties of our station or to the exercise of other virtues According to this rule, the body should be supported so as to be equal to the burthens of the Christian's vocation, whatever that may be ; and in our voluntary fasts and watchings and other bodily austerities we should keep to the rule of not doing anything which may stand as a hindrance to the

(2) Singularity should be avoided

(3) Extremes should be avoided

duties of that state in which we are placed by God. This is the teaching of St. Thomas, who explains this matter with his usual exactness. For after proposing the question whether a man can sin by too much fasting and abstinence, he answers 'That according to the philosopher Aristotle we must judge differently of the end, and of the means that conduces towards that end For that which is sought as the end is to be sought for without limit or measure, whereas in those things which we seek as a means we should keep to some measure or limit proportionate to the end we have in view Thus, a physician strives to produce health, which is his end, to the greatest possible amount, but he uses medicine in so far only as it is fitted to produce health. We should therefore keep in mind that in the spiritual life the love of God is the end, and that fasts and watchings and other bodily exercises are not followed as an end, for, as it is said in the Epistle to the Romans, *The kingdom of God is not meat and drink*, but they are made use of as necessary to the end—that is to say, to tame the concupiscence of the flesh . . . If, however, anyone should so weaken his body by fasts and vigils and other austerities that he cannot fulfil the duties of his calling, that he cannot preach if he be a preacher, or teach if he be a doctor, or sing if he be a chanter, and so of the rest, without doubt he sins . . The maceration of our body, for instance, by vigils and fasts is not accepted by God, except so far as it is a work of virtue. And it is this so far as it is done with due discretion in order that concupiscence may be restrained and nature may not be too heavily pressed on'

(4) In regard to those who belong to any conventual institution, they have not to omit the austerities prescribed in their rule; in regard to others, the manner of their bodily austerities is not one, but many, according to the various constitutions of their body, the various degrees of their strength, the various dispositions of their minds, and the different occasions and incitements which they have to virtue, since some have fewer impediments and others more. He who would not go wrong must not follow his own judgment, but the counsel of others in the practice of mortification. St. Theresa, in speaking of excessive bodily mortifications, condemns those which are not disclosed to our spiritual director, or which are not left off at his command 'The same,' she says, ' happens in the case of indiscreet and ill-arranged penances, which lead us to think that we are more penitent than others or that we are doing something. If we go on with them, concealing them from the confessor or superior, or saying that we will leave them off, but not doing so, they are clearly a temptation' To the office of a prudent confessor it belongs to take into consideration whether any real impediments exist against the penitent's making use of this or any other kind of mortification and penance, in order that, as St Basil says, ' we may not, under the pretext of bodily necessity, pursue our own pleasure '[1]

(4) Religious should follow their rule, seculars should follow the advice of their confessors

What has been said with regard to the measure of these austerities is to be understood of voluntary bodily mortifications In connection with these, however, we have to refer to pains and sufferings

[1] See 'Treatise on Heroic Virtue,' chap. IX

that are unavoidable and inseparable from our nature, and the right use we should make of them towards our spiritual advancement. These may be included under the title given them by Father Tyrrell, S.J., 'The Gospel of Pain,' whose teaching on this head brings out clearly the true spirit of Christian mortification and self-denial, as will be seen from the following extracts.

[6. 'The Gospel of Pain,' by Rev. Father Tyrrell, S.J.]

6. 'The whole aim of humanitarians is to lessen the amount of pain in the world, but in no wise to teach men to bear pain, much less to value it, to court it, to be in love with it, as St. Theresa was. They seek to raise the standard, not of happiness (which, indeed, they lower), but of *comfort*, thus implicitly making comfort, or freedom from hardships and bodily sufferings, if not the essence, at least an essential condition of happiness. They strive to make men less accustomed to privations and inconvenience, and therefore more impatient and intolerant of such as are inevitable; to make the conditions of contentment ever more manifold and complex, and therefore more rarely realized, more easily disturbed. Our estimate of good and evil is largely taken from those with whom we dwell, and our enjoyment and suffering depend on that estimate. Thus, we marvel at what our forefathers put up with in the way of discomfort; we admire their patient endurance of various inconveniences, injustices, oppressions which to us would be quite unbearable; and, forgetting that the conditions of contentment are far more subjective than objective, we fancy that our ancestors must have been as miserable as we should now be in the same circumstances. Instead of inuring men to the rough climate of this mortal life, humani-

tarianism has accustomed them to wraps and muffles, and rendered them susceptible to every little change of temperature—poor, frail, pain-fearing creatures."[1]

The same author, from this view of pain and suffering, asks us to turn to the mystics, to the prophets and seers of all ages, and to inquire of them for the law of life, and tells us that the answer will be that of St. Theresa: *Aut pati, aut mori* (Either suffer or die). The same is the answer of religion 'For even the very body itself must be exalted, purified, and spiritualized by suffering, by fast and vigil and penance ; it must be subdued, tranquillized, and, as it were, put to sleep, before it is an apt medium for communication between this world and the other, before it is attuned to be a fit instrument of God's Holy Spirit. The spiritual man understands the deep things of the spirit because they are spiritually apprehended, but the animal man never rises beyond the laboured methods of reason ; he knows nothing of the instincts of love, of that quick intuition which leaps to the truth, from crag to crag, and pinnacle to pinnacle, where others crawl and clamber and stumble. *Dilectus meus venit mihi saliens super montes* (My beloved comes to Me leaping across the mountains). "What man can know the counsels of God or who can divine His will ? For the thoughts of men are timid, and their foresight is uncertain, because the corruptible body weighs upon the soul, and its earthen tenement drags down the mind with its many thoughts." As far as she can shake herself free from the embrace of this body of death, so far can the soul fly to the embrace of Truth, her Spouse and her Life: *Aut pati aut mori.*'[2]

[1] 'Hard Sayings,' pp 139, 140 [2] *Ibid*, p 147

Again, the same author instructs us how to deal with sufferings and sorrows, and confirms his teaching by quotations from Thomas à Kempis ' Christ's primary mission with respect to the sufferings and sorrows of life was not to relieve them, but to teach men to bear them, to value them, to thank God for them. There are two ways of dealing with difficulties and trials by changing ourselves or by changing our surroundings ; by running away from hardships or by adapting ourselves to them and nerving ourselves to bear them. There is no question as to which is the wisest course If we fly from our cross, it is only to fall into the arms of another. Go where we will, we carry ourselves with us, the source of most of our trouble. Until we change ourselves no change of circumstances will avail. *Imaginatio locorum et mutatio multos fefellit*, says à Kempis (Many have been deluded by the imaginary advantages of change) Men are constantly laying the blame of their own faults on their surroundings ; ever fancying that they would be perfectly happy in some other place ; ever keen-eyed to their present grievances and prospective advantages ; ever blind to their present advantages and prospective grievances, always loath to face the inevitable truth that life is a warfare upon earth ; that it is essentially a cross which must be borne, whether willingly or unwillingly ; that there is no other way to life and to true internal peace but the way of the Holy Cross and of daily mortification. ' Walk where you will, seek what you will ; yet you will find no higher way above, no safer way below, than the way of the Holy Cross. Arrange and order everything according to your own likings and fancies, and yet you will always find something that you have to suffer, whether willingly or unwillingly, and thus you will always find the Cross. You will have to put up either with bodily pain or with spiritual troubles. At one time you will feel abandoned by God, at another you will be tried by your neighbour, and, what is worse, you will often be troublesome to yourself. Nor yet can you be released or relieved by any remedy or comfort, but needs must bear it as long as God wills . . Run where you will you cannot escape : for wherever you go you carry yourself along with you, and so everywhere you will always find yourself. Turn where you will, above or below, within or without, yet in every corner you will find the Cross, and everywhere you will need to exercise patience if you want to possess inward peace and deserve an everlasting crown If you carry the Cross willingly, it will carry you, if you carry it unwillingly, you make a burden for yourself and weight yourself still more, and yet bear it you must. If you cast off one cross, you will surely find another, and perhaps a heavier one. Do you imagine you are going to escape what no man ever yet escaped ? . . . You are sore mistaken if you expect anything else but to suffer trials, for the whole of this earthly life is full of miseries and hedged round with crosses. Make up your mind that you will have to endure many adversities and all sorts of inconveniences in this wretched life, for so it will be with you wherever you are, and so you will surely find it wherever you lie hid . . . When you shall have got so far that tribulation is sweet to you and savours of Christ, then indeed it will be well with you, and you will have discovered paradise upon earth. As long as suffering is an evil in your eyes, and you try to run away from it, so long will you be unhappy, and whithersoever you fly the need of further flight will still follow you. But if you settle down to the inevitable, namely, to suffering and dying, things will quickly mend and you will find peace. . . . Had there been anything better or more useful for men's souls than suffering, surely Christ would have taught it by word and example. . . . And, therefore, let this be the final conclusion of all our study and investigation, that it is of necessity through many tribulations that we are to enter the Kingdom of God" ("Imitation of Christ," ii., 12)"[1]

[1] 'Hard Sayings,' appendix, p 456 *et seq*

CHAPTER VIII

PURIFICATIONS—ACTIVE AND PASSIVE

1. AMONGST the exercises of preparation for contemplation, we have different purifications to which the soul should be subjected. These purifications are called *active* and *passive*. The *active* purifications belong to the remote preparation of the soul for the higher gifts of contemplation. They are called *active* because they are effected by the labour of the soul itself, helped by Divine grace, and in order to distinguish them from the *passive purifications*, which are the extraordinary means which God employs to purify the soul from its stains, and to prepare it proximately or immediately for those exceptional graces of the supernatural order. All those holy efforts, mortifications, labours, and sufferings, by which the soul, aided by the grace of God, endeavours to reform the mind, body, heart, and the whole sensitive appetite, and to fit itself for the contemplation of heavenly things, are included in the name of active purifications.

But whatever the soul may do to dispose itself for contemplation, all its mortifications and all its labours will not suffice. This is the work of the right hand of God, and it is effected by purifications which mystical writers term *passive*. These passive puri-

marginal note: 1 The meaning of active and passive purification

fications consist in an accumulation of aridities, temptations, and of other external and internal trials which God by a singular providence sends to the soul, that in a certain violent way the rebellious appetites may be subjected to reason, vicious habits and imperfections may be corrected, so that thus tried and purified it may be properly disposed for the influx of heavenly contemplations. As the imperfect soul before being admitted into heaven must pass through the pains of purgatory and be cleansed from its least stain, so in like manner the soul here on earth before enjoying the contemplative vision must undergo passive purgations or purifications.[1]

We shall study and explain these passive purifications later on. We have now to give our attention to the active purifications, which, according to the Abbé Lejeune, mystics distinguish or divide into four kinds, which impart to the soul four kinds of purity—namely, purity of *conscience*, purity of *heart*, purity of *spirit*, and purity of *action*. Under each of these four heads some short instructions may be written, and, as far as possible, the subjects treated under each will be kept distinct.

The dark nights described by St. John of the Cross.

2. In the works of St. John of the Cross these purifications are called *nights*. According to his plan of teaching, the soul, before reaching the Divine light of perfect union, has to pass through a dark night, or, rather, the soul passes through two principal nights. The Saint explains why he uses the expression *night*. 'The journey of the soul to the Divine union is called night for three reasons. The first is derived from the point from

[1] Voss, 'Scaramelli Compend,' p. 162.

which the soul sets out — the privation of the desire of all pleasure in all things of this world by an entire detachment therefrom. This is as night for every desire and sense of man. The second, from the road by which it travels—that is, faith, for faith is obscure, like night, to the intellect. The third, from the goal to which it tends—God, incomprehensible and infinite, Who in this life is as night to the soul. We must pass through these three nights if we are to attain to the Divine union with God . . . These three nights are but one divided into three parts. The first, which is that of the senses, may be likened to the commencement of night when material objects begin to be invisible; the second, of faith, may be compared to midnight, which is utter darkness; the third resembles the close of night, which is God, when the dawn of day is at hand.'[1]

In the following chapter of his work the Saint further explains in another way why he selected the term 'night' and applied it to each of the purifications to which the soul is subjected. He says 'The privation of all pleasure to the desires in all things is here called night. For as night is nothing else but the absence of light, and, consequently, of visible objects, whereby the faculty of vision remains in darkness unemployed, so the mortification of the desires is as night to the soul. For when the soul desires itself those pleasures which outward things furnish to the desire, it is, as it were, in darkness without occupation. As the faculty of vision is nourished by light and fed by visible objects, and ceases to be so fed when the light is withdrawn, so

[1] 'The Ascent of Mount Carmel,' chap. xi

the soul by means of the desire feeds on those things which, corresponding with its powers, give it pleasure; but when the desire is mortified, it derives no more pleasure from them, and thus, so far as the desire is concerned, the soul abides in darkness without occupation.

'This may be illustrated in the case of all the faculties of the soul. When the soul denies itself the pleasure arising from all that gratifies the ear, it remains, so far as the faculty of hearing is concerned, in darkness without occupation, and when it denies itself in all that is pleasing to the eye, it remains in darkness so far as it relates to the faculty of sight. The same may be said of the other senses, so that he who shall deny himself all satisfaction derivable from external objects, mortifying the desire thereof, may be said to be in a state which is as night, and this is nothing else but an entire detachment from all things . .

'I call this detachment the night of the soul, for I am not speaking here of the absence of things—for absence is not detachment, if the desire of them remain—but of that detachment which consists in suppressing desire and avoiding pleasure. It is this that sets the soul free, even though possession may be still retained. The things of this world neither occupy nor injure the soul, because they do not enter within, but, rather, the will and desire of them which abide within it. This is the night of the sensual part of the soul.'[1]

Purity of conscience explained. 3. By purity of conscience is meant that disposition of soul which excludes every deliberate venial sin and every affection for the least venial sin. This

[1] 'The Ascent of Mount Carmel,' chap. iii.

does not signify that from time to time the soul may not fall into venial sin, but that it is in the habitual disposition not to commit one deliberately, to repent immediately after falling into such sins, and to avoid the occasions of them. On this subject Father Baker gives us several paragraphs of minute instruction, of which I shall quote only two. 'If,' he says, 'it were required to perfection in a contemplative life that a soul should be entirely free from venial defects, it would be impossible to attain unto it, considering the incurable frailty of our nature, the frequency of temptations, and the incapacity which is in the soul to be in a continual actual guard over herself. True it is that, by perseverance in spiritual prayer accompanied with mortification, such defects become for number more rare, and for quality less considerable; but though prayer and mortification should continue never so long, a soul will find occasion and a necessity to be in continual resistance against her perverse inclinations, and in such combats will sometimes come off with loss.

'Venial sins, therefore, are not inconsistent with perfection, although they should be committed never so oft out of frailty, subreption, or ignorance; but if if they be committed deliberately, advisedly, customarily, and with affection, they render the soul in an incapacity of attaining perfection in prayer,' etc. Further on he adds: 'A necessity likewise there is (upon supposition of aspiring to perfection) to mortify all deliberate affections to any, even the least venial defects and deordinations of our souls. This duty of mortification (or purification) requires of us that, deliberately and customarily, we neither admit into our minds internally vain thoughts nor outwardly speak or exercise acts of vain love, vain hope, vain fear, or vain sorrow; and all is vain that is not referred to God or is not done for Him.'[1]

St. John of the Cross, that most experienced of mystical writers, speaking on the voluntary desires that are hurtful to the soul, says 'All the voluntary desires—whether of mortal sins, which are the most grievous, or of venial sins, which are less so, or imperfections, which are still less so—must be banished away, and the soul which would attain to perfect union must be delivered from them all, however slight they may be. The reason is this. The estate of Divine union consists in the total transformation of the will into the will of God in such a way that every movement of the will shall be always the movement of the will of God only. This is the reason why in this state two wills are said to be one—my will and God's will—so that the will of God is also that of the soul. But if the soul then cleaves to any imperfection contrary to the will of God, His will is not done, for the soul wills that which God wills not. It is clear, therefore, that, if the soul is to be united in love and will with God, every desire of the will must first of all be cast away, however slight it may be; that is, we must not deliberately and knowingly assent with the will to any imperfection, and we must have such power over it and such liberty as to reject every such desire the moment we are aware of it. I say knowingly, for without deliberation and a clear knowledge of what we are doing, or because it is not wholly in our power, we may easily give way to imperfections and venial sins . . . It is of such sins as these not

[1] 'Holy Wisdom,' pp. 204-208

so entirely voluntary that it is written · *A just man shall fall seven times, and shall rise again.*[1]

'But as to those voluntary and perfectly deliberate desires, how slight soever their objects may be, any one of them not overcome is sufficient to prevent this union. I am speaking of the unmortified habit thereof, because certain acts occasionally have not so much power, for the habit of them is not settled; still, we must get rid of them, for they, too, proceed from habitual imperfection. Some habits of voluntary imperfections, so far as they are never perfectly overcome, impede not only the Divine union, but our progress towards perfection.

'These habitual imperfections are, for instance, much talking, certain attachments, which we never resolve to break through—such as to individuals, to a book or a cell, to a particular food, to certain society, the satisfaction of one's taste, science, news, and such things. Every one of these imperfections, if the soul is attached and habituated to them, results in serious injuries to our growth and progress in perfection. Yea, even if we fall daily into many other imperfections greater than these, provided they are not the result of the habitual indulgence of any evil inclination, we should not be so much hindered in our spiritual course as we are by this selfish attachment of the soul to particular objects; for while the soul entertains it, it is useless to hope that we can ever attain to perfection, even though the object of our attachment be but of the slightest importance.'[2]

4. By purity of heart is here meant that which consists in keeping the heart free from all attach- *4. Purity of heart explained*

[1] Prov. xxiv. 16.
[2] 'The Ascent of Mount Carmel,' chap. xi.

ment to creatures, not only from sinful attachment, but even from innocent attachment when this divides with creatures the heart that should be given to God alone. The heart is to be understood as the symbol of our affections, and, above all, the symbol of love, and therefore the more our hearts are detached from the love of creatures and free from the troubles and intricacies of natural affection, the more completely they can be given to God. A divided heart cannot attend to contemplation. Contemplation means the sweet repose of the heart and the spirit in God, and that heart cannot rest in God that is still bound by earthly attachments, according to the words, *Where thy treasure is, there also will be thy heart.* I do not think that it is possible to keep our references to purity of heart quite distinct from what may be said with equal truth of purity of conscience, and it is not at all necessary to do so, as they both mean one and the same thing, only with some shades of difference, according to the manner in which the writer may view them or choose to treat of them

The following instructions and reflections of St. John of the Cross may well be applied to the purity of heart as well as to the purity of conscience, inasmuch as both these signify the purification of our souls from attachment to creatures 'How sad it is,' says the Saint, 'to see certain souls, like vessels richly freighted, full of good works, of spiritual exercises, virtues, and gifts of God, which because they have not the courage to break with certain tastes, attachments, or affections—these are all one —never reach the haven of perfect union! And yet it would cost them but a single vigorous flight to break the thread of their attachment or to shake off the reward of desire. It is a matter of deep regret, when God has given them strength to burst other and stronger ties—those of vanity and sin—merely because they will not detach themselves from trifles which God has left for them to break away from for love of Him, and which are no more than a single thread, that they should for this neglect their own advancement and the attainment of so great a blessing. And what is still more deplorable, because of such attachments, not only do they not advance, but, so far as perfection is concerned, they fall back, losing in some measure what they had already gained with so much labour. For it is well known that, on the spiritual road, not to go on overcoming self is to go backwards, and not to increase our gain is to lose. This is what our Lord would teach us when He says, *He that gathereth not with Me scattereth.*[1] He who will neglect to repair the vessel that is but slightly cracked will at last lose all the liquor it may hold ; *for he that contemneth small things shall fall by little and little*,[2] and, *Of one spark cometh a great fire.*[3] One imperfection is enough to beget another, and this other others again. We shall never see a soul negligent in overcoming a single desire which has not also many other desires arising out of the weakness and imperfection from which the first proceeds. There have been many persons who by the grace of God had made great progress in detachment and freedom, and yet because they gave way, under the pretence of some good—as of society and friendship—to petty attachments, have thereby lost the spirit and sweetness of God,

[1] St Matt xii. 30.   [2] Ecclus xix 1.   [3] Ecclus xi 34.

holy solitude, and cheerfulness, and have injured the integrity of their spiritual exercises so as not to be able to stop before all was gone. All this has befallen them because they did not root out the principle of pleasure and of the sensual desires, keeping themselves in solitude before God.'[1]

The heart being the symbol of love, when we are speaking of purifying it we must understand that the love of our hearts must be pure and holy. Love, we are told, is at the root of all other passions, and natural love is the source of innumerable evils. The remedy, according to Father Baker, for deordinations proceeding from natural and inordinate love of creatures 'is to have a new contrary Divine principle imprinted in our hearts by which we should be averted from the falsely seeming happiness that self-love promises us in creatures, and converted to our first and only end, which is God, and this can be no other but Divine love or charity shed abroad in our hearts by the Holy Ghost. This charity is an universal cure of all our disorders, producing the like effects in us with respect to our true end that self-love did to a false end. It raises and employs, when need is, all other passions anger against our own negligence, ingratitude, etc ; hatred against the devil and sin, that hinder our conversion to God, etc. And it is the root of all our good actions for giving us an inclination, desire, and tendency to union with God ; from thence it is that we regulate and direct all our actions to Him. Hereupon St. Paul ascribes to charity the acts of all other virtues. *Charity*, saith he, *is patient, is kind, long-suffering*,

[1] 'The Ascent of Mount Carmel,' chap. xi., book 1

it doth nothing unseemly, it rejoiceth in the truth, etc.'[1]

5. Purity of spirit includes, according to the Abbé Lejeune, two things: the *purification of the imagination* and the *purification of the memory.* It is that which the soul effects, or is effected in the soul, by moderating and controlling the imagination and memory, so as not to allow these to be occupied with vain images of senseless or dangerous objects.

(1) This purification is exercised by the will on the imagination in the first place, to prevent its wanderings, and to banish from that faculty all foul, profane, and ridiculous images and figures. The imaginative faculty is compared to a painted hall with many images and pictures, some foul, some profane, and others ridiculous, monstrous, and deformed; and man entertains himself in painting them, taking pleasure in beholding them, enticing the understanding to gaze upon them, and often drawing it into sinful thoughts and desires—into that which is called *delectatio morosa*, a continuing or lingering delight in a matter either of carnality, as De Ponte says, or in revenge, ambition, and avarice, delighting one's self with the imagination of those things as if they were present. It stands to reason that the soul disturbed by such images and distracting objects is not a fit subject for recollection and for repose in God. Thus writes De Ponte concerning the dangers of the imagination.[2] But it is not so much of the imaginations that are sinful or that are likely to lead to sins that we speak when we wish to explain the purification of this faculty

[1] 'Holy Wisdom,' p. 244
[2] Part 1, 'Meditat.,' 27, point 3

The strength of imagination exaggerates our sufferings. Father Tyrrell says well: 'Suffering would be desirable enough were it not for reflection [or, I should say, imagination], which magnifies it and joins its several pangs into one charge of woe, and brings those that are past, and even those that are future, to bear upon the present, and crushes us with pain, of which nine-tenths belong to the world of ideas.'

We are directed by the devout Blosius how to regard and to deal with involuntary movements and imaginations when he observes 'Sometimes even souls that are more perfect will feel inordinate movements in their inferior nature or animal senses to which their whole reason and will are opposed, a temporary rage in the inferior nature whilst the superior man is at peace. Such things do occur, and are displeasing to the will; but let not that soul imagine that the grace of God has left her. For God often promotes the salvation of His elect by things that to the sufferer seem contrary to salvation. Hence He sometimes permits those foul and infernal temptations that are a horror to the soul. Amidst such involuntary trials the devout soul will resign herself to God, adhere to God, and abide in her superior nature, and will omit neither her good works nor the Holy Communion, for as long as the soul refuses her consent she suffers no injury. The imagination may be beset even with blasphemies and other absurd follies, suggestions of the evil one, and they may almost seem to speak with a human voice; still let the soul not trouble herself any more than if they were so many flies buzzing about the face, and let her turn to God. If they grow urgent and vehement, sign the cross, look to our Lord's Passion, and say to Him *Keep my heart immaculate, that I may not be confounded*."[1]

(2) Purity of spirit signifies also the control which the will should exercise over the memory. We are told that the part of the memory in the spiritual life is of sovereign importance. This faculty, according as it is well or badly directed, or according as it is subjected to control or left free, can be the source of much good or of much evil to the soul. The memory is the place where good and bad are stored up, and these can be called into action every moment—the good to assist the soul in its ascent to God, or the bad to hinder its progress and to paralyze its efforts. Owing to original sin, the memory, like the other powers of the soul, is weak and defective, and somehow it more easily retains vain and dangerous recollections than those which are useful and holy. We are not called upon to account for this, but we know by experience that such is the case. Images and spectacles that disturb our senses are painted and retained in the storehouse of the mind, also injuries received, resentments, rancours, which can be revived in a moment. It is, therefore, necessary to purify the memory of all these dangerous recollections or to keep them under the control of the will; for where these are kept alive in the mind there is no room for the recollection of God's perfections, of Christ's sufferings, and of the other objects of Divine contemplation.

(2) The purification of the memory

This purification means the suppression of ex-

[1] Blosius apud Ullathorne, 'Christian Patience,' lect. viii, p. 154.

cessive preoccupation of the mind about temporal things, anxiety for the future, and all those things that disturb our peace of mind and conscience

'Beware of anxiety,' writes Bishop Ullathorne, 'the very sound of the word "anxiety" is painful Next to sin there is nothing that so much troubles the mind, strains the heart, distresses the soul, and confuses the judgment. Anxiety is the uneasiness and trouble of mind to which we give way because of some difficulty of which we cannot see the solution, or because of some uncertainty respecting one's self or another, or because of some future event of which we are uncertain. It is more than uneasiness and disturbance, more than solicitude, and it is attended with fear and perplexity, and inclines the soul to sadness. It has a certain paralyzing influence, compressing the soul with the ligaments of fear, suspense, and uncertainty that impede and stifle the freedom of her powers. St Gregory describes it by a strong figure as "strangling the throat of the mind." A modern writer has described it as "fright spread thinly through the soul."[1] The purification of the memory means to get rid of anxieties, of excessive preoccupation of the mind about temporal matters, vain fears for the future, and all such things by which the memory distracts the mind and engages the attention of the understanding, and prevents the soul from devoting itself to God and to Divine things The remedy to be applied is to keep the memory well supplied with spiritual and supernatural objects, such as the Passion of our Lord, the Holy Eucharist, the Blessed Virgin, the Guardian Angels, the graces

[1] 'Christian Patience,' p 128

received in the past at the time of prayer, and at Holy Communion. We are also directed to make use of ejaculatory prayers as the means of overcoming the distressing and useless remembrances that disturb the soul and retard its progress.

Mystical writers tell us that this purification of the memory is a requisite condition for progress in the way of perfection, and an indispensable preparation for contemplation. And independently of these, it has many other immediate advantages, some of which are enumerated by Lejeune, such as the protecting the soul against temptations; the deliverance of the soul from anxieties as to earthly cares and temporal affairs which choke the good seed; the disposing of the soul for the action of grace; and, in fine, it is the means of bringing peace and tranquillity to the soul. It frees the soul from the thoughts of profane and useless or dangerous subjects, and thus removes the serious obstacles which so often hinder its advancement in perfection, and prevent its union with God in the prayer of contemplation.

CHAPTER IX

ACTIVE PURIFICATIONS (*continued*)

<small>1. Purity of action</small> 1. This purity of action is the fourth of the various kinds of purity which is mentioned as the fruit or result of active purifications. It is a quality which is not to be regarded as affecting the material action, so much as the motives which inspire and sustain it. This purity consists in acting for the love of God or according to the order of God. It is not difficult to see that this kind of purity is required as a preparation for contemplation. Contemplation is no ordinary grace, and it requires more than ordinary attention to the motives of our actions that they be performed for the love of God, and that our intentions be purified with regard to them. They should proceed from the love of God in the beginning, and be continued afterwards through that same motive.

This purity is the result of the other three, because our actions will be pure in their motives in so far as they proceed from purity of conscience, purity of heart, and purity of spirit. But besides these means of securing purity in our actions, one or two others are mentioned as direct and immediate means. The first of these is to watch over with special attention the beginning of the action, that it may not proceed from passion or self-love or from a purely natural inclination In such a case it is not done for God, but for our own pleasure. It is, therefore, advisable for our greater perfection, at the beginning of each action, especially of each important action, to renew our intention, to purify it, and to supernaturalize it. This teaching is common amongst spiritual writers, but from a theological point of view we have to say that, when our thoughts and actions are given to God by the morning offering, they belong to Him, and may be said to proceed from His love so long as our intention is not withdrawn or interrupted, even though we may not advert to its renewal frequently during the day. Spiritual writers have more fear of our weakness and changeableness than theological writers, and therefore some of them speak of this renewal of our intention as something indispensable at the beginning of each action, in order that the action be pure in the sense understood above The habitual intention suffices for the goodness of the action and that it be meritorious. The actual intention is not always possible, and cannot therefore be said to be indispensably necessary for its perfection or its purity. As a second means of securing this purity of action, we are advised to renew the intention of doing it for the love of God sometimes during the action or work, when this means a continuous occupation, or at all events to guard against self-love, self-interested and natural motives creeping into our actions when we want those actions to be entirely disinterested and entirely supernatural Many actions, it is true, begin in the spirit, and, as St. Paul says, end in the flesh —that is to say, many actions directed to God, in the beginning, in their progress deviate from the right motive, and end with self. It is for this reason that vigilance is necessary always in the course of our actions and employments, and hence we are recommended to call to mind often the presence of God, also, that we ourselves are the creatures of God, made for Him alone, that all our activity as well as our being is from Him, and that of ourselves we are nothing and have nothing

Vanity the vice to be avoided

2 The special vice which causes deordination and want of purity in our actions is vanity, and it is against this we have to fight, whether it proceeds from occasions outside ourselves or from our own interior. The vanity occasioned from outside is the inordinate desire of the esteem of men, the thirst for approval, for praise, for admiration and love, which would infect our best works, and render fruitless those works which in appearance are, and which otherwise would be, the most meritorious. Vanity from within is subtle, and therefore the more dangerous. It is called by Lejeune pride of comparison, and causes us to measure ourselves constantly with others, to prefer ourselves to them, and to glory in our superiority; or, when our inferiority is evident, then this vanity causes sadness, susceptibility, jealousy, and uncharitableness. Nothing can be more opposed to contemplation than this twofold vanity. There is an absolute incompatibility between vanity and contemplation, and this gift can find no place in a vain soul. This is evident in itself, and for this reason mystical writers dwell so much on the necessity of humility as a preparation for this great and extraordinary gift of God. 'Whosoever,' says the author of the 'Scale of Perfection,'

'disposeth himself to serve God in a contemplative life without this virtue (humility), either in true will or in the feeling of affection, will, like a blind man, stumble on the road, and never attain thereto. The higher he may climb by bodily penance and other virtues, if he hath not this humility, the lower will he fall. For, as St Gregory saith "He that cannot perfectly despise himself hath never yet discovered the humble wisdom of our Lord Jesus Christ"'[1]

3. To aid us in obtaining the different kinds of purifications above described, we are reminded that it is necessary each day to take an exact account of our dispositions and our faults by an examination of conscience. The examination of conscience is a very efficacious means for effecting the purification of the soul, and for this reason it may be well to remember some directions and admonitions given by prudent and experienced spiritual guides on this subject.

The examination of conscience.

The necessity of this examen is insisted upon by all, but too much self-examination would be as injurious to the spiritual state as it is to our physical state of health. For instance, it would be injurious to the soul were a person to be always, or nearly always, examining the conscience, or to turn the whole mental prayer into a kind of examination of conscience; and it would also be injurious to neglect entirely the examination of conscience except when we prepare for confession. Beginners in the way of perfection, thoughtless persons, and those subject to many defects by neglecting to examine the conscience, would thereby seriously retard their progress in virtue, and remain in a condition little

[1] 'Scale of Perfection,' p. 28.

adapted for the gift of contemplation, as the obstacles in the way of this exercise are not removed. A short time should, therefore, be devoted each day to this examination, and the examination should be occupied about, not only our theological faults, but also our imperfections and secret tendencies or inclinations. In this way we shall know ourselves and our failings, and be able each day to repair our defects by resolutions against them, and by obtaining the grace through prayer to persevere to the end in a continual amendment of life.

In the case of scrupulous souls, it is prescribed that this examen, in order to be beneficial, should be rather of the heart than of the head, and ordained to a renewal of confidence in God and to strengthen good resolutions, and not to cause anxiety or discouragement. It should be short and limited to a certain time, and ought never to be prolonged to an indefinite length of self-examination. There are some souls who cannot turn to God without falling at the same time into this examination; and we are admonished that such a tendency is disastrous, and is calculated to destroy the spirit of prayer, and with it the development of the spiritual life. In every case the examination should conclude with an act of sorrow and sincere regret for our sins and defects, and a firm, serious, and calm purpose of amendment in the future.

Lejeune, referring to the first book of the 'Obscure Night' of St John of the Cross, tells us that in the twelfth chapter we can find a useful lecture for those who wish seriously to profit by the examen of conscience. In that chapter St. John of the Cross places all the defects or faults of beginners under the seven capital vices, and he shows in outline how the goods of the supernatural order, so precious in themselves, can be depraved by being used improperly, and may be turned aside by our defects from the complete design for which they were intended. The human *Ego* (*I*) has the same influence over these unless they are well guarded, as it has over temporal goods. It can alter their nature, and change them from being an element of perfection into an occasion of imperfection. The human *Ego* attaches to these spiritual goods the same kind of irregularity and disorder as it attaches to material things, and from this disorder arises a series of sins having for their object that which is wholly spiritual, and corresponding to like sins in the material order. Thus, we can distinguish *spiritual* avarice, *spiritual* luxury, *spiritual* gluttony, etc. St John of the Cross is speaking of desires which suffice to injure the soul and of desires that are not mortally grievous in the particular paragraph referred to by Lejeune, but desires, as he says, that are matter of venial sin or known imperfection, and these, he tells us, occasion many positive and negative evils to the soul. He mentions some specific evils belonging to the particular vices of sensuality, avarice, vainglory, and gluttony which they generate, as well as the evils common to other vices. Thus, according to him, the chief and proper fruit of sensuality is defilement of body and soul, the principal and direct result of avarice is trouble; darkness and blindness are the immediate effect of vainglory, and the primary and direct result of gluttony is weakness in those things that pertain to virtue. With the text of the 'Ascent of Carmel' before me, I fail to discover that the Saint restricts his teaching to *spiritual* avarice, *spiritual* luxury, etc., as interpreted by Lejeune. But without any such restriction I can see with him that these are included under the vices named, even though the grosser sins of the same kind are not excluded, and that the lesson to be learned and the point to be demonstrated are nevertheless one and the same, which that author inculcates, namely that spiritual sins offer as many and as great dangers as the grosser sins that come under observation, and that in our examination we have to enter into the hidden depths of our souls, and discover how we use the supernatural goods and blessings as well as the natural ones, and whether we permit the *Ego*, ourselves and our natural inclinations to misdirect or abuse them.

4. Warning against being too much occupied with self

4. After stating the reasons and necessity of this self-examination, I may now give a few words of warning against the practice of being occupied too much with self and with self-introspection, even in regard to the affairs of our conscience, and I am fortunate to find all that need be said on the subject well and clearly written by Bishop Ullathorne, on whose teaching and authority we can rely with such complete confidence.

'It may be taken as a maxim, that whatever fosters selfishness disposes the soul to sadness There is a habit of self-introspection too much indulged in by many well-meaning persons that is disastrous to the spirit of religion, cheerfulness, and generosity. Self-knowledge is invaluable; yet it is not obtained by peering into our own darkness, but by seeing ourselves as we are reflected in the Divine light We shall never find what we are by dwelling in our own troubles and making them whilst we are dwelling in them, but by getting our mind above them and dwelling on the goodness of God, when that Divine goodness will teach us what we are by comparing ourselves with Him But when we dwell upon ourselves alone, and dwell in ourselves apart from the view of God, the truth is hidden from us, and we feel nothing but discouragement. Souls that act thus cling to themselves, discouraged, saddened, and disheartened; with their eyes bent upon their breast, they see but themselves, and that in the shallowest way, it is only by looking to God that they can see themselves truly. "Know yourself," says St. Catherine of Siena, "not in yourself, but in God, and God in you;" then you will find what in the sight of God you are

'Much and solicitous occupation with one's self produces much consciousness of one's self, and this breeds a sense of self that greatly interferes with the sense of God It gives not the true, but a fictitious, sense of one's self through means of the imagination, so that we alternately hug our self-complacency and our miseries, instead of looking with cheerfulness to God for their remedy. For instead of cleaving with the heart to God, such souls cleave to themselves with self-love, and suffer more from the subtleties of sadness than they know They are afraid to quit the sandy shores of their nature, and to leave the sense of themselves behind them, that they may launch forth in generous faith and confidence upon the ocean of God's goodness and mercy.

'Moreover, this incessant self-introspection and consciousness of self greatly impedes the spirit of duty as well as devotion. These laborious self-inspections cannot have that *very good heart which, hearing the word of God, keeps it, and brings forth fruit in patience.* For that very good heart is unselfish, open, loving, patient, cheerful, generous. *Seeking not her own, but what is profitable to many,* and diligent in all duties for God's sake. This clinging to self-consciousness leaves patience defective, humility defective, and charity defective, for how can one be subject to God or adhere to God when internally engaged with the feeling of one's self? Rolled up into one's self like the snail in its slimy shell, the soul can neither open herself to God nor to her neighbour. She is too much engaged with her selfish feelings to look to God with serene eyes, or to feel after Him with a loving heart. And the soul suffers—suffers from internal corrosion, suffers from depression and sadness, suffers from irritation and impatience, suffers from the want of a Divine air to breathe in, suffers from anxiety and loss of cheerfulness. But the cheerfulness of perfect charity, better than all those anxieties of self-introspection, better than all those cleavings of self-love to self, would keep away temptations and evil, and purge the fancy of its megrims. The irritability which in idle and self-conscious persons produces so much disorder would find its legitimate escape in useful works and services, consulting the health both of body and soul.'[1]

Thus far Bishop Ullathorne, whose words may be taken to heart by all pious souls as a protecting influence against the habit of too much introspection of, and occupation with, one's self and one's own feelings and state and condition of spirituality. Let

[1] 'Christian Patience,' pp. 134, 135.

us examine our consciences in regard to the faults committed each day, the occasion of these faults, and the dispositions with which we renew the resolution of amending our lives and making progress in virtue. But as to victories gained over ourselves or as to our good actions, we are advised not to dwell too long on the remembrance of them, lest presumption and vanity take that time to steal into our hearts. Let us leave our good works, whatever they may be, in the hands of the Divine mercy, and think more of doing our duty with greater fervour for the future

5. It may be asked, therefore, how we are to know ourselves, because we are told that spiritual progress depends on two things in general—to know ourselves and to know God. Bishop Ullathorne teaches us how to know ourselves when he quotes the words of St. Catherine of Siena 'Know yourself not in yourself, but in God, and God in you.' How this is to be done is well explained by another venerable ecclesiastic of the Benedictine Order, who is of very great assistance to us in our endeavours to understand and expound the secrets of the spiritual and mystical life I mean the Rev. W. Hilton. In 'The Scale of Perfection,' treating of the manner in which a man comes to know his own soul, he says. 'A soul that would know spiritual things needs first to have the knowledge of herself, for she cannot have the knowledge of a thing which is above herself unless she has first the knowledge of herself. And this she has when the soul is so gathered into herself and so separated from the sight of all earthly things, and from the use of her bodily senses, that she feeleth herself as she is in her own nature—that is, without a body. If, then, thou desirest to know

5. How to know ourselves

and see what thy soul is, thou must not turn thy thoughts upon thy body to seek it by imagination there, and to feel as if it were hidden within thy heart as thy heart is hidden and contained within thy body. If thou seekest it thus, thou wilt never find it. The more thou seekest to find and to feel it, as thou wouldst find a bodily thing, the further thou art from it. For thy soul is no bodily thing, but an invisible life, not hidden or contained within thy body, as a less thing is contained or hidden within a greater; but it containeth and quickeneth the body, and is much greater in power and in virtue than is the body. If, then, thou wouldst find it, withdraw thy thoughts from all bodily things, and from the care of thy own body, and from all thy five senses, as much as thou canst, and think upon the nature of a reasonable soul spiritually. And as thou wouldst reflect upon any virtue in order to acquire a knowledge of it, such as justice, humility, or any other, even so consider thy soul as a life immortal and invisible, who hath in itself the power to know the sovereign verity and to love the sovereign goodness, which is God. When thou feelest this, then wilt thou feel somewhat of thy true self. Seek thyself in no other place, for the more fully and the more clearly thou thinkest of the nature and the worthiness of a reasonable soul and of its operations, the better wilt thou see thyself.

' It is very hard for a soul that is ignorant ever to have this sight and knowledge of itself, or of an angelic nature, or of God. It betaketh itself immediately to imagining a bodily shape, and it fancieth that thereby it will arrive at the sight of itself, or of God, or of spiritual things. But this is not possible, for all spiritual things are seen and known by the understanding of the soul, and not by the imagination. As the soul seeth by her understanding that the virtue of righteousness consists in giving to everyone that which he ought to have, even so, and just in such a manner, may the soul see itself by the understanding.

'Nevertheless, I say not that thy soul should continue to rest in this knowledge, but by means of it shall it seek a higher knowledge above itself, and that is, the nature of God. For the soul is as a mirror, in which thou shouldst behold God spiritually. And therefore must thou first of all find thy mirror and keep it bright and clean from fleshy filth and worldly vanity, and hold it up well from the earth, that thou mayest see it and our Lord therein also.'[1]

[1] 'Scale of Perfection,' pp 249, 250.

CHAPTER X

PASSIVE PURIFICATIONS

1. Meaning of passive purifications

1. In the beginning of Chapter VIII. we have given a description of passive purifications as distinguished from active purifications. Therein we have stated that these purifications are the special work of God, and that they consist in aridities, temptations, and in external and internal trials which God sends to prepare the soul for contemplation, and to purify it the more in order to make it more worthy of the holy union with God which takes place in contemplation. Inasmuch as the whole man to be reformed and purified consists of a sensitive part and an intellectual or spiritual part, both these parts must have their own purification. Hence the distinction between the passive purification of the senses and the passive purification of the spirit. We have to treat of them separately.

2. The passive purification of the senses

2. This purgation or purification has for its material object or its subject-matter, as the name implies, the sensitive part of man's nature, both as to its affection and as to its apprehension. In the sensitive part there is an affective quality which is called the appetitive faculty, or that of desire, and includes what are known as the emotions, feelings, or passions (the *passiones concupiscibiles* and *iras-*

cibiles of the scholastics) and their acts, and there is also in this part the apprehensive or cognoscitive element which is located in the senses both external and internal. The sensitive purification takes place in both these portions of our sensitive nature as the recipient of the pains and punishments

We have to note, however, that, even though the purification of the senses is distinguished from the purification of the spirit, in practice and according to experience, the one is never found without the other, so that in the purification of the senses there is always something of the purification of the spirit, and to determine what kind of purgation afflicts the soul it will be necessary to judge by that one which prevails or is the more evident. It is rarely that a soul is subjected to both purifications at the same time and to the same extent or precise purpose or intent

The passive purification of the senses, according to St. Thomas, is an aridity which arises from the withdrawal of God, of the sensible feeling of grace, so that the soul imagines that all its perfections and the sources of good works have failed, and it fancies that all which it does is of no value, although this is not the case, because it is enriched all the time with greater helps of interior grace leading it to patience, according to the words of the Psalmist · *He hath turned rivers into a wilderness, and the sources of waters into dry ground.*[1] The subtraction of sensible grace is followed in this kind of purification by various kinds of trials and sufferings, so that the soul is thrown into darkness and aridity Oppressed with sorrow and a sense of misery the soul experiences

[1] Ps cvi 33

great difficulties and great sufferings. This arises from the fact that before this it has been advancing in the spiritual way amidst sensible favours and consolations, carried along, as it were, by a favourable wind in its progress towards perfection, and that, too, in spite of ordinary difficulties and trials which it felt itself able to overcome successfully and joyfully; now, however, it feels itself abandoned and desolate, and although sustained in patience and in reality strengthened by greater helps than before, it nevertheless experiences bitterness instead of sweetness, thorns instead of roses, sorrows instead of delights, and it finds no joy or solace either in heavenly or in earthly things, so that it remains in darkness and in the shadow of death. Such a devout person as the one we suppose, through devotion, has renounced earthly pleasures, especially all those that cannot be enjoyed without danger of sin, and he finds himself deprived of, and shut out from, all spiritual pleasures, and also annoyed by many temptations from all sides. He feels himself poor and miserable after being spiritually rich and happy, he has not taste or relish in the practice of virtue, and regards himself as tepid, or even forsaken, by God.

This state is a trial sent by Almighty God. It is felt as an evil and a punishment, and God is certainly the cause of it. In a twofold sense He may be the cause of what is called the evil of punishment or suffering Punishment taken as an infliction of suffering by contrarieties and crosses comes from God as an acting agent; but inasmuch as it consists in withholding favours and graces, it comes from Him, not as an agent, but as the result of not being influenced by such perfecting gifts It belongs to Him and to His Divine will either to grant or to withhold His favours, and passive purification consists in withholding sensible devotion and the interior feeling of His grace, and the actual infliction by Him of sensible pains and sufferings. Pains and sufferings may also be regarded in a twofold light, either as punishments for past sins, or as medicine, not only to cure evil habits as the remnants of past transgressions, but also to promote spiritual health and strength ; and according to this view a person is sometimes punished without fault or sin, but never without a cause Passive purification is therefore a medicinal punishment to promote some good. It may be inflicted without fault, but not without reason or cause, and is ordained to advancement in virtue This purification may be compared to the twofold nature of the pains of purgatory—namely, the pain of sense and the pain of loss.

3. These three things are experienced in the passive purification of the senses—viz., weariness, aridity, and desolation. They are opposed to the three blessings or favours which beginners often experience in meditation—namely, devotion, sweetness, and consolation

(1) Weariness is opposed to devotion, and it means a dislike of prayer, together with a feeling of langour and sadness in all those things that belong to the worship and service of God It is to feel tired of well-doing and sad in the matter of spiritual things. This uneasiness begets sloth or arises from sloth, but is to be found in the sensitive part of our nature. It is the repugnance or rebellion of the flesh against the spirit. We do not now speak of

the sloth which is sinful—namely, that which makes a man omit some duty which is obligatory—but of the feeling of sloth which the soul resists and overcomes, and in this way it may be the occasion of merit When it is the effect of passive purgation it is to be regarded as a punishment or trial sent by God. It is this which causes the soul of a humble man to feel as if he were rejected by God, and to experience such anguish that he has no longer any inclination either to pray, or to do good, or to work

Bishop Ullathorne proposes two remedies for this state of sadness and weariness—prayer and endurance He says · 'The great remedy for sadness is prayer, for, as sadness arises from a morbid clinging to one's self, prayer is the most effective way of detaching one from that inordinate self-adhesion, and of drawing one off from one's self to God, whilst it obtains the grace to overcome this vile clinging to one's own disorder *If any one of you be sad,* says St James, *let him pray.*[1] But as it is in the nature of sadness to loathe the remedy of prayer, this can only be begun by an effort, and by beginning with vocal prayer, which, as the soul becomes freer and more detached from self, will lead to mental prayer

'There is a quality of endurance which, owing to its great value as a discipline of the soul, calls for special remark That quality is the power of waiting Whenever the mind is anxious, or in a state of suspense or uncertainty, it finds that state painful and restless, and has a disposition to rush out into action ; but as this action is without due light and is unreasonable, it is sure to commit us to folly. A soul that is patient waits with calm endurance for light

---

[1] St. Jas v 13

before acting, and in virtue of this calm and patient endurance suffers no pain or anxiety, because the soul possesses herself and waits for light, and when the mind waits patiently for light, sooner or later it is sure to come. Trials of mind affect us more deeply than pains of body, and if we give way to anxiety such trials become troubles, and are immensely increased, but this cannot happen to those patient souls who, regardless of human respect, feel that they are in the hands of God and are encircled with His Fatherly providence, and that all things are in His disposal. When we see not our way through some trial or difficulty, we have only to look to God, and to wait in patience, and in due time His light will come and guide us. This very attitude of waiting, this very patience of expecting, will dispose the mind to receive, and the will to rightly use, the needful light.'[1]

These remedies prescribed by the venerable Bishop for ordinary sadness may with advantage be applied in cases of weariness and sadness sent by God, which are experienced in the state of passive purification.

(2) Aridity is opposed to the sweetness experienced by beginners in their prayers and spiritual duties. It is called also sterility and dryness. This aridity or dryness takes place in the sensitive feelings when God, wishing the soul to advance from the state of beginners to a more perfect state, transfers His communications from the sensitive feeling to the spirit, and changes these feelings themselves into spiritual. The spiritual communications, being of a superior order and of another nature of which the sensitive nature is incapable, are to be regarded as

(2) Aridity

[1] 'Christian Patience,' pp 136, 137.

substantial rather than pleasant, and they never superabound or overflow into the sensitive element or part of our nature. Hence the senses and feelings remain void and dried up, as it were, whilst the spirit is refreshed and nourished. Even the spirit itself in the beginning has no taste or relish for these communications, but, rather, feels weariness and reluctance towards them on account of the sudden change. It has been accustomed to sensible feelings, and these have ceased, so that the soul does not seem yet strong enough or perfect or pure enough to appreciate the purely spiritual emotions, if we may call them by that name. The aridity arises from the fact that the sensible feelings of Divine communications have been lost or withdrawn, and the soul cannot just yet enjoy the purely spiritual food which is imparted to it to dispose it for greater favours and greater perfection. This may be illustrated by the example of the Israelites, who at first did not like the light heavenly food of the manna, but hungered after the fleshpots of Egypt. They had not got accustomed to the new food, and had not quite lost their taste for the old. We can quite understand that greater perfection is needed in the soul to relish things pure and spiritual and removed from sense and sensible experiences and feelings. The more spiritual and the purer it becomes, the better will it be able to enjoy these favours, to value them, and to use them with great advantage for itself as well as for others in promoting God's greater glory.

(3) Desolation

(3) The third punishment resulting from passive purification is desolation, which is contrary to the consolation experienced by beginners in their prayers

and spiritual duties. This is a species of sickness in the inferior nature in its endeavours or aspirations for heavenly things, by reason of which no joy or pleasure is experienced from spiritual things. To distinguish this from the two other punishments of passive purification, we may consider the three various stages in which souls find themselves. Sometimes a man feels disinclined for prayer, and even unfit for that holy exercise, and then he suffers from weariness, and he is said to be tepid and undevout. Sometimes he is inclined to pray, but on entering upon the consideration of holy things he feels nothing like the influence of meditation or affection. This man is afflicted with dryness, and though he is truly devout, he is nevertheless sterile or in the state of aridity. At other times it happens that one is ready and prompt in the Divine service, and is suffused or enriched with holy reflections and affections in prayer, or to the understanding and the will ; but the inferior part remains poor and hungry, and thus opposition and contradiction is experienced, the soul is deprived of sensible devotion, and desolation is the result. In this state a man suffers by passive purification. He elicits affections of love and of the other virtues, but not sweetly nor easily, but with an effort and with a feeling of affliction ; and these acts are not yet so intense, because the inferior powers do not concur with them, and sometimes are in opposition to them. The time of prayer drags along slowly, and he is kept in the place of prayer and perseveres in the exercise, not by any predilection or liking for it, but as a matter of duty and by the force of reason and conscience. He is just like a sick man who has no relish for food, and if he were to obey his appetite he would take none whatever, but through necessity and the wish to get well and strong he forces himself to eat. Thus, the desolate soul, not through any inclination or pleasure, but convinced by reason and its own necessity, devotes itself, even in sorrow and difficulty, to spiritual exercises. A person in this state ascends the mountain of prayer, but he has to creep along on his hands and knees, not carried along swiftly by the vehicle of sensible devotion, nor raised aloft to the summit on the wings of consolation. And although the earth does not produce in his heart the thorns and briars of evil affections, and it may be that it germinates good fruits of holy thoughts and affections, it does not produce those spontaneously nor easily, but our subject has to eat his bread in the sweat of his brow, and to labour hard and constantly during this period of passive purification [1]

'There are trials,' says Bishop Ullathorne, 'laid on devout souls from which every drop of sensible sweetness seems to be extracted. The one sense left is the sense of desolation. In this most purifying trial the suffering soul shares her Lord's desolation on the Cross Yet is there a way still left to see the will of God, to acquiesce in the trial, to understand its justice, to wait with patient endurance the coming of God, and meanwhile to see the hand of God. Great is the pain, the privation, and the pressure, yet the soul can desire and pray, and feel her poverty, abiding in the resigned attitude of waiting and endurance, and she is conscious of the Divine wisdom expressed in the words of Ecclesiasticus *Wait on God with patience, join thyself to God and*

[1] See 'Mystica Theol Divi Thomæ,' disp viii, art. 3

endure, that thy life may be increased in the latter end.[1]

'Magnificent is the patience of faith under such a trial well endured, and the more so because the sufferer sees not the virtue of his endurance ; it is only beheld by the helping angels What the soul sees is her native poverty ; what she desires is the Divine goodness What she feels in the depth of her spirit is an infusion of the gift of endurance. Then will the heart say to God with the Psalmist . *Hear, O Lord, my voice, with which I have cried to Thee. Have mercy on me and hear me. Thy face, O Lord, will I still seek Turn not Thy face from me . I believe to see the good things of the Lord in the land of the living Expect the Lord, do manfully, and let thy heart take courage, and wait for the Lord*[2] See how the soul is drawn to God by the trial that seems to take her from Him. The voice seeks Him, the heart seeks Him, the face seeks Him, the wants of the soul seek Him, the desolation seeks Him , patience pleads, endurance pleads, the expectant waiting of the soul pleads, and love pleads, in them all. And when all these pleadings have purified the spirit, and drawn every purified desire from self to God, then God shows His face to the soul in the great benignity and sweetness of His visitation.'[3]

[1] Ecclus 11 3   [2] Ps xxvi 7-9, 13, 14
[3] 'Christian Patience,' p. 138

CHAPTER XI

PASSIVE PURIFICATION OF THE SENSES (*continued*)

God the efficient cause of passive purifications

1. The efficient cause or agent of the passive purifications described in the foregoing chapter is God Himself. This manner of His dealing with devout souls is accounted for by spiritual writers, when they tell us that it is a sign that He wishes to consummate the perfection of the work of sanctity which He has begun, and dispose the soul for intimate union and for close friendship with Him. He is compared to a wise and experienced nurse by some mystical writers. In the beginning He feeds the soul with the sweet milk of devotion, and enriches her with sensible favours and graces, that later on He may increase the spiritual life with more solid and substantial food, and in this sense we are to understand the words of St Paul. *I gave you milk to drink, not meat for you were not able as yet. But neither indeed are you now able, for you are yet carnal.*[1] And to this our Saviour also alluded, when He said to His disciples *I have yet many things to say to you, but you cannot bear them now But when He, the Spirit of truth, is come, He will teach you all truth.*[2] Amongst others, St. Bonaventure well describes this manner of acting by

[1] 1 Cor III. 2 [2] St John xvi 12, 13.

PREPARATION FOR CONTEMPLATION

which God leads novices and beginners in the spiritual life. The beneficent God, whose delights are to be with the children of men, freely imparts these delights to His faithful servants from their youth—that is, in the beginning of their conversion or their spiritual life. But, alas! some of them become contumacious when elated by spiritual consolations—they despise others; and some turn not to good account these favours, for they are desirous of praise, and, yielding to the vice of boasting, they become hypocrites. And when they endeavour to seem better than they are, they oppose themselves to God and rashly usurp to themselves His glory. The good God, therefore, knowing how useful temptations and trials are for man, first gives him the consolations of sweetness, by which he is afterwards sustained from yielding to temptation, and by which he is moved always to return to them and to seek to recover that which he has lost. Thus a man setting out on a journey strengthens himself by a good refection, lest he should faint by the way; thus Peter was brought to Thabor, there to see the glory of the transfiguration of Christ, that afterwards, when Satan would try him and sift him as wheat, he might be mindful of the sweetness he had felt, and remain faithful to that God Whose glory he had witnessed and Whose kindness he had experienced; thus the children of Israel received the heavenly food of manna in the wilderness, that they might be sustained in their long and wearisome journeys and strifes.[1]

2. To show the Divine purpose in withdrawing sensible consolations from those who have to be

[2] Spiritual gluttony described by St John of the Cross

[1] St Bonaventure apud 'Mystica Theol Divi Thomæ,' 1 307.

firmly established in virtue and prepared for the higher communications of the Spirit, let us turn to the teaching of St. John of the Cross, and, omitting other things, let us direct our attention to what he calls spiritual gluttony and its imperfections. Speaking of persons who indulge in such imperfections, he says

'When they communicate, they strive with all their might to find some sensible sweetness in the act, instead of worshipping in humility and praising God within themselves. So much are they given up to this that they think, when they derive no sensible sweetness from Communion, they have done nothing, so meanly do they think of God, neither do they understand that the least of the blessings of the Most Holy Sacrament is that which touches the senses, and that the invisible grace it confers is far greater; for God frequently withholds these sensible favours from men that they may fix the eyes of faith upon Himself. But these persons will feel and taste God, as if He were palpable and accessible to them, not only in Communion, but in all their other acts of devotion. All this is a very great imperfection, and directly at variance with the requirements of God, which demand the purest faith

'They conduct themselves in the same way when they are praying, for they imagine that the whole business of prayer consists in sensible devotion, and this they strive to obtain with all their might, wearying out their brains and perplexing all the faculties of their souls. When they miss that sensible devotion they are cast down, thinking they they have done nothing. This effort after sweetness destroys true devotion and spirituality, which consists in perseverance in prayer, with patience and humility mistrusting self, solely to please God And therefore, when they once miss their accustomed sweetness in prayer, or in any other act of religion, they feel a sort of repugnance to resume it, and sometimes cease from it altogether. In short, they are like children who are not influenced by reason, but by their inclinations. They waste themselves in search after spiritual consolation, and are never satisfied with reading good books, taking up one meditation after another, in the pursuit of sensible sweetness in the things of God. God refuses it to them most justly, wisely, and lovingly ; for if He did not, this spiritual gluttony on their part would grow into great evils. For this reason it is most expedient that they should enter into the obscure night, that they may be cleansed from this childishness.

'They who are bent on sensible sweetness labour under another great imperfection—weakness and remissness on the rugged road of the cross ; for the soul that is given to sweetness naturally sets its face against the pain of self-denial. They labour under many other imperfections also, which have their origin here, of which our Lord will heal them in due time through temptations, aridities, and trials— elements of the obscure night.'[1]

What St. John of the Cross has said of the imperfections of spiritual gluttony may be applied to all other defects and inordinate desires, and the same Divine purpose may be discovered in the purifications applied to the soul. In the words of

[1] 'The Obscure Night of the Soul,' book 1, chap vi

the same Saint, to avoid prolixity, we need not enlarge on them here.

<small>3 Some particular reasons for these purifications</small>

3. Besides the general reasons assigned for these purifications, namely, those common to active purifications, such as the subjection of the body to the soul and the sensitive appetite to reason, some particular motives may also be assigned

(1) An angel of Satan may transform himself into an angel of light, God permitting him, and he may mix up his influence with the communications of sensible consolations, and lead into error inexperienced beginners. He can act on the imagination and represent imaginary forms, and excite the feelings in such a way that what proceeds from the passions may be mistaken for spiritual favours.

(2) Then, sensible devotion may often proceed from natural dispositions, as well as from the suggestions or action of the evil spirit, so that consolations that come in this way may easily be mistaken and wrongly attributed to the Holy Spirit.

(3) We ought never to set too much value on such delights and sensible emotions, or take occasion of pride from them even when they proceed from God, because they are often granted to the imperfect, and sometimes to sinners; besides, even when confined to the friends of God, they are proper to beginners, and these have to be purified from their imperfections in order to obtain greater and more perfect communications.

(4) These sensible communications and consolations may prove too strong for some people, and injure the health by weakening the head or heart and breaking down the constitution, so that beginners, by reason of such weakness, are rendered

unfit for spiritual exercises, and have to give up the practices of devotion. Those who are really weak in body may with advantage, however, sometimes withdraw themselves from the occupation of devotion and mental exercises that cause great efforts and labour to them by reason of their weakness, but they must not omit devotion altogether, or exempt themselves from their spiritual exercises for slight indispositions or fanciful fears about their health.

4. We have to consider some questions bearing upon these passive purifications of the senses, that may serve to explain further their nature and the part which they take in the preparation of souls, either for contemplation or for the higher degrees of perfection. We have first to consider their severity All mystical writers agree in telling us that these purifications are severe and very painful. St. Theresa, speaking of the sufferings of the contemplative way, says : ' I tell you, daughters, those of you whom God leads not in this way, that, as far as I have seen and understood from those who walk in it, they do not carry a lighter cross than you, and that ye would wonder at the ways and manner whereby God crosses them. I know both concerning one sort and the other, and understand clearly that the afflictions God lays on the contemplative are intolerable, and of such a kind that, unless He give them this repast of quiet (food or strength of interior delights or consolations), they could not be endured. And it is manifest, that since it is true that whom God loves much He leads in the way of afflictions, and those, the more He loves them, the greater still, it seems not credible that He abhors as

These purificatio severe

to this contemplative persons, because He with His own mouth commends them and accounts them His friends. It is folly, then, to imagine that He admits into friendship with Him persons living delicately and without troubles; nay, I am confident God sends them greater crosses And since He leads them through so uneven and rough a way that sometimes they conceive they are lost, and must begin again to set forth anew, they have need that His Majesty should afford them some refreshment, and this not of water, but wine; that so inebriated with this celestial wine they may not consider what they suffer, and may be able to endure it.'[1]

The Saint here signifies that God, Who disposes all things with love and sweetness, does not permit these sufferings to be continual, and that He exchanges them for or intermingles with them spiritual consolations. St John of the Cross teaches that there are vicissitudes of joy and sorrow, but that the sorrow is often renewed with greater intensity. 'And so it comes to pass,' he says; 'for when the soul is most secure, it is then plunged at once into another affliction, heavier, darker, and sadder than the previous one, and which, perhaps, will be of longer duration. The soul again is convinced that all goodness is gone from it for ever. Experience cannot teach it; the blessings that flowed out of its former trials, during which it thought that its sufferings would never end, cannot prevent it from believing, in its present trials, that all goodness has perished from it, and that it will never be again with it as it was before. Its present convictions are so strong, grounded on actual feelings, as to destroy

[1] 'The Way of Perfection,' chap xviii

within it all occasions of joy. Thus, the soul in this purgation, though it seeks to please God and is ready to die for Him a thousand deaths—for souls thus tried love God with great sincerity—nevertheless finds no relief, but, rather, an increase of pain therein. For seeking God alone to the exclusion of aught else, and seeing its own miserableness to be so great, it doubts whether God be not angry with it. It cannot then persuade itself that there is anything in it worthy of love, but, rather, is convinced that there is that in it which should make it hateful, not only in the eyes of God, but of all creatures also for ever; it grieves to see within itself sufficient grounds why it should be abandoned of Him Whom it so loves and so longs for.'[1]

We have, however, to note concerning the severity of these sufferings, that St. Theresa and St. John of the Cross speak from experience, and in all probability they themselves suffered all the pains of this passive purification, and knew others who had passed through the same fire of suffering, yet, speaking with theologians who examine and lay down rules for all classes of the faithful, high and low, in the spiritual order, we have to state that not all the purgations, nor the same, nor with the same intensity, are applied by God to all souls called to contemplation or to perfect union with Him. Even as to time and duration no fixed rule can be prescribed. These purifications may last for many years, sometimes continuously, and sometimes with intervals full of consolations. Long and severe purifications are usually the signs and forerunners of sublime contemplation. St John of the Cross gives us the

[1] 'The Obscure Night,' book ii., chap vii.

result of his experience and sound knowledge where he says: 'But how long the soul will continue in this fast and penance of sense no one can with certainty tell. It is not the same in all men, neither are all men subjected to the same temptations These trials are measured by the Divine will, and are proportioned to the imperfections, many or few, which are to be purged away, and also to the degree of union in love to which God intends to elevate a particular soul. That is the measure of its humiliations, both in their intensity and duration.

'Those who are endowed with the capacity for suffering and who have force sufficient to endure are purified in more intense trials and in less time. But those who are weak are purified very slowly with weak temptations, and the night of their purgation is long; their senses are refreshed from time to time lest they should fall away These, however, come later to the pureness of their perfection in this life, and some of them never. These persons are not clearly in the purgative night nor clearly out of it, for though they make no onward progress, yet, in order that they may be humble and know themselves, God tries them for a season in aridities and temptations, and visits them with His consolations at intervals, lest they should become fainthearted and seek for comforts in the ways of the world.

'From other souls, still weaker, God, as it were, hides Himself that He may try them in His love, for without this hiding of His face from them they would never learn how to approach Him. But those souls that are to go forwards to so blessed and exalted a state as this of the union of love, however quickly God may lead them, tarry long, in general, amidst aridities, as we see by experience."[1]

According to Cardinal Bona, Hubert of Casseli spent fifteen years under passive purifications, St. Theresa, eighteen ; St Francis of Assisi, only two ; St. Clare of Montefalco, fifteen ; St. Catherine of Bologna, five ; St. Magdalen of Pazzi, five at first, and afterwards sixteen more ; the Blessed Balthazer Alvarez, sixteen years also [2]

5. We have to remark also that aridities, afflictions, and tribulations such as we have been describing are not always to be regarded as passive purifications, nor are all souls who endure them called to contemplation. For all souls who serve God are in this life subject to such trials and sufferings, and all are not called to contemplation. If it is found that souls who fall into sin and are tepid in the service of God are afflicted in this way, we must not regard it as a sign of subsequent contemplation, but rather as warnings to lead to emendation of life. Even when dereliction is perceived in beginners, it is not a sign of contemplation ; but in the perfect it is to be regarded in that light, although it is commonly admitted that the most perfect souls may have to undergo all the passive purifications, and never receive in this life the gift of contemplation , for not all the Saints were mystics and contemplatives, and some of those who were not mystics equalled in sufferings sent by and endured for God the greatest of the mystical Saints. This we must admit when we hold that virtue in a heroic degree may be practised without contemplation, and that

5. Not always a sign of a vocation to contemplation

---

[1] 'The Obscure Night,' book 1, chap xiv
[2] Lejeune, 'Manuel de Théol Mystique,' p. 230.

contemplation as a free gift of God is not necessary for heroic sanctity

We must not, therefore, expect after the purification of the senses that the soul will always be raised to delightful contemplation, because this only happens when the purification is ordained by God to contemplation, and this is not always the case. For it may happen that this purification is ordained to the perfection of the soul, and in this case the result is perfect meditation, not contemplation. As to visions, locutions, revelations, etc., as they are gifts *gratuitously* given, they do not always follow infallibly— God gives them to whom He pleases, when He pleases, and according to the designs of His wise providence.

When contemplation is the end to which all these passive purifications are ordained, then the result is that which is so beautifully described by St. John of the Cross.

6. Effects of these purifications

6. 'The soul which God is leading onwards enters not into the union of love at once when it has passed through the aridities and trials of the first purgation and the night of sense. It must spend some time, perhaps years, after quitting the state of beginners in exercising itself in the state of proficients In this state, like a man released from a rigorous imprisonment, it occupies itself in Divine things with much greater freedom and satisfaction, and its joy is more abundant and interior than it ever experienced in the beginning before it entered the sensitive night. Its imagination and faculties being no longer tied down, as hitherto, to spiritual thoughts and reflections, it now rises at once to most tranquil and loving contemplation, and finds spiritual sweet-

ness without the fatigue of meditation. But as the purgation of the soul is still somewhat incomplete in the chief part—the purgation of the spirit being wanting, without which, by reason of the mutual connection between our higher and lower nature, man being an individual, the purgation of sense, however violent it may have been, is not finished and perfect—it will never be without some aridities, darkness, and trials, sometimes much more severe than in the past, which are, as it were, signs and heralds of the coming night of the spirit, though not so lasting as that night. . . .

'That sweetness and interior delight which the proficients find so easily and so plentifully come now in greater abundance than before, overflowing into the senses more than they were wont to do previous to the sensitive purgation And as the senses are now more pure, they can taste of the sweetness of the spirit in their way with greater facility; but since the sensitive part of the soul is weak, without any capacity for the strong sense of the spirit, they who are in the state of proficients are liable, by reason of the spiritual communications which reach to the sensitive part, to great infirmities and sufferings and physical derangements, and consequently weariness of mind, as it is written *The corruptible body presseth down the mind*.[1] Hence the communications made to these cannot be very strong, intense, or spiritual, such as they are required to be for the Divine union with God, because of the weakness and corruption of the sensitive parts which has a share in them.'[2]

Lastly, it has to be noted that these salutary

[1] Wisd., ix 15.   [2] 'The Obscure Night,' book II, chap IV

effects are granted only to those souls who have passed through the difficult ways of the obscure night of the same with fidelity. If during the time of trial the soul should grow negligent and careless, if it should give up its devout practices, and if it should resist temptations only remissly and tepidly, and if it should bear the aridities, the sufferings and trials, in an imperfect manner, it not only will not reach the state of contemplation, but it will not make one step towards that degree of perfection for which God intended to prepare it by means of these remedies, and it will probably remain during a whole lifetime in an imperfect state; and this is a matter which should be kept in mind, not only by the individual souls themselves, but also by their confessors and spiritual guides.[1]

7. The need of spiritual direction in time of purification

7. It is at this juncture of the spiritual life that the soul has absolute need of a good and wise confessor or spiritual guide. This I can say on the authority of St. John of the Cross and of St. Theresa The former writes as follows with regard to this need

'When God effects the change of which I have spoken, when He leads the soul out of the way of sense into that of the spirit, from meditation to contemplation, when it is helpless so far as its own powers are concerned—that is, during the aridity of the night of sense—spiritual persons have to endure great afflictions, not so much because they are in a state of aridity, but because they are afraid that they have missed the way, thinking that they are spiritually ruined and that God has forsaken them, only because they find no support or consolation in holy

[1] Voss, 'Compend Scaramelli,' p 170.

things. Under these circumstances they weary themselves, and strive, as they were wont, to fix the powers of the soul with some satisfaction upon some object of meditation. They think when they cannot do this, and are not conscious of their labour, that they are doing nothing—but with great dislike and interior unwillingness on the part of the soul, which enjoys its state of quietness and rest—while they change from one condition they make no progress in the other, because by exerting their own spirit they lose that spirit which they had in tranquillity and peace. They are like a man who does his work over again, or who goes out of a city that he may enter it once more, or who lets go what he has caught in hunting that he may hunt it again. Their labours are vain, for they will find nothing, and that because they are turning back to their former habits

'Under these circumstances, if they meet with no one who understands their case, these persons fall away and abandon the right road, or become weak, or at least put hindrances in the way of their further advancement, because they make efforts to proceed in their former way of meditation, fatiguing their natural powers beyond measure They think that their state is the result of negligence or of sin All their efforts are now in vain, because God is leading them by another and very different road—that of contemplation. Their first road was that of discursive reflection, but no imagination or reasoning can reach the second.'[1]

St. Theresa recommends a director who is both pious and learned She gives it as her opinion that,

[1] 'The Obscure Night,' book 1, chap. x

if the choice of confessors or directors lies between a pious and unlearned man and a learned man, the latter is to be preferred. Her pronounced opinion is against the half-learned. She says: 'I have found by experience that it is better for directors who are virtuous and full of holy manners to have no learning at all, rather than a little; because those who have none will not trust themselves without asking the opinion of others who are learned, and neither could I trust them myself. But I was never deceived by any truly learned man, and even those others had no desire of deceiving me, but they erred only because they knew no better. I thought they were capable of guiding me, and that I was not bound to do anything but believe them, as what they told me was in accordance with the general opinion and gave me more liberty. If they had been more strict with me, I was so wicked that I should have chosen other confessors. . . . I think that Almighty God, on account of my sins, allowed my confessors to deceive me, and to be deceived themselves. And I also deceived many others by telling them the very same things which had been told me.'[1]

From these extracts we may understand the need of guidance in the spiritual life, and that confessors and directors, besides the knowledge of dogmatic and moral theology, should acquire a good, substantial knowledge of ascetical and mystical theology as well, and also we may understand the great prudence, piety, and knowledge which are required for the proper guidance of souls in the higher paths of the spiritual life.

[1] 'Life of St Theresa,' chap. v.

CHAPTER XII

PASSIVE PURIFICATIONS OF THE SENSES CAUSED BY SECONDARY AGENTS

GOD Himself is the direct cause of the aridities and sufferings that follow from the withholding of the sensible consolations of grace, and of the other trials of the obscure night of the senses referred to and explained in the foregoing chapters. Sometimes He makes use of secondary causes or instruments, or permits them, to inflict purifying pains on devout souls. Sometimes He permits the devil to tempt and torment them; sometimes natural causes are applied for their purification; sometimes He makes use of other men as His agents, and in a thousand ways these can trouble and afflict holy souls.

1. The office of the demon is to injure and torment the souls of men, and even the just are exposed to his temptations. This diabolical persecution, in the case of souls undergoing the passive purification of the senses, is exercised in three grades—that is, by temptations, by obsession, and by possession of their bodies. And in such cases the temptations are more than ordinary, and even increase to such an extent as to inspire horror and surprise.

[1] The devil as agent

2. I shall follow Scaramelli in referring only to some of these temptations, as it would be impossible to mention all.

2 Diabolical temptations

(1) As the theological virtues are the foundation and principle of all perfection, the devil puts into action all the strongest machinery of his temptations against them. Against faith he excites the mind by persuasions or arguments against Catholic dogmas, so as to suggest doubts about the existence of God, against the mystery of the Holy Trinity, against the immortality of the soul, etc. It is narrated of one holy person, whose purification was very severe and cruel, that, appearing to be as an angel of light, the devil suggested to her most perfidious heresies, and proved them by many plausible reasons; and represented the precepts of the Decalogue as unjust, imprudent, and barbarous, and that with so much clearness and subtlety that her director, to whom she made known her difficulties, was astonished. Then, again, when he sees the soul afflicted and suffering from aridity, dryness, and anxiety, he tries to make it believe that God is unjust and cruel in treating one so devoted to Him with so much severity. To these suggestive representations it is advisable to make no reply, and not to endeavour to refute the error, because the devil is very clever, and he can easily deceive by false reasons and arguments, and he is likely to outwit most people by his natural ability and his keen insight into their weakness and ignorance. Besides, a soul in a state of darkness and dereliction and full of trouble is not, humanly speaking, capable of normal good reasoning. It is, therefore, the best plan to turn our back on the devil, and to raise up our mind and heart to

(1) Against the theological virtues

God, and to make short general acts of faith, such as: 'I believe all that God has revealed and that the Church teaches'; or, 'I believe, Lord; help my unbelief' As to the virtue of hope, there is scarcely a soul attacked by Satan who is not made to feel sentiments of distrust, and to whom sometimes thoughts against hope are not suggested. The enemy places before the eyes not only past sins, but also present imperfections; and he does not make them appear in that clear light which comes to the soul from the Divine light, by which it is moved to humble sorrow and peaceful hope; but he makes them appear in his own gloomy light, and represents heaven closed, hell open, God angry, and all lost By means of the aridities and tribulations he tries to persuade the soul that God has abandoned her, that she has consented to temptations, that she has sinned mortally, and is already in the hands of the demon or given up to him Thus agitated in the interior sense and excited to desperation, the soul may be compelled or forced to break forth into exterior acts of desperation for which they cannot be held responsible.

These temptations to despair are most dangerous, and the only way to overcome them is to have recourse to God, Who will not abandon one under such dreadful afflictions, and to make short acts of hope, or at least to repeat the words of holy Job: *Although Thou shouldst kill me, I will trust in Thee*[1] One must not be disturbed by the feelings which may be contrary to those expressed sentiments in the inferior part, because God only regards the free acts of the will, and these He accepts.

[1] Job xiii. 15.

The most terrible temptations of all are the attacks of the devil against charity. Into some souls the devil tries to instil the spirit of blasphemy, so that they feel inclined to utter impious words against God and against the Saints. He fills the ears of others with blasphemous words, so that they can scarcely hear their own words, as often happened to St. Mary Magdalen of Pazzi during the recital of the Divine Office. To some others he represents God as their implacable enemy, and thus endeavours to move the hearts of devout souls to dislike, and even hatred, of Him. He tries to excite in the souls of others the spirit of murmuring against God, as in the case of Job, who, pierced with the thorns of this temptation, exclaimed · *I cry to Thee, and Thou hearest me not: I stand up, and Thou dost not regard me.*[1] We are not to think that this most patient and holy man gave any assent of the will to wicked murmurings, but that he only manifested the perverse feelings produced by the demon in the inferior part of his nature. There have also been some examples in which we find it mentioned that the demon represented to the phantasy and painted before the imagination of holy persons foul and unbecoming pictures, even when they were praying before the images of Christ and His Saints, so that he might impel them to irreverence towards sacred things. This also happened to St. Mary Magdalen of Pazzi, who was tempted to blasphemies and to profanity even when praying before the Blessed Sacrament

As these and the like temptations cause the greatest repugnance to the soul, they are not

[1] Job xxx 20.

usually regarded as very dangerous, and therefore those who experience them are advised not to fear them, nor to allow themselves to be anxious or disturbed about them ; but with great peace let them elicit acts of the contrary virtues, and despise all these diabolical suggestions ; let them offer up suppliant prayers to God and submit themselves entirely to His Divine will. God will accept and reward this oblation.

(2) As he attacks the theological virtues with the full force of his evil intent, so does the demon attack also the moral virtues by inflaming the human passions and evil inclinations. Sometimes he excites persons undergoing purification to anger, to impatience, indignation, and the like, so that companions and domestics fear to go near them lest they should break out into words or acts against charity. Sometimes the demon tempts them to gluttony, as he did our Divine Lord in the wilderness, when he said to Him *If Thou be the Son of God, command that these stones be made bread.*[1] Sometimes he tempts devout souls to pride, and this with all his might, it would appear. He suggests to them the glory of being reputed a Saint, so that the whole world may know them, during prayer he can move the feelings and sense so that false ecstasies may be occasioned, and apparitions even presented, so that spiritual pride and vanity may be instilled into the soul and nourished there.

What we have said with regard to these vices may be said also of all other vices, for there is no virtue which the devil does not attack with more or less violence. Some of the sufferers are especially

[1] St. Matt. iv 3.

worthy of commiseration, and these are good, observant, religious men and women, who are sometimes violently tempted to leave the cloister, to renounce their state of life, to return to the world, and to enjoy all its pomps and vanities; all such evil suggestions come from, or at the instigation of, the evil spirit.

To all these may be added the terrible torment to the soul which arises from the fear and apprehension that she has consented to these temptations, that she has lost the grace of God, and from the painful impression that she has committed mortal sins. Hence arise most acute remorse, tortures, and anxieties of conscience, which the innocent soul will bear with her usual patience. It will torture itself at this time by reasoning and thinking, to suffer, and to suffer without fruit, and to suffer under the feeling of having offended God grievously, must certainly be to souls, whose sole purpose in life is to be united with God and to keep themselves unstained by sin, a bitter cup of sorrow and affliction. The cause of the feeling of dereliction is God, but it is the demon who tempts to despair, and who is permitted to stir up the evil passions and inclinations into revolt and disorder.

3 How to regard and resist these and other temptations (by Father Baker)

3 Father Baker gives us useful directions as to how we are to regard and to resist such temptations. He says. 'A well-minded soul ought to consider that the simple passing of such thoughts or imaginations in the mind is no sin at all, though they should rest there never so long without advertence, but only the giving a deliberate consent to them. Neither is it in the power of a soul either to prevent or to banish them at pleasure, because the imagination is

not so subject to reason that it can be commanded to entertain no images but such as reason will allow, but it is distempered according to the disposition of the humours and spirits of the body, and sometimes also the devil is permitted to inject or raise images to the disquieting of tender souls, but he can force none to consent to these suggestions proceeding from them.

'There is less danger of consenting unto temptations merely spiritual, such as are thoughts of blasphemy, despair, etc., and consequently less likelihood of scrupulosity from a suspicion of such consent. Though sometimes they may be so violent and so obstinately adhering that the fancy will become extremely disordered, and the soul will think herself to be in a kind of hell, where there is nothing but blasphemy and hating God.

' Her best remedy is quietly to turn her thoughts some other way, and rather neglect than force herself to combat them with contrary thoughts, for by neglecting them the impression that they make in the imagination will be diminished. She may do well also by words or outward gestures' (that is, when alone, and the gestures should not be absurd), 'to signify her renouncing and detestation of them, as in a temptation of blasphemy let her pronounce words and express postures of adoration of God, praise, love, etc.; let her also be the more diligent in frequenting the choir, continuing more carefully in postures of humility before Him. And, doing thus, let her banish all suspicions of having consented as being morally impossible.

' Certain it is that, however troublesome and horrid soever such temptations may seem to be, yet they, being quietly resisted, or, rather, neglected, do wonderfully purify the soul, establishing Divine love most firmly and deeply in the spirit. Moreover, by occasion of them the superior soul is enabled to transcend all the disorders and tumults in inferior nature, adhering to God during the greatest contradictions of sensuality.

'As for the other sort of inferior temptations, which are more gross, causing oft disorderly motions and effects in corporal nature, it will be more difficult to persuade timorous souls that they have not consented, both by reason that such imaginations are more pertinacious and sticking to the corporal humours and spirits, and also because inferior nature is powerfully inclined to a liking of them; yea, and after the resistance made by reason, yet such images continuing in the fancy and such motions in the body, the mind will be stupefied, and the resistance of reason will oftimes be so feeble as that in the opinion of the person it will pass for no resistance at all, yea, rather the soul will be persuaded that she has deliberately consented, considering the continuance of them, after that she was fully awake and had reflected on them.

'Notwithstanding, unless in such souls the reason do not only reflect upon the sinfulness of such impure thoughts, if consented to, but likewise unless in the very same instant that she makes such a reflection her will be deliberately moved to the approving of them, they may be assured that there has passed no culpable consent to them. Again, if the general disposition of such souls be such as that seldom or never either speeches or deliberate actions do proceed from them conformable to such impure imaginations, they may confidently judge that there is no danger of having incurred a mortal sin.

'Above all things, the devout soul is to be careful that she may not be disheartened by occasion of such temptations from pursuing constantly her appointed recollections the best she can, notwithstanding that then, above all other times, such thoughts will throng into her mind, so that she will think it almost unlawful to appear before God, being full of such impure images. But she is to consider that now is the proper time to show her fidelity to God. No thanks to her if she adhere to God when nature makes no opposition, but rather finds a great gust in it. But if amidst these tempests of corrupt nature she will firmly adhere to God when such adhesion becomes so extremely painful to her, this is thanksworthy; then she will show herself a valiant soldier of our Lord, and worthy of that testimony that He gives of her, Who has judged her fit and capable of encountering such furious enemies.

'A great blessing and happiness it is that in all internal confusions, obscurities, etc., we can always make an election of God with the superior will, which, being effectually done, whatsoever disorders are in the imagination or in inferior nature, they do rather increase than prejudice our merit.'[1]

4. The foregoing remarks are applicable to all temptations, whether they proceed from the devil or from ourselves, and here I wish to notice one special point that concerns temptations, namely, whether devout souls should ever seek or promote assaults of the inferior powers or raise passions in order to repress them

4. Temptations not to be sought for nor promoted

[1] 'Holy Wisdom,' pp 284-286

In the 'Spiritual Combat' we find the following statements 'First, whenever thou art assailed by the impulses of sense, oppose a valiant resistance to them, so that the superior will may not consent. Secondly, when the assaults have ceased, excite them anew, in order to repress them with greater force and vigour. Then challenge them again to a third conflict, wherein thou mayest accustom thyself to repulse them with contempt and abhorrence. These two challenges to battle should be made to every disorderly appetite, except in the case of temptations of the flesh.'[1]

It is against the second of these statements that some warning is needed, and that warning is given as well as sound counsel by Father Baker, whose teaching in this matter is the surest and the safest. After advising especially beginners in the spiritual life in all times and occasions as much as lies in them to suppress all passions, he says:

'I do the more earnestly recommend the practice according to this advice, because I find that some good spiritual authors do counsel a quite contrary proceeding as a remedy and means to subdue passions. For they would have souls willingly and purposely to raise them in sensitive nature, and when they are come to a certain height, then by the strength of reason and motives of religion to quiet and pacify them again. As, for example, in case of an injury received, they advise that we should call to mind all the circumstances and aggravations that are apt to kindle indignation and resentment; and as soon as the passion is inflamed, then to suppress it by considerations of the example of our Lord, and His

[1] 'The Spiritual Combat,' chap. xiii.

precept of charity to enemies, of the dangerous effects of revenge, and the blessed reward of patience, etc. The like they say concerning a sensual desire to any object; they would have it represented with all its allurements and charms, so as to move a strong inclination in sensitive nature, and this being done, presently to suppress such inclinations by strong resolutions and contrary practices. Only they forbid this practice in the passion of sensual impurity, which must not be revived upon any pretence whatsoever.

'To perfect souls this advice may be proper, who have an established dominion over their passions; but as to the imperfect, if they should conform themselves to it, two great inconveniences could scarce be prevented, viz., (1) that they would be in danger either to be unwilling or unable to restore peace unto their minds once much disquieted; (2) by an advised and earnest representation of such objects as do raise passions in their minds they do thereby fix more firmly in the memory the images of them, and by that means do dispose the said images to return at other times against their will, when perhaps the reasons and motives to repress them will either not be ready or the soul in no disposition to make use of them; or if it should be willing, it is to be doubted that then such motives will not prove efficacious.

'Therefore, imperfect souls may do best to deal with all passions as they ought with those of impurity, namely, to get the mastery over them by flying from them, and, if they can, forgetting them.'[1]

I should certainly extend these directions to the

[1] 'Holy Wisdom,' pp 210, 211.

most perfect as well as to the imperfect, as I do not understand how anyone can be justified in occasioning dangers and temptations to themselves without a sufficient reason, and I do not consider it a sufficient reason to do this for the purpose of putting virtue to the test, or of proving how strong our resistance can be, or as a preparation for future encounters. There shall never be wanting dangers and temptations to any souls in this world, and there will never be any necessity to go in search of these or wilfully to start them, especially by stirring up feelings or passions that are counted material sins when not wilful, and may easily become formal sins when wilfully caused This would seem to be the doctrine laid down by Father Baker himself further on in his book, where he says : 'Nevertheless, we must not voluntarily seek temptations, for *qui amat periculum peribit in eo* (he that loves danger shall perish therein), saith the wise man. God will not deny spiritual strength to resist and make good use of temptations that by His providence befall us—yea, although it was by some precedent fault and negligence of ours that they befell us; but He has made no promise to secure us in a danger into which we voluntarily run.'[1]

5 The visible ways in which the demons are permitted to tempt and try the servants of God

5. We have said that in three ways the assaults of the evil spirit may be directed against devout souls for the purpose of purification—namely, by temptations, such as we have described, by obsession, and by possession. These two—namely, obsession and possession—have more immediate relation to the body than to the soul, and show themselves by many visible manifestations.

[1] 'Holy Wisdom,' p 284

Schram explains the difference between *obsession* and *possession*. He tells us that the possessed are also obsessed, but that it is not to be understood that the obsession strictly taken means also possession. The *obsessed* are those in whom the devil is not, but who are subjected to many and extraordinary vexations of the devil acting from without; the *possessed* are those in whom the devil is, and in whose bodies he exercises various operations, God permitting him. These are called also *demoniacs* and *energumens*.

(1) The passive purification of the sensitive or inferior nature is sometimes effected by demoniacal *obsession*, and this is the case when the devil, not from within, but from without, is permitted to tempt, vex, and torment a man in some extraordinary and visible manner. This he does in various ways, as we read in the lives of many Saints. Sometimes he presents horrid visions before the eyes; at other times the ears are tortured by terrible noises or wicked words of blasphemy; and at times the whole body is afflicted by excruciating pains and sufferings brought on by the demons. Ribet says that obsession is one of the ordinary means of this passive purification. Schram states that it is a species or kind of the purification of the senses, but I should hesitate to state with Ribet that it is an ordinary form of this purgation in the sense that such obsessions are to be expected generally in cases of vocations to contemplation or to the higher grades of perfection. That the Saints of God have been tried in this way cannot be doubted, and from their example we may learn how this means of purification is permitted by Almighty God, and how it may

(1) Diabolical obsession

be turned to good account. Benedict XIV., treating on this subject, says :

'The servants of God while upon earth have not only for the most part felt in their members the law which fighteth against the mind, but by the permission of God have endured many afflictions at the hand of the devil. In the life of St. Hilarion, written by St. Jerome, after relating the temptations with which the devil tormented him when he was a boy, he thus proceeds : " One night he heard the crying of children, the bleating of sheep, the lowing of oxen, the wailing as if it were of women, the roaring of lions, the tramp of an army, and the portentous sound of many voices, that he might be overcome through terror at the noise before he saw anything. He understood the artifices of the devil, and, falling on his knees, made the sign of the Cross of Christ on his forehead. . ."

'In the life of St. Anthony the Great, written by St. Athanasius, we find the following, related by St Anthony himself: " I have sometimes seen the devil in lofty stature, daring to call himself the power and the providence of God, and saying to me, 'Antony, what dost thou wish me to give thee?' But I, spitting in his face, armed with the name of Christ, threw myself upon him, and his lofty form vanished between my hands. Frequently, too—I do not deny it—I have been beaten by devils, but I sang, ' No one shall separate me from the love of Christ.' At the sound of that word they became angry, and were routed, not by mine, but by the power of Christ, Who said, *I saw Satan fall like lightning from heaven.* . "

'In the Bull of canonization of St. Philip Neri we read "And although the ancient enemy of the human race did very frequently manifest himself to him in a horrible shape in order to terrify him, he, always brave and undaunted, triumphed gloriously over him, and retained true peace and tranquillity which he interiorly enjoyed." Other relations of a like kind are to be found in the reports of the Auditors of the Rota in the causes of St Francis Xavier, St. Mary Magdalen de Pazzi, and St. Francesca Romana. For if Christ was led by the Holy Spirit into the desert, if He of His own will submitted to be tempted, not so far as consent, but only to the struggle and the victory; if He suffered the devil to take him up to the pinnacle of the Temple or to a high mountain, as we read in St. Matt. iv., if these things were done by Him, so that no one, however holy, should think himself free or safe from temptations, and that He might teach us how to overcome the temptations of the devil, as, after St. Hilary and St. Augustine, St Thomas teaches, it ought to be matter of surprise to no one that we often read in sacred history and the Acts of the Saints that they were tempted by the devil in various forms and under various appearances'[1]

That souls may not yield to the fear, consternation and sadness which the devil causes in this way, we are exhorted to renew our confidence and our trust in God, and to remember, first, that God never permits the devil to harm us as much as he can, and as much as he would, as the power which he has of injuring us is restricted by God Thus,

[1] 'Treatise on Heroic Virtue,' vol ii, pp. 29, 31

when He permitted the devil to afflict His servant Job, He said to him: *Behold, all that he hath is in thy hand: only put not forth thy hand upon his person.*[1] And when He allowed him this greater power against His servant, He added: *Behold, he is in thy hand, but yet save his life.*[2] Second· God never permits anyone to be tormented in body, or tempted in soul, beyond that which he is able to bear, according to the words of St. Paul· *God is faithful, Who will not suffer you to be tempted above that which you are able: but will make also with the temptation issue, that you may be able to bear it.*[3] The more horrible the vexations, the more vehement the temptations, the greater and the stronger is the Divine aid. Third 'It is of great importance,' says Bishop Ullathorne, 'to understand that, when evil spirits tempt us, they have no power allowed them except on the corporal senses and on the imagination. They cannot act in the substance of the soul without the soul's consent It is equally important to understand that, though the imagination acts on the mind, it has its origin from the corporal senses. When this was explained to St Theresa, it became an epoch of light in her spiritual life She then understood how to manage her imagination, and what degree of importance was to be attached to what St. Paul calls the spirit of the flesh'[4] By these reflections souls persecuted by the evil spirit may be consoled and comforted. They are recommended also to employ the ordinary means left by our Divine Saviour to the Church and to the faithful against the infernal powers. prayer, mortification,

---

[1] Job i. 12
[2] Job ii. 6
[3] 1 Cor x. 13.
[4] 'Christian Patience,' p. 213

the Sacramentals—in particular, holy water and the sign of the Cross; and in some rare cases exorcisms may be permitted and recommended in cases of obsession, especially when they take the form of preventing people from going to church, or to confession and Communion, or when the devil excessively tortures and afflicts the soul. The ritual exorcisms by the law of the Church are reserved to priests, and even priests are not allowed to make use of them in casting the devils out of possessed or obsessed persons, without the leave of the bishop, and then they are admonished not to have recourse to this ceremony without sufficient grounds for believing that the person is really possessed or tortured by diabolical obsession.

(2) Diabolical possession is not regarded ordinarily as one of the passive purifications to which persons are subjected in preparation for contemplation. The reason assigned for this is that in this possession the use of reason and liberty is suspended, and thereby the exercise of perfection, whilst passive purgation is always carried on by free and meritorious acts. St. Augustine tells us that sin is usually the cause of these possessions. It is seldom that God permits His devout servants to be subjected to this trial. The Abbot Moses, of whom St Gregory the Great speaks, and many other authors, teach that these possessions are in no way a preparation for contemplation; but that they are inflicted as a punishment, it may be for some light faults, even, when God wishes to inspire His servants with extreme horror for such faults. If it should happen that possession may be noticed as a prelude to contemplation, we should hold that contemplation

would be granted had there been no such punishment, rather than suppose it to be a preparation for contemplation. Nevertheless it is not, absolutely speaking, impossible that this species of diabolical tyranny might be the means of passive purgation; for God knows how to draw good out of evil, and to give to the punishment a purifying power, according to the designs of His justice and goodness [1]

[1] Ita Ribet, vol. 1, p 395

CHAPTER XIII

THE PURIFICATION OF THE SENSES BY TRIALS FROM NATURAL CAUSES

1. It remains for us to treat of great trials and adversities which are occasioned sometimes by men, and sometimes by necessary natural causes, such as sickness, poverty, privations, etc. When afflictions of this kind dispose and prepare a person for perfection and contemplation, they ought to be ordained to that end by special providence, because they are sometimes sent as punishment, and then they do not appertain to the purification of which we treat. 1. Purification by natural causes

(1) Benedict XIV. takes two Scriptural examples to illustrate how God makes use of these trials and crosses for the greater purification of His servants. The first is that of holy Job, who was tried by the evil spirit as well as by so many natural causes. The history of this holy man and his dreadful sufferings is well known, but the learned Pontiff represents his case so well for our purpose that we may, without fear of unnecessary repetition, quote his words. (1) Exemplified by holy Job

'Job,' he says, 'was free from all wickedness, not only in act, but in thought, and had made a compact with his eyes not even to look at a virgin. Yet, when Satan stood among the sons of God, or the

Angels, before the Lord, and being asked if he had considered the virtues of Job, he had answered that Job was just because the Lord had prospered him, but that he would depart from justice if he fell into trouble. He obtained permission to make trial of the virtues of Job, provided he did not hurt him. Upon this the Sabæans entered the land of Job, slew his husbandmen, plundered his cattle; fire fell from heaven and consumed his sheep, three bands of Chaldæans carried away his camels, and his sons and daughters, feasting in the house of their elder brother, were all killed. When Job had said in his sorrow that he had come naked out of his mother's womb, and that naked he should return, and had blessed God Who had given him all things and had taken all things away, Satan stood again before the Lord, and being asked if he had admired the patience of Job in so many and so great afflictions, he answered that man would give everything for his life, insinuating that if Job were deprived of it he would fall away from God. The Lord permitted him to afflict Job still further, only he must spare his life. Upon this he was afflicted with ulcers and a disease which, Piveda says, was a combination of two or three and thirty disorders, and Bartholinus, in his book " De Morbis Biblicis," has enumerated therein twelve kinds of disease. To this were added the rebukes of his wife and the reproofs of his friends, who accused him of sin, and advised him to return to God by penance and humbly to acknowledge the Divine justice. Afterwards Satan was withheld from inflicting further evils upon him; his worldly substance was doubled, sons and daughters were born to him, and God granted him a happy death. Notwithstanding the impious assertion of Jews and sectaries that the history of Job is a parable and a fiction, its truth is unquestionably proved from the prophecy of Ezekiel and the Epistle of St. James, as St. Thomas in the prologue to his commentaries on the Book of Job clearly shows.'[1]

(2) To the history of Job in the Old Testament succeeds that of Lazarus in the New. *(2) By Lazarus* Full of sores which the dogs licked, he lay at the door of the rich man; but his soul was carried by the Angels into Abraham's bosom, and the rich man was buried in hell. When the rich man, tormented by the flames, lifted up his eyes, and afar off saw Abraham with Lazarus in his bosom, he asked him to have pity upon him, to send Lazarus to dip his finger in water and to cool his tongue. We know that interpreters are not agreed here, for some think this a parable, and others a true history, which is the more probable opinion, because in parables the names of persons are not expressed, but Lazarus is mentioned by name, and because Christ uttered no parables concerning the things of the next life, but of those things that are obvious to sense; and, further, because in honour of this very Lazarus, as a Saint and patron of lepers, there are many ancient churches in divers places Benedict XIV. goes on after this to give a summary of St. John Chrysostom's homily on Lazarus. In that homily St Chrysostom enumerates the cruel torments and afflictions of Lazarus: 'the first, poverty, was so extreme that he could not obtain the crumbs that fell from the rich man's table; the second, the sores that covered him; the third, his desertion by all; the fourth, his lying at the

[1] 'Treatise on Heroic Virtue,' vol. ii, pp 3, 4

gate of the rich man, who feasted sumptuously every day; the fifth, his being considered unworthy of a word or look from the rich man, who abounded in all worldly goods; the sixth, the absence of all companions in his misery; the seventh, the obscurity of faith and of the hope of resurrection in that age, which after the coming of Christ wonderfully sustains and strengthens the faithful in their sorrows; the eighth, his suffering these things, not once or for one day, but for many days continuously; the ninth, the loss of reputation, for many thought that he suffered on account of great sins, all of which, like another Job, as if he were of adamant, he endured with a brave and unvanquished spirit.'[1]

These two examples of Scripture history may serve to give us some knowledge of the tribulations and afflictions which may befall the just, and of the patience and endurance with which they have to be borne.

2 Bodily disease the means of purification sickness

2. We can only take for our consideration a few of the trials of this life, because it would be impossible to speak of all. The first of these means which God sends for the purification of the senses may be set down as bodily diseases. Sometimes these are sent by God that man may change his ways, forsake sin, and be converted to his Creator; but they are also sent to prepare souls for greater perfection and for contemplation. Nearly all the contemplative Saints not engaged in external works of charity towards their neighbour were afflicted by such infirmities. We may mention St Lidwiges or Lidwina, Virgin of Schiedam in Holland, St. Clare, St. Theresa, St. Catherine of Siena, and St. Rose of Lima, as

[1] 'Treatise on Heroic Virtue,' vol. ii, pp. 6, 7.

examples. 'Chastisements fall in five ways,' says St. Augustine, 'that the merits of the just may be increased, as in the case of Job, that virtue may be kept in safety, and temptations of pride resisted, as in the case of St. Paul, for the correction of sin, as the leprosy of Mary; for the glory of God, as in the man born blind, or as a judicial punishment, as in the case of Herod.' To this kind of purification belong the loss of members or of the bodily senses, such as the blindness of Tobias; also corporal deformity or disfigurement is inflicted, that the soul may be the more detached from the world and its vanities.

'A sick person,' says Father Baker, 'is to account himself after an especial manner in God's hands, as His prisoner, chained as it were by his own weakness, disabled from the ordinary solaces of conversation, walking, etc., debarred from eating what pleases the palate, become profitable to none, troublesome and chargeable to many, exposed ofttimes to bitter pains and sharper remedies of such pains, etc, a grievous indeed, but yet a happy prison this is to a soul that will make good use of it, for unless the internal taste of the soul also be depraved, she may by this occasion immensely increase in spiritual liberty, health and strength, by accepting with indifference these incommodities, and mortifying her natural exorbitant desire of remedies, not desiring to escape but where and after what manner God shall ordain.

'But to speak more particularly touching the duties of a soul during sickness, she is to assure herself of this one thing, whether she think that her sickness may justify her neglect of her spiritual exercises of mortification and prayer (the essential duties of an internal life); if these be not continued as well in sickness as in health, the soul herself will become the more sick of the two, and exposed to greater danger than the body, for most certainly if sickness do not produce good effects of patience and resignation, etc., in the soul, it will produce the quite contrary, and such effects cannot be produced but only by the exercise of mortification and prayer.'[1]

Loss of friends and relatives

3. Another source of suffering ordained for purification may be mentioned, namely, the loss of friends or relatives by death, or some equally sorrowful and painful privation or loss; and on this point let us remember the wise advice and admonition of Bishop Ullathorne: 'There is one form of sadness which is criminally prolonged by dwelling persistently on the memory of some great affliction, loss, or disappointment, to the unhinging of the soul and the neglect of present duties. The image of that event is kept before the mind with all its circumstances, and is allowed to oppress the heart until the features bear the fixed stamp of a cherished sorrow. What is worse, that fond entertainment of saddened memory prolonged through years is mistaken by the mourner for virtue, as it seems to imitate the virtues of constancy, endurance, and perseverance. The understanding is misled, as well as the heart, by the enduring strain of self-love and sadness. But this is a sin against the providence of God, Whose hand is in all events; against the soul herself, whose powers it unnerves and depraves; and against that cheerful performance of our duties, for which the soul loses her freedom by brooding on events past recall.'[2]

[1] 'Holy Wisdom,' p 470   [2] 'Christian Patience,' p 134

4. Of other kinds of persecutions and purifications, we may say with Benedict XIV. : 'Were we to make mention of the loss of goods, reputation, friends and kindred, and of ridicule, this chapter would scarcely have an end.' He then goes on to relate some instances of these sufferings which the servants of God have to endure. He says · 'We find in the second report of the Auditor of the Rota on the virtues of St. Theresa, that she was sometimes so abandoned by all that no one would hear her confession. In the report of the cause of St John of God, we find that he in the beginning of his conversion, when, for the sake of mortification, he rolled himself in the mud, was by many regarded as a madman, that he suffered very greatly from boys, who pelted him with dirt and stones and injuriously treated him in every way. In the report in the cause of Blessed Jerome Æmilian, we find that he, though of noble birth and of military renown acquired in the defence of his country, when he was converted and used to go forth in coarse garments, pale and dirty, to collect alms for the orphans, was received with jeers, insults, hisses, and contumely, and followed as a madman by a wanton mob of children. Finally, in the life of St Lewis, King of France, it is related that when the Ambassador of the Count of Gueldres to the King of France returned home, and was asked whether he had seen the King, he replied, laughing : " I saw that miserable Papist of a King dressed in furs, with a cowl on his shoulders." '[1]

Further on we find in the same work of Bene-

[1] 'Treatise on Heroic Virtue,' vol. ii., p. 16

dict XIV. instances of persecutions inflicted on the Saints, sometimes by pagans or heretics, sometimes by wicked Catholics, and sometimes even by good men and good, but deceived, Catholics.

'To the first kind must be referred the persecutions of St. Francis Xavier, when he preached the Gospel to the Indians, of which mention is made in the report in his cause.

'To the second kind of persecution we must refer those things which are related of St. Benedict in his life by St Gregory the Great—how at one time the priest Florentius and at another certain monks attempted to give him poison to drink. To this kind, also, is to be referred the contention of Brother Elias, Vicar-General of the Franciscans, with St. Francis himself, the founder of the Order, whom he ventured to accuse in the presence of many of his brethren as the destroyer of his Order, and with St Anthony of Padua, whom he put in prison St. Anthony escaped to Rome and appealed to the Holy See, where, after a judicial inquiry before the Pope, the matter was at length terminated by the deposition of Brother Elias from the generalship of the Order, which had been conferred upon him after the death of St. Francis, and by the election of a new General in the presence of the same Pontiff . . .

'To the third kind must be referred the following In the report in the cause of St. Philip Neri much is related of what he endured at the hands of some of the principal persons in Rome in the times of the Sovereign Pontiffs Paul IV. and Pius V, when some accused him of vainglory, because in the time of the carnival, attended by a great concourse of men, he visited the seven churches; and others, of foolish speaking in his sermons.

'We read of some Saints that they were suspected of heresy, accused before the tribunal of the most Holy Inquisition, and committed to its prisons. In the second report in the cause of St. Theresa we find this · "When she was staying at Seville, she and her companions, charged with many things that were false, were denounced to the Holy Inquisition."

. Cardinal de Lauræa, of famous memory, makes mention of some servants of God whom God permitted to be sometims unjustly punished by their ecclesiastical superiors, who were themselves deceived. "Some just persons are, by the permission of God, purified and mortified by their superiors, ill-informed, and these, too, of ecclesiastical and even the highest rank, of whom, especially among religious, I could write a lengthened history." The same is observed by Theophilus Raymond, when he inquires whether persecution in a community is the most dreadful of all. On this subject may be read the life of the Venerable Abbot Barreri, from which we learn that when, through envy of some of his monks, he was judiciously condemned by the Apostolic Delegate, and deposed from his rank for the space of seven years, he most patiently bore it; and, lastly, when the matter had been referred to the venerable servant of God, Cardinal Bellarmine, and the fraud of the witnesses had been discovered, he was, with the approbation of the Sovereign Pontiff, declared innocent, and restored to his honours and dignities.'[1]

Besides the remedies already prescribed for other

[1] 'Treatise on Heroic Virtue,' vol II, pp 35, 37.

trials and sufferings that come from God, or are permitted by Him, great and special patience is necessary under persecutions of this kind. In these we have constantly to keep before the mind the example of Jesus Christ. In sorrows, in bodily infirmities, in persecutions from others, from enemies and from friends, and from those of our household, and even from ecclesiastical superiors, the most efficacious remedy is to be found in assiduous meditation on the Passion and sufferings of our Divine Redeemer. In all His bitter sufferings He has left us an example of patience more efficacious than any other motive to lead us to imitate Him.

Whether one is allowed to excuse or justify himself

5. The question arises as to whether the injured person is allowed to excuse and justify himself, or to seek solace from others by complaining. Useless complaining and murmuring are always against the spirit of true Christian forbearance. Generally speaking, complaints are useless, and murmurings are always, not only useless, but wrong. Unless the glory of God and the good of souls require the persons persecuted to justify themselves with humility and modesty, it is always better that they should, after the example of Christ, bear their sufferings in silence and commit their defence with a lively faith to God, saying: *Deliver me, O Lord, and set me beside Thee, and let any man's hand fight against me*,[1] or, *If armies in camp should stand together against me, my heart shall not fear. If battle should rise up against me, in this will I be confident.*[2] Experience proves that excuses serve only to increase the irritation of adversaries, and in some way to confirm their accusations, and thus

---

[1] Job xvii. 3   [2] Ps xxvi. 3.

expose the innocent to further blame and opposition The best rule, then, to follow is to overcome adversaries by humility, to restrain them by patience, to reply to their detractions and calumnies by silence. In His own time God will justify His servants, and in the meantime these merit great reward by their patient sufferings.

I have said, when the glory of God and the good of souls require it, the most just and the holiest should defend their cause against detractors, evil-minded and wicked-tongued people. These do not confine their detractions and calumnies to penitents only, but they extend them to good, holy priests as well, and that, too, in matters connected with their ministerial duties. They say, when finding fault with devout people, that the confessors and directors are indiscreet, deficient in learning, too credulous, wanting in discretion and prudence, and even insinuate other suspicions. Now, when the holy ministry is attacked in this way, followers of Christ are not permitted to dissimulate, or to give any appearance to the common saying, 'Silence gives consent.' The good of the faithful, whose pastor he is, the good of the Church, and God's glory, will not allow a man to remain quietly in such circumstances, under false accusations and insinuations. If possible, the guilty persons should be found out, and, if possible, also punished. This, however, is not always possible, as we live in an age of anonymous letters and other underhand methods of ruining the good name of our fellow-man. The false accusations and imputations should, however, be denied for the sake of the good of souls and of the good name of the priestly office. If the matter be only personal, or affect only the individual and not injure anyone else, silence may be kept, and this form of persecution offered to God, and the cause committed to Him, as said above. But never should we give up our charge because of such contradictions, but, despising all such murmurings and the vain words of men, the priest's duty is to prosecute his work with courage and fortitude, and in spite of all opposition, either from devils or from wicked men, believing in his heart the truth of those Divine words *Blessed are ye when they shall revile you, and persecute you, and speak all that is evil against you, untruly, for My sake ; be glad and rejoice, for your reward is very great in heaven. For so they persecuted the prophets that were before you.*[1]

6. The value of patient and resigned suffering (Blosius)

6. With the pious and experienced Bishop Ullathorne we may now sum up the value of patient and resigned suffering in the language of the devout and learned Blosius

'(1) Nothing more valuable can befall a man than tribulation, when it is endured with patience for the love of God ; because there is no more certain sign of the Divine election But this should be understood quite as much of internal as of external trials, which people of a certain kind of piety are apt to forget.

'(2) It is the chain of patient sufferings that forms the ring with which Christ espouses a soul to Himself

'(3) There is such a dignity in suffering for God's sake that we ought to account ourselves unworthy of an honour so great.

'(4) Good works are of great value ; but even

[1] St Matt v 11, 12 See Voss, 'Comp Scaramelli,' p. 221

those lesser pains and trials that are endured with peace and patience are more valuable than many good works.

'(5) Every sorrowful trial bears some resemblance to the most excellent Passion of our Lord Jesus Christ, and when it is endured with patience it makes him who endures it a more perfect partaker of the Passion of his Lord and Saviour

'(6) Tribulation opens the soul to the gifts of God, and when they are received tribulation preserves them.

'(7) What we now suffer God has from eternity foreseen, and has ordained that we should suffer in this way, and not in any other way. Would He allow the least adversity to fall upon His children or to come within them, or the least breath of wind to blow upon them, that He saw was inexpedient for their salvation? Heat and cold, hunger and thirst, infirmities and afflictions—all these and each of them, whenever they befall the servants of God, come not only to purify, but to adorn their souls.

'(8) The artist lays his lines and colours in lights and shades upon the canvas to set forth some beautiful production of his genius. The noble maiden is adorned with rich garments set with gold and jewels for her nuptials. So God adorns His elect, whom He separates unto Himself, investing them with the magnificent virtues produced by sufferings, like those with which He adorned His well-beloved Son. Wherefore all affliction and bitterness must be borne with cheerful patience, as they are so much better than the pains of purgatory or the eternal flames

'(9) One of the friends of God has said · " When

anyone feels affliction or sorrow, and is humbly resigned to God, this resignation is like a harp that gives out sweet-sounding notes, and the Holy Spirit brings out a canticle that resounds melodiously, though secretly, in hearing of our Heavenly Father. The lower chords, strung in the inferior nature of the man, send forth low and mournful notes of grief, but the higher chords, strung in the superior powers of the soul, are full of devotion, and resound with the free and soaring notes of patient resignation to the glorious will of God. The sensible nature is crucified, and sighs over its sufferings; but the rational spirit praises God in peace For those fiery afflictions that consume the marrow and bones prepare the soul for close union with God, and as fire prepares wax to receive new forms, these trials prepare the soul to receive a better likeness of God. Nothing can receive the form of another until its own form is put away; and before the Divine Artist can imprint the most noble image of His glory on the soul, the soul must give up the image of the old Adam with pain and suffering, that she may be supernaturally changed and transformed. The Almighty prepares her, therefore, for this happy transformation by severe adversities. Having decreed to adorn her, after this Divine transformation, with the Divine gifts, so great a change cannot be effected by soft and soothing baths, but by plunging her into a sea of bitterness."

'Yet all are not brought into the same depths of interior trial, nor are all subjected to the like accumulation of external afflictions. These are God's special favours marked out for great perfection, and consequently for a large share of the Cross and glory of Christ. To these Divine purifications it may be truly said that *many are called, but few are chosen.* Feebler souls are treated in gentler ways Some God conducts more in the way of consolation than in the way of the Cross, others, because of their stronger nature, require greater purification ; others, again, because faithful to the gift of fortitude, can endure more for the love of God. But in this world or in the next must every soul be perfectly purified before her admittance to the open glory of God

' It by no means follows that the strongest natures, whether strong in body or in mind, have the greatest share assigned them of the Cross and sufferings of Christ. These favours are granted to those who are faithful to the strongest graces. Hence we often see them bestowed on persons of feeble frame or of simple mind, in whom, as true lovers of the Cross, grace triumphs over nature in admirable ways. St Gertrude was divinely instructed, that sometimes when God would favour a soul by abiding with her, when she is not constant in abiding with Him, He sends her troubles or pains of body or soul to change her spirit, that she may be able to abide with Him. These are the mysterious ways of God's grace and goodness *For the Lord is nigh to them who are of contrite heart.*[1] And of such He says. *He shall cry to Me, and I will hear him. I am with him in his trouble.*'[2]

[1] Ps xxxiii 19
[2] Ps xc 15 See Blosius, ' Institutio Spiritualis,' chap. viii, sect 3, apud 'Christian Patience,' p 155 *et seq*

CHAPTER XIV

THE PASSIVE PURIFICATION OF THE SPIRIT

<small>1. The meaning of this kind of purification</small>

1. THOMAS A VALLGORNERA, the author of the 'Mystica Theologia Divi Thomæ,' well explains what is meant by the passive purification of the spirit or of the intellective part of man. He speaks of it as having four causes, like the passive purification of the sensitive part. These four causes he designates by the usual scholastic names—material and formal, efficient and final—and in explaining these he gives us the true meaning of this kind of purification.

<small>(1) Its material cause</small>

(1) By the material cause he means the subject or the recipient faculties of the soul in which this purification operates. These are the two superior or intellectual faculties—namely, the intellect or understanding and the will—and these do not need any corporal organism for their existence, and they remain with the soul in the state of separation from the body. They are essential powers or faculties of the soul, but, like the soul itself in this life, they are confined to the body, and they therefore need the help of the organic powers and senses for their operations. The intellect has for its object truth, and it abstracts from present, past, and future in tending towards its object. The will has good in its universal sense for

its object, and does not regard it in the same light as the sensitive appetite. The soul, therefore, according to these spiritual powers, is the subject in which the passive purgation is effected, and it is on this account designated the material cause.

(2) The formal cause of this purgation is the clear light of contemplation which penetrates into the very centre of the soul and heart, and brings under our knowledge all its hidden faults and imperfections; and by this revelation it causes much torture and pain to the soul by involving the mind in darkness of spirit, and reducing the will to a state of abjection and anguish. It involves the intellect in darkness, because by means of this clear light it detains or confines it to the consideration of its own defects, and prevents its elevation to Divine and heavenly things, and thus it becomes absorbed in the thick, cloudy darkness of its own miseries, and it cannot find relief or rescue itself from this state of darkness. The will is reduced to a state of deep affliction and dejection because it detects so many infirmities and evils in itself, and becomes horrified at the thought of being itself the cause of them. It sees its sins multiplied like the sands of the sea, and therefore thinks itself unworthy to look up to heaven; then, also, it understands better the enormity of the wickedness of sin, and even venial sins appear to the soul in all their true and real malice. All this afflicts the devout soul, and causes sufferings more terrible and bitter than any which have ever been experienced during the process of the passive purification of the senses. The trial may be more and more severe when a soul is conscious of great sins in the past or when it sees in a

true light before God how it brought upon itself, through its own fault, all past punishments and heart-breaking sorrows and afflictions. Souls who are conscious of innocence and not conscious of faults may have some secret consolation or comfort arising from a latent knowledge that all the persecutions and trials, whether from devils or men, are for their perfection and purification; but those who know they have deserved them all, and far more, must cling to the notion that they are real punishments, they cannot so easily be persuaded that, having neglected and rejected or abused graces so much in the past, God now intends to make them Saints, and to raise them up by special favours to intimate union with Him even in this life. Yet this has happened, and many of the greatest contemplatives and many of the greatest Saints have been penitents, and some of them had not to wait an unusual period of time, either, before they were raised to a high degree of virtue and holiness; but I have no hesitation in asserting that their purification of spirit was the hardest ever endured, and theirs was the most bitter cup of suffering during the course of their holy lives afterwards. They could expect no sympathy from creatures, and in spite of the adverse opinion of men and of the whole world, and in the face of the pity of the virtuous and just—a pity galling to human nature—they indeed have had to tread the winepress alone. Had they been innocent, it would not be so hard to bear these things, because the soul knows itself to be right before God and cares very little for public opinion or human respect; but the soul that knows the opinion of the world and of men to be just in condemning it, and that it has deserved

PREPARATION FOR CONTEMPLATION

it all, experiences, to my mind, the most trying ordeal of all in the process of the purification of the spirit

(3) The efficient cause of this purification is God, merciful and just, Who by purifying the souls of His elect disposes them for more perfect union with Him (3) Its efficient cause

(4) The final cause is the intimate union of the soul with God, for which this passive purification of the spirit prepares and disposes the soul (4) Its final cause

2. Bishop Ullathorne describes for us this kind of purification when he writes of the purification of the intellect and of the will. 'The purgation of the intellect,' he says, 'is effected by that withdrawing of Divine light which leaves the soul in obscurity, except in what regards the light of conscience, and the soul more clearly sees that this light is in the hands of God to give or to take away We put many images of vanity into that light and many reflections of self-love, and make the holy light a mirror in which to admire our own mental efforts, forgetful that it is by God's gift of light that we believe, and think, and obtain knowledge and understanding. But when darkness comes upon the mind, we find ourselves out; we see that our light comes from God, and that by no labour of our own can we produce a single ray of its illumination. We are left to faith and to the light of justice needful to guide us on our way and we learn how insignificant our mental efforts are without the light of God The pride of intellect is mortified and humbled; the intellect itself is purified of its vanities and conceits and from the reflected image of self-love; and when the cheering light returns, it comes more serene into a purer mind, so that we make our prayer and con- This purification described by Bishop Ullathorne

duct our operations with truer dependence on the Divine illumination. Thus, the intellect is purged from pride and vanity that we may see the truths of God and the laws of wisdom with purer eyes, and respond to them with greater fidelity.

'The purgation of the will is effected by the crucifixion of our inordinate loves and desires. This is accomplished by the sufferings, privations, and disappointments which the will has to endure in things that tend to God. When the dispositions of the will have been thus purified from seeking their own way in the things of God, and when the desires of nature have been cleansed away from impeding the will of God in that soul, the soul accepts all privations and sufferings here below with indifference. The gift of charity is purified from the interests of nature and self-seeking, and divested of all its accidental incumbrances, the flame of Divine love obtains an increase of purity and force, of fortitude and patience, that gives it wonderful capacity both for unity with God and for every good work.'[1]

We have said that the formal cause of this purification is a clear light, which penetrates into the very soul, and causes it unspeakable pain and affliction. St. John of the Cross, writing on this wonderful manner of the Divine action, shows how the Divine light can effect in the soul darkness, and be for that particular soul the cause of its torture.

Why the Divine illumination is called 'night' by St. John of the Cross.

3. 'Why do we call the Divine light which enlightens the soul and purges it of its ignorances the obscure night? I reply that the Divine wisdom is for two reasons, not night and darkness only, but

[1] 'Christian Patience,' pp 219, 220

pain and torment also to the soul. The first is, the Divine wisdom is so high that it transcends the capacity of the soul, and therefore is in that respect darkness. The second reason is based on the meanness and impurity of the soul, and in that respect the Divine wisdom is painful to it.

'To prove the truth of the first reason, we assume a principle of philosophy, namely, the more clear and self-evident Divine things are, the more obscure and hidden they are to the soul naturally. Thus, the more clear the light, the more does it blind the eyes of the owl, and the stronger the sun's rays, the greater the darkness of our visual organs; for the sun, in its own strength shining, overcomes them, by reason of their weakness, and deprives them of the power of seeing. So when the Divine light of contemplation shines into the soul, not yet perfectly enlightened, it causes spiritual darkness, because it not only surpasses its strength, but because it obscures it and deprives it of its natural perceptions. . . .

'Because the light and wisdom of contemplation is most pure and clear, and because the soul within which it shines is impure and dark, that soul which is the recipient must greatly suffer. Eyes afflicted with humours suffer pain when the clear light shines upon them, and the pain of the soul, by reason of its impurity, is immense when the Divine light shines upon it. And when the rays of this pure light strike upon the soul in order to expel its impurities, the soul perceives itself to be so unclean and miserable that it seems as if God had set Himself against it, and itself were set against God. So grievous and painful is this feeling—for the soul feels as if God had abandoned it—that it was one of the heaviest afflictions of Job when he was in his trial *Why hast Thou set me opposite to Thee, and I am become burdensome to myself?*[1] The soul sees distinctly in this clear and pure light, though obscurely, its own impurity, and acknowledges its own unworthiness before God and all creatures; and what pains it still more is the fear that it has that it will never cease to be unworthy, and that all its goodness is gone. This is the fruit of that profound depression under which the mind labours, in the knowledge and sense of its own wickedness and misery. For now the Divine and obscure light reveals to it all its wretchedness, and it sees clearly that of itself it can never be otherwise. To the same effect are the following words of the Psalmist *For iniquities Thou hast chastised man, and Thou hast made his soul pine away as a spider*[2]

'In the second place, the pain of the soul has its sources in its natural and spiritual weakness; for when the Divine contemplation flows within it with a certain vehemence, in order to strengthen it and subdue it, it is then so pained in its weakness as almost to faint away, particularly at those times when the Divine contemplation seizes upon it with a greater degree of vehemence; for sense and spirit, as if bowed down by a heavy and dark burden, suffer and groan in agony so great that death itself would be a relief. This was the experience of Job when he cried · *I will not that He contend with me with much strength, nor that He oppress with the weight of His greatness.*[3] The soul bowed down by this burden of oppression feels itself so removed out of

[1] Job vii 20 [2] Ps xxxviii 12 [3] Job xxiii 6

God's favour that it thinks—and it is so in truth—that all things which consoled it formerly have utterly failed it, and that no one is left to pity it. Job, in like circumstances, has said: *Have pity upon me, have pity upon me, at least you my friends, because the hand of the Lord hath touched me*[1] Wonderful and piteous sight! So great are the weakness and impurity of the soul that the hand of God, so soft and so gentle, is felt to be so heavy and oppressive, though neither pressing nor resting on it, but merely touching it, and that, too, in His mercy; for He touches the soul not to chastise it, but to load it with His graces.'[2]

I may here state that, when in the above extract the soul is said to be impure, it is in relation to the perfect purity which God requires in it, not that it is stained by the guilt of sin. Souls in this state are always to be considered in a state of grace and charity, yet are not pure in the sense that the angels themselves are not pure in the sight of God. Moreover, we have to understand that passive purification does not take away from the soul essential devotion, but only now one and again another accidental devotion, or the agreeable feeling of devotion, the soul all the while continuing to serve God with fidelity and eagerness, and to be agreeable or pleasing to Him.

4. According to St. John of the Cross, the purification of the spirit takes place usually after the purification of the senses. The night of the senses being over, the soul for some time enjoys the sweet delights of contemplation; then, perhaps when least expected, the second night comes far darker and far more miserable than the first, and this is called the

[1] Job xiv 21   [2] 'The Obscure Night,' book ii, chap v

purification of the spirit. God seems to grant the interval of peace and delight that the soul may acquire renewed strength and fresh courage to sustain the afflictions of the second purification. As, however, God follows no certain rules in the sanctification of souls, but leads almost each soul by a particular way to contemplation or to the degree of perfection to which it may be destined, no time can be assigned with any certainty for the purification of the spirit. We read in the life of St Angela of Foligno that she went through the two, namely, the purification of the sense and of the spirit, at the same time. This appears to have been the case also with St Mary Magdalen of Pazzi, though Scaramelli hesitates about asserting this with any security or certainty.

St. John of the Cross also teaches that very many souls pass through the purification of the senses, but few undergo the purification of the spirit. This seems to be in accordance with the opinion of St. Theresa, who, speaking of the prayer of quiet, says: 'There are many souls who arrive at this degree of prayer, and few who go beyond it, and I know not who is in fault; but of this I am sure, there is none on the part of God, for since His Majesty does a soul the favour of bringing her to this degree, I cannot believe He would cease to bestow many more favours, were it not through some fault of her own.'[1] Therefore, it appears that the purification of the senses is directed to, and sufficient for, the lower degrees of contemplation, such as the infused prayer of quiet; and that the purification of the spirit is ordained to, and necessary for, the more sublime

[1] 'Life of St. Theresa,' chap. xv

degrees of contemplation. And since few souls are elevated to this great sublimity, so few are called upon to pass through the most trying and most desolate way of the second purification.

5 It must be to this passive purification of the spirit that we have to refer what Father Baker calls 'the great desolation,' and to which he devotes a whole chapter. He places it after Divine communications and sublime familiarities between God and His chosen souls, especially after the first passive union He thus speaks of the great desolation ' A soul having once experienced such extraordinary Divine favours will be apt to say with the Psalmist . *I shall never be moved, Thou, Lord, of Thy goodness hast made my hill so strong.* But if she think so she will find herself strangely deceived , for as the whole course of a spiritual life consists of perpetual changes, of elevations and depressions, and an extraordinary consolation is usually attended by succeeding anguish and desertion, so above all other times this so supereminent and so comfortable a Divine visitation is commonly followed by a most terrible unexpected desolation, a desolation so insupportable to souls unprovided or unaware of it, that many, not enabled or not well instructed how to behave themselves in it, have lost all heart to prosecute internal ways, and so bereaving themselves of the benefits of all their former exercises and Divine passive inactions have returned to a common extroverted life.'[1]

This same author then gives a woeful description of the desolation and suffering of the soul in this state of what he calls pure sufferance , but as I have

[1] 'Holy Wisdom,' p 536

---

5 The great desolation by Father Baker

already page after page been describing miseries and desolations and trials of every description, I need not continue to repeat words for the sake of signifying aggravated sufferings of every kind; and it may relieve the monotony of these descriptions for the sake of non-mystical as well as mystical readers if I here add some words of comfort from the same chapter of 'Holy Wisdom' in which all the woeful sufferings are described.

'The truth is that in this case of desolation the soul doth by her free will, or, rather, in the centre of the spirit beyond all her faculties, remain in a constant union and adhesion to God, although no such union do appear to her; yea, though it seems to her that she is not only estranged, but even averted from God, and by virtue of that most secret but firm adhesion she makes election of God as her only good, which may to any but herself sufficiently appear by her carriage during that state; for she breaks not out into any murmurings, she seeks not to comfort herself by admitting any inordinate external solaces, nor doth anything deliberately by which to rid herself from such an afflicting estate sooner or otherwise than God would have her do. She practises tranquillity of mind in the midst of a tempest of passions in the sensitive nature; she exercises resignation without the least contentment to herself therein; she learns patience in the midst of impatience, and resignation in the midst of irresignation; in a word, she yields herself as a prey unto Almighty God, to be cast into the most sharp purgatory of love, which is an immediate disposition to an established state of perfection.'[1]

[1] 'Holy Wisdom,' p. 540.

6. St. Bonaventure enumerates the temptations which assail souls in this state, and concludes his enumeration with consoling words, as follows 'First there is the withdrawal and poverty of devotion, second, a difficulty in well-doing; third, a distaste which a man experiences in every good work; fourth, a temptation to impatience with God, fifth, which he says is most dangerous, when grace has been a long time withheld, a man amid the anxious desires of recovering it, as if weary, relaxes in his efforts to recover it, and under the pretence of patience ceases from seeking further help, thinking, with a sort of indignant humility, that he is unworthy of such a grace, because God may have destined him for other external works, from which it comes to pass that he abandons the interior life, finally there is the sixth, which includes more doubts about the Catholic faith, despair of God's mercy, a spirit of blasphemy against God and the Saints, and of laying violent hands on, and destroying, one's self, and the hesitation of a querulous conscience, refusing measures of relief from these evils' In another place he explains dryness of spirit in these words. 'It very frequently happens to those who are given to devotion, that the more efforts they make to have this grace of devotion, the less they have it, and when they have the more vehemently strived, the more dry and hard of heart they become.' The Saint, after relating the fruits of these afflictions, thus concludes the subject 'God sometimes purifies the hearts of devout persons by the withdrawal of that consolation, the want of which is their greatest affliction, that being thus purified they may become more fit to receive a more abundant grace in this

life, and glory in the life to come, although they may not have deserved this affliction by any special fault.'

7. The effects of this purification

7. 'Cardinal de Lauræa says that the fruit of this passive purgation of the just is an increase of grace, fortitude in suffering, union with God, and the attainment of glory. Then, after showing that not only beginners, but also those who are advanced, and the perfect, are liable to these temptations, he thus consoles the spiritually minded and the contemplatives: "Let not those who are spiritually minded and contemplative be alarmed at these trials of the passive purgation and external temptations, which are sent to them either in soul or body by the will or permission of God; neither let them from this suppose that they are abandoned by God or less loved, or hated by Him; but let them call to mind that the Saints of the Old and New Testament were so purified by God to the increase of their grace and glory."'[1]

With regard to the effects of this purification, let us attend to the unerring and clear teaching of that master of mystical theology, St. John of the Cross. He teaches us that this purification has a twofold result it removes the obstacles which oppose the union of Divine transformation, and then it procures the union itself in an eminent degree. 'I find it necessary,' he says, 'here to observe that this purgative and loving knowledge, or Divine light, is to the soul which it is purifying, in order perfectly to unite it to itself, as fire is to fuel which it is transforming into itself. The first action of material fire

[1] See Benedict XIV., 'Treatise on Heroic Virtue,' vol ii, pp 43-46

on fuel is to dry it, to expel from it all water and moisture. It then blackens it and soils it, and, drying it by little and little, makes it light and consumes away its accidental defilements which are contrary to itself. Finally, having heated and set on fire its outward surface, it transforms the whole into itself, and makes it beautiful as itself. Thus, fuel subject to the action of fire retains neither active nor passive qualities of its own, except bulk and specific weight, and assumes all the qualities of fire. It becomes dry, then it glows, and glowing burns; luminous, it gives light, and burns much lighter than before. All this is the effect of fire.

'We theorize in this way concerning the Divine fire of contemplative love, which, before it unites with and transforms the soul into itself, purges away all its contrary qualities. It expels its impurities, blackens it and obscures it, and renders its condition apparently worse than it was before. For while the Divine purgation is removing all the evil and vicious humours, which, because so deeply rooted and settled in the soul, were neither seen nor felt, but now, in order to their expulsion and annihilation, are rendered clearly visible in the obscure light of the Divine contemplation, the soul—though not worse in itself, nor in the sight of God—seeing at last what it never saw before, looks upon itself not only as unworthy of the Divine regard, but even as a loathsome object in the eyes of God.'[1]

The same holy master of the mystical life shows us also the effects of this purification on the soul and its powers, in the following manner. 'The sensitive and spiritual desires are lulled to sleep and

[1] 'The Obscure Night,' book ii, chap. v.

mortified, unable to relish anything human or Divine, the affections are thwarted and brought low, incapable of excitement, and having nothing to rest upon; the imagination is fettered, and unable to make any profitable reflections, the memory is gone, the intellect is obscured, the will is dry and afflicted, and all the faculties are empty; and, moreover, a dense and heavy cloud overshadows the wearied soul, and alienates it, as it were, from God. This is the obscurity in which the soul says it travels securely.

'The cause of this security is evident, for usually the soul never errs, except under the influences of its desires, or tastes, or reflections, or understanding, or affections, wherein it generally is overabundant, or defective, changeable, or inconsistent, hence the inclination to what is not becoming it. It is therefore clear that the soul is secure against error therein, when all these operations and movements have ceased. The soul is then delivered not only from itself, but also from all its other enemies--the world and the devil—who, when the affections and operations of the soul have ceased, cannot assault it by any other way or by any other means

'O spiritual soul, when thou seest thy desires obscured, thy will arid and constrained, and thy faculties incapable of any interior act, be not grieved at this; but look upon it rather as a great good, for God is delivering thee from thyself— taking the matter out of thy hands; for however strenuously thou mayest exert thyself, thou wilt never do anything so faultlessly, perfectly, and securely as now — because of the impurity and torpor of thy faculties—when God takes thee by the hand, guides thee safely in thy blindness along a road to an end thou knowest not, and couldst never travel guided by thine own eyes and supported by thy own feet.'[1]

8 We are to learn from the examples of the Saints how to bear all these crosses and trials. There is nothing new or extraordinary to be prescribed, except what has been said with regard to bearing other crosses and trials, and this is well and clearly described for us by Benedict XIV., speaking of the Saints He says .

8 The manner in which souls should act in this state

'It is fully proved from their acts that they not only bore courageously and with equanimity what men did to them, but endured patiently the scourges of our Lord Himself, when He withdrew from them the comfort of His presence, and removed Himself from them so that a most broad wall seemed to intervene between Him and them. Then they confessed themselves to have deserved more grievous afflictions; they hid themselves in God, remained unmoved in their desolation, sought for comfort foolishly in no mortal creature or thing, but comforted themselves only with those words which Christ Himself has said *Thy will be done*. By the help of Divine grace they resisted the temptations of the devil; by the advice of their spiritual directors they examined into the sources of their desolation . if these proceeded from their own fault and negligence, they laboured by penance to do away with them and amend; if from the assaults of the devil, they bravely resisted them , if from the Divine will, they waited in patience, and did not abandon or diminish their prayers, but increased

[1] 'The Obscure Night,' book ii , chap xvi

them after the example of Christ, *Who, being in an agony, prayed the longer.* They prayed that the will of God might be done, and thought that desolation came from Him that they might obtain the enlightenment of their mind, greater knowledge of Divine things, humility, fortitude, and inflamed charity."[1]

[1] 'Treatise on Heroic Virtue,' vol. ii, p 54

CHAPTER XV

THE PASSIVE PURIFICATION OF THE SPIRIT (*continued*)

1. THE purification of love is called by Ribet the last passive purification of the spirit. The comparison of St. John of the Cross which we cited in the foregoing chapter gives us clearly to understand that this purification is united with ardent love, which clarifies the soul and leads it to contemplation. The fire which penetrates into the most interior recess of the soul at first remains hidden, but by degrees it manifests itself in bright, warm rays and in flames. So long as the obscurity lasts, the soul is not aware of the fire that consumes and transforms it; but when the smoke vanishes and the bright flames appear, then the soul becomes conscious of it, and continues its purification with redoubled activity, and with a sorrowful admixture of light, of desires, and of hopes. This is the trial that prepares the soul for the highest degrees of the contemplative life. We must have recourse to St John of the Cross to express this doctrine in words which do not easily suggest themselves to an ordinary writer·

' Here the soul speaks of the fire of love which, in the night of painful contemplation, seizes upon it as a material fire on the fuel which it burns. This

[marginal note: 1. The purification of love—its degrees]

burning, though to a certain extent resembling that which takes place in the sensitive part of the soul, is still, in one sense, as different from it as the soul is from the body, the spiritual from the sensitive. For this is a certain fire of love in the spirit whereby the soul in its dark trials feels itself wounded to the quick by a certain impression and foretaste of God . .

'The mind is now conscious of a deep affection of love, for this spiritual burning produces the passion itself And, inasmuch as this love is infused in a special way, the soul corresponds only passively with it, and thus a strong passion of love is begotten within it. . .

'Here we perceive in some degree how great and how vehement is this burning of love in the spirit when God gathers and collects together all the strength, faculties, and desires of the soul, spiritual and sensitive, so that their harmonious combination may direct all its energies and all its forces towards the real and perfect fulfilment of the first commandment of the law, which comprehends within its scope the whole nature and gifts of man.

'When all the desires and energies of the soul are thus recollected in this burning of love, and the soul itself touched, wounded, and set on fire with love in them all, what must the movements and affections of these desires and energies be when they are thus wounded and burning with love, and when that love does not satiate them, when they are in darkness and doubt about it, and suffering also, beyond all question, a more grievous hunger after it, in proportion to the past experience of it? For the touch of this love and of the Divine fire so dries up the spirit and enkindles its desires for satisfying its thirst that it turns upon itself a thousand times and longs for God in a thousand ways, as David did when He said: *For Thee my soul hath thirsted, for Thee my flesh, O how many ways*,[1]—that is, in desire. Another version reads: *My soul thirsteth after Thee, my soul is dying for Thee.*[2]

From this description we may understand how the soul can suffer through the pangs of love, and it only remains for us, after the example of mystical writers, to classify or to give the degrees of these purifying qualities of love which are enkindled in contemplation. These degrees are placed in an order of progression; they differ from each other, and belong to successive states of contemplation. They are chiefly three in number, which I find explained under the names given to them by mystical writers. I find them designated and explained as clearly as the subject admits by Father Voss in his compendium of Scaramelli's 'Directorium Mysticum.' The three headings are: (1) The Inflammation of Love; (2) The Wounds of Love; (3) The Languor of Love.

(1) We have to bear in mind that we do not mean by the inflammation of love what is essential to the habit of charity as it exists in the souls of all the just, but we speak of an accidental form or quality of that love. The substantial inflammation of this exists in the souls in the beginning of their spiritual purification. It consists of a great esteem for the Divine goodness, a promptness in the will to undertake great things for God with the pure

(1) The inflammation of love

[1] Ps. lxii. 2. [2] 'The Obscure Night,' book ii., chap. xi.

intention of pleasing Him and doing His will in everything. In course of time this love, which the soul has not at first felt, because it was hidden and latent, begins to reveal itself to the interior spirit with vivacity, ardour, and yet with anguish and suffering towards God. This the Angelic Doctor calls the accidental inflammation of love. The descriptions of St. John of the Cross, already quoted from chapters xiii. and xi. of the 'Obscure Night,' represent it forcibly. The sacred fire pervades the whole soul and inflames it with the passion of love so that it vehemently desires the object of that love and seeks Him in a thousand ways; it expects Him in all its actions, thoughts, and words; its affection is in continual motion, because it aspires to be always united with the Infinite Good.

The anguishes or pains of this love are so great because at the time when this inflammation takes place all the powers of the soul and of the sensitive appetite are despoiled of every affection, and dried up, and unable to relish any other thing, either heavenly or earthly. Thus, the starved will embraces with all its strength the love infused into it by God, and this at a time when the intellect is in darkness and the soul fears it may be abandoned by God. The soul wounded by Divine love becomes the more inflamed the more it fears not being loved by Him Whom it loves so much.

It may appear strange that a soul enveloped in darkness, that does not seem to know God by reason of this darkness, can seek with such intense love to be united to Him even when it thinks itself rejected by Him. But we must remember that the soul in this darkness always knows God, although the knowledge is obscure. It is therefore able to love Him, and to love Him more than it knows Him. And as this inflammation of love is infused by God, we can conclude that it need not be measured by, nor proportioned to, the knowledge. Again, that it should love God at the time that it feels itself rejected is quite intelligible, and can be proved by the experience of natural love for a creature.

During this purification the intellect also is sometimes refreshed by some certain illumination, and then, by the inflammation of the will and the enlightenment of the intellect, a sweet and strong love is produced, which is the beginning of union, and which is granted only towards the end of the purifying process. The inflammation of the will, however, precedes the enlightenment of the intellect the heat of love known as the inflammation or enkindling is not continuous, but arises only at intervals; it does not affect the bodily health like those which are experienced after the passive purification of the senses. The effect of this purification is the same as that explained by St. John of the Cross by the comparison he makes use of with regard to the action of fire upon fuel. This heavenly light first obscures the soul, then it purifies it from its stains, and finally by its flames it elevates it to sublime contemplation, and transforms it into intimate union with God and with His Divine image.

(2) Besides the inflammation or enkindling of love there are also the wounds of love, inflicted not in the heart, but in the spirit, and in order to purify it the more and to dispose it for the great grace of

(2) The wounds of love

union This wounding of the soul is described by St John of the Cross 'How can we say that God wounds the soul when there is nothing to wound, seeing that it is all consumed in the fire of love? It is certainly marvellous; for as fire is never idle, but in continual movement, flashing in one direction, then in another, so love—the function of which is to wound so as to cause love and joy—when it exists in the soul as a living flame, darts forth its most tender flames of love. . . . This wounding, therefore, which is the "playing" of the Divine Wisdom, is the flames of those tender touches which stir the soul continually—touches of the fire of love which is never idle. And of these flashes of the fire it is said that they wound the soul in its inmost substance.'[1] In another place the Saint represents to us in poetical language the complaint of the wounded soul 'Why, after wounding this heart, hast Thou not healed it?' The enamoured soul complains, not of the wound itself—for the deeper the wound the greater is its joy—but that the heart, being wounded, is not healed by being wounded unto death The wounds of love are so deliciously sweet that if they do not kill they cannot satisfy the soul, they are so sweet that it desires to die of them, and hence it is that it says. 'Why, after having wounded this heart, hast Thou not healed it?' That is, why hast Thou struck it so sharply as to wound it so deeply, and yet not healed it by killing it utterly with love? As Thou art the cause of its pain in the affliction of love, be Thou also the cause of its health by a death from love, so the heart, wounded by the pain of Thy absence, shall be healed in the delight and

[1] 'The Living Flame,' stanza 1, line 2.

glory of Thy sweet presence."[1] This wound, we are told, does not touch the body, but only the spirit; but by reason of body and soul being united and affected by each other, through it the life even of the body would be endangered were it not that God sustains and strengthens it.

When in this state, the least cause, such as a word or a thought, may produce these thrusts which wound the soul. And it sometimes happens that the soul loses power, not only over the external senses, but even the internal faculties remain suspended from their actions. The sorrow occasioned by the spiritual wounding may vanish in a short time, or it may last for whole hours. And though the desire of dying in order to be perfectly united to God may be in the superior part, yet the inferior part clings to life, and does not desire to be deprived of it.

There is no need of any imagery of the phantasy in this dolorous wound of love such as we wish to represent, because, as I have repeated, all is accomplished in the spirit. Nevertheless, God has deigned to favour some beloved souls in such a way as to represent to them in vision that which they felt in the inmost soul. St. Theresa saw a seraph who transfixed her heart with a flaming dart or arrow which caused her great pain and sorrow. In her case and in like cases the representation was only imaginary, and signified what the soul experienced in a spiritual manner at the time, for the wound is not corporal, but spiritual, as is its pain.

(3) The languor of love by which God adorned the spirit of St. Theresa and disposed her immediately

(3) The languor of love

[1] 'A Spiritual Canticle,' stanza IX.

for the heavenly espousals is a most ardent and eager desire of God, seemingly absent, through which the soul of the lover is brought to the agony of death. This desire does not depend on any human power or exercise, but is infused by God, and it elevates the soul above all creatures and above itself. The soul finds itself, as it were, in a vast solitude, in which it seeks not the society of creatures, but rather refuses and rejects that society because it desires only God. God in that solitude presents Himself to the soul from afar, and this tortures it. It has not, and it does not wish to have, the society of creatures. Apparently, it has not, and it cannot have, the society and possession of God which it most ardently desires. St. Theresa, afflicted by this anguish or languor, at times lost the use of her senses, and for some days would be so oppressed by severe pangs of sorrow and pain as to be at the point of death. Nevertheless, she used to say that this grievous suffering, like all other pains of love, gave pleasure and delight to the soul, so that after once experiencing it one would never wish to be without it. This martyrdom of the spirit does not always impress itself in the same degree upon the soul, but it is sometimes greater, sometimes less. Although the languor of love and the wound of love agree in many ways, they are distinct in other respects. The wounds of love are effected suddenly and in a moment, but the languor, although it comes on suddenly, increases gradually. First it places the soul in solitude, then in a state of anxious desire, and finally in a state of mortal agony. The wounds are formed by the touch of love and by the intellect, and they excite the inflammations or enkindlings of love; languor is produced by the intellect alone, and it remains without the inflammations of love.

By this purgation the old man is put off, so far as this is possible here below, so that nothing is now in the way of the union of the soul with God. All inordinate affections, inclinations, and imperfect habits are eradicated, as are also all adhesions and affections, whether for heavenly or earthly things, apart from God. The soul, thus cleansed and purified from all the infirmities and imperfections which it had contracted from nature or through its own fault, can now be elevated to that union with God, and undergo the most complete spiritual transformation that can be enjoyed by souls in this life.

The languor of love may be made clearer to our minds by the description of the threefold pain of the soul given by St John of the Cross. Beginning with a line of the stanza in which the soul says, speaking of God, 'Tell Him I languish, agonize and die,' the Saint writes 'There are three necessities of the soul, namely, languor, agony and death, for the soul that truly loves God with a love in some degree perfect suffers threefold in His absence in the three powers—the intellect, the will, and the memory. In the intellect it languishes, because it does not see God, Who is the salvation of it, as the Psalmist saith: *I am Thy salvation.*[1] In the will it agonizes, because it possesses not God, Who is its comfort and delight, as it is written: *Thou shalt make them drink of the torrent of Thy pleasure*[2] In the memory it dies, because it remembers its privation of all the goods of the intellect, which are the vision of God, and of the delights of the will, which are the

[1] Ps xxxiv 3   [2] Ps xxxv 9.

fruition of Him, and that it is very possible also that it may lose Him for ever because of the dangers and changes of this life. In the memory, therefore, the soul labours under a sensation like that of a death, because it sees itself without the certain and perfect fruition of God, Who is the life of the soul, as it is written *He is thy life*.[1]

The fruits and benefits of this state 2. For the comfort and consolation of devout souls who experience the bitterness of the passive purification of the spirit, or what Father Baker calls 'the great desolation.' I may quote this writer's summary of the fruits and benefits flowing from this state when it is supported with patience and tranquillity. These fruits and benefits, he tells us, are wonderful '(1) For, first, hereby the devout soul obtains a new light to penetrate into the mystery of our Lord's desertion in the garden and on the cross, and from this light a most inflamed love to Him; now she ceases to wonder why He should deprecate a cup so mortally bitter as this, and that it should work such strange effects on Him, or that He should cry out, *Eli, Eli, lamma sabactani*, and by this desertion of His (which lasted till the very last moment of His life) she hopes to have an end put to hers (2) Now she learns by experience to make a division between the supreme portion of the spirit and inferior nature—yea, between the summity of the spirit and the faculties of the same, for that portion of her by which she cleaves to God seems to be another third person distinct from herself that suffers, complains, and desires, for she choses God, and at the same time fears that her will chooses and consents to sin. She is mightily supported by God,

[1] Deut xxx 20 See 'Spirit. Cant, stanza ii, line 2

and yet she thinks Him utterly estranged and separated from her. Thus at last she perceives that she can operate without any perceptible use of her faculties. (3) Hereby she learns a perfect disappropriation and transcendence, even of the highest gifts and graces of God, and a contentment to be deprived of the greatest blessings that God has to bestow on her (except Himself) (4) The sight of the inexpressible weakness and perverseness of nature, left to itself, without any sensible influences of grace upon the inferior faculties, produce in her a most profound humility and hatred of herself. (5) Lastly, by this most sharp purgatory of love she enters into a state of most perfect confidence in God, of tranquillity of mind, and security of God's unchangeable love to her, not to be disturbed by any possible future of affliction. For what has a soul left to fear that can with a peaceable mind support, yea, and make her benefit of, the absence of God Himself?'[1]

3 St. Paul of the Cross, who was so well taught in the school of suffering by lessons so constant, so strong and efficacious, has left us some useful instructions on the method of profiting from sufferings such as these, which he termed precious Some of his sayings and sentiments on this subject may here be subjoined for our direction and edification [3 Sentiments and directions of St Paul of the Cross with regard to the passive purification of the spirit]

'What a great honour God does us,' he writes, 'in making us walk in the path by which His Divine Son walked!'

'Make great account,' he says, writing to a friend, of these exterior and interior trials. The little garden of Jesus will then be flourishing by the

[1] 'Holy Wisdom,' p 540

virtues that are exercised. When the cross is most afflicting and wounding, it is the best; when suffering is most deprived of comfort, it is the purest; when creatures oppose us the most, we approach more nearly to God. . . . He is not worthy of Divine contemplation who has not suffered and vanquished some great temptation.'

Again he writes 'Afflictions, fears, desolations, aridity, abandonments, temptations, and other trials, are an excellent broom, that sweeps from your soul all the dust and mire of the imperfections that are concealed from you. Work, suffer, be silent, do not show resentment; these are maxims of the Saints and of high perfection.'

He writes as follows to a priest: 'Has your reverence ever seen a rock in the sea beaten by the storm? A wave comes furiously and strikes it. What happens? There is the rock. Another more furious wave comes, and strikes it on every side. What becomes of it? There is the rock. After the storm, if your reverence notices the rock, you will see that the waves of the storm have washed and purified it from all defilement it has contracted during the calm weather. Henceforward I wish you to be a rock. A stormy wave comes—be silent. See, a hundred and a thousand come—be silent; and the most I give you leave to say is, "Father, I am thine." O dear, O most sweet will of God, I adore Thee.'

'These little trials,' he writes to one of his penitents, 'corporal and spiritual, are the first steps of that high and holy ladder which is mounted by great and generous souls, which they ascend step by step till they reach the top, where they find the purest suffering without comfort from heaven or earth ; and if they are faithful in not seeking consolation, they pass from this pure suffering to the pure love of God without mixture of any other thing. But very few and rare indeed are the happy souls that reach the step I speak of. Ah, a soul that has received heavenly favours to find herself stripped of everything ! Yet more, to go so far as to seem to herself abandoned by God, to think that God no longer loves her, no longer cares for her, and that He is very angry ! Hence, it appears to such a soul that everything else she does is ill done. Ah, I cannot explain myself as I could wish ! It is enough for you to know, my child, that this is almost the pain of loss, if I may so speak, a pain beyond every other torment But if the soul is faithful, what treasures does she gain ? These storms pass away, and she reaches the true, sweet, beloved embraces of the Divine Lover, Jesus Then God treats her as His spouse, then are celebrated between God and the soul the sacred espousals of love Oh, what treasures ! But you, my child in Jesus, are not yet at the first step of the ladder. I have written this, however, that you may not be alarmed if God should place you in any state of pure suffering without comfort ; but then more than ever be faithful to God, and never leave off your accustomed exercises.'[1]

[1] 'Life of St Paul of the Cross,' Oratorian Series, vol ii, chap xxv

PART III

THE DEGREES OF CONTEMPLATION

INTRODUCTION

AFTER having treated of the nature, the object, the causes, and the effects of contemplation, and also of the preparation, both active and passive, by which the soul is disposed for the acts of contemplation, it remains for us to examine its several degrees, or what Scaramelli calls contemplation in particular or according to its species.

1. Voss, in the compendium of Scaramelli, says in his introduction to this department of contemplation that contemplation is by acts, and these acts are either distinct or indistinct. Contemplation is by distinct acts, when God so clearly manifests some hidden truths that they are understood in a particular manner, and perceived in objects present to the mind, as happens in visions, locutions, and revelations. Contemplation by indistinct acts is that which represents its Divine object generally, and in a kind of luminous obscurity. This latter, he tells us, is really and truly contemplation. This, he says, is the elevation of the mind to God and to Divine things, joined with the simple, admiring, and loving intuition or view of these Divine things in which formal contemplation consists. Contemplation is improperly applied to that which is made by distinct acts, according to this author, because this is an intuition or view of Divine things without being

_{1. Contemplation by distinct and indistinct acts as explained by Scaramelli}

always loving or proceeding out of charity, as sinners have sometimes been favoured with heavenly visions Inasmuch, however, as these extraordinary favours have a connection with contemplation properly so called—for they are often bestowed during contemplation, and more often granted to contemplatives than to sinners—they come within the scope of mystical theology, and they are always dealt with by mystical writers in their treatises on this science. We shall therefore devote the last part of this work to their examination and explanation. We have in this place to notice that contemplations by distinct acts are not more perfect than contemplations by indistinct acts; they are simple, though extraordinary, favours of God, each of which depends upon His will, and have no necessary connection with contemplation by indistinct acts, nor order of dignity that can admit of grades in comparison with it. Neither have they naturally any order or gradation of dignity among themselves, although some of these gifts are more perfect than others, as will be seen when we come to examine them.

Contemplations by indistinct acts are closely connected with each other, and the soul ascends from one degree to another in order. They thus form steps or degrees of which the one following is more perfect than the preceding. It has to be understood always that the gradation is not always necessary, and that we have no laws by which the degrees must follow one another according to an established order. They are the free gifts of God, and He sometimes elevates souls to the highest degree of contemplation, without their being necessitated to ascend by gradual steps or to pass through the lower degrees, but this is not His ordinary way of acting with devout souls. The grades of contemplation are by way of progress, of spiritual or supernatural advancement in the knowledge and in the love of God, or in knowledge and love through contemplating God as true and good. As souls can advance always more and more in the knowledge and the love of God, it follows that the degrees of contemplation are innumerable. They are restricted to a certain number and classified by mystical writers, but in this classification we find much difficulty both by reason of the subject itself and by reason of the different arrangements and the different nomenclature adopted by these writers.

2. We need not be surprised to find these diversities in the writings of mystical authors after we read what Father Baker says in explanation of this, and how he accounts for it :

2 The diversities of mystical writers with regard to the degrees of contemplation, and with regard to the names used explained

'Generally mystic authors write according to their own experience in their own souls when they treat of the several degrees of prayer, and the several manners of the Divine operations in souls, in such degrees, as if the same instructions would serve indefinitely for all others, whereas such is the inexplicable variety of internal dispositions that the same course and order in all things will scarce serve any two souls. Therefore if the indiscreet readers, without considering their own spirits and enlightenment, shall upon the authority of any book tarry too long in an inferior degree of prayer, when God has fitted them and does call them to a higher, or in a foolish ambition shall, being unprepared, presume to a degree of prayer too sublime and spiritual for them, there will be no end of difficulties, doubts, and consultations.'

With regard to the nomenclature, the same worthy author says: 'Mystic writers, in expressing the spiritual way in which they have been led, do oft seem to differ extremely from one another; the which difference, notwithstanding, if rightly understood, is merely in the phrase and manner of expression. And the ground hereof is, because the pure immaterial operations of perfect souls in prayer, and especially the operations of God in souls in which they are patients only, are so sublime that intelligible words and phrases cannot perfectly express them, and therefore they are forced to invent new words, the best they can, or to borrow similitudes from corporal things, etc., to make their conception more intelligible; and thus does each one according to the manner that he finds or conceives in himself, or according to his skill in language. No wonder, therefore, if there seems to be diversity among them. Hereupon the author of "The Cloud" observes that great harm may come by understanding things literally, grossly, and sensibly, which, howsoever they be expressed, were intended and ought to be understood spiritually.'[1]

Father Baker's opinion as to the degrees of contemplation

3 Further on in his work he seems to disavow any attempt on his own part to explain the degrees of contemplation in the following paragraph:

'I know that some mystic authors do constitute several distinct states following active contemplation. As Barbanson makes mention of the state of the Divine Presence in the soul, and after that of the manifestation of God to the spirit, etc., and in all these great variety of ascents and descents, etc., likewise F. Ben. Canfield, in his last and most

[1] 'Holy Wisdom,' pp 88, 89

perfect state of the essential and supereminent will of God, makes mention of several distinct exercises, as denudation and active and passive annihilation, etc These authors, perhaps, spoke according to the experience of the Divine operations in their own souls, and with regard to their particular manner of prayer. Therefore I conceive that what they deliver needs not to be esteemed a common measure for all, neither will I deny but that there may be distinct states (some of which I will mention), as the great desolation, etc., but it will be to no purpose to search closely into them. These happy souls, whom God shall so highly favour as to bring them to the mount of vision and contemplation, will have no need of light from anyone but God to conduct them in those hidden Divine paths, and the inexperienced will reap but little profit from such curious inquiries.'[1]

4. It is true, indeed, that contemplation is not a science developed from absolute laws and principles like natural sciences, nor can its degrees be classified with great exactness and distinctness, as the Spirit of God is not confined to any one method in the operations of His grace. He gives or He retains and He distributes His favours where and when He wills, according to His good pleasure and according to the infinite mystery of His love. Yet from the writings of His Saints themselves, who have experienced the various degrees of contemplation, theologians have been able to arrange these favours according to some order or classification, admitted, I think, as to its substantial and essential parts by all, though with great variety of opinions with regard

4. The classification of the degrees of contemplation diverse

[1] 'Holy Wisdom,' p 508

to accidental points and names and in some details of explanation. With few exceptions, they teach that the contemplative life advances by successive degrees, and that this is the general rule. Exceptions in this, as in other things, may be said to prove the rule.

This classification, no doubt, presents great difficulty to one who is himself without actual experience of these higher degrees of spirituality, and who is anxious to know the nature of these operations for his own sake as well as for the sake of others. He can only gain this knowledge from approved sources and from the teaching of authors who have been trained and who have trained others in the mystical way. When he finds the same standard authors giving different groups and different modifications of the various degrees, it is hard to know which one to adopt and to follow so as to secure the most satisfactory guidance and the surest result.

Ribet gives a list of the best-known classifications by the most celebrated mystical writers, and explains the system of each briefly. In that list we find the names of Richard of St. Victor, St. Bonaventure, Gerson, St. Theresa, St. Francis of Sales, Father Alvarez de Paz, Philip of the Most Holy Trinity, St. Alphonsus, Father Schram, Fathers Godinez and Scaramelli. To each of these a system of classification of degrees is attributed, extracted from their published works. Their systems seem to me to agree substantially, but there are differences in the order in which they are given, as well as in the divisions and subdivisions. It would be no easy matter to reconcile them all, or to indicate any new plan that would include them all, or to give any new solution more luminous and better founded than any given by these great Saints and holy writers.

5. I shall therefore select from among the various systems, as my standard for the arrangement of the degrees of contemplation, and for the nomenclature to be used, that of Scaramelli, as given by Father Voss in the compendium of the 'Directorium Mysticum'—not that I am to be understood as judging it better than any of the others, or as placing it before them; but it seems to me less complicated than some of them, and that author adopts a method of treatment that commends itself to an ordinary scholastic theologian. In adopting his classification of the degrees of contemplation and of the mystical names applied to various steps or grades, it will not be necessary to confine ourselves to his explanations and developments of the said degrees. For these we can avail ourselves of the further explanations given in the writings of the Saints and of other mystical authors, and I think that in this way we may be able to obtain an accurate and full explanation of all that we need to know concerning the ordinary and general rules by which devout souls are elevated to the heights of contemplation and of union with God

We must not expect or pretend to know all that the soul experiences in each degree, for even the favoured souls themselves cannot tell us. And in this kind of contemplation, as we have said, they see God and Divine things in a sort of luminous obscurity, of which Father Baker reminds us in the following passages when he speaks of the highest union of the soul with God in this life.

'Of these intellectual passive unions, the supreme

5 Scaramelli's classification and nomenclature adopted

and most noble that may be had in this life is that whereby God is contemplated without any perceptible images by a certain intellectual supernatural light darted into the soul, in which regard it draws much towards an angelical contemplation; for herein, though God be not seen as He is, yet it is clearly seen that He is, and that He is incomprehensible.

'Mystic authors call this a Divine passive union rather than contemplation, a union far more strait and immediate than any of the former, a union exercised more by the will than by the understanding, although the effect thereof be to refund great light into the understanding, notwithstanding which light, yet the understanding's contemplation is said to be *in caligine*, in which darkness God is more perfectly seen, because there is nothing seen that is not God, yea, according to the doctrine of mystics, this union passes both the understanding and will, namely, in that supreme portion of the spirit which is visible to God alone, and in which He alone can inhabit a portion so pure, noble, and Divine that it neither hath nor can have any name proper to it, though mystics endeavour to express it by divers, calling it the summit of the mind, the fund and centre of the spirit, the essence of the soul, its original portion, etc.'[1]

From these statements, in which all other writers agree, we may conclude that no writer can give a clear knowledge or understanding of the real state of heavenly things experienced by contemplative souls. The favoured souls themselves, even when raised to the most exalted union and to the highest sphere of supernatural light that can be enjoyed here

[1] 'Holy Wisdom,' p 532

on earth, are still said to be *in caligine;* how much more may ordinary theologians be said to be *in caligine* when endeavouring to describe and explain what passes between souls and God, and their mutual relations in the different degrees of contemplation! This reflection may conciliate impartial readers, especially when they are assured that in all that we write concerning these degrees we attempt nothing new, but endeavour to walk faithfully in the beaten track made known to us by experienced and holy contemplatives through their works.

CHAPTER I

THE FIRST THREE DEGREES OF CONTEMPLATION

FIRST DEGREE: THE PRAYER OF RECOLLECTION.

THE first degree of supernatural contemplation is the prayer of recollection.

<small>1. Meaning and explanation of the prayer of recollection</small>

1. Recollection is twofold: one which we acquire by our own industry, inasmuch as the soul enters into itself and represents God present to it and fixes all its interior powers on Him. The other does not depend on our own industry, but on grace infused in an extraordinary manner, by which God summons together for attention the powers of the soul distracted by many things. This is the kind of recollection which is called the first degree of infused contemplation. It is defined: 'A pleasant and sudden recollection of all the interior faculties or powers in the very centre of the soul by which God, through a lively faith, manifests Himself.' It is produced by a certain light and sweetness infused by God into the intellect and the will, which unites and retains the internal senses to which it overflows in delight before God, Who manifests His perfections to the interior soul. On this recollection of the internal senses, the external senses become also restrained, so that the eyes become closed though the person

has not wished to close them, the ears do not hear, and the body remains immovable.

'As sheep, hearing the voice of the pastor, come to him,' says Scaramelli, 'as the needle turns itself to the magnet and adheres to it, so all the powers of the soul, when God, manifesting His presence, calls them, at once centre around and adhere to Him, absorbed by His presence. Then the wandering memory becomes quiet, the distracted intellect becomes collected in contemplating Him, then the vacillating will becomes firm and rejoices in Him Even the external senses are withdrawn from their objects, and in their own way seem to see, to taste, and to enjoy God present in the soul.'

This recollection usually takes place suddenly, so that the soul, as St Theresa teaches, perceives all its powers collected in God before it has begun to think of God. Hence it follows that this prayer is infused, and not acquired. We are told, however, that it cannot as yet be designated contemplation, but its beginning, or, rather, the Divine vocation to infused contemplation. In this prayer we are not to omit meditation and the operations of the intellect; but these ought to be very quiet and tranquil, lest the peace and serenity through which God communicates great good to the soul should be disturbed. The effects of this prayer are · greater detachment of the soul from worldly and perishable goods, and a greater love of prayer and solitude. The soul, having experienced how sweet the Lord is, despises earthly things and seeks the presence of God in solitude. Scaramelli, whom we have chosen as our guide in this matter, gives a few admonitions which we have here to note.

Admonitions concerning this kind of prayer

2. He reminds us, first, that in this recollection the powers of the soul are not suspended from action; on the contrary, the intellect can at the time reflect and reason, and the will can love, give thanks, and humble itself, and it ought to do these things. With great calmness the intellect should consider its own insignificance and God's greatness, and the will also should make its acts with great quietude. If the soul should with anxiety and solicitude disturb itself about these acts, it would hinder the Divine operation, and this must never be done.

Secondly, he says that, if God should call a person to this recollection when engaged in vocal prayer, he should either suspend the prayer altogether or continue it very quietly and peacefully. The first is to be done when the vocal prayers are voluntary and not prescribed by any rule, and when they are found to impede the Divine operation. The second is to be followed in the case of prescribed vocal prayers. The rule is to be followed, and the prayers of precept are not to be discontinued.

Thirdly, he observes that when this interior recollection is frequent it is to be regarded as a sign of the Divine vocation to infused contemplation, and the soul has to be treated with greater care and solicitude. The time of prayer might be lengthened; the soul, as far as possible, should remain in solitude apart from worldly distractions and worldly concerns, and generously continue the exercises of the solid virtues of mortification and humility.

Finally, he remarks that for souls called by God to recollection in this peculiar manner it is necessary that they help themselves by endeavouring to practise recollection. Let them do so by observing in their prayers the practice of regarding God as in themselves, and not seeking for Him outside themselves. There, in their own hearts, as in His own living temple, He may be found, loved, and adored.

3. St. Theresa, in her admirable work 'The Way of Perfection,' describes the prayer of recollection in the following manner.

3. The prayer of recollection described by St Theresa

'It is styled "of recollection" because in it the soul recollects all the faculties and enters within herself with her God, and there her Divine Master comes much sooner to instruct her and bestow upon her the prayer of quiet than in any other manner; for placed there with Him she may meditate with herself on the Passion, and there represent the Son and offer Him to the Father, and not weary of the understanding by going to seek Him on Mount Calvary, or in the Garden, or at the Pillar. Those that in this manner can shut up themselves in the little haven of their soul, where He abides that created heaven and earth, and shall inure themselves not to behold or stay where those exterior senses distract them, let them believe that they walk in an excellent way, and that they shall not fail to arrive to drink water from the fountain, for thus they go far in a little time. . . .

'In like manner, if the recollection be true, it is very clearly discerned, for it produces a certain operation (which I know not how to explain: whoever hath it will understand), so that it seems the soul rises up from play (such she seeth the things of this world are), and, taking an opportunity, mounts up and, like one that retreats to some strong fort to be out of fear of the enemy, withdraws the senses from these exterior things, and in such sort quits them that (though unawares) the eyes close up not to behold them, the more to open the sight of the eyes of the soul. Accordingly, whoso walks by this way, almost always in prayer, keeps the eyes shut; and it is an admirable custom for many things, because it is forcing one's self not to behold things here below. This [shutting of the eyes] is only at the beginning of such recollection, for afterwards it is needless, then more force is required to open them. The soul seems to fortify and strengthen herself at the body's charge, and to leave it alone and enfeebled, and thence draws even provision for it.'[1]

In her life she narrates how she experienced the presence of God in her soul. She says

'Being one day in prayer, on the festival of the glorious St. Peter, I saw standing very near me, or, to speak more properly, I felt and perceived (for I saw nothing at all, either with the eyes of my body or of my soul), that Christ our Lord was close by me, and I found it was He Who spoke to me as I thought. As I had been up to this time extremely ignorant as to whether there could be any such vision, I fell at first into a great fear, as I could do nothing but weep; but presently our Lord gave me comfort by speaking only one word, and I found myself, as I was wont, very quiet, with great delight and without fear. It seemed that Christ went always by my side; but the vision not being imaginary, nor represented in any form to the imagination, I perceived not in what shape He was, though I found and felt very sensibly that He was always on my right side; that He was the witness of whatever I did, and that if I were recollected, even a little, or,

[1] 'The Way of Perfection,' chap xxviii

THE DEGREES OF CONTEMPLATION

rather, unless I were very much distracted, I could not help understanding that He was near me. . . .

'But if, as I say, I saw our Lord neither with the eyes of the body nor of the soul (because it was no imaginary vision), how can I understand and assert more clearly that He was near me, than if I had actually seen Him? It seems as if a person were in the dark and saw not another who stood near him, or as if the person were blind. This is something of a comparison, though not much, for even if a person were blind he might know another was present by his other senses, because he could hear him speak or stir, or he might touch him. But here there is nothing at all of this, nor is there darkness; but our Lord's presence is represented to the soul by a sign clearer than the sun itself, and yet no sun or brightness is seen, but only a certain light, which, without our seeing it, illuminates the understanding that the soul may enjoy so great a good.'[1]

Second Degree: Spiritual Silence.

It seems that spiritual silence is not regarded as a distinct degree of prayer or contemplation, but it is given as such by Alvarez de Paz, and by Scaramelli on his authority.

1. It is a form of contemplation which holds a middle place between the prayer of recollection and the prayer of union, as inferior to the latter and superior to the former. It is a suspension in which the powers of the soul are not lost as to action, but astonished, they adhere to God in silence and admiration. In the prayer of recollection the intellect is

[1] 'Life of St. Theresa,' chap. xxvii.

Spiritual silence a form of contemplation holding a middle place between the prayer of recollection and the prayer of quiet

not drawn away from meditating and reasoning, nor is the will prevented from making acts of petition, of thanksgiving, of praise and oblation; and both these powers can produce their acts without doing violence to themselves. But when in the recollected soul the light of the intellect and the love of the will increase, then the intellect remains fixed in the admiration of God, and the will becomes immersed in His love, so that neither faculty proceeds with its other acts. The intellect and will can by doing violence to themselves, not only proceed to other acts, but they can even withdraw from the Divine object on which they are so happily engaged, and attend to external things In this prayer of silence the phantasy rendered insensible does not disturb the soul by its importunate imaginations, but, participating of the consolation that fills the intellect and will, it remains quiet, silent, and contented; the intellect transfixed in admiration of the great things manifested to it in such clear light by God does not discourse or reason. The will with full contentment rests in its love. The sensitive appetite even enjoys a complete calm, so that silence reigns in the whole interior man, a silence that is pleasing and comforting

Its cause and effects

2. The cause of this silence is a certain Divine light in the intellect, and an intense love in the will by which these powers remain filled and immovable in admiration, without exercising their own acts for the time being. The soul, we are told, then sees and hears. Its seeing is by a simple and delicate beholding in which God is perceived after the manner described by St. Theresa as given above. The soul hears when in quietude, it attends to God,

Who speaks to the heart by His light, by His inspirations, and sometimes even by express words. The effects of this prayer of silence are the same as the effects of the prayer of recollection, but they are more perfect, in so far as the light of the mind and the love of the will are greater and richer in this degree of prayer. Hence it withdraws the heart more from attachment to earthly things, it increases the love of prayer and solitude, and intensifies the purpose of serving God always.

Thomas à Vallgornera places this spiritual silence under the prayer of recollection, and in his explanation of its nature, its cause, and its effects he agrees in all particulars with the explanation here taken from Scaramelli. It may indeed be said to be a more advanced form of the prayer of recollection, and it has no characters very distinct from that degree of prayer; but there is no reason why this form may not be designated a degree, and why we may not adhere to the classification that places it as the second degree of contemplation. The lines on which some of these degrees are marked off do not appear to be very exactly determined.

3. The special directions given by Scaramelli in regard to the prayer of silence are

3. Special directions concerning the prayer of silence

(1) In the prayer of recollection persons are advised to continue to exercise the intellect and the will with peace and tranquillity; in this prayer they are advised not to exercise them, but to hold them suspended in the admiration and love which God imparts to them. If, moreover, in this state the attention of the soul should be excited in such a manner as to signify that God wishes to speak to the heart, then no impediment should be placed in

the way of the Divine communication. Let the voice of God be heard Care, however, must be taken that the suspension of the powers does not proceed from affectation or the human efforts of the soul, which may sometimes happen, in which case the error should be corrected, and the person should be obliged to return to the exercise and the acts of the understanding and the will.

(2) If after a short time the brightness or clearness of the light and the ardour of love should cease, and with these the suspension of the other powers, the soul should at once return to reflection, colloquies, prayers and oblations, and the other ordinary acts of this kind It is useless to force one's self under such circumstances to continue the prayer of silence, so that it is important that one knows well when to be silent and to contemplate, and when to exercise the powers of the soul according to the movement of the Holy Spirit.

(3) The suspension of this silence lasts only a short time, like all supernatural suspensions. SS Bernard and Gregory and Hugo of St Victor teach that it does not exceed half an hour. Wherefore, should it happen that the powers of the soul remain suspended and bewildered in this spiritual silence for some hours, the work is not of God, but brought about by one's own efforts, and the person so affected should be admonished to lay aside the delusion and to apply the powers to act in accordance with the usual spiritual exercises It sometimes happens that after the soul returns from silence to activity it is drawn into silence again, and in this way, with intervals, the prayer of silence may last longer and be prolonged.

4. The remarks of St Francis de Sales on the amorous recollection of the soul in contemplation may be applied equally to the prayer of silence, and throw some further light on both degrees. He says·

'The recollection of which we speak is the work of love, which, being first aware of the presence of God by the sweetness diffused in the heart, obliges the soul to unite her powers and attention, and to direct them to her Beloved. All this is effected with ease and pleasure, love communicating to the soul an inclination to direct all her powers to God, Who attracts them with so much sweetness. The infinite goodness of the Almighty attracts and binds all hearts more powerfully than cords and chains can fasten and restrain the body.

'We must also observe that this recollection is not always produced by the sweet conviction that God is present in the heart; other causes may produce a similar effect provided they tend to place the soul in the Divine presence. In attentively considering the Sovereign Majesty of God, Who beholds us, we are sometimes seized with so lively a feeling of respect and delicious fear that all our interior powers are immediately concentrated and recollected in themselves, just as the unexpected presence of a great Prince recalls the wandering thoughts of the most distracted mind, and produces the exterior respect and reverence due to the dignity of the person present.'

The Saint then quotes an example to illustrate this degree of contemplation. He tells that he knew a person favoured with this gift of recollection· 'No sooner was she spoken to in the tribunal of penance, or in a private conference on the mysteries of our religion, or any part of Scripture calculated to remind her forcibly of the presence of God, than she immediately entered into herself so profoundly that it was with difficulty she afterwards finished what she had begun to say or replied to the observations made to her. Persons who beheld her in these circumstances would have supposed her deprived of life, the use of her senses remaining suspended until it pleased her Divine Spouse to terminate the state of profound recollection, which varied in the period of its duration.'[1]

Third Degree. The Prayer of Quiet.

The prayer of quiet is given by all mystical writers, and in their explanations we find agreement and uniformity. It is a degree of prayer not so easily understood or explained, on account of the errors of the quietists and the semi-quietists, who brought the word into discredit, and for this reason we should give it special attention and consideration in our treatment. Let us try to understand in the first place what is the nature of the prayer of quiet as experienced and taught by the Saints.

[The nature of the prayer of quiet explained]

1. The prayer of quiet, according to Scaramelli, is a certain rest, peace, and internal pleasantness proceeding from the depths of the soul, and overflowing to the corporal and sensible powers, which arise from the fact that the soul not only approaches God, but even feels His presence. The cause of this prayer is not a simple act of faith produced by

[1] 'Treatise on the Love of God,' book vi, chap vii

the ordinary helps of grace, by which the soul believes God to be intimately present; but it is the gift of wisdom, which by its light shows God present, and makes the soul not only to believe Him present, but to experience His presence by a most pleasing sensation of the spirit. The purpose of the gift of wisdom is to render God present to the soul in a peculiar spiritual manner, and the act of the gift of wisdom is to contemplate God, not in any way, but in affection with a certain experimental sweetness The soul then understands, in a certain way, different from the mode of knowing through the senses, that God is so near to her, that if only she were a little nearer she would be one with Him by complete union Hence the difference between the prayer of quiet and that of silence. This has its origin from the intellectual light suspending the soul, the former arises from a certain experience of love whereby the will perceives and tastes God present with it. From this sense of the Divine presence there is caused a great quiet, great peace, and a sweet delight, which, springing from the very centre of the soul where God makes His presence felt, expands itself into all the powers and faculties of the soul. So great is the suavity and peace that the soul, perfectly satisfied, desires nothing more, and with the Spouse in the Canticles she repeats : *I sat down under his shadow whom I desired, and his fruit was sweet to my palate* [1]

2. St Theresa endeavours to explain to her daughters the prayer of quiet, and she goes into the explanation very minutely, so as to make them understand it the better She writes·

2. St Theresa's description of this prayer

[1] Cant ii 3

'This prayer of quiet, according as I have heard it practised, or our Lord hath pleased to let me understand it—perhaps that I might tell it you—is that in which, it seems to me, our Lord begins to make known that He hath heard our request, and begins already to give us His kingdom here, that we may really praise and sanctify Him, and procure that all may do the same. This is a thing supernatural, and which we cannot acquire with all the diligences we use, because it is the settling of a soul in peace, or, rather, our Lord, to speak more properly, puts it in peace by His presence, as He did just Simeon, for all the faculties are calmed.

'The soul understands, after a manner far different from understanding by the exterior senses, that she is now joined near to God, so that within a very little more she will attain to the being made one with Him by union. . . . The just Simeon saw no more of the glorious little Infant Jesus than one so poor and wrapped up in swaddling-clothes, and with so few attendants to go in procession with Him, that he might rather think Him the son of a mean person than the Son of the Heavenly Father. But the Child Himself made Himself known to him. Just so the soul understands Him here, though not with like charity, for she herself knows not how she understands, but that she seeth herself in the kingdom— at least, near the King Who is to give it to her—and the soul seems struck with such a reverence that she dares not then ask anything.

'It is a kind of mortifying interiorly and exteriorly, so that the exterior man—I mean the body, that ye may the better understand me—would not stir at all, but, like one arrived almost at his journey's end, rests to be able to travel again, for here the forces to this purpose are redoubled. A very great delight is perceived in the body, and a great satisfaction in the soul. She is so delighted with merely seeing herself near the Fountain, that even without drinking she is already satisfied. There seems to be nothing more to be desired by her, the faculties so quiet that they would not stir; everything seems to disturb her loving. Yet they are not lost, for they think near Whom they stand, for two of them are free, the will here is the captive, who, if she can feel any pain in this condition, it is to see that she is to return to her former liberty. The understanding would understand no more but one thing, nor the memory employ itself about any more. Here they perceive this alone is necessary, and all things besides disturb them. They would not have the body move, because they conceive so they should lose their peace, and therefore they dare not stir. Speaking troubles them. In saying only one *Pater Noster* they will sometimes spend an hour . . . They seem not to be in the world, and they would neither see nor hear it, but only their God Nothing troubles them, nor, it seems, can do so. In some, whilst this lasts, with the satisfaction and delight contained therein, they are so inebriated and absorbed that they remember not that there is anything more to desire, but that they say with St. Peter *Lord, let us make here three tabernacles.*'

3. The Saint continues the description, and gives us another aspect of this state which appears to be active—that is, the soul can attend to other things whilst being engaged in the prayer of quiet ' In this prayer of quiet God sometimes doth another

<small>The soul active in this state.</small>

favour, very hard to be understood unless there be great experience, but if there be, those that have it will presently understand it, and it will afford them great consolation to know what it is, and I believe God doth this favour together with that other. When this quiet is great and for a long time, it seems to me that, unless the will were attached to something, it could not continue so long in that peace, for it happens we go a day or two with the satisfaction and do not understand ourselves (I speak of those who have it). And, indeed, they see, they are not taken up entirely in what they do, but that they want the main—that is, the will—which seems to me to be united with God, and leaves the other faculties free that they may attend to things of His service—and for this they have then more ability; but for treating of matters of the world they are stupid, and fools, as it were, sometimes. This is a great favour to whomsoever our Lord doth it, for the active and contemplative lives are conjoined. Our Lord is then served of all, for the will is busy at her work without knowing how she works, and continues in her contemplation; the other two powers serve in the office of Martha, so that she and Mary go together. I know a person whom our Lord often put into this condition, and because she knew not what to make of it she asked a great contemplative, who told her it was very possible, for it had so befallen him. Therefore I think that, since the soul is so well satisfied in this prayer of quiet for the most of the time, the power of the will must needs be united to Him Who alone is able to satisfy it."[1]

[1] 'The Way of Perfection,' chap. xxxi.

It is evident from St. Theresa's teaching that there may be much activity in this prayer of quiet, and it is in this sense she is understood by St Francis of Sales. Writing on this subject, he says . ' However, we must not imagine that we are in danger of forfeiting this holy quiet on account of movements, either of mind or body, in which levity and indiscretion have no share. For, as St Theresa observes, it is a species of superstition to be so jealous of our repose as to refrain from coughing, and almost from breathing, for fear of losing it. God, Who is the Author of this peace, will not deprive us of it for such motions of the body as are unavoidable, or even for involuntary distractions and wanderings of the mind Though the understanding and the memory may escape the bounds of restraint, and wander on strange and useless thoughts, yet the will, when once attracted by the charms of the Divine presence, will still continue to enjoy the same delights It is true that the calm is not then so perfect as it would be if the understanding and memory were in union with the will. Yet a real spiritual tranquillity is certainly and effectually enjoyed, since it resides in the will, which governs all the powers of the soul. We have seen a person who in this prayer of quiet certainly was most intimately attached and united to God, and yet whose understanding and memory were so perfectly free and had so little share in this interior occupation that she distinctly heard and remembered everything said near her, though she was unable either to reply or to detach herself from God, to Whom the application of her will alone united her. Yet so closely was she attached to Him that she could not be distracted from her sweet occupation without experiencing great regret, to which she gave vent in sighs and tears; this occasionally happened also amidst the repose of holy quiet.'[1]

<small>4 The sense in which this form of prayer is called passive</small>

4. I may add to the expositions of these two great Saints that in this quiet we are not to understand that even the will is inactive, as during the time it is capable of eliciting fervent affections and aspirations. Although the form of prayer may be called *passive*, which we have to understand in the sense that God reveals Himself to the soul by a supernatural species impressed on her, in which He is the only Agent and she the patient; not as if, when a soul does contemplate God, she were not in some sort active, but because by no dispositions or preparations that the soul can use can she assuredly procure them; but when God is pleased graciously to communicate them, the soul is taken out of her own disposal, and does and must see and think only what God will have her, and this no longer than His good pleasure is such.[2]

We may conclude this chapter with the following admonition of St Francis de Sales 'When the will is attracted and sweetly restrained by the happiness it derives from the presence of God, it should not endeavour to recall the other powers when they are diverted from this object; thus to separate from its Divine Spouse would be to sacrifice its repose. Its efforts to recall the attention of these volatile powers would also prove vain and ineffectual Besides, nothing is more efficacious in bringing them back to their duty than the tranquil

---

[1] 'Treatise on the Love of God,' book vi, chap x.
[2] See 'Holy Wisdom,' p 520.

perseverance of the will in holy quiet, because the heavenly sweetness diffused in the heart, as a perfume whose fragrance is gradually communicated to all the powers of the soul, invites them to return and unite themselves to the will, that they may share in its happiness.'[1]

[1] 'Treatise on the Love of God,' book vi, chap x

CHAPTER II

ERRORS OF FALSE MYSTICS IN REGARD TO THE PRAYER OF QUIET

Many instructions and directions are given regarding this degree of prayer, and in connection with it, regarding contemplation in general, in order to protect souls, against deception and error in this extraordinary way of sanctity. For the safe guidance of souls, it may be well that they be warned especially against the systems of false mysticism, as exhibited in the quietism of Molinos and the semi-quietism of Fénelon, and in this place it may be useful to give the history of these false systems, and explain the sense in which they have been condemned by the Church. For this purpose I shall give the following account by the Rev. Alban Butler of the errors affecting the prayer of quiet, which is well worthy of the attention of all who, in their perusal of works upon this subject, would avoid the errors of false mysticism.

[1] Rev. Alban Butler's account of the errors of quietism and semi-quietism (1) The errors of quietism

1. 'In books of devotion the errors of false mystics or quietists and semi-quietists are carefully to be guarded against.

'(1) The heresy and fanaticism of quietism was broached by Michael Molinos, a Spanish priest and spiritual director in great repute at Rome, who in

[398]

his book entitled 'The Spiritual Guide' established a system of perfect contemplation. It chiefly turns upon the following general principles. (*a*) That *perfect* contemplation is a state in which a man does not reflect either on God or on himself, but passively receives the impression of heavenly light without exercising any acts, the mind being in perfect inaction and inattention which the author calls quiet, which principle is a notorious illusion and falsity; for even in supernatural impressions or communications, how much soever a soul may be abstracted from her senses and insensible to external objects which act upon their organs, she still exercises the understanding and will in adoring, loving, praising, or the like, as is demonstrable both from principle and from the testimony of St. Theresa and all true contemplatives (*b*) This fanatic teaches that a soul in that state desires nothing, not even his own salvation, and fears nothing, not even hell itself This principle, big with pernicious consequences, is heretical, as the precept and constant obligation of hope of salvation through Christ is an article of faith. The pretence that a total indifference is a state of perfection is folly and impiety, as if solicitude about things of duty was not a precept, and as if a man could ever be exempt from the obligation of that charity, which he owes both to God and himself, by which he is bound above all things to desire and to labour for his salvation and the eternal reign of God in his soul A third principle of this author is no less notoriously heretical, that in such a state the use of the Sacraments and good works become indifferent; and that the most criminal representations and motions in the sensitive part of the soul are foreign to the superior, and not sinful in this elevated state, as if the sensitive part of the soul was not subject to the government of the rational or superior part, or as if this could be indifferent as to what passes in it. Some will have it that Molinos carried his last principle so far as to open a door to the abominations of the Gnostics, but most excuse him from admitting that horrible consequence (see Fathers Avrigny, Honoré of St. Mary, etc.). Innocent XI., in 1687, condemned sixty-eight propositions extracted from this author as respectively heretical, scandalous, and blasphemous. Molinos was condemned by the Inquisition at Rome, recalled his errors, and ended his life in imprisonment in 1695 (see Argentre, "Collect. Judiciorum de novis erroribus," t. iii., part ii., p. 402; Stevaert, "Prop. Damnat.," p. 1).

(2) The errors of semi-quietism.

'(2) Semi-quietism was rendered famous by having been for some time patronized by the great Fénelon. Madame Guyon, a widow lady, wrote an essay and short method of prayer, and Solomon's Canticle of Canticles, interpreted in a mystical sense, for which, by order of Louis XIV., she was confined to a nunnery, but soon after set at liberty. Then it was that she became acquainted with Fénelon, and she published the Old Testament with explanations, her own life by herself, and other works—all written with spirit and a lively imagination. She submitted her doctrine to the judgment of Bossuet, esteemed the most accurate theologian in the French dominions. After a mature examination, Bossuet, Bishop of Meaux; Cardinal Noailles; Fénelon, then lately nominated Archbishop of Cambray; and Mr. Tronson, Superior of St. Sulpice, drew up thirty articles concerning the sound maxims of a spiritual life, to which Fénelon added four others. These thirty-four articles were signed by them at Issy in 1695, and are the famous Articles of Issy (see Argentre, "Collectio Judiciorum de novis erroribus," t. iii.; Du Plessis, "Hist. de Meaux," t. i., p. 492; "Mémoires Chronol.," t. iii., p. 28). During this examination Bossuet and Fénelon had frequent disputes for and against disinterested love, or Divine love of pure benevolence. This latter undertook in some measure the patronage of Madame Guyon, and in 1697 published a book entitled "The Maxims of the Saints," in which a kind of semi-quietism was advanced. The clamour which was raised drew the author into disgrace at the Court of Louis XIV., and the book was condemned by Innocent XII. in 1699, on March 12, and on April 9 following by the author himself, who closed his eyes to all glimmerings of human understanding to seek truth in the obedient simplicity of faith. By this submission he vanquished and triumphed over his defeat itself, and by a more admirable greatness of soul over his vanquisher. With the book, twenty-three propositions extracted out of it were censured by the Pope as rash, pernicious in practice, and erroneous, respectively, but none were qualified heretical.

'The principal error of semi-quietism consists in this doctrine, that in the state of perfect contemplation it belongs to the entire annihilation in which a soul places herself before God, and to the perfect resignation of herself to His will, that she be indifferent whether she be damned or saved, which monstrous extravagance destroys the obligation of

Christian hope. The Divine precepts can never clash, but strengthen one another. It would be blasphemy to pretend that because God, as an universal Ruler, suffers sin, we can take a complaisance in this being committed by others. God damns no one but for sin and final impenitence; yet while we adore the Divine justice and sanctity, we are bound to reject sin with the utmost abhorrence, and deprecate damnation with the utmost ardour, both which by the Divine grace we can shun. Where, then, can there be any room for such a pretended resignation, at the very thought of which piety shudders? No such blasphemies occur in the writings of St. Theresa, St. John of the Cross, or other approved spiritual works. If there are, or seem to be, expressed in certain parts of some spiritual works, as those of Bernieres or in the Italian translation of Bondon's "God Alone," these expressions are to be corrected by the rule of solid theology. Fénelon was chiefly deceived by the authority of an adulterated edition of the "Spiritual Entertainments of St Francis of Sales,' published at Lyons in 1628 by Drobet. Upon the immediate complaint and supplication of St. Frances Chantal and John Francis Sales, brother of the Saint, then Bishop of Geneva, Louis XIII. suppressed the privilege granted for the said edition by letters patent given in the camp before Rochelle in the same year, prefixed to the correct and true edition of that book made at Lyons by Cœurceillys in 1629 by order of St. Frances Chantal. Yet the faulty edition, with its additions and omissions, has been sometimes reprinted, and a copy of this edition imposed upon Fénelon, whom Bossuet, who used the right edition, accused of falsifying the book (see "Mém. de Trev." for July, anno 1558, p. 446).

(3) 'Bossuet had several years before maintained in the schools of the Sorbonne, with great warmth, that a love of pure benevolence is chimerical. Nothing is more famous in theological schools than the distinction of the love of *chaste desire* (*concupiscentiæ*) and of *benevolence*. By the first a creature loves God as the creature's own good—that is, upon the motive of enjoying Him, or because he shall possess God and find in Him his own complete happiness; in other words, because God is good to the creature himself both here and hereafter. The love of benevolence is that by which a creature loves God purely for His own sake, or because He is in Himself infinitely good. This latter is called pure or disinterested love, or love of charity; the former is a love of an inferior order, and is said by many theologians to belong to hope, not to charity, and many maintain that it can never attain to such a degree of perfection as to be a love of God above all things, because, say they, he who loves God merely because He is his own good, or for the sake of his enjoyment, loves Him not for God's own uncreated goodness, which is the motive of charity, nor can he love Him more than he does his own enjoyment of Him, though he makes no such comparison, nor even directly or interpretatively forms such an act, that he loves Him not more than he does his own possession of Him, which would be criminal and extremely inordinate; so this love is good, and of obligation as a part of hope, and it disposes the soul to the love of charity. Bossuet allowed the distinct motives of the love of *chaste*

<small>(3) The love of chaste desire (*concupiscentiæ*) and the love of benevolence.</small>

desire and *benevolence*, but said no act of the latter could be formed by the heart, which does not expressly include an act of the former, because, said he, no man can love any good without desiring to himself at the same time the possession of that good, or its union with himself, and no man can love another's good merely as another's. This all allow, if this other's good were to destroy or exclude the love of his own good. Hence the habit of love of benevolence must include the habit of the love of desire. But the act may be, and often is, exercised without it, for good is amiable in itself, and for its own sake, and this is the general opinion of theologians. However, the opinion of Bossuet that an act of the love of benevolence or of charity is inseparable from an actual love of desire is not censured, but maintained also by Father Honoratus of St Mary ("Tradition sur la Contempl.," t. iii., c. iv., p. 273). Mr. Norris carries this notion so far as to pretend that creatures in loving God consider nothing in His perfections but *their own* good (Letter ii., on Divine Love, p. 8). Some advised Fénelon to make a diversion by attacking Bossuet's sentiments and books at Rome, and convicting him of establishing theological hope by destroying charity. But the pious Archbishop made answer that he never would inflame a dispute by recriminating against a brother, whatever might have seemed prudent to be done at another season. When he was put in mind to beware of the artifices of mankind, which he had so well known and so often experienced, he made answer, "Let us die in our simplicity" (*Moriamur in simplicitate nostra*). On this celebrated dispute the ingenious Claville ("Traité du Vrai Mérite") makes this remark, that some of those who carried the point were condemned by the public as if they lost charity by the manner in which they carried on the contest; but if Fénelon erred in theory, he was led astray by an excess in the desire of charity. By this adversity and submission he improved his own charity and humility to perfection, and arrived at the most easy disposition of heart, disengagement from everything in the world, bowed down to a state of pliableness and docility not to be expressed, and grounded in a love of simplicity which extinguished in him everything besides. Those who admired these virtues in him before were surprised at the great heights to which he afterwards carried them, so much he appeared a new man, though before a model of piety and humility. As to the distinction of the motives in our love of God, in practice, too nice or anxious an inquiry is generally fruitless and pernicious, for our business is more and more to die to ourselves, to purify our hearts, and employ our understanding in the contemplation of the Divine perfections and heavenly mysteries, and our affections in the various acts of holy love, a boundless field in which our souls may freely take range. And while we blame the extravagances of false mystics, we must never fear being transported to excesses in practice by the love of God. It can never be carried too far, since the only measure of our love to God is to love without measure, as St. Bernard says. No transports of *pure* love can carry souls aside from the right way, so long as they are guided by humility and obedience. In disputes about such things, the utmost care is necessary that charity be not lost in them, that envy and pride be guarded against, and that sobriety and moderation be observed in all inquiries, for nothing is more frequent than for the greatest geniuses in pursuing subtleties to lose sight both of virtue and good sense and reason itself See Bossuet's works on this subject, t. vi., especially his " Mystici in Tuto ", also Du Plessis ("Hist. de l'Eglise de Meaux," t. 1, p. 485), the several lives of Fénelon, etc.'[1]

Some of the errors in particular condemned by the Holy See

2. In addition to the foregoing clear, wise, and authoritative exposition of the errors of quietism and semi-quietism, I may subjoin here for greater security some other particular errors of those systems condemned by the Holy See. Molinos taught, and was condemned for so teaching, that true interior life consists in annihilating the powers of the soul: 'Opertet hominem suas potentias annihilare; et hæc est vita æterna.' All active operations he condemned as being offensive to God. 'Velle operari active est Deum offendere.' Thus, the operations of knowledge and of love, according to him, even when directed to God, are displeasing to Him, thus denying the old primitive truth, that the end for which God hath made us is to know Him, to love Him, and to serve Him, and affirming that the whole duty of men is to do nothing and to attempt nothing. In the seventh of the condemned propositions he forbids all meditation on the four last great truths—Death, Judgment, Hell, and Heaven In the twelfth of his impious propositions he asserts that whosoever has given up his free will to God ought to have no care about anything, neither about

[1] Note to 'Life of St John of the Cross,' November 24, and quoted in full in Guy's edition of 'The Scale of Perfection.' note, p 45 *et seq*

hell nor paradise, nor ought he even to have any desire about his own perfection, nor about the acquisition of virtues, nor about his own sanctification and salvation, all hope of which he ought to drive away. In the fourteenth the prayer of supplication is forbidden, and it is declared that our Divine Lord's command, *Ask, and ye shall receive*, is not meant for interior souls, which are to have no will, whereas asking implies a wish to obtain what is asked for, and is therefore an imperfection. Thanksgiving is forbidden in the next proposition, and others follow which it is beyond our present purpose, and certainly far from our desire, to allude to.

The second proposition condemned by Innocent XII., taken from the 'Maxims of the Saints' by Fénelon, is that which declared that in the state of the contemplative or unitive life every interested motive of fear and love is lost · 'In statu vitæ contemplativæ seu unitivæ amittitur omne motivum interessatum timoris et spei.'[1]

Against all these errors of false mystics we must bear in mind that all should enter with energy and activity upon the exercises of the spiritual life ; that all have to accept of the three degrees of an interior life, purgative, illuminative, and unitive, which are rejected by Molinos in the twenty-sixth of his condemned propositions as being the height of absurdity ; that all have to follow the kind of prayer proper to one or other of these states, and to take the warning against cessation of prayer, in which all have to persevere in spite of every temptation and obstacle

[1] 'Holy Wisdom,' edition by Right Rev Abbot Sweeney, note, pp 490-492

The preceding and the following instructions with regard to the degrees of contemplation may be the better understood by giving the landmarks within which our doctrine must be confined; and the errors being once clearly known, a great safeguard is provided for devout souls in their progress towards perfection and sanctity.

CHAPTER III

THE FOURTH, FIFTH, AND SIXTH DEGREES OF CONTEMPLATION

FOURTH DEGREE: THE INEBRIATION OF LOVE.

AFTER the prayer of quiet there follows, according to St. Theresa, what mystics call the *inebriation of love*, which belongs to the prayer of quiet in its more elevated degree. This inebriation is a jubilation excited in the soul by an excess of love, and the joy of the soul overflows to the senses and reveals itself externally by sallies and eccentricities that resemble the effects of material inebriation.

Scaramelli divides this inebriation into imperfect and perfect. The imperfect does not properly belong to this degree of prayer, but he explains it in connection with it in order to enable us the better to understand the perfect.

1. The imperfect inebriation is a certain devotion [1] of love and joy from which, as from strong wine, the fervour of spirit becomes so exuberant that it cannot be contained within itself. It therefore manifests itself in unusual ways, such as by cries, tears, laughing, singing, dancing; and these outbreaks are by sudden fits and incoherently. It is of this St. Theresa speaks when she cries out:

'O my God! in what state is a soul when she

[1] Imperfect inebriation

finds herself raised to this degree of prayer; she would wish to be changed into so many tongues in order to praise You, O Lord! She utters a thousand holy extravagances, always endeavouring to please You Who hold her in this state. I know a certain person who, though she was no poetess, made very feeling verses *extempore*, declaring the sweet pain she suffered; and these were not composed by her understanding, but the better to enjoy that glory which gave her so delightful a pain. She complained thereof to God, and she wished both her whole body and soul could be torn in pieces to show the joy she felt in pain. What torments could then be placed before her which she would not gladly endure for the love of her Lord?[1]

In the imperfect form this inebriation affects the senses and the heart principally, although its cause is the interior devotion of the soul. It is granted to souls not yet purified, and it is called imperfect because it proceeds from a less pure light and is felt chiefly in the inferior or sensitive part of the soul.

Perfect inebriation of love

2. The perfect inebriation of love which is given only to the perfect—to those who have already been cleansed by the passive purifications, either entirely or for the most part—is a sublime species of contemplation, consisting in a high degree or form of the prayer of quiet, which produces so delightful, so sweet, and so joyful a love in the soul that it becomes dead to all earthly things, and, as it were, taken out of itself, and thus it falls into a state of delicious delirium or wise folly, and is on this account said to be inebriated with love.

St. Theresa's words will teach us more of this

[1] Her Life, chap. xvi.

state than any amount of cool theological explanation. After describing this state of prayer and the joy thereof, she goes on to say.

'I think I have not at all exaggerated anything respecting the joy which our Lord is pleased a soul should experience in this place of banishment, for all that I have said is very mean in comparison with the reality. Blessed be Thou, O Lord, for ever! May all creatures praise Thee for ever. Be now pleased, O my King, and I humbly beseech Thee that, since even now, while I am writing, I am not out of this holy and celestial frenzy (which through Thy goodness and mercy Thou grantest to me as a favour without any merit of mine) either all those with whom I converse may become fools for Your love, or permit me no more to converse with any person; or so order, O Lord, that I may have nothing more to do with things of the world, or take me quite away from it. O my God! this Thy servant can no longer endure so many afflictions, which she sees come upon her when she has Thee not. If she *must* live, she desires to have no ease in life, and, indeed, Thou dost not give her any. She desires to be free from the body; eating is insupportable to her, sleep afflicts her. She sees that her whole life is passed in satisfying the body, and that now no one but Thee can truly delight her. She seems to live against nature itself, since she no longer desires to live in herself, but in Thee. O my true Lord and my glory! how light, and yet how very heavy, is the cross which Thou hast prepared for those who have arrived at this degree! It is light because it is sweet, and it is heavy because at certain times no patience in the world can endure it. And yet the soul would never desire to be free from it, unless it were that she might find herself with Thee. And when she remembers that she has not served Thee in anything but that by living she may thereby be able to serve Thee, she would gladly endure a burden much more heavy, and would be content not to die until the end of the world. She cares not for any rest or repose provided she can do Thee any little service. She knows not what to desire, though she knows well that she desires nothing but Thee.'[1]

St. John of the Cross, in his own beautiful words and imagery, describes this degree, both in its imperfect and perfect form, when he draws out the comparison between old and new wine. Beginners he compares to new wine, and the perfect to old, and after applying the doctrine he intends to teach to the two spiritual states, he concludes as follows

'For this cause an old friend is of great price in the eyes of God: *Forsake not an old friend, for the new will not be like him.*[2] It is through this wine of love, tried and spiced, that the Divine Beloved produces in the soul that Divine inebriation, under the influence of which it sends forth to God the sweet and delicious outpourings. The meaning of these three lines [of the stanza], therefore, is as follows "At the touch of the fire" by which Thou stirrest up the soul, and by the spiced wine with which Thou dost so lovingly inebriate it, the soul pours forth the acts and movements of love which Thou producest in it."[3]

It sometimes happens that holy persons, under

---

[1] Her Life, chap xvi [2] Ecclus ix 14
[3] 'A Spiritual Canticle,' stanza xxv, in the English version.

the influence of this perfect inebriation, like the imperfect, cannot contain themselves, and manifest their interior joy externally by unusual and extraordinary actions. Especially this is the case with those of tender disposition, as exemplified in the lives of St. Francis of Assisi, St Paul of the Cross, St. Peter of Alcantara, and many others This holy excess often reveals itself in the desire of suffering for God. St. Ignatius, Martyr, manifests it in his martyrdom. It is also shown in the words of St Lawrence addressed to the tyrant who was causing his death by urging him to greater cruelty, and it serves to explain the joy of the martyrs generally in facing their torments, and the Divine impulse by which they sometimes sought them. This holy state does not reach the degree of union, but, as I have said, it belongs to the prayer of quiet in its highest degree. During it, as I wish to avoid any semblance of quietism or semi-quietism in these pages, I must say that the powers of the soul remain free, and are not entirely suspended, because the soul can always exercise its acts towards God, in praising, loving, and honouring Him Though under this spiritual influence, while it lasts it cannot well divert itself to other things. We are told that the state may last sometimes for a day, sometimes even for two or three days, but not with the same force or vivacity, and not, I think, without interruptions, so that the soul may occupy itself properly with other necessary duties.

3. Amongst the effects of this species of contemplation, besides the fortitude which the Martyrs displayed in their torments, we may conceive that other holy souls also receive an increase of this gift

3 Effects of this degree of contemplation

of the Holy Ghost, and all who experience this inebriation receive new and increased courage and strength to do great things for God. It has been noticed by others as well as by St Theresa that a person entirely without poetic fancy or poetic skill may often compose, under this influence and inspiration, graceful and sublime hymns and canticles. The Psalms and the Canticle of Canticles are quoted as Scriptural examples, but, of course, they have the special inspiration as well which belongs to the Sacred Scripture. Above all, this heavenly favour enkindles and inflames the love of God in the soul, so that it breaks forth into desires, praises, and a thousand ardent affections and aspirations towards God, all of which are so many acts of the virtue of charity, meriting new and higher graces by their repetition and by the fervour with which they are elicited.

Fifth Degree Spiritual Sleep.

1. Spiritual sleep described by the example of natural sleep

1. After the example of St. Theresa, many mystics place this spiritual sleep as one of the degrees of contemplation. This is done by Alvarez de Paz, St. John of the Cross, and Scaramelli, whose order we are following. It derives its name from its similarity to natural sleep, and is explained by Richard of St. Victor by the characteristics and effects of natural sleep. 'Besides,' he says, 'what natural sleep effects in the exterior man, this the spiritual sleep effects in the interior man. Bodily sleep overcomes the senses, closes the eyes, the ears, and the other senses, and rests all the members. As by natural sleep all the senses of the

body slumber, so by this sleep of the interior man all the senses or faculties of the mind are overcome. It absorbs at the same time the imagination, the thoughts, the understanding, the memory. It is the peace of God which, according to the Apostle, surpasses all understanding.'[1] This sleep encloses the soul, as it were, in the embraces of the beloved, where it rests upon His breast. The spiritual sleep, therefore, consists in the absorption of the interior powers—namely, of the phantasy, the understanding, the memory, and the will itself—in the Divine love, so that the soul loves without knowing how it loves, and by that love enjoys a delicious foretaste of heavenly love. It does not love entirely without knowing, because, according to the axiom of philosophers, there cannot be love of that which is unknown; but as the heat of love increases the attention of the intellect is arrested, and its reflection upon its actions. But, nevertheless, it is because its acts are so simple and delicate that the soul from which they proceed does not notice them. The powers of the soul are not lost, but they slumber. They act, but they do not know how they act. The soul in this state can say with the spouse in the canticle: *I sleep, and my heart watcheth*[2] I sleep because the eye of the mind appears closed to understanding, but I feel that heart in love in the embraces of the Beloved.

2 The effects of this spiritual sleep into which the soul is led by God are similar to those attributed to the perfect inebriation of love. But, besides, there

[2] Its effects

---

[1] Phil iv 7 Richard of St Victor apud Voss, 'Compendium Scaramelli,' p 272

[2] Cant v 2.

accrues to the soul from this benefits which may be compared to those which the body derives from natural sleep. As the body by its sleep is refreshed, its powers renewed, and rendered more fit for subsequent labours, so by the spiritual sleep the soul is refreshed and invigorated to do and to suffer more for God.

<small>3 The pure spiritual light which causes the rest of the soul</small>

3 There is another phase of this spiritual sleep represented by Scaramelli, which does not, like that just mentioned, proceed from the perfect inebriation of love, but which consists in a certain oblivion of all things which is caused by a pure spiritual light which penetrates the soul, holding it intent on and occupied with God in such a manner as to exclude every other attention and reflection.

St. John of the Cross, in the fourteenth chapter of the second book of the 'Ascent of Carmel,' describes and illustrates this state. He shows us how the soul may be unconscious of particular thoughts, how it may be unconscious of time and place, how God may suspend the faculties of the soul, and yet how the soul is not idle, because conscious of God by love. I shall make room for one paragraph from that chapter · 'This forgetfulness occurs when God in a special way suspends the faculties of the soul. This does not often occur, for this knowledge [the light spoken of] does not always fill the soul. It is sufficient for our purpose that the intellect should be abstracted from all particular knowledge, whether temporal or spiritual, and that the will should have no inclination to dwell upon either. This sign serves to show that the soul is in this state of forgetfulness, when the knowledge is furnished and communicated to the intellect only. But when it is communicated to the will also, which is almost always the case in a greater or less degree, the soul cannot but see, if it will reflect thereon, that it is occupied by this knowledge; because it is then conscious of the sweetness and love therein, without any particular knowledge or perception of what it loves. This is the reason why this knowledge is called loving and general; for as it communicates itself obscurely to the intellect, so also to the will, infusing therein love and sweetness confusedly, without the soul knowing distinctly the object of its love. Let this suffice to show how necessary it is for the soul to be occupied by this knowledge in order that it may leave the way of meditation, and to feel assured, notwithstanding the appearance of doing nothing, that it is well employed if it observes the signs of which I am speaking. It appears, also, from the illustration of the sun's rays full of atoms, that the soul is not to imagine this light to be the most pure, subtle and clear when it presents itself to the intellect more palpably and more comprehensibly. For it is certain, according to Aristotle and theologians, that the more pure and sublime the Divine light is, the more obscure it is to our understanding.'

Scaramelli goes on to tell us that the soul immersed in this sleep can continue its prayer for many hours in perfect forgetfulness of everything, and without adverting to what it is doing. After the prayer it has forgotten what it was doing, where it was, and how it spent so much time; it seems to it that the hours have passed so quickly. It often happens that the devout soul is troubled with scruples about having wasted time, or about some other delusion, and the director may also be puzzled if he be ignorant of these things. But provided it was not a state of natural sleep, or that it has not resulted from some unusual and natural stupidity, which can easily be detected by the result, the person ought to rest assured that he has been favoured by Almighty God, by what is known as spiritual sleep, which is one of the degrees of infused prayer

The genuineness of this prayer is known by its fruits. In this prayer the soul may know that it is elevated to God, that it is alienated from earthly things and abstracted from imaginary forms and figures It also experiences in itself a profound peace and an interior quiet, and feels itself better prepared for the exercise of solid virtues. In this sense the soul may exclaim '*I have watched, and am become as a sparrow all alone on the housetop.*[1] I have watched in my sweet slumber, and I found myself solitary in the depth of my soul, and abstracted and alienated from all things, God alone excepted'

4. What St Francis de Sales says of 'liquefaction' applies to this spiritual sleep

4. We may use the language of St Francis of Sales, and apply what he says of the liquefaction or flowing of the soul in God to this spiritual sleep When the complacency we take in the object of our affections has reached the greatest height to which it can attain, it reduces the person who loves to a kind of spiritual impotence, so that the soul, feeling herself, as it were, dissolved and unable any longer to subsist in herself, takes refuge in the object of her love, and flows like balm, which by melting loses its solidity and consistency.

[1] Ps ci 8.

'In this operation the soul does not bound or dart towards God; she is not joined to Him by means of union [the Saint means contemplative union], but sweetly and gently flows into the paternal heart of her God, as fluids move onwards as long as their progress is not impeded.

'This was undoubtedly the disposition of St. Paul; it was his ardent love and zeal for the glory of the Son of God which caused him to exclaim: *I live, now not I, but Christ liveth in me.*[1] *Our life is hidden with Christ in God.*[2] Suppose that a drop of water were thrown into a sea of perfume, and that this drop had life and power to describe its situation, would it not joyfully exclaim: O men, who wonder at my lot, it is now that I begin to live; or, rather, it is not I who live—it is this immense ocean which lives in me. My existence is quite concealed in its abyss.

'We cannot say of the soul thus dissolved in God that this dissolution causes her death; she could not find death in Him Who is the very source and principle of life, but she no longer lives by her own life or in herself. The stars are not deprived of light in the presence of the sun, they only cease to shine in our eyes; the great luminary of the day then shines in them, and their light is concealed in his. Thus, when the soul is engulfed in God she is not deprived of life by having lost herself in Him, but it is God who lives in her, in consequence of this loss.

'Such was the disposition of the Philips of Neri and the Francis Xaviers, when, unable to support the abundance of heavenly consolations, they con-

[1] Gal. ii. 20. [2] Col. iii. 3.

jured the Almighty to retire from them for a time; that is, they implored that while He permitted them still to remain in their exile for the promotion of His glory He would enable them to live and converse with creatures, which could not be easily accomplished as long as their life continued entirely hidden and absorbed in Him.'[1]

Sixth Degree: The Anguish and Thirst of Love.

After God has enriched the soul loved by Him with the gifts of infused prayer—namely, of recollection, of silence, and of quiet—after he has often inebriated it with His holy love, and after, perhaps, it has found spiritual sleep in His embrace, ordinarily speaking, He does not at once join it to Him in the joyful union of love, but, wishing to be first ardently desired by it, He sends an anguish and thirst of impatient love into the soul, by which the soul, being as it were consumed, is attracted or drawn to Him. The anguish of this love is a strong, lively desire of the soul, wholly or almost wholly purified, for that God already tasted and loved, but not yet possessed. If the desire is permanent it is called the thirst of love, for according to the mystical sense the *anguish* is a transient desire of God, and the *thirst* is a permanent desire of God. This anguish and thirst are excited in the soul when, being already to some extent purified, it knows God as the greatest good by the gift of understanding, Whom before it regarded by the gift of wisdom as the most lovable Being. Now

[1] 'Treatise on the Love of God,' book vi, chap xii

the soul, knowing the sweetness of God by its present light and its past experience, is inflamed by such a desire and thirst of love that it sometimes breaks forth into extravagant desires towards its God.

There are three kinds of this anguish and of this thirst—that of beginners, of proficients, and of the perfect.

1. The anguish and thirst of beginners usually happens after the soul has by generous mortification passed through the active purification, when it has not been tried as yet by the passive purification, and its anguish is imperfect, full of anxiety and solicitude, joined with headache and weariness. It is of this St Theresa speaks when she says: 'Such I myself had in the beginning, and they [the anguishes] always left my head so disordered and my soul so wearied that sometimes I was not able for several days to return to the exercise of prayer.' She adds the following words of sound advice for those who may suffer as she did 'We should therefore use great discretion at the beginning in order that everything may go on with sweetness, and the soul may be taught the way of exercising herself interiorly, we must also endeavour as much as we can that the exterior may be avoided.'[1]

2. In the more proficient—that is, the souls who have been purified by the passive purgation of the senses—the anguishes are more spiritual, although they are yet felt in the senses. They are purer and more lively than in the case of beginners. Of this state of anguish and thirst St. John of the Cross speaks when he says 'The longings of the soul

[1] Her Life, chap xxix

for God are so deep that the very bones seem to dry up in that thirst, the bodily health to wither, the natural warmth and energies to perish in the intensity of that thirst of love. The soul feels it to be a living thirst. Such also was the feeling of David when he said *My soul hath thirsted after the strong living God.*[1] It is as if he had said, My thirst is a strong living thirst. We may say of this thirst that, being a living thirst, it kills. Though this thirst is not continuously but only occasionally violent, nevertheless it is always felt in some degree.'[2]

3 Of the perfect

3 This anguish and thirst are stronger in those of the progressive state than in beginners, but it is not so great as that of the perfect—namely, of those who have passed through the passive purification of the spirit and of the senses, and who are now near their union with God. 'This burning and thirst of love,' says St. John of the Cross, 'inasmuch as it now proceeds from the Holy Ghost, is very different from that of which I spoke in the night of the senses. For though the senses also have their part in this, because they share in the afflictions of the spirit, yet the root and living force of the thirst of love are felt in the higher portion of the soul—that is, in the spirit—conscious of what the soul feels, and of the absence of what it desires; still, all the pains of sense, though incomparably greater than those of the sensitive night, are as nothing, because of the interior conviction that one great good is wanting, for which there is no compensation possible.'[3]

---

[1] Ps xvi 3   [2] 'The Obscure Night,' book I, chap xi
[3] *Ibid*, book II, chap xiii

This thirst and burning is sometimes concealed in the interior of the soul, and therein produces an infirmity or sickness of love in the same way that thirst and want produce weakness and sickness of body. Sometimes, however, it affects the bodily powers and dries them up with its excessive heat, so that the bodies of those persons appear sickly and delicate, and they are subject to lethargies and languors. It always happens that this thirst, whether hidden in the soul or experienced in the body, is accompanied with great suffering, which, however, is at the same time so sweet and precious that the soul never wishes to be deprived of it.

The end for which God afflicts the soul with such anguishes, thirst, and impetuosity of love is twofold: First, in order to purify the soul from all impediments still hidden within it to the Divine union;[1] secondly, that the soul may be dilated and rendered more capable of receiving the greatness of that love by which it becomes entirely engulfed and transformed in God. Wherefore the soul is exposed to these trials and hardships until it is perfectly established in the union with God which is called spiritual matrimony, because up to this state it requires to be more and more purged and purified. Although God may unite it to Himself by a certain bond of love, although He may elevate it to Himself by ecstasies and raptures, although He may adorn it with the ornaments of a spouse, after the lapse of the time of these favours the soul returns to its former thirst and desire. In the state of habitual union only are all these bitter anguishes satiated,

[1] See the 'Passive Purification of the Spirit,' Part II., Chapter XV.

and in it only does the soul enjoy constant serenity with God. We have to understand, however, that the anguishes of the perfect only, and not those of beginners or the more proficient, dispose the soul proximately for this union. Those other anguishes dispose the souls for certain peculiar favours, but not for immediate union with God.

<small>4 How the wounds of love act upon the soul, explained by St Francis de Sales</small>

4. St. Francis de Sales, speaking of Divine love and of what he calls the wound of love, explains in an easy manner how this acts upon the soul 'Those who have long and faithfully exercised this sacred virtue sometimes receive a kind of wound which God Himself inflicts on those whom He designs to raise to an exalted perfection He presses and solicits the soul by powerfully attracting her to His sovereign goodness and exciting feelings of ardour which she had never before experienced, and which produce great astonishment.

'The soul thus animated exerts all her endeavours to wing her flight towards the Divine Object Who so strongly attracts her towards His Divine Majesty. But she soon perceives that her efforts are insufficient, that she cannot soar as high as she aspires, and that her love for God is far from having attained the perfection she desires. Who can express the extreme anguish which she experiences from this conviction ? Invited on one side to her Beloved, and restrained on the other by her own weakness and the weights of the miseries of this mortal life, she longs for the wings of the dove that she may fly away and be at rest But these ineffectual desires only serve to torment her ; they keep her suspended between efforts to bound to her God and weakness which prevents her from doing so The great Apostle experienced this struggle when he said: *Unhappy man that I am, who shall deliver me from the body of this death ?*[1]

'In this case it is not the desire of an absent blessing which wounds the soul; she feels that the God Whom she loves is present, that He has already introduced her into the mystical cellar, where He keeps His precious wine, and that He has implanted in her heart the sacred standard of love But God, Who sees that she is wholly His, ceases not to pursue her, and from time to time He wounds her with new arrows by imparting to her a conviction that the God of her affections is infinitely more amiable than loved.

'This soul then endures inexpressible anguish, because she sees that the ardour of her love is nothing in comparison of her desire, and that the God Whom she sighs to love in proportion to His infinite amiability will never be sufficiently or worthily loved. She makes new efforts, but each succeeding endeavour, rendering her more sensible of her weakness and misery, renews and augments her suffering.

'A heart thus transported with love for God allows no limits to its desire of loving Him, and yet acknowledges that comparatively with what the Almighty deserves it can neither worthily love nor sufficiently desire to love Him This insatiable desire is like an arrow which pierces it. The wound it inflicts occasions a sweet pain, because those who ardently desire to love take pleasure in this desire, and would consider themselves most unfortunate if they did not incessantly sigh to love what is

[1] Rom vii 24

sovereignly amiable. Desire produces sorrow; yet the happiness which results from desire renders pain pleasing and agreeable

'Such is the conduct of God with regard to souls inflamed with charity; He continually extracts from His enchanting beauty burning arrows with which He designs to wound their hearts. These darts are rays of light, which show them that their love is in no degree equal to the amiability of its object. Those who love God without desiring to be consumed with still more ardent charity do not yet love Him sufficiently; those who are satisfied with the measure of their love are far from having reason to be so.'[1]

[1] 'Treatise on the Love of God,' book vi, chap. xiii

CHAPTER IV

THE SEVENTH DEGREE OF CONTEMPLATION

Seventh Degree: The Mystical and Simple Union of Love.

The mystical union of which we now speak is in its kind the most perfect act of contemplation. It is great and admirable, and almost incomprehensible, and, as Voss says, can only be explained by comparisons and similitudes. We have first to treat of the nature of mystical union.

1. To explain mystical union, it is necessary to consider the various ways in which God can be united to our souls.[1]

The first union to be mentioned is the physical, real, and inseparable union which naturally exists between God the Creator and the creature. God is intimately united to all creatures by His *presence*; He sees all by His wisdom and knowledge, and He rules and governs all by His providence. This is not the mystical union of which we here treat.

The second union is that which exists between God and the just soul by means of sanctifying grace, by the habits of the infused virtues, and by the gifts of the Holy Ghost. This union is far superior to, or more noble than, the former union, but it is not yet mystical union.

[1] The various ways in which the soul can be united to God

The third union consists in perfect charity, effective charity, by virtue of which the soul conforms itself most perfectly to the will of God. It is the union of conformity and of similitude between the will of God and that of man which is called Christian perfection, to which all are invited. But this is not what is understood as mystical union.

There is a fourth manner of union mentioned, which is pantheistic, which imagines the essence of the soul to be transmuted into the Being of God. Almaricus, a theological doctor of Paris, taught that such a union existed between God and the contemplative soul. The doctrine was condemned by Innocent III., and it is rejected at once by sound reason as an impossibility.

2 The mystical union of love explained

2. Finally we come to the mystical union of love, which is explained by Scaramelli as follows. This wonderful and sublime union consists in the experimental love of God, so intimate that the soul, without losing anything of its physical and natural being, is divested of its own affection and is wholly lost in God. He says that mystical union consists in the experimental love of God, and not in perfect charity, because, as Alvarez de Paz well remarks, there are many perfect men in the Church who have perfect charity to whom neither the gift of contemplation nor the gift of this union is given. Although perfect charity and the love of union are one and the same thing in substance, they differ as to accidents; for the love of union is communicated not in an ordinary way, but in a peculiar way, and it is extraordinary. It is an experimental love, so that the soul perceives the sensation of God in a true, loving, and spiritual manner, and in no way according to

animal nature. In this union the same author, quoting Hugo of St Victor, says the soul is, as it were, divided; the animal nature remains its nothingness, and the spiritual nature is raised to the greatest height, it is divided from the lowest depth of its nature that it may be raised up to the summit, it is taken asunder from the lower element that it may be united with God. The animal operations cease that the soul may be occupied only with spiritual operations. Therefore in the spiritual part only is the presence of God perceived.

Since, however, in the prayer of quiet and in the other infused prayers the presence of God is perceived in a spiritual manner, in order that the union may be distinguished from them, this author says in his definition that the experimental and spiritual perception is so very intimate in this union that the soul is wholly lost in God, and this is the proper characteristic of the union. The soul is not lost, it does not abandon or relinquish itself as to its substance and as to its being, nor can its substance be transformed into the substance of God, but it relinquishes itself as to the knowledge and sense of itself, and it is transformed into God as to the deep and profound sense of love which it experiences in Him. The soul in this union relinquishes itself as to knowledge because intent on God, the Divine light deprives it in a way of all knowledge of itself and all reflection on its own operations It relinquishes itself as to all sense of itself, because the sense of this experimental love is so sweet and delightful that it absorbs the whole spirit, so that it can only enjoy God alone, and in this way it is said to be lost or immersed in God. Then the soul no longer perceives itself, but only God in itself, and thus it becomes transformed in God. To be transformed means to put off one form and to assume another To give up or put away one's being in order to assume another is called essential transformation ; to put away or remove an accident of one's self and to assume another is accidental transformation. In this sense we can call that transformation affective or one of affection, in which the soul loses all sense and affection of everything else and of itself, and assumes the Divine affection, or feeling, or sense, or whatsoever the experimental perception of this love of God in the soul may be called Such is the transformation of the soul in God—not an essential transformation, but affective or one of affection.

In this state, according to the manner explained by Hugo of St Victor, when the mind is alienated from itself, when it is rapt up in the abode of the Divine sanctuary, when it is on all sides surrounded by the flames of Divine love and is wholly on fire, it puts off itself entirely, and puts on a certain Divine affection or spiritual clothing, and becomes transformed into a new glory The soul, in the words of St Francis of Sales, becomes liquefied, and flows into the bosom of God.

Explanations of recent French writers, as Ribet and Lejeune, may serve to enable us to understand more clearly what is meant by the mystical union They may be set down in the following order

Sanctifying grace establishes a wonderful union between God and man, in virtue of which man is said to participate of the Divine nature, and this may be almost called a theological axiom.

This Divine life dwells in us without our being

directly conscious of it. Its presence makes itself manifest occasionally by the superhuman energy which it imparts, and by the victories which it enables us to gain—victories of the supernatural order. But so long as we live our earthly lives we can never perceive directly and immediately the Divine realities. The veil will be removed entirely only in heaven. We only know that the life of grace and the life of glory are the same, and that the difference betwen them is the same as that which exists between adolescence and maturity, as it is expressed by Bossuet Glory, according to him, is only a certain revelation of our life hidden in this world, but which will appear in all its entirety and perfection in the other

Between the obscurity of faith and the full light of glory are placed the pleasures of mystical union. As M. Ribet explains, God, without unveiling Himself entirely, can impart to the soul to which He is united a more or less lively feeling of this union, in such a way that the soul will not only believe by the adhesion of faith in the communication of the Divine life which grace imparts, but it will *see*, *feel*, and *taste* the ineffable union which is effected between it and God The consciousness of this union which the contemplative soul experiences is different from that which the beatified soul enjoys, it is not so complete nor so glorious as this latter. Faith does not disappear, as in one respect the vision and the enjoyment do not exist yet. The obscurities of faith, however, seem in the act of union to vanish, according as light and possession are perceived to increase.

Two elements enter into the composition of

beatitude—the vision and the love of God. Of these two elements, it is the second which predominates in mystical union. It is for this it sometimes receives the name of *fruitive* union, because the soul relishes God and enjoys Him without possessing the full vision of Him.[1]

<small>3. Various grades of this union</small>

3. In this mystical union there are various grades distinguished from each other, not only as to greater or less perfection, but also as to the mode by which these degrees unite the soul with, and transform it in, God. The first of these degrees is called simple union, which is the mystical union in its lowest degree, and of which we have to treat before we attempt to explain the more advanced grades, known as ecstatic union and perfect union or spiritual marriage

<small>4. The prayer of simple union</small>

4. After the explanation given of mystical union in general, we may define the prayer of simple union as a very intimate union of the soul with God, without the suspension of the external or bodily senses, accompanied with a true, indubitable, and most pleasant perception of God present in the centre of the soul.

That which is most precious in this union is not the pleasant perception and happiness which results from it, but it is the union itself or the transformation of the soul in God. This transformation takes place really in every soul gifted with sanctifying grace, and such souls become more or less perfect according to the greater or less degree of sanctifying grace which elevates the soul, and advances it in its spiritual or supernatural life. Hence it follows

---

[1] 'Manuel du Theol Myst,' Lejeune, chap vi , 'La Mystique Divine,' M Ribet, vol. 1, p 257

that the union of which we speak—that is, the union with the perception of the presence of God and with the joy which this perception imparts—is in no sense necessary for sanctification or for sanctity. One can have grace, and have it in the same eminent degree, without experiencing this perception and joy; one can be very holy and not experience nor enjoy the mystic union. This union, nevertheless, remains, and is to be regarded as one of the most precious graces which God bestows upon a soul, and it is a sign that the soul thus endowed has attained a high degree of perfection. It is not to beginners, nor to those who have taken the first steps in the way of perfection, that God thus reveals His presence. We have, however, always to keep in mind that it is a gift entirely gratuitous, and that God has not promised to give it to any soul, no matter how perfect or how holy that soul may be. It is granted only to the perfect, but not to all the perfect [1]

There are three questions to be examined in regard to this prayer of simple union (1) Whether the powers of the soul are suspended during the time; (2) whether the senses of the body are suspended during the same prayer; (3) how this prayer differs from the prayer of quiet.

(1) With regard to the first question, namely, whether all the powers of the soul are suspended during the time of this prayer, Scaramelli, on the authority of St. Theresa and of other mystic writers, says that they are all in some way and to some extent suspended, and he goes on to explain in what way and to what extent. The intellect is suspended in such a way that it cannot wander to the considera-

(1) Whether the powers of the soul are suspended during it

[1] Ita Lejeune, 'Manuel de Théol Myst,' p 177.

tion of other objects, nor can it reflect upon its own acts. Its action does not cease entirely, as some authors have taught, because it remains fixed and occupied in the sublime contemplation of God, and is suspended only as to acts which have not God as their object. The will is suspended in the sense that it is in some way changed into the will of God, but not so as to lose its own liberty. Although in this sublime communication it remains immovably adhering to God by a love fixed upon that object, it can, however, absolutely speaking, cease from that act. In the view of the scholastics, the will for the time being may lose its liberty (*quoad specificationem*) as to different acts, so that it cannot elicit other acts; it retains, however, its liberty (*quoad exercitium*) as to the exercise of the act of love, so that it can cease from that act, or it retains the power of suspending the act of love, and this suffices for merit and for liberty. In the beatific vision it cannot resist the act of love, by reason of the force and efficacy by which it is absorbed in God, but in the mystical union it can resist, as I have said, and merit an increase of grace during the prayer of union, and no one would think of depriving a soul of its merit during the time of this most holy exercise and communion with God. The phantasy is entirely lost, or, rather, suspended, during the time, as Scaramelli distinctly says, but he adds, when this suspension and full union holds the soul captive for a short time, one or other of the powers is awakened again. Thus, the phantasy, by some imagery or vision presented to it by God, begins once more its operation; or the intellect, again, excited by an intellectual vision, or by some distinct understanding of some individual object imparted to it by God, resumes its operation as to that object. Then the suspension and union are no longer complete, as to all the powers, but only as to the will, which continues submerged and lost in God even when the other powers are engaged with their distinct and peculiar operations. With these remissions and interruptions the powers may repeatedly be suspended and lose themselves wholly in God.

(2) With regard to the second question—namely, whether the senses of the body are entirely suspended as to their acts during the simple mystical union—we have the following statements of St. Theresa, which may serve as an answer given by her whose authority is so great and who herself experienced that holy contemplation 'The soul finds herself almost sinking under a sweet and most excessive delight, accompanied with a kind of fainting, so that the breath begins to fail, and also all corporal strength, not, indeed, accompanied with great pain, but in such a manner that even the hands cannot be moved; the eyes are closed without our having any desire to close them, and when they are open the soul sees nothing distinctly. If she can read, she is unable to tell a letter, and she knows not how to pronounce it properly. She sees, indeed, there are letters; but, as the understanding does not help her, she knows not how to read, though she should desire. She hears, but understands not what she hears. Thus, she receives no benefit at all from her senses, but only that they will not allow her to take the full enjoyment of her pleasure, and accordingly they do her more harm than good. As to speaking, it is useless to attempt it,

(2) Whether the senses of the body are suspended during it

for she cannot form words; and even if she could, she has no strength to pronounce them, because all her bodily strength is gone, while that of the soul is increased that so she may the better enjoy her glory The exterior delight which she feels is both very great and very evident. This prayer, however long it may last, produces no inconvenience—at least, I feel none, nor do I remember when our Lord bestowed this favour upon me, however ill I might be, that I ever found myself worse. I was, on the other hand, much better. But what harm can so great a blessing do? Its effects are so manifest that one cannot doubt it augments the vigour of the soul, since our Lord took away all her bodily strength, though attended with such great delight in order to leave her still greater strength.'[1]

Because of the partial loss of the use of the external senses, this simple union of love is called incipient and imperfect ecstasy. Ecstasy, as we shall see, supposes the total suspension of the external senses, a suspension which is not produced by the prayer of simple union.

(3) The difference between the prayer of simple union and the prayer of quiet

(3) The difference between the prayer of simple union and the prayer of quiet is stated to be in many particulars by Thomas a Vallgornera. I shall mention only two (1) In the prayer of union all the powers of the soul are more often suspended from their natural operations, in order that, united entirely to God, they may with complacency attend to what they see and hear, and enjoy the interior delight; but in the prayer of quiet the intellect and imagination are more often wandering, and although they can be more easily recalled than in the prayer

[1] Her Life, chap xviii

of recollection, their temporary aberrations nevertheless afflict the soul, and disturb its quiet and peace. (2) In the prayer of quiet, the soul, dreaming as it were, doubts whether those things which it perceives are true or only the fictions of the imagination, or whether they are communications from God or from the demon transforming himself into an angel of light ; but in the prayer of union neither the imagination nor the memory nor the intellect can impede this good, nor can the demon mix himself up in it or impede its good effects That is. I think, the greatest consolation to the soul who may be favoured in this way

Scaramelli distinguishes the prayer of simple union from that of spiritual sleep by reminding us that in this latter all the powers are, as it were, asleep, but that in the former the intellect is wide awake, and very much alive by reason of the heavenly light which illumines it, and the will also is very excited and inflamed with the love of God He says that the great difference between the prayers already explained and the prayer of mystic union consists in this—that in the former the soul, although immersed in God, lives still to itself, and it is not transformed in God except in this prayer of union In the state of union alone can the soul truly say *I live, now not I, but Christ liveth in me* [1]

5. The wonderful effects of this simple union are explained by St. Theresa by the similitude of the silkworm, which is transformed into a butterfly ' As soon as in this prayer it [the worm or creature] becomes sufficiently dead to the world, it comes

<small>5 The effects of this kind of prayer</small>

---

[1] Gal ii 20

forth a white butterfly. Oh wonderful greatness of
God! How changed does the soul come forth by
having been only for a short time (never, in my
opinion, a full half-hour) immersed in the greatness
of God and united closely to Him! I tell you the
truth she now does not know herself, for you must
remember that there is the same difference here as
there is between an ugly worm and a beautiful
butterfly The soul knows not how she could merit
so great a favour or whence it could come She is
so desirous of praising God that she would be willing
to annihilate herself and endure a thousand deaths
for His sake. She immediately begins to wish to
endure great afflictions, and she cannot do otherwise ; her desires of penance, solitude, and of all
men knowing God, are excessive, and on this account
she feels great pain in seeing Him offended . .
Oh, how strange is it to behold afterwards the restlessness of this butterfly, though in all its life it was
never more at ease nor more calm! This is an occasion of praising our Lord, that it knows not where
to rest nor to settle, and having before enjoyed
such repose, it is disgusted with all that it sees on
earth, especially when God often allows it to drink
of this wine it gains more and more almost every
time. Now it no longer esteems the works which
it used to do when a worm, viz., forming its cell by
little and little. Its wings have now grown How,
then, as it is able to fly, can it take pleasure in
creeping along? All it can do for God seems little
in proportion to its desires. It does not wonder
much at what the Saints did and suffered, because
it understands by experience how our Lord assists
and transforms a soul in such a way that she does

THE DEGREES OF CONTEMPLATION 439

not seem the same nor to be of the same shape, because the weakness which she seemed to have before in doing penance she perceives is now no more, but has become strong. The ties which bound her to her friends, relations, or estate (which, when she was desirous of leaving, neither acts nor resolutions were sufficient to remove), are now entirely broken in such a manner that she is displeased to be obliged to do what is barely necessary in this respect, lest she might seem to be resisting the will of God.'[1]

The Saint also tells us regarding this union that in it 'God makes the soul quite stupid in order to imprint the deeper in her true wisdom; hence she neither sees nor hears nor understands nor perceives all the time she is in this state, and this time is short, and, indeed, it seems to her shorter than it is. God so fixes Himself in the interior of this soul that when she comes to herself she cannot but believe she was in God, and that God was in her. This truth is so deeply rooted in her that, though many years may pass away before God bestows the like favour upon her, she never forgets it.'[2]

6. Sacramelli treats of what he calls the *Divine touches* of the soul under this seventh degree, and thus connects them with the prayer of simple union, though, so far as I can understand, they may occur in all the higher degrees of contemplation, especially in all the degrees of mystical union. What Sacramelli calls *Divine touches* of the soul are those experiences which are designated spiritual impressions by St. John of the Cross.

6. The Divine touches of the soul explained

[1] 'Interior Castle,' Fifth Mansion, chap. ii
[2] *Ibid*, chap. i

To souls elevated to the mystical union are granted frequently spiritual touches or impressions, which consist in a true, real, but spiritual perception by which the soul feels God in its very centre and enjoys Him with great delight. In these the soul approaches to God, not only by an act of faith enlightened by the gift of wisdom (for, as the Angelical Doctor teaches, the gift of wisdom makes the contemplative soul near to God), but by a spiritual and experimental act it touches and feels God, as it were

For the explanation of these I have to refer to the Venerable Louis de Ponte, as I understand him to refer to these spiritual impressions when he writes as follows concerning the means by which God communicates Himself to souls in prayer

'As the body has its five exterior senses with which it perceives the visible and delectable things of this life, and takes experience of them, so the spirit, with its faculties of understanding and will, has five interior acts proportionable to these senses, which we call seeing, hearing, smelling, tasting, and touching spiritually, with which it perceives the invisible and delectable things of Almighty God, and takes experience of them, from which springs the experimental knowledge of God, which incomparably exceeds all the knowledge that proceeds from our reasonings, as the sweetness of honey is much better known by tasting a little of it than by using much reasoning to know it And so by these experiences mystical theology is obtained, which is the savoury wisdom and science of God, in such way that St. Denis says of divine Hierotheus that he had knowledge of Divine things, not only by the doctrine of the Apostles, nor only by his industry and discourse, but by *affection* and *experience* of them, which is obtained by means of the five interior senses, of which the Scripture makes much mention, and the holy Fathers, especially St. Augustine, SS. Gregory, Bernard, and others, whose sayings St. Bonaventure copiously alleges in his treating of the seven ways to eternity, in the sixth way.'

The venerable author then acknowledges that he borrows from St. Bonaventure's work somewhat of that which he states, and he goes on to explain the spiritual senses and how the soul may be said to *see, hear, smell, taste,* and *touch* God spiritually. When he comes to this last, he says

'The fifth manner of God's communicating Himself is by a spiritual *touching*—touching with His loving inspirations the recesses of the heart, and our Lord joining Himself to the soul with such gentleness and affection as cannot be expressed but by those similitudes of which the Book of Canticles makes mention, which I omit, lest our grossness should be dazzled with so much tenderness; but yet all rest in this saying of the Apostle St. Paul, that *he that is joined to the Lord* is become *one spirit* with Him,[1] for God interiorly embraces him with the arms of charity, and cherishes him, giving him inward testimonies of His presence, of the love that He bears him, and of the care that He has of him, with great tokens of peace and very familiar friendship. And whosoever perceives himself so favoured embraces within him God Himself with the arms of love, saying with the bride, *I held Him,* and *I will not let Him go.*[2] And here are

[1] 1 Cor. vi. 17.   [2] Cant. iii. 4.

exercised those tender colloquies, those petitions with groanings unspeakable, and those acts called *anagogical*, high elevated in matter of spirit, which our Lord grants of His singular grace to whom He pleases; but these have not to be ambitioned, but received when they shall be given, as already has been said.'[1]

7. Explanation of the mystical union by St John of the Cross

7. In further elucidation of, and as our guide in, this, as in all matters concerning the mystical union, let us attend to the following explanation of St. John of the Cross. He says

'We must therefore remember that from all these impressions, whether the Divine touches which cause them be rapid or continuous and successive, there flows frequently into the intellect the apprehension of knowledge or understanding, which is usually a most profound and sweet sense of God, to which, as well as to the impression from which it flows, no name can be given. This knowledge comes sometimes in one way, sometimes in another, now most deep and clear, again less so, according to the nature of the Divine touches which occasion the impressions, and according to the nature of the impressions of which it is the result.

'It is not necessary to waste words here in cautioning and directing the intellect, amid this knowledge, in faith to the Divine union For as these impressions are passively wrought in the soul, without any co-operation on its part, so also the knowledge which results from them is passively received by the intellect Philosophers apply the term "passible" to the intellect, independently of its

[1] 'Introduction to Mental Prayer,' chap. vi

own exertions. In order, therefore, to escape delusions here, and not hinder the benefits of these impressions, the intellect ought not to meddle with them, but to remain passive, inclining the will to consent freely and gratefully, and not interfering itself. For, as in the case of successive locutions, the activity of the intellect can very easily disturb and destroy this delicate knowledge, which is a sweet supernatural intelligence, which no natural faculty can reach or comprehend otherwise than by the way of recipient, and never by that of agent No effort, therefore, should be made, lest the intellect should fashion something of itself, and the devil at the same time effect an entrance into the soul with false and strange knowledge. He is well able to do this through the channel of these impressions, by taking advantage of the bodily senses Let the soul be resigned, humble, and passive, for as it receives passively the knowledge from God, so will He communicate it of His own good pleasure when He sees it humble and detached By so living the soul will put no obstacles in the way of the profitableness of this knowledge for the Divine union and that profitableness is great. All these touches are touches of union which is passively effected in the soul'[1]

[1] 'The Ascent of Mount Carmel,' book II, chap xxxii

CHAPTER V

THE EIGHTH AND NINTH DEGREES OF CONTEMPLATION

ST THERESA treats fully of ecstasies, trances, and raptures in the Sixth Mansion of the 'Interior Castle,' and I think most mystical writers since her time have made use of her instructions when treating on these subjects. I have, however, to continue the plan of the degrees of contemplation as adopted by Scaramelli, and to draw from the works of Benedict XIV. clear doctrine, reasons, and illustrations, in order to proceed with my subject in a manner to suit the plan of the work and to suit my own intelligence. The order adopted may be a little adorned and illustrated by extracts from St Theresa and other mystical writers.

EIGHTH DEGREE: ECSTATIC UNION.

1. Ecstatic union, Scaramelli says, is that mystical union which abstracts the soul entirely from the senses; not, however, with violence, but with sweetness. In this degree of prayer the use of the senses is entirely lost, as the word 'ecstasy' indicates. We have seen in the preceding chapter that, in the prayer of simple union, the external senses are left free, or, at all events, they are not entirely closed or

marginal note: 1. Ecstatic union

absorbed. In ecstasy they are altogether bound up, so as to be incapable of acting. St. Francis de Sales assigns the reason of this state when he says

'The attractions of the uncreated beauty and eternal goodness are infinitely sweet and amiable. Yet at the same time they are so powerful and efficacious, and so completely engage the attention of the mind, that they seem not only to fascinate, but even to ravish and carry the soul beyond her natural limits. When, on the other hand, we consider the ardour with which a soul in these circumstances yields to the Divine attractions, she seems not only to consent to their influence, but even to quit her natural sphere and bound into the bosom of God.'[1]

The distinction between simple union and ecstatic union is, as I have said, that in this latter the senses are asleep, and the soul is abstracted from them entirely, in the former, as we have seen, this is not the case. The abstraction or loss of the senses is not always a sign of ecstasy, because in the spiritual sleep the use of the senses is lost; but there is a great difference between this and ecstasy, because in the spiritual sleep all the powers of the soul and of the body are absorbed, but in ecstasy the intellect and will are illumined and very active. Besides, the supernatural communications made to the soul in ecstasy are far greater and more sublime than those communicated in spiritual sleep

2. Benedict XIV., quoting St Augustine and *The nature and St. Thomas, teaches us very definitely the nature character of ecstasy and character of ecstasy. According to this author, St. Augustine, describing ecstasy, says, 'It is the

[1] 'Treatise on the Love of God,' book vii, chap iv

withdrawal of the mind from the bodily senses'; and in another place he says: 'Ecstasy is a transport of the mind which sometimes results from fear, sometimes, too, through revelation, by withdrawing the mind from the bodily senses, so that the spirit may perceive what is shown to it. A person is said to be in ecstasy when he is beside himself This happens in two ways, according to the apprehensive and according to the appetitive faculty, as we shall show out of St Thomas. Ecstasy, in the faculty which subserves knowledge, is said to be or to exist *formally*, as they say, because by interior meditation on one subject the intellect is withdrawn from others ; in the appetitive power it exists *casually*, for the vehemence of the affection absorbs the soul, and suffers it not to have the control of itself Thus St. Thomas speaks " I reply that a man is said to be in ecstasy when he is beside himself, which happens relatively to the apprehensive and the appetitive faculty."

'With reference to the apprehensive faculty, a man is said to be beside himself when he is without the knowledge which belongs to him, either because he is raised to a higher state, as a man when he comprehends certain things which are above sense and reason is said to be in an ecstasy, in so far as he is beside the connatural apprehension of reason and sense, or because he is brought down to a lower, as when a man becomes furious or mad he is said to be in an ecstasy. With respect to the appetitive part, a man is said to be in an ecstasy when the desire of anything is carried to another, going in a certain way out of itself. The first ecstasy is caused by love, by way of disposition, in so far as it causes a man to meditate on the object loved An intense meditation on one subject withdraws him from others, but the second ecstasy is caused by love directly. St. Thomas furthermore teaches "That the vegetative powers of the soul do not operate through the soul being intent thereupon, as the sensitive powers, but in a natural way, and therefore in a rapture, abstraction therefrom is not necessary, as it is from the sensitive powers, by the operations of which the intentness of the soul upon intellectual understanding would be diminished."[1] This goes to show that the vegetative power does not necessarily cease its operations during ecstasy

3 According to Richard of St. Victor, Divine ecstasy may proceed from three sources—from admiration, from great joy, from great love—which Henry Harphius explains at length 'It is great admiration when the soul is led beyond itself, irradiated with the Divine light, sustained in admiration of the highest beauty, is thrown out of itself, and raised up to sublime things Great love is it when the human mind burns with so great a fire of heavenly desires that the flame of interior love, increasing above human measure, releases the soul from its former state, and raises it up to heavenly things. Great joy is it when the human mind, filled with the abundance of interior sweetness, utterly forgets what it is, what it was, and, carried away into a superhuman affection, becomes a stranger to itself.'[2]

3 Ecstasy proceeds from three sources

---

[1] 'Treatise on Heroic Virtue,' vol III., pp. 232-34, English translation

[2] Apud Benedict XIV, 'On Heroic Virtue,' vol III, p 267

With regard to the cessation of the vital and nutritive powers, the following note may be added.

'Although it is not essential to raptures and ecstasies that the vegetative and vital powers of the soul be impeded and bound up, as the sensitive and the animal powers are bound up, as St. Thomas says—because the vital powers do not, like the animal powers, require the soul or any general power to be intent upon them—nevertheless, because the spirits retire and collect themselves within by an operation so intense as that which takes place in an ecstasy, the vital operations also become impeded—that is, digestion and nutrition—as it clearly appears in him who immediately after meals betakes himself to study or any other mental exercise.'[1]

Ninth Degree. Rapture.

[Distinction between ecstasy and rapture]

1. According to St. Thomas, rapture is more than ecstasy: it is accompanied with violence. He thus speaks: 'Rapture involves something more than ecstasy, for ecstasy means "simply out of one's self," whereby a man is placed beyond his usual orderly condition; but rapture further involves violence. . . Silvius, however, says that violence is not essential to rapture, but that it is sufficient that it show something like violence.' Cardinal Bona explains the subject better: 'This, then, is the difference between rapture and ecstasy: this withdraws the mind from the senses more sweetly, the former more powerfully, and with a certain violence to the soul.

[1] Baldelli, quoted by Benedict XIV, 'Treatise on Heroic Virtue,' vol. iii, p. 247

most rapidly and powerfully withdraws it from sensible things, carries and bears it aloft to the intellectual vision and love of invisible things. The mystics explain this violence to be a certain violent motion of the body—namely, as when they who are abstracted from the senses are raised up into the air, and so remain for a time raised up from this earth. This explanation is adopted by Cardinal de Lauræa.

'It is enough to have pointed this out, for, according to Cardinal de Lauræa, the terms "ecstasy" and "rapture" are generally indiscriminately used, and Cardinal Durant has made the same observations: "We may assume it as certain that doctors in theology sometimes apply the terms 'ecstasy,' 'transport,' and 'rapture' to the same thing, and that even in the Holy Scriptures they are at times so used." Father Baldelli also says the same "The Holy Scripture speaks of ecstasy thus understood as being identical with transport and rapture, and they are mentioned as being the same, as St. Thomas observes, although the term 'rapture' expresses a certain force and violence, and yet it is more properly attributed to the intellect than to the will, as to suffer violence and force is more peculiar to the former than to the latter, according to the same holy Doctor." [1]

2. The teaching of Benedict XIV. as regards the different kinds of ecstasy is well and clearly summarized and expressed by Henri Joly in his work entitled 'The Psychology of the Saints':

'In his treatise on beatification and canonization Benedict XIV. distinguishes three kinds of ecstasy

[1] 'Treatise on Heroic Virtue,' vol iii, pp 237-239

natural ecstasy, which is a malady ; diabolic ecstasy, and Divine ecstasy

'In order to discern one from the other, it is necessary to watch the symptoms which precede the phenomenon, those which accompany it, and the results of whatever kind which follow upon it

(1) Natural ecstasy

'(1) If the ecstasy recurs periodically and at stated intervals, if in course of time the ecstatic becomes paralyzed, or is struck with apoplexy or any similar disease, if the ecstasy is followed by lassitude, inertness of the limbs, heaviness of the mind, intellectual density, and loss of memory, if the countenance becomes pale and livid and spiritual depression ensues, then we may be sure that the ecstasy was a purely natural one, we may be still more certain of it if, in consequence of earthly desires being aroused, the person becomes subject to fits of grief and pain.

(2) Diabolic ecstasy

'(2) Diabolic ecstasy may be recognised if the subject is a man of bad life, or if the attack is accompanied by excessive distortion of the limbs, by a disorderly (and not, as in the case of Divine ecstasy, a merely unusual) bodily disturbance, and still more if these movements are in the slightest degree unseemly. We may suspect diabolic ecstasy if the person can bring on or arrest the attack at will, if he speaks like a man whose mind is affected, if it appears as though someone else were speaking with his mouth (*quasi alius loquatur per eum*), if, after apparent alienation of mind, he is unable to repeat what he said, and, lastly, if the seizure comes on frequently in public places.

(3) Divine ecstasy

'(3) The absence of all the above symptoms is a testimony in itself to the Divine character of the ecstasy. All doubts will vanish if the words of the ecstatic tend only to excite others to the love of God, and if, when consciousness returns, he shows himself to be more and more strengthened in charity, humility, and in peace of mind

'Once admit that an ecstasy is Divine, and it is easy to see how much it owes to a supernatural agency. If, as our religion teaches us, the least virtue requires the help of grace, how great must be the grace required to produce states such as these! There are, however, spiritual causes which effect a sort of personal preparation for this sublime state. Benedict XIV. tells us of three (as above)—intensity of admiration, greatness of love, and strength of exaltation or joy. This does not sound very much like the state of collapse which many people consider to be the chief characteristic of ecstasy.

'With regard to the suspension of the functions of the organs and faculties, this author remarks "In all accounts given by the Saints (who have experienced ecstasies) we are able to distinguish between two orders of faculties or operations That the inferior operations, even breathing, are suspended is true It is also true that this state of the body may, according to the natural constitution and temperament of the person, be accompanied by phenomena which are absolutely similar to those produced by the different kinds of ecstasy doctors study and diagnose in their patients. But, in the words of St. Theresa, while the soul is asleep as regards earthly things, it is awake to the things of heaven. 'I have noticed,' she says, 'that the soul has never more light to understand the things of God than in this sort of rapture.' 'It is true,' she adds, 'that if anyone asks me how it is that, while our faculties and senses are as much suspended (in their operations) as if they were dead, we are able to hear or understand anything, I can only answer that this is a secret which God has reserved, with many another, to Himself.' She is none the less positive that during a rapture the soul feels itself to be illuminated. The understanding stays its discursive operations, but the will remains fixed in God by love—it rules as a sovereign. It is then that the apparent vacuum in the mind is filled up by visions. They are sometimes purely intellectual visions, which are rather an intense realization of the presence of God, and of the ineffable effects which it produces on the soul. More often they are visions of the imagination and of the inward sense. The latter, though no doubt more liable to illusions, are more in keeping with the weakness of our nature; for when the vision ceases, the soul, with the help of the images which still remain in the mind, is more able to recall the vanished scene." This author adds in a note "According to St. Theresa, intellectual visions last longer, and when they are thus protracted the state which accompanies them cannot properly be called an ecstasy." We shall treat of visions in the next part of our work

'We must not lose sight of these two characteristics of ecstasy in the Saints—the sleep of the senses, and the awakening of the higher faculties. If the former alone is present, it is a sign of false ecstasy; if the latter accompanies it, and because it does so, we recognise Divine ecstasy.'

I shall give one more extract from this author, in

which he contrasts the extraordinary phenomena of false and true mysticism

3. 'With regard to the extraordinary phenomena in false and true mysticism alike, the best authorities are agreed that in both cases there exists a fixed process, a connected whole, with which the unexpected occurrence blends itself without destroying the economy of nature nearly as much as is supposed It is highly probable that this occurrence is the culminating-point in a series of states, as well as the starting-point in a series of others; and the same may be said of certain decisive actions in everyday life, which are dependent upon a more than ordinary exercise of our free will. In like manner modern pathology teaches that, although the germ of disease may come from outside, it is none the less received by a prepared organism, which, according to the manner in which it is disposed, either preserves and develops or else eliminates it. Now take the case of the false mystic Unable to control his imagination, excessive in his austerities, and therefore subject to melancholy, covetous of exceptional favours, undisciplined in prayer, more anxious to love, and especially to think himself beloved, than to exercise himself in humility and patience, he in a way deserves to become the victim of illusions; and when they occur, he does his best to prolong their disastrous effects upon his faculties. The true mystic, on the contrary, is humble and prudent, and careful to preserve a just balance in all things. He is convinced that he ought to offer as well as ask, to give as well as receive, and therefore he "devotes himself to the service of God with manly courage."[1]

[side note: 3 The extraordinary phenomena of false and true mysticism contrasted]

[1] St Theresa

He will not acknowledge the Divine nature of his own visions, excepting in so far as they enable him to advance in virtue. He knows very well that in the matter of his own perfection, however large a share he may ascribe to the action of God, he can never arrive at it without personal effort He perseveres in his efforts in spite of all the obstacles he encounters, both in himself and from others

'He is well aware of these obstacles, for in this, no less than in other things, it is astonishing to see with what certainty, good sense, and accuracy the Saints have detected, treated, and cured false ecstasy. They know the symptoms well The mixture of physical weakness and dreariness, that prostration of strength increased by a collapse of will-power, that melancholy in which the soul is either beguiled or tyrannized over by fixed ideas, those illusions of the imagination in which an ordinary fainting-fit is mistaken for ecstasy, that half-wished-for state of delusion which is the offspring of a mysticism in which pride has too large a share, or of desires, ill sustained by a defective energy and prudence. The Saints have described all this, dreading it both for themselves and for those they had to direct.'[1]

The above remarks may serve to guide us in detecting false ecstasy better than laying down any minute rules for particular cases, and they may serve also as prudent admonitions for all who may have experienced these marvellous communications, and for those who have to deal with such favoured souls.

On the authority of Benedict XIV, who quotes

[1] 'Pyschology of the Saints,' chap iii, p 87 *et seq*

from authentic records, we may state some other characteristics of Divine ecstasies.

4 (1) The signs of a Divine ecstasy are principally to be derived from his conduct who is subject to them. A Divine ecstasy takes place with the greatest tranquillity of the whole man, both outwardly and inwardly. He who is in a Divine ecstasy speaks only of heavenly things, which move the bystanders to the love of God; on returning to himself he appears humble and, as it were, ashamed; overflowing with heavenly consolation, he shows cheerfulness in his face and security in his heart, he does not delight at all in the presence of bystanders, fearing lest he should thereby obtain the reputation of sanctity; for the most part, while he is at prayer or at Mass, or after receiving the Eucharist, or while he hears of God or paradise, he falls into an ecstasy or trance.

<small>4 Some other characteristics of Divine ecstasies</small>

(2) Divine raptures are not long, but frequently brief, as Cardinal Bona and Thomas of Jesus show. The circumstances which precede, attend, and follow ecstasies are to be diligently considered.

(3) 'The ecstatic and the rapt remember what has happened to them during their ecstasy and rapture.' On this point it has to be remarked, if through want of a perfect memory, or want of power to relate those things which he saw, the ecstatic cannot tell or write his experience, we are not to conclude that the ecstasy was not a true one. As Pignatelli observes, God does not grant to the ecstatic the power of relating, unless it be his duty to prophesy and reveal for the good of others. Wherefore St. Paul speaks of himself in his rapture, that *he heard secret words which it is not granted to*

man to utter, of which Tertullian says: 'The condition of them was that they were to be revealed to no man,' which is confirmed by Cardinal de Lauræa'

<small>5 Whether the acts of an ecstatic are meritorious</small>

5 It is a question among theologians whether the ecstatic gains merit by acts of the intellect during the ecstasy, as seeing, and of the will, as loving Cardinal de Lauræa says that the ecstatics gain merit by the acts which precede the ecstasy, as they are free, employed upon a good object and circumstances as are the other acts of religion and faith, but that they gain no merit by those acts which occur during the ecstasies, for these are not free. Suarez, on the contrary, maintains that they are free, and therefore meritorious, and herein he is followed by Father Anthony of the Annunciation and Gravina. From what has been said of the merit of acts performed during the prayer of simple union, we may conclude with Suarez that the acts which occur during ecstasy are meritorious Freedom *quoad specificationem* is not required, nor is freedom to sin required for merit, and how could we suppose those most fervent acts of the will performed through God's special grace during such a favoured time to go without merit?

<small>6 Spiritual espousals between God and the soul</small>

6 What is designated by mystical writers as the spiritual espousals between God and the soul takes place in this degree of contemplation and during rapture. It is signified by St. John of the Cross in the 'Spiritual Canticle,' stanza xiv., where, speaking of a very high estate and union of love whereunto God is wont to elevate the soul, he calls it the spiritual espousals of the Word, the Son of God And he says: 'In the very beginning of this, the

first time that God so elevates the soul, He reveals to it great things of Himself, makes it beautiful in majesty and grandeur, adorns it with graces and gifts, and endows it with honour, and with the knowledge of Himself, as a bride is adorned on the day of her espousals. On this happy day the soul not only ceases from its anxieties and loving complaints, but is, moreover, adorned with all grace, entering into a state of peace and delight, and of the sweetness of love, in praise of the magnificence of the Beloved, which the soul recognises in Him, and enjoys in the union of the espousals.'

By way of explaining these words of St. John of the Cross and the reason of the name 'espousals,' Scaramelli says that God takes to Himself some specially loved souls as His spouses, and in the prayer of rapture enters into espousals with them, and this has happened sometimes with external tokens and signs which are used in celebrating earthly espousals This is narrated of St. Catherine of Siena, of St. Catherine, Virgin and Martyr, St Magdalen of Pazzi, St. Angela of Foligno, of whom it is narrated that God placed a ring on their fingers in token of love and of mutual fidelity.

In further explanation of the application of this name, it has to be noted that holy souls who are consecrated to God by vows are called the spouses of Christ, although they have not been elevated to the mystical union, but it is not of these we speak here. The true spouses of Christ are those privileged souls whom God by rapture introduces into the presence of His majesty, and unites Himself to them as a sign or pledge of future spiritual matrimony, and who are in this way transformed into a more perfect image of their Divine Spouse and wholly consecrated to Him. Thus it is espousals are celebrated between God and the soul. This union, although most close and intimate, is not yet spiritual or mystical matrimony, because it is yet separable, and the spiritual matrimony for which the espousals are a preparation may be called in a certain sense the inseparable union of the soul and God.

When it is said of certain souls that the espousals had been celebrated in a visible or sensible form, or by some sensible sign, such as the putting the ring on the finger, we have to understand that the name of 'espousals' cannot strictly be given to the visible or sensible apparition. This can be regarded only as a sign of the espousals to be celebrated in future or already celebrated between the soul and God. This Divine espousal can only be celebrated spiritually. God is a Spirit. The soul, called to the intimate union which is called espousal, must be divested of everything of an inferior nature, that in spirit alone it may be united with the Divine Spirit

7. The effects of the spiritual espousals

7. This great privilege may perhaps be better known to ordinary people by what the Saints tell us of its effects, some of which are bestowed on the soul during the union, others are experienced afterwards. During the union or rapture, the soul, with all its powers and acts, is submerged, absorbed, and lost in an abyss of light, serenity, peace, and of interior quiet and sweetness, and then, as St. Theresa tells us, after a man has returned to himself, for one, or two, or even three days the powers will remain

bewildered and absorbed, and, as it were, engulfed in God—that is, if the rapture has been great [1] God opens up to the espoused soul His secrets; He shows her a vision of the eternal kingdom, and of immortal glory united with a joy that cannot be imagined. He imparts to her sublime and most pure intellectual visions. He infuses into her clear, subtle, and elevated notions of Himself and His perfections, which bring with them great relish, great joy and sweetness, so that the soul seems to enjoy the heavenly beatitude, not only by seeing it, but by a foretaste of it. The visions may also be imaginary, but of a very exalted nature, and I cannot better represent those imaginary and intellectual visions than in the words of the great St. Theresa, who experienced and enjoyed them. Writing after one of these raptures, she says of the soul, 'It seems to her that she has been altogether in another region quite different from this world in which we live, and there another light is shown her very different from this here below; and though she should employ all her life long in trying to form an idea of this and other wonders, yet it would be impossible to understand them. She is in an instant taught so many things together that, though she should spend many years in arranging them in her thoughts and imagination, she could not remember the one-thousandth part of them. This is not an intellectual but an imaginary vision, and it is seen with the eyes of the soul much better than we see things here with the eyes of the body, and without words certain things are discovered to her. If she should see any of the Saints, she knows them as

[1] Her Life, chap. xx

well as if she had conversed with them for a length of time.

'At other times, together with what she beholds with the eyes of the soul, other wonders are there represented to her by the "intellectual vision," particularly a multitude of Angels with their Lord, and without seeing anything with her corporal eyes, by a wonderful knowledge which I cannot express, this of which I am speaking and many other things are represented to her which are not to be mentioned Whoever shall experience these things himself, and shall have better abilities than I possess, may perhaps be able to explain them, however difficult they may appear to be. Whether all these things take place in the body or no I cannot say; at least, I would not swear it is in the body, nor that the body is without the soul'

The soul is not severed from the body even in a Divine ecstasy or rapture, for though it be certain that the Divine power could sever it therein and again restore it to the body, and whether it so happened or not when St. Paul was in ecstasy or rapture, he confesses that he knew not. It is not necessary that the separation of soul and body should attend upon a Divine ecstasy, seeing that God, in virtue of His infinity, is present to every soul, and so may reveal to it what He wishes to reveal in ecstasy without severing it from the body, and as we never read that the souls of so many prophets who have been in ecstasies, and so many other servants of God who have been entranced, were separated from their bodies.[1]

'I have often thought how, when the sun is in the

[1] Ita Benedict XIV, 'Treatise on Heroic Virtue,' vol. iii, p 236

heavens, his rays have such force that without the sun changing his place they immediately reach this world, and so it is here, for the soul and the spirit (which are one and the same, just as the sun and the rays are), though remaining in her place—that is, in the body—may by virtue of the heat communicated to her from the true Sun of Justice soar above herself in the superior part.'

Speaking of the effects upon the soul after such raptures, the Saint says:

'As the soul is, as it were, out of herself, as far as I can understand, great secrets are revealed to her, and when she returns to her senses, it is with such immense gain, and with such contempt for all earthly things, that everything seems mean to her in comparison with what she has seen.' Ever after she lives in the world with great regret, and she cares not at all for any of those things which once used to seem beautiful to her. It seems as if our Lord was pleased to show her something of that land towards which she is going (as those of the people of Israel who were sent beforehand to the land of promise brought back things that showed the nature of the country), in order that she may endure the difficulties of this journey, and may know where she must hasten to find repose. And though that which passes away so quickly may seem to you not very profitable, yet so great are the benefits it leaves in the soul that he only who has experienced them can tell their worth. Hence we may clearly see that these things do not come from the devil, and that they should come from our own imagination is impossible, since the devil can represent nothing which leaves in the soul such great effects. Such peace, such quiet and profit, and especially three things, are left in a high degree.

'The first is a knowledge of the greatness of God, for the more we see of it the more we are able to understand it. The second is the knowledge of ourselves, and humility in considering how base we are in comparison with the Creator of so many wonderful things, and how we have dared to offend Him, how we dare not look upon Him. The third is a contempt for all earthly things, unless there be some she can apply to the service of so great a God

'These are the jewels which the Spouse begins to give His bride, and they are so valuable that she will be most careful of them, for these visions are so engraven in her memory that I believe it is impossible for her to forget them till she gets possession of them for ever, unless it be through her own fault. But the Spouse who gives them to her is able to bestow His grace upon her, so that she may never lose them But to return to the courage of which she stands in need, do you think it so trifling a matter? The soul really seems separated from the body because she sees the senses lost, and does not understand for what purpose It is necessary, then, that He Who gives all the other gifts should give *this* also You will reply "This fear is well rewarded." I say the same. May He be blessed for ever Who can give so liberally, and may His Majesty be pleased to grant that we may be worthy to serve Him.'[1]

I may conclude this chapter in the poetic language of St John of the Cross, enriched as it is with Scripture quotations ·

[1] 'Interior Castle' Sixth Mansion, chap v

'Such, then, is the state of the blessed soul in the bed of flowers, where all these blessings and many more are granted it. The seat of that bed is the Son of God, and the hangings of it are the charity and love of the Bridegroom Himself. The soul now may say, with the bride *His left hand is under my head*.[1] And we may therefore say in truth that such a soul is clothed in God and bathed in the Divinity, and that not, as it were, on the surface, but in the interior spirit; and filled with the Divine delights in the abundance of the spiritual waters of life, it experiences that which David says of those who have drawn near unto God *They shall be inebriated with the plenty of Thy house, and Thou shalt make them drink of the torrent of Thy pleasure, for with Thee is the fountain of life*.[2] This fulness will be in the very being of the soul, seeing that its drink is nothing else than the torrent of delight, which is the Holy Spirit, as it is written *And he showed me a river of water of life clear as crystal, proceeding from the throne of God and the Lamb*.[3] The waters of this river, which is the very love of God, pour into the soul and make it drink of the torrent of love, which is the spirit of the Bridegroom infused into the soul in union Thence the soul in the overflowing of love sings the following stanza:

> '" In the innermost cellar
> Of my beloved have I drunk, and when I went forth
> Over all the plain
> I knew nothing,
> And lost the flock I followed before "'[4]

---

[1] Cant ii 6 [2] Ps. xxxv. 9, 10 [3] Apoc xxii 1.
[4] A 'Spiritual Canticle,' Stanza xxvi

CHAPTER VI

THE TENTH DEGREE OF CONTEMPLATION

TENTH DEGREE: PERFECT UNION OR SPIRITUAL MARRIAGE

<small>1 Spiritual marriage explained in general</small>

1. ST. THOMAS speaks of spiritual marriage when explaining the words of St Paul: *This is a great Sacrament, but I speak in Christ and in the Church*[1] He says that the Sacrament of which the Apostle writes, that of matrimony, is a great Sacrament—that is, a sign of a sacred thing, namely, of the union of Christ and the Church. According to this holy Doctor, the words of the Apostle signify chiefly spiritual marriage, although secondarily they signify the Sacrament instituted by our Lord, or the sanctification of the union of wedlock. This is a holy state, and it signifies the union of Christ with His Church, and it is from this resemblance and through the grace of the Sacrament that the blessings of human marriage are secured. Christ is not only the Spouse of the Church, but He is the Spouse of the soul.

'When Adam slumbered, God drew from his side a helpmeet to him, and being altogether made for him, soul and body, inexplicable without him.

[1] Eph v 32

God drew the soul of man from His own side, and she is restless till she returns thither again. The soul is God's spouse, made for His embrace, made to bring forth in herself His Word, His Image, His beloved Son; and the passion of the purest and noblest heart of man is but the far-removed symbol of the ardent love of God for His spouse. To Him her whole being cries out : " Thou hast made me for Thyself as the casket for the jewel, as the mirror for the sun, as the eye for light, as the ear for sound, as the harp for music My mind craves for truth, and Thou art the Truth, my will for good, and Thou art the Good; my heart for love, and Thou art Love; mine eye for beauty, and Thou art the Beautiful, my ear for music, and Thou art Song; my soul for eternity, life, and salvation, and Thou art Eternity, Life, and Salvation."[1]

Thus writes the Rev George Tyrrell of the soul and her spouse

In general, the union of the Holy Ghost with the Church and with just souls is called spiritual and Divine marriage, and the Church and just souls are called the spouses of the Holy Ghost. The Holy Ghost unites souls to God by charity, as He is the Love of the Father and the Son. It is He Who vivifies our souls by grace, as He is the *life-giving Spirit*. And it is for these reasons that He is called the Spouse of the Church in general, and of each faithful soul in particular.

Besides giving love and fecundity, the Holy Ghost promises and imparts to His spouses the most excellent gifts. He unites them so closely to

[1] 'Hard Sayings,' by Father Tyrrell, S J 'The Soul and her Spouse'

Himself that He makes them partakers of the Divine Nature,[1] and He raises them up to His own condition and dignity. It is by Him that the Church and devout souls are adorned and enriched by the Divine gifts of wisdom, understanding, fortitude, counsel, knowledge, piety, and the fear of the Lord. It is by Him that the Church and just souls are made fruitful and beget so many spiritual children, and produce so many examples of virtue, the fruits of good works performed through the vivifying force of sanctifying grace. It is He, in fine, Who protects the Church and her devout children by sheltering them under His special care, and by making them trust in His almighty and Divine power.

Our Saviour is also called the Spouse of the Church and of souls, and the expression 'spiritual marriage' may with greater reason, be applied to Him than to the Holy Ghost, because of the hypostatic union of the Word with human nature, and the real and affectionate union of Jesus Christ with our souls in the Holy Communion. In the sacred Scriptures we find the name Spouse of the Church and of our souls more often applied to our Saviour than to the Holy Ghost. The Church is called the Body of which Christ is the Head. He has promised to remain always with her, even to the end of time. She is His fruitful spouse, the mother of countless children, whom she has brought forth and nurtured in her virginal bosom. They are more numerous than the stars of the firmament, and they fill heaven and earth, so that we may address to her the words of the prophet *Lift up thy eyes round about, and see:*

---

[1] 2 Pet 1 4   See 'Manual of Ascetical Theology,' pp 37-39

all these are gathered together, they are come to thee: thy sons shall come from afar, and thy daughters shall rise up at thy side[1]

The nuptials of the Divine Lamb are not confined to the Church in general; they are contracted with all the faithful who are her perfect members by charity, and especially at the time when they receive Him in the Holy Eucharist. By this Sacrament, and by His heavenly gifts communicated through it, He unites Himself entirely to us in the closest of unions. He demands gifts from us, faith, hope, and charity; but these gifts He Himself has given, and He continues to increase them and all other holy virtues in our souls. When we think of this special union with our Saviour, and the intimate union established between our souls and the Three Divine Persons of the Blessed Trinity by grace and charity, we can understand fully the sense in which spiritual marriage is used in sacred Scripture and in the writings of the Fathers of the Church, and the sense in which our souls are called the spouses of God, and especially of our Saviour Jesus Christ.

After these few words of explanation to show the appropriateness of the expression *spiritual marriage* as applied to just souls in general, we may proceed to consider it as applied by mystical writers to the highest degree of contemplation.

2. The union of the soul with God is accomplished by grace, but its full enjoyment is reserved for glory. Nevertheless, even here below God imparts, when it is His good pleasure, to some favoured souls a perception or consciousness more or less vivid of His alliance with them. When this consciousness

[2] The nature of spiritual marriage in its mystical sense, and its difference from spiritual espousals

[1] Isa. lx. 4.

is transitory, it is either simple or ecstatic union, according as the soul remains mistress of itself or is thrown into a rapture which suspends the use of the senses and of its powers.

When this consciousness becomes continual and permanent, we have what is called the spiritual marriage, or the most perfect union of the soul with God which it can experience here below. It is this most elevated state which St. Theresa describes in the seventh and last mansion of the 'Interior Castle' It is from this work chiefly, the fruit of the experience of the Saint, that we have to learn most of those things taught by mystics concerning this highest degree of contemplation

From this work we learn, in the first place, the difference between spiritual marriage and the spiritual espousals. Spiritual marriage is a *permanent* perception or consciousness, as I have said, of the presence of God in the soul and His union with it, while the spiritual espousals is a transitory feeling or perception of that presence which ceases with the Divine motion which causes it.

Writing of the spiritual marriage, St. Theresa says

'More cannot be said [of this state, as far as can be understood] than that the soul becomes one with God; for, as He Himself is a spirit, His Majesty is pleased to discover the love He has for us by making certain persons understand how it extends, in order that we may praise His greatness, because He has vouchsafed to unite Himself to a creature in such a way, that as in the marriage state husband and wife can no more be separated, so He will never be separated from the soul. The spiritual espousals is different, for this is often dissolved, and so also is

THE DEGREES OF CONTEMPLATION

union; for though "union" is the joining of two things into one, they may at last be divided, and may exist apart. We generally see that this favour of our Lord quickly passes away, and the soul afterwards does not enjoy that company—that is, so as to know it. But in that other favour of our Lord this is not the case, for the soul always remains with her God in that centre.'

The Saint also teaches us that the difference between the spiritual marriage and the spiritual espousals is to be known not only from the respective duration of the sense of these unions, but also from their intensity, that of the spiritual marriage surpassing all other unions in its intensity, and this she illustrates as follows·

'Let us suppose "union" to be two *tapers*, so exactly joined together that the light of both make but one light; or that the wick, light, and wax are all one and the same, but that afterwards one taper may be easily divided from the other, and then two distinct tapers will remain, and the wick will be distinct from the wax. But here [in the spiritual marriage] it is like water descending from heaven to a river or spring, where one is so mixed with the other that it cannot be discovered which is the river water and which the rain-water. It is also like a small rivulet running into the sea, whose waters cannot be separated from each other, or as if there were two windows in a room at which one great light entered, but which, though entering divided, yet makes but one light within. This is, perhaps, that which St Paul means when he says, *He who adheres to God is one with Him*, alluding to this sublime marriage, which presupposes that God is united to the soul by union. He likewise says *Mihi vivere Christus est, et mori lucrum* (To me to live is Christ, and to die is gain.) I think the soul may say the same here.'[1]

As to the permanent character of the consciousness of this union, it may be asked whether it is to be understood in its strict sense. No. The permanence is not to be understood as if the presence of the Holy Trinity were constantly manifested to the soul with the same perfection and with the same evidence as on the first and subsequent occasions when the favour is bestowed upon the soul. If it were to continue in that way, the soul could never do anything else, and it could not live amongst men. It should go out of the world. But although the vision of the Holy Trinity is not always in the same high degree and with the same intensity, the soul, nevertheless, every time that it thinks of itself finds itself in this Divine company. The example is given of a person who, being in the company of others in a bright apartment, when the windows of the apartment are closed he cannot see those present, but he knows and feels certain of their presence. Thus it happens to the soul which has reached this degree of union. It may be further asked whether the soul can return to the vision at will or whenever it pleases. The answer is, No; this is not in the power of the soul. It is our Lord alone who can again open the windows of the understanding and impart the spiritual light and vision, and there is no such thing as a habit imparted to any soul by which it can elicit the acts of spiritual marriage at will. We have no example of a habitual state of this

[1] 'Interior Castle' Seventh Mansion, chap. ii.

THE DEGREES OF CONTEMPLATION

union other than the state of sanctifying grace in which the soul is constituted by Almighty God. 'You must not suppose, Sisters,' says St Theresa, 'that the effects I have mentioned are always in the same degree in these souls, for on this account I said that our Lord sometimes leaves them in their natural condition.'[1]

3. The impression or feeling of the presence of God and of the Divine union does not exclude every interruption, either the interruptions caused by natural sleep, which suspends the exercise of the contemplative life, or the interruptions when awake caused by external occupations and duties which demand attention. Schram observes that it is only in comparison with the inferior degrees of union, in which God appears only rarely and, as it were, furtively, that spiritual marriage is said to be a stable and permanent state. But it may be called a permanent union even though the soul has not consciousness of it by absolute continuity, just as two loving souls who are faithful to each other and who are rarely absent from each other may be said to be always together and never separated. We may understand the sense of the permanent nature of this union better after we know how the union is effected. According to St. Theresa, the spiritual marriage is effected by a special visitation of the Blessed Trinity and its indwelling in the centre of the soul, and by a special union of the soul with the Word Incarnate. Let us read the description in her own words:

How spiritual marriage is to be understood as a stable and permanent state

'When she [the soul] is brought into this mansion by an intellectual vision, all the Three Persons of the

[1] 'Interior Castle'. Seventh Mansion, chap. iv.

Most Holy Trinity discover themselves to her by a certain way of representing this truth. This is accompanied with a certain inflaming of the soul, which comes upon her like a cloud of extraordinary brightness. These Three Persons are distinct, and by a wonderful knowledge given to the soul she, with great truth, understands that all these Three Persons are one substance, one knowledge, and one God alone. Hence, what we behold with faith the soul here (as one may say) understands by sight, though this sight is not with the eyes of the body, because it is not an imaginary vision. All the Three Persons here communicate themselves to her, and speak to her, and make her understand those words mentioned in the Gospel, where our Lord said that He, and the Father, and the Holy Ghost, would come and dwell with the soul that loves Him and keeps His commandments.

'O my Lord! what a different thing is the hearing and believing of these words, from understanding in this way how true they are! Such a soul is every day more astonished, because these words never seem to depart from her, but she clearly sees (in the manner above mentioned) that they are in the deepest recess of the soul (how it is she cannot express, since she is not learned), and she perceives the Divine company in herself.

'You may imagine that the soul is so out of herself, and so absorbed, that she can attend to nothing. On the contrary, she is more occupied than formerly, in whatever relates to the service of God; and when she is not engaged, she is still with this delightful company; and if the soul be not wanting to God, He will never fail (in my opinion) manifestly to discover His presence to her, will not forsake her, so that she should lose it, and well may she think so, though she does not cease to use more care than ever in endeavouring not to displease Him in anything.'[1]

4 Besides the vision of the Holy Trinity in the interior of the soul, according to the teaching of St. Theresa there appears to be also a twofold vision of the sacred humanity of our Lord, one imaginary, and the other intellectual The Saint says · [The twofold vision of our Lord in this state]

'The first time God bestows this favour His Majesty is pleased to discover Himself to the soul by an imaginary vision of His most sacred humanity, in order that she may fully understand it, and be not ignorant that she receives so immense a gift To others He may appear in another form, to her of whom we speak[2] our Lord showed Himself immediately after she had communicated, in a figure of great splendour, beauty, and majesty, just as He was after His resurrection. He said to her, that now was the time she should consider His affairs as hers, and that He would take care of hers. Other words were uttered, more fit to be felt than spoken '

After this she speaks of an intellectual vision of our Lord which is proper to the spiritual marriage She says that that which is experienced in this is far different from any other union. For our Lord appears in the centre of the soul, not by an imaginary, but an intellectual vision, though it is more subtle than those I have mentioned before. Such did He appear to the Apostles, without

[1] 'The Interior Castle' Seventh Mansion, chap 1
[2] The Saint, no doubt, alludes to herself Ibid, chap 11

entering in at the door, when He said to them, *Pax vobis.*[1] I must note that the apparition to the Apostles was very sensible and external, and the Saint here probably means that the entering in through the gift of His glorified body—*subtility*—signifies in some way the imperceptible manner of His appearance in the soul by the intellectual vision, and the manner of His entering therein.

I may also, in this place, again call attention to the special sense in which the Divine word may be called the Spouse of the soul by reason of His sacred humanity. When we say that the Word Incarnate has the special relation of spouse towards souls united to God by sanctifying grace and all the degrees of grace, we must always bear in mind that there is not physically or in reality any manner of union of the soul with the Son that excludes the Father and the Holy Ghost, or any union effected by grace in our souls that is not common to the Three Divine Persons. The Holy Ghost is called the Spouse of our souls by appropriation in one sense, and the Son may by appropriation in the sense explained—namely, by reason of His union with humanity—be called also the Spouse of our souls. This doctrine in no way can affect what mystical writers say with regard to the intellectual vision of the Word Incarnate and the spiritual alliance of the soul with Him, because this signifies that the favoured soul in contemplation experiences, perceives, and, as it were, feels these operations of grace and their manifestation; whilst others, who are not contemplatives, and who have never had a vision, may in reality possess the same perfect

[1] 'Interior Castle' Seventh Mansion, chap. ii

union and alliance with the Spouse of their souls, Christ Jesus, as well as with the whole Trinity of Persons. We may from this explanation understand what follows, which, according to Lejeune, is an extract from Scaramelli

5 'In short, two things only seem essential to the perfect union of which we treat the first is the intellectual manifestation of the Most Holy Trinity and the consciousness of the indwelling of the Three Persons in the centre of the soul, the second is, the revelation of the Word, also by intellectual vision, with speech and testimonies which assure the soul that He has raised it to the dignity of His spouse. It does not signify whether the two apparitions be simultaneous or whether one be before the other, provided the alliance between the Word and the soul be entered into in the presence of the Holy Trinity Nevertheless, according to the logical order, it is the Trinity which appears first, in order to prepare the soul for this union, and in testimony of it.'[1]

In the compendium of Scaramelli by Voss I find the following further explanation given in reference to this matter 'Although the imaginary vision of our Redeemer, according to the narratives of St. Theresa, ordinarily occurs in this supreme union, I do not think it is necessary, nor that it intervenes always It seems to me sufficient that there be perceived the intellectual vision of the Trinity, by which the indwelling of God in the soul is established, and the intellectual vision of the Divine Word, together with the spiritual locution,

<small>5 The two things essential to this perfect union</small>

[1] Scaramelli, apud Lejeune, 'Manuel de Theologie Mystique,' p 210

by which the mutual and reciprocal consent is signified, and by which is indicated the indissoluble union of love between these spirits—the soul and Christ. And even though the imaginary vision of the sacred humanity of our Redeemer intervene, we have to understand that the close union is with the Word alone, spirit with Spirit, and not a bodily union St. Bernard and St. John of the Cross in declaring the substance of this union make no mention of the imaginary vision, but speak of the Word and the Divinity alone. I do not, therefore, consider the imaginary vision necessary, but only the intellectual vision, and this I consider necessary and sufficient"[1]

[1] Voss, 'Compend Scaramelli,' p 330

CHAPTER VII

THE GRACES AND EFFECTS OF THE SPIRITUAL MARRIAGE

1. THEOLOGIANS consider the grace granted to the soul in the spiritual marriage as a new mission of the Holy Ghost to the soul. The ordinary and common increase of grace does not constitute a new mission of the Holy Ghost, but, according to the teaching of theologians, extraordinary graces, and even graces *gratuitously given*, do signify a new mission, and as a consequence this great grace, which holds the highest place among extraordinary favours, is to be regarded as a new mission of the Holy Ghost to the soul. This signifies a new and sublime manner of indwelling of the Most Holy Trinity in the centre of the soul. [1. Spiritual marriage signifies or implies a new mission of the Holy Ghost]

2. We are not to suppose that the soul thus favoured is thereby rendered entirely impeccable, for it can notwithstanding its special favour fall into defects, and even into great sins, and thus turn away from its heavenly Spouse. There is no physical impossibility of separating the soul from God, because it retains its liberty; but there is a certain moral impossibility by reason of this most perfect union with God. The soul, as we have learned, before this union has put away all evil habits and over- [2. Whether the soul in this state is impeccable]

come all evil passions through the help of grace. It has accustomed itself to the exercise of all virtues, and even attained to heroic degrees in this respect. Moreover, God never unites to Himself in this holy union a soul that is not first prepared by a series of special and efficacious graces that it may be able to respond faithfully to His love. For these reasons we may say that, though the soul can, absolutely speaking, sin, it is not likely to do so, and it may be said to be morally impossible for it to be so perfidious and unfaithful. If we add to these the consideration of the graces and favours bestowed by God upon the soul in this exalted state, the familiar manner in which He reveals to it His Divine secrets, the manner of His intimate dwelling in the very centre of the soul, and the consciousness of that indwelling, it seems almost impossible for such a soul with full deliberation to choose that which is evil and to neglect the exercise of virtue, to which it is with so much fervour and devotion attracted and impelled.[1] We may therefore hold that the soul is impeccable whilst the act of perfect union lasts; but we need not hold that outside that act it is always so intent upon God and so united to Him that it may not fall into some imperfections and venial sins. The venial sins, however, when committed by such souls are usually without full advertence.

Ecstasies and raptures in this degree

3. Mystical authors agree in stating that the phenomena of ecstasy or rapture, though not impossible in the spiritual marriage, are extremely rare. St. Theresa says in regard to this subject:

'I am astonished to see that, when the soul gets

[1] Voss, 'Compend Scaramelli,' p 324

so far, all raptures are taken from her, except at some few times. This taking away of the raptures, which I here speak of, relates to the exterior effects which these cause—such as losing our sense and heat, though some persons tell me that these are merely accidents of the raptures, which in reality are not taken away, since the interior effect is rather increased. Hence, the raptures cease in the manner I have mentioned, and there are no more ecstasies nor flights of the spirit, if they come at all, it is very seldom, and almost never in public, nor do the great opportunities of devotion given to her help her herein as they once used to do; hence, if she beheld a devout picture, or heard a sermon (which seemed almost as if she did not hear it), or listened to music, she was so troubled, like the poor butterfly, that everything frightened her and made her take wing.'[1]

The reason of this is quite intelligible, because the cause of ecstasy is the insufficiency of the power of the soul to respond both to the visions which ravish it and to the organic functions from without at the same time, but when the interior powers grow stronger and it becomes accustomed to the supernatural communications, then it can contemplate without failing or weakness the visions which before caused the rapture or ecstasy

4 The question is asked whether the soul in the enjoyment of the spiritual marriage can be certain of its salvation It is certain, and of faith, that no one can be certain of His salvation without a special revelation from God Such a revelation, we know, can put at rest all the doubts and uncertainty of the

[1] 'Interior Castle' Seventh Mansion, chap III

soul on this question. God can assuredly grant this favour, in order to render the practice of heroic virtues and the bearing of severe trials more sweet and easy to His elect. The question to be decided is whether God gives this special revelation to all souls who are raised up by Him to the degree of union known as spiritual marriage. On this point, according to Lejeune, mystical authors are divided. Some attribute to the mystical marriage only those choice graces which render their fall more difficult, but leave them uncertain as to their salvation. Others believe that God in the sublime act of spiritual marriage reveals to the soul its state of grace and its predestination. St. Theresa explains herself on this point. She says

'I may seem to mean that the soul by obtaining this favour becomes *secure* as regards her salvation, and does not afterwards relapse But I do not say any such thing, and whenever I speak on this subject, and seem to mean that the soul is secure, my words must be understood thus : so long as the Divine Majesty holds her in His hands, and she does not offend Him. I know for certain that, though she see herself in this state, and though it may continue some years, she does not therefore think herself secure, but, rather, she has greater fears than formerly, and is more careful to avoid any small offence against God . . . She also has such ardent desires of seeing Him, and such continual pain and confusion to see how little she does, and how much she is obliged to do, that it is no small cross, but a great mortification ; for, in doing penance, the greater it is the more delight does the soul feel.'[1]

[1] 'Interior Castle : Seventh Mansion, chap. ii

The certainty and security may be experienced when the soul is engaged in the act of this highest degree of contemplation, but God permits it afterwards at other times to have fears and doubts about its experiences and revelations, or it is permitted to forget this particular revelation as to its salvation so that it may continue to work out the great affair of salvation in fear and trembling. That which limits this certitude with regard to salvation to the time of the act of perfect union seems to be the more probable opinion.

5 The following enumeration of some of the effects of the spiritual marriage may be given according to the teaching of St. Theresa and St John of the Cross.

5. The effects of the spiritual marriage

The first effect is profound peace and undisturbed tranquillity. 'Whatever the Lord does to the soul,' says St. Theresa, 'and all that He teaches her, passes in such quiet, and without noise, that it seems to me to resemble the building of Solomon's Temple, when no noise was heard; and so in this temple of God, for this mansion is His, wherein He and the soul sweetly enjoy each other in the most profound silence.'[1] We must not, however, suppose that these souls are free from all tribulation and anxiety, as they cannot be spouses of Jesus crucified without the cross, but all their afflictions and troubles are confined to the senses and to the bodily powers, and do not penetrate into the centre of the soul. There peace and quiet and the enjoyment of God reign.'

The second effect is that aridities and interior tribulations of spirit no longer molest these souls *Winter is now past, the rain is over and gone.*[2] For

[1] Seventh Mansion, chap III.   [2] Cant. II 11

such souls the winter of hardness and dryness, the cold of desolation and the frost of fears, weariness and anguish, as Scaramelli expresses it, have now passed away. The soul now rejoices in great consolations, and enjoys with great delight its union with God, and if He should sometimes send it aridities, which seldom happens, they last but for a short time, and during that time the soul knows that God is with it and converses with it in its interior

The third effect is the subjection of the inferior or sensitive part of the soul to the superior part, not, indeed, to the same extent as that complete subjection of the body to the spirit which belonged to the state of innocence. The inordinate appetites are kept under control, the affections of the soul are well regulated, the imagination or phantasy is also rightly disposed and confined within due bounds, so as not to distract the soul by its wandering and by its importunate and inopportune representations

The fourth effect is that God in the depth of the spirit moves the soul by His secret inspirations. He directs, rules, and governs all its operations, so that it can truly say with the Apostle *I live, now not I, but Christ liveth in me.*[1]

The fifth effect is that the soul becomes forgetful of itself. St. Theresa gives this as the first effect of perfect union. Speaking of the soul, she says 'The first effect is a forgetfulness of self, so that she truly seems, as I have said, no longer to exist; for she is affected in such a way that she neither knows herself, nor remembers that there is either heaven, or life, or honour destined for her, being entirely engaged in seeking the glory of God. .

[1] Gal ii 20

But,' adds the Saint very wisely, 'do not imagine, daughters, that on this account she neglects to take any care about *eating* and *drinking* (which are a great torment to her), and doing everything to which she is obliged by her state of life. We are speaking of *interior* things, for as regards exterior works little can be said. It is rather an affliction to her to consider how all that she is able to do by her own strength is a mere nothing. Whatever she understands would conduce to the honour of our Lord she would not omit for anything in the world.'[1]

The sixth effect consists in perfect conformity to the will of God. Nothing disturbs this soul any longer, because she has fully and entirely submitted her will to the will of her Divine Spouse. Even the desire of seeing and enjoying Him is in perfect submission to His Divine will.

The seventh effect is a great desire for suffering, which St. Theresa explains as follows: 'This desire for suffering, is not like what the soul formerly had, for that used to disturb her. The desire which such souls have that God's will may be done in them is so excessive that they receive with pleasure whatever His Majesty sends them. If He wish them to suffer, they are content; if not, they do not torment themselves about it, as they used at other times. Those souls feel great joy when they are persecuted, for then they enjoy more peace than that I have ever spoken of before, and they do not feel the least hatred against their persecutors—nay, they conceive for them a particular affection ; so much so that, if they see them in affliction, they feel

[1] Seventh Mansion, chap. iii.

it keenly, pity them, and most sincerely recommend them to God, on condition that He would in exchange bestow these afflictions on themselves in order that they might not offend His Majesty.'[1]

The eighth effect is great and notable zeal for the honour of God and the salvation of souls 'Such souls,' St Theresa says, 'desire to benefit, if they can, some other soul; hence, they not only do not desire to die, but to live many years on earth, and to endure very great crosses, in order that our Lord by this means may be honoured, however little And though they were sure, when the soul leaves the body, immediately to enjoy God, they make no account of this, and think as little on the glory which the Saints possess. They do not desire it at present, since all their glory consists in their being able to assist, in something, their crucified Lord, especially when they see Him so much offended, and so few who, disengaged from all other things, have His honour truly at heart.'[2]

6 Concluding remarks on Part III from St Theresa and St John of the Cross

6 I shall conclude this chapter and my treatise on the degrees of contemplation by some extracts from the works of the two great mystical authors St. John of the Cross and St. Theresa. St. Theresa will teach us that the highest mystical union is not to be regarded as an idle or fruitless state 'The desires of these souls do not now run after consolations and delights, because they have Christ our Lord with them, and His Majesty now lives in them. It is manifest that, as His life was nothing else but a continual torment, so He makes ours

---
[1] Seventh Mansion, chap III
[2] *Ibid* See Voss, 'Compend Scaramelli,' *pro his effectibus*, p 330 *et seq*

such—at least, by desire—and He leads us as being feeble, though in other things, when He sees it necessary, He gives us strength. . . . When they become negligent, our Lord Himself excites them, so that it is clearly seen that this impulse (or I know not what to call it) proceeds from the interior of the soul, as I mentioned when speaking of impetuosities. Here it is done with great sweetness, but it comes neither from the fancy nor from the memory, nor any other thing, whereby one can discover that the soul did nothing on her part. This is so usual, and happens so often, that one may very easily observe it. For as a fire, however large it may be, does not send forth its flame downwards, but upwards, so this internal motion is here discovered to proceed from the centre of the soul, and thus it excites the faculties."[1]

Again she says: 'It will be well, Sisters, to make you acquainted with the end for which our Lord bestows such great favours in this world; and though you might understand this by the effects, if you considered them well, yet I wish to repeat it here again to you, that so none of you may think it is only to caress such souls (which would be a great mistake), since His Majesty cannot bestow a greater favour upon us than to give us a life to be spent in imitation of that which His beloved Son spent on earth. Hence, I consider it certain that these favours are given to strengthen our weakness, that we may be able to suffer something for His sake. We have always noticed that those who have been nearest to Christ our Lord were the most afflicted. Consider what

[1] Seventh Mansion, chap. iii

His glorious Mother suffered, and the glorious Apostles.'[1]

She continues further on in the same chapter 'You may imagine, perhaps, that I speak of beginners, and that these may afterwards take their rest. But I have already told you the rest which these souls possess in their interior is given them because they possess so very little in the exterior. For what end, think you, are those inspirations—or, to speak more correctly, those aspirations and messages—which the soul from her interior castle sends to the people around the castle, and to the other mansions which are outside that in which she resides? Is it, do you think, that they may send themselves to sleep? No, no, no! for then it excites a fiercer war, to keep the faculties, the senses, and all that is corporeal, from being idle, than it did when she suffered from them; for then she knew not the immense benefit which afflictions bring, and these, perhaps, have been the means employed by God to advance her so far. And as the company which she enjoys gives her greater strength than ever (for, as Daniel says *With the holy thou wilt be holy*), no doubt but that she, by becoming one with the strong, through so heavenly a union of Spirit with spirit, must needs receive strength both for suffering and dying: it is very certain that with the strength which she thence derives she assists all those within the castle, and even the body itself.'[2]

St. John of the Cross, in the thirty-ninth stanza of the 'Spiritual Canticle,' gives us some insight into the soul which is united to God in the spiritual

---

[1] Seventh Mansion, chap. iv.   [2] *Ibid.*

marriage He first speaks of the love of the Holy Ghost uniting it with the Blessed Trinity.

'The breathing of the air! This is a certain faculty which God will then bestow upon the soul in the communication of the Holy Ghost, Who, like one breathing, elevates the soul to His Divine aspiration, informs it, strengthens it, so that it may breathe in God with the same aspiration of love which the Father breathes with the Son, and the Son with the Father, which is the Holy Ghost Himself; Who is breathed into the soul in the Father and the Son in that transformation so as to unite it to Himself; for the transformation is not true and perfect if the soul is not transformed in the Three Persons of the Most Holy Trinity in a clear, manifest degree This breathing of the Holy Ghost in the soul, whereby God transforms it in Himself, is to the soul a joy so deep, so exquisite, and so sublime, that no mortal tongue can describe it, no human understanding, as such, conceive it in any degree, for even what passes in the soul with respect to the communication which takes place in its transformation wrought in this life cannot be described, because the soul, united with God and transformed in Him, breathes in God that very Divine aspiration which God breathes Himself in the soul when it is transformed in Him.'

St. John then goes on to explain how the perfect in this life taste the joy of heaven·

'In the transformation which takes place in this life, this breathing of God in the soul, and of the soul in God, is of most frequent occurrence, and the source of the most exquisite delight of love to the soul, but not, however, in the clear and manifest degree which it will have in the life to come. This, in my opinion, is what St. Paul referred to when he said *Because you are sons, God hath sent the Spirit of His Son into your hearts, crying, Abba, Father.*[1] The blessed in the life to come and the perfect in this thus experience it. Nor is it to be thought impossible that the soul should be capable of so great a thing, that it should breathe in God as God in it, in the way of participation. For granting that God has bestowed upon it so great a favour as to unite it to the Most Holy Trinity, whereby it becomes like unto God, 'and God by participation, is it altogether incredible that it should exercise the faculties of its intellect, perform its acts of knowledge and of love, or, to speak more accurately, should have it all done in the Holy Trinity together with It, as the Holy Trinity Itself? This, however, takes place by communication and participation, God Himself effecting it in the soul, for this is to be transformed in the Three Persons in power, wisdom, and love, and herein it is that the soul becomes like unto God, Who, that it might come to this, created it in His own image and likeness.'

We have to understand St. John as laying down clearly the Catholic doctrine that God and the soul are one, not by fusion of nature, but by identity of will—that is, of love—and this he teaches in the following words:

'Nor are we to suppose from this that our Lord prayed that the Saints might become one in essential and natural unity as the Father and Son are, but that they might become one in the union of love, as the Father and the Son are one in the oneness of their

[1] Gal. iv. 6

love. Thus, souls have this great blessing by participation which the Son has by nature, and are therefore really gods by participation, like unto God and of His nature St. Peter speaks of this as follows: *Grace to you and peace be accomplished in the knowledge of God and of Christ Jesus our Lord as all things of His Divine power, which appertain to life and godliness, are given us through the knowledge of Him Who hath called us by His own proper glory and virtue. By Whom He hath given us most great and precious promises. that by these you may be made partakers of the Divine nature*[1] Thus far St Peter, who clearly teaches that the soul will be a partaker of God Himself, Who will effect within it, together with it, the work of the Most Holy Trinity, because of the substantial union between the soul and God And though this union be perfect only in the life to come, yet even in this, in the state of perfection to which the soul is supposed now to have reached, some anticipation of its sweetness is given it in the way I am speaking of, though in a manner wholly ineffable.'[2]

[1] 2 Pet 1, 2-4 [2] 'A Spiritual Canticle,' stanza xxxix

PART IV

MYSTICAL PHENOMENA DISTINCT FROM CONTEMPLATION

INTRODUCTION

As has been stated in the introduction to Part III., the act of contemplation may be either distinct or indistinct. In that part we have treated of contemplation according to its various degrees, or the contemplation which, according to Scaramelli, is by indistinct acts. In Part IV. we have to treat of the contemplation which, according to the same authority, is by distinct acts. He calls the acts distinct because their objects are particular, and presented to the mind in some distinct and definite form by visions, locutions, and revelations. He reminds us that the term 'contemplation' is improperly applied to these acts, that they are said to be connected with it only because they more frequently take place during contemplation than at other times, and because these favours are bestowed more frequently upon contemplatives than upon others, and for these reasons they are usually explained by theologians in their treatises on contemplation, and they certainly belong to the science of mystical theology, as they are extraordinary favours granted to some whom God chooses to raise up above the ordinary way of His grace in the supernatural life of the soul here on earth, and they are extraordinary manifestations of His goodness and His love for men, and of His mysterious dealings with them in the supernatural order.

It seems, however, to me that the heading and title under which Scaramelli classes these phenomena is not intelligible without some explanation such as I have given. The second part of the second book he entitles 'Concerning Contemplation which is effected by Distinct Acts, or, Of Visions, Locutions, and Revelations.' I think it well to omit the first part of this title, as it is confusing, and I can retain the second part as included under the general title given above. Visions, locutions, and revelations may be called mystical phenomena distinct from contemplation, and yet connected with it in the manner I have explained. It is under this title that Ribet treats of these phenomena after having studied and written on the mysteries of contemplation, which, as he truly says, is the substance, the centre, and the end of the mystical life.

This learned author places or divides these phenomena into three classes—namely, those that belong to the intellectual order, those that belong to the affective order, and those that relate to theology, and he deals with each of these classes of phenomena in a very minute, accurate, and exhaustive manner He accounts for his classification of the phenomena and for his divisions and subdivisions in a logical and scientific preamble. He says

'These phenomena of which man is the subject appear in his soul and in his body.

'The soul is not a blind, but a seeing activity. It sees and it acts It sees in order to act, whence result, as it were, two principles of life, one of which is destined to nourish the other and to enlighten it by showing it its end.

'The body is composed of an assemblage of organs which put the soul in communication with the exterior world in respect to information and action.

'The intellectual life, the affective life, the organic life, form three aspects of human life

'The supernatural and mystical action of God on man is directed principally and finally to the will, to draw it and subject it to the ineffable union of charity. But, according to the order by which all reasonable nature is ruled, this action passes first through the understanding, and again returns to it with a luminous flash of love And then both—namely, the intellectual movement and the affective movement—obedient to the law which attaches the soul to the body, exercise on the organs a glorious radiance, at the same time the senses on their part convey to the soul from without innumerable influences.

'According as the supernatural action has its principal home or seat in the understanding, the heart, or the body, the facts are classed or characterize themselves by their predominant aspect.

'We can therefore arrange all the mystical phenomena under one or other of these three forms —the intellectual life, the moral life, and the sensible life. Let it not be forgotten that this classification is not rigorous or exclusive, for many of the facts or phenomena may occur and recur either simultaneously or successively in the three orders [1]

[1] 'Les Phénomènes Mystiques,' vol ii , preamble.

The phenomena may be classified as thus outlined, but is it necessary, it may be asked, to be continually going back to the rules of grammar, and to be puzzled with ever-recurring grammatical terms, in treating of any advanced subject in literature or science? Is it necessary to be ever reminding readers of first principles, and reducing all our propositions and our facts to them, in order thereby to make them more easily understood? The process is wearisome, and is likely to become entangled with repetitions and inconsequences, especially in a subject-matter in which the phenomena cannot be confined within the limits of the class or form to which it is assigned, and when one form cannot be kept distinct from another except as to its aspect or the mode of regarding it.

All the phenomena to which I think it necessary to direct attention in this part may be classed under the following heads (1) Visions, (2) Spiritual Locutions, (3) Revelations, (4) Prophecies, (5) Miracles

These are familiar words, and we cannot well mistake their general meaning. Through these God has from the beginning communicated with His creatures in an extraordinary manner. All supernatural religion is founded upon revelations, and its credibility is founded upon prophecies and miracles. Dogmatic theology is the science to which they belong, and which treats of them in their relation to Christianity, and from which it draws its arguments in proof of the religion of Christ, and in establishing the notes and attributes of the Church of Christ, and in this respect they do not come immediately under the scope of the science of mystical theology properly so called. This department of theology has to consider them in so far as they relate to the sanctification of souls, and as the extraordinary means used by Almighty God in His communications with individual souls, indirectly intended for their own salvation, and directly for the salvation or the good of others. They come under what are known as the graces *gratis datæ—gratuitously given*—of the Holy Ghost, which are not intended as the motives of our faith, and which do not belong of necessity to the whole Church so as to claim the assent of all the faithful. They are, therefore, to be regarded by this branch of theology as private visions, private revelations, private prophecies, and miracles, as they have been wrought in the Church in every age from its foundation up to the present through the instrumentality of the Saints and servants of God.

These have to be considered and proved by Scriptural references, their characters as to their genuineness and their Divine origin have to be examined, and the nature of the faith we have to place in them and the reverence and respect which we have to entertain for them have to be examined, and in this way we may be able to understand God's mysterious communications with men in the supernatural order by means of these mystical phenomena.

CHAPTER I

ON VISIONS AND APPARITIONS

The notion of visions

1. ACCORDING to St. Thomas, we can take a name in a manifold sense. In one sense it may be taken according to its etymology or first imposition, in another, according to usage. Thus, with regard to the name 'vision,' which in its primary sense signifies the act of the sense of sight, still, because of the excellence and the certitude of that sense, the name by usage was extended in its meaning to signify the knowledge of the other senses; and ultimately it came to be used to signify even the knowledge of the intellect, according to the words *Blessed are the clean of heart, for they shall see God.*[1]

Voss says that a supernatural and extraordinary vision is the intuition or view of some object presented to us by God in some singular way.

Cardinal de Lauræa, speaking of visions and revelations, instructs us as to some distinction to be made between them. He tells us that visions may be said to be revelations, especially if they be of a secret, future, present, or past subject; and on the part of God, Who shows these things, or the devil deceiving, they may be called revelations, and on

[1] St Matt v. 8

the part of man, who receives them, visions. Cardinal Bona says that the terms 'vision' and 'apparition' may be used for one and the same thing; but there is this difference: that an apparition is that which presents itself to our contemplation, but without our knowing what it is, but a vision is that the understanding of which is given also with the external apparition. Apparition is the exhibition of an object known or unknown, and in a vision there is an interior indication which corresponds to the representation made. There will be no necessity to introduce this distinction in the course of our further explanations, as what we have to say will apply equally to visions and apparitions.

We have already seen that visions, both intellectual and imaginary, often occur in the ecstatic degree of contemplation, but let us attend to what Benedict XIV. says

'It has been well observed by Cardinal de Lauraea that visions are not always connected with ecstasies He says that visions, apparitions, and revelations are not always and of necessity connected with ecstasies and raptures and simple contemplation This he maintains on the ground of reason and of fact In the Holy Scriptures visions and apparitions are promised to no class of persons, and in the second place, on the ground of fact, many contemplatives, and in particular those of acquired contemplation, and many ecstatic and enraptured, neither had nor ever have either visions, or apparitions, or revelations, but only illuminations, with reference to the object of their contemplation.'[1]

[1] 'Treatise on Heroic Virtue,' vol iii, p 283

2. The different kinds of visions

2. Benedict XIV., quoting from a manuscript of Father Baldelli, gives us the common teaching of theologians with regard to the different kinds of visions

'We must understand, as is taught by St. Augustine, St. Thomas, St. Isidore, and Dionysius the Carthusian, that visions are of three sorts bodily, with the eyes of the body; ideal, with the imagination and fancy; and intellectual, with the intellect alone. Of the first kind was the vision of Moses when he saw the bush on fire and not burnt, and that of Baltassar the king (Dan v.) when he saw the handwriting on the wall. Of the second kind was that of St. Peter when he saw the sheet (Acts x), that of St. John in the Apocalypse (1), that of Ezekiel (xxxvii) when he saw a plain full of the bones of the dead, which stood up on their feet, an exceeding great army; that of Isaias (vi.) when he saw God on His throne, and the Seraphim, and the altar from which the live coal was taken to cleanse his lips; and many others of other prophets. And, according to Dionysius the Carthusian, the same are generally those in which the dead appear to persons in their sleep, and bid others to give them burial and the like, and those likewise which, even awake, some see, who are usually disordered in mind, as madmen. And if, perchance, in similar visions it happens that future or other events are seen which could be seen naturally, and by the natural intervention of images, he says that this takes place only by the ministry of Angels, God thus willing or permitting Lastly, of the third order was that of St. Paul when he saw the Divine essence without the intervention of images and representations.'[1]

3. St. Augustine says that these three visions have their own order of perfection and degree, stating that the first—namely, the bodily vision— has need of the second—namely, the ideal vision— because the external senses do not perform their functions without the concurrence of the internal powers. The second has need of the third in order that a correct judgment may be formed of those things which are in the imagination and apparent. Finally, the third, as the most perfect, although it is ordinarily attended by the second, seeing that in this life nothing can be perceived without images, yet it has no need of it, and can of itself exist without it, as in the case of St. Paul. St. Thomas well observes that these apparitions or ideal visions, if they occur during sleep, are called dreams; if during waking, but while the subject of them is abstracted, visions. In dreams as well as visions the soul is occupied with images only, whether wholly or in part, and rests in them as if they were not images and similitudes of things, but the things themselves. And herein a dream or vision differs from prophecy, if perchance that is effected by means of symbols and similitudes of things; for the soul of the prophet does not rest in the symbols and similitudes, but passes beyond them in a prophetic light; because, knowing them to be symbols and appearances, it arrives at the understanding even of the things signified and shadowed by them, as it is written, *A word was revealed to Daniel . . . and he*

[3] The three kinds do not exclude each other, but are often found together

---

[1] 'Treatise on Heroic Virtue,' pp. 305-307

understood the word, for there is need of understanding in a vision.[1]

How these visions may be joined together under the three forms in the same subject or recipient may be shown by the example of the wise men, although the object of one of the forms was different from the object of the other two. A star appeared to their natural sense of sight. They received at the same time an intellectual intimation or vision of the signification of this external sign, and after they had acknowledged and adored the infant God they were by an imaginary vision admonished in a dream to return by another way to their own country.[2]

4. By reason of their dignity or excellence, the intellectual vision holds the first place, and that of the imagination is superior to the bodily vision. We have a further explanation of these three kinds of visions, in which their order is signified, given by Benedict XIV.

'The term "bodily" is applied to that which comes under the cognizance of the sight as well as that of the other senses, according to St. Augustine "To see is properly a property of the eyes. But we apply the word also to the other senses, when we apply them for purpose of understanding. We say not only, see what shines, which the eyes alone can receive, but also see what sounds, see what smells, see what tastes, see how hard it is." Ideal vision, which St. Augustine calls spiritual, is effected through species or figures and images of things existing in the imagination itself, which are so disposed by the operation of God or of an Angel

[1] The order of these visions

[1] Dan. x 1 [2] Ribet, 'La Mystique Divine,' vol ii, p 7

as to represent clearly the object proposed, light being infused from on high for the understanding of what they mean. And it is effected also through new species never before received, but sent by God or Angel; and this ideal vision may take place during waking or sleeping.

'Lastly, intellectual vision is the most clear manifestation of Divine things, which is perfected in the intellect alone without figures and images, and it takes place either when the human mind is illuminated by the grace of the Holy Ghost, that it may understand those things which in the bodily or ideal apparition are represented by sensible signs, or when the Divine mysteries are perceived immediately by species infused into the intellect by God.'[1]

5 I find one difficulty proposed for solution in respect of ideal apparitions The apparition, as has been said, may be purely imaginative or bodily—that is, externally visible to the senses. In the first case, he who has the vision is the only one that perceives it. Then either he knows it is not real—that is to say, external—or he believes that it is real and becomes the dupe of a hallucination. This word 'hallucination' is the favourite word of those who would explain away all the visions contained in the lives of the Saints

Now, it is true that the Saints had visions that were purely imaginative, but they knew that they had no exterior sensible existences, and they knew also that they had the full consciousness that they were produced by a Divine communication, and they were not, therefore, the victims of hallucinations. Hallucination supposes an error by which a man

[1] 'Treatise on Heroic Virtue,' vol III, pp 305, 306

believes that to exist outside which alone comes from the imagination or which passes only through the imagination. The man who discerns a Divine action which really exists in the interior, acknowledges its existence there and knows that it does not affect the external senses, cannot with justice be said to be labouring under a hallucination. In this case the vision has an objective reality, even though it is not apparent to the external senses.

The imaginative or ideal vision does not behold an object which does not exist in the imagination, but it is the perception by the brain or mind of an object which makes an impression on it. Not only is there no opposition between an imaginative vision and a bodily one, but there is a great affinity between them. In both we recognise a spiritual agent external to the soul; in the first form of vision the agent acts only upon the brain; in the second it acts upon the organs of the body: in a hallucination it does not intervene at all. The imagination alone is the sole cause of the phenomena which appear.

Moreover, the Saints, as we have said, had many other visions that were not purely imaginative. They had bodily visions that were seen by others as well as themselves, though the apparitions were granted as favours to them, and they had visions that left sensible and perceptible marks upon them that could be witnessed by others.[1]

6. According to St. Thomas and most theologians, these visions or apparitions are of the nature of true miracles.

According to the established order of things, this world must remain under the shadows of faith; con-

[1] 'Le Merveilleux Divin,' Dom B M Maréchaux, pp. 240, 241

sequently, according to the laws of nature and the ordinary laws of providence, God does not manifest Himself in a visible manner, and the inhabitants of heaven do not appear to their brethren on earth unless to fulfil some extraordinary mission or design of Divine providence. It was this that made St. Augustine say that the martyrs could not assist the living by their own natural powers without special help from God. The law which separates the two worlds is a general one, and equally applies to God, our Lord, to the souls in heaven, and to the celestial spirits. In itself the work accomplished may be natural, but as it regards us it is an equivalent miracle, since according to the manner in which it is effected it is against the law of nature, or the ordinary law, which does not permit a man to put himself in this kind of communication with superior beings except by faith and prayer.

Whenever, then, God, or the Angels, or the Saints manifest themselves to us either in a mental or bodily vision, however natural may be the act by which we see or experience such a vision, we are no longer in the regular or ordinary way of nature, but under the influence of an extraordinary and supernatural agency.

Nevertheless, the miracle varies according to the different visions. The corporeal presents nothing of the marvellous in the subject which receives it. He sees, hears, touches, by an exercise natural to the senses. The prodigy is altogether in the external manifestation of an object which does not belong to the ordinary course of things here below. In the intellectual vision, on the contrary, the prodigy is in the very act of cognition, and in the faculty from which it proceeds. The recipient cannot doubt but that he is in the region or atmosphere of the extraordinary supernatural perception and influence

As regards the imaginative or ideal vision, this seems to be miraculous from a twofold aspect. The recipient exercises upon it his interior senses or powers with elements, or, at least, with conditions that take him out of the natural sphere. At the same time, the external agent which impresses the imagination, although in itself it acts according to the laws of nature, nevertheless, it establishes with the recipient a relation which is not in the normal or usual course of providence—a relation which consequently must be regarded as miraculous.[1]

7 How visions or apparitions are to be regarded in general

7 Our conduct with regard to visions or apparitions may be viewed either on the part of the recipients of these favours, or on the part of others who have to direct souls, or who hear or read of such things in the lives of the Saints.

(1) Not to be desired

(1) These things have not to be desired by individual souls. This is the advice of all spiritual guides and teachers, as is well shown by Benedict XIV.

‘That which relates to not seeking after visions or desiring them may be corroborated by the authority of St Bonaventure, whose words are these "To some it seems safer not to seek them, not to be too ready to trust them when offered Sometimes to esteem them lightly as less profitable, so as to regard them, if true, with indifference, if false, not to lean on them, that they may not be deceived" Gerson also speaks in the same way,

[1] Ribet, ‘La Mystique Divine,’ vol. ii., p 18.

saying that we must humbly renounce them, and giving us the following formula for doing it "Let it be said reverently with Peter, *Depart from me, for I am a sinful man, O Lord*,[1] for I am vile, unworthy of Thy visions, which I neither seek or accept, but reject. Let me see Thee in heaven, not here; my whole reward is the Lord God, and that is sufficient What have I to do with visions of Thee in this world?" A little before he says "Someone will object to me the words of the Apostle, *Extinguish not the spirit*.[2] If the vision, then, be from the Holy Ghost, and nevertheless is rejected, what is this but to resist the Holy Ghost and to choke this rising grace? But, indeed, the Holy Ghost, Who gives Himself to the humble, will never withdraw Himself on account of this humiliation He will enter, rather, and in His good pleasure, and will lead the soul that is vile in its own eyes triumphantly on high and without any wrinkle of hypocrisy."

'St. Philip gave the same advice, as we learn from his life, written by Father Bacci, where, among other things, we read thus "He advised, and very frequently commanded, his penitents to repel them with all their might, that they should not suppose that they thereby displeased the Divine Majesty, for this is one way of ascertaining the true vision from the false." St Vincent Ferrer in his treatise on the spiritual life, quoted by Gravina, says "For such a desire [the desire for visions] cannot be found without the root of pride and presumption—yea, of temptation to curiosity with respect to Divine things

---

[1] St Luke v. 8. [2] 1 Thess v 19.

—nor without some vacillation and uncertainty in matters of faith."[1]

(2) Confessors not to be too credulous, nor too incredulous in these matters

(2) With regard to confessors and spiritual directors, the advice given is that they be neither too credulous nor too incredulous. They should not believe without examination and serious inquiry every tale of vision that they hear, nor give credence too easily in cases where there is great danger of deception, as happens with certain weak, fanciful, and hysterical persons. On the other hand, they should not reject every vision or supernatural apparition as a vain, foolish imagination or a diabolical delusion. It is true in the matter of visions delusions may take place very easily, because they can be created by the imaginations of some people, or by the deceits and frauds of the devil, or by the malice of hypocrites; but all these ought not to make them incredulous, but, rather, cautious, prudent, and circumspect, and they should endeavour to understand how to distinguish true from false visions and how to examine them carefully.

All persons favoured by God in this way are reminded of the necessity of communicating their visions to learned men—men not too credulous, but, rather, timid, or I should say cautious. 'Let them,' says St. Bonaventure, 'seek the advice of the wise only, and of but few.' 'Among other signs,' says Benedict XIV, 'by which the visions, apparitions, and revelations of St Bridget are accounted Divine, that is mentioned, namely, that she used to submit all to the judgment of wise men, as Cardinal Torquemada says in the prologue to these revelations "She submitted with great humility the whole to

[1] 'Treatise on Heroic Virtue,' vol. iii, pp. 353, 354.

the examination, judgment, and correction of her spiritual father, and other spiritual fathers and wise prelates of the Church."'

Seeing that these souls need direction and advice, and also that in the opinion of all they should seek advice and be guided by it, it follows that the spiritual father should receive them kindly, listen to them with patience, and give them wholesome counsel On the other hand, it appears that they may be severe, according to the advice of Gerson and other eminent spiritual teachers whom Benedict XIV. quotes. Gerson, I think, must refer to a false mystic or to someone who is full of pride and vanity, when he advises as follows :

' Beware, then, whoever thou art who hearest or givest advice, that thou dost not praise that person, nor commend him, nor admire him as a Saint, and worthy to receive revelations and to work miracles Resist him, rather, chide him harshly, treat with contempt him whose heart is exalted and whose eyes are lofty, so that he walketh in great matters and in wonderful things above himself. Let him not seem to himself to be such an one as may work out his own salvation not in the human way of others, according to the teaching of the Scripture and the Saints, and according to the dictates of natural reason, unless he presumes to have counsel and thinks he has it, not only from Angels, but from God, not even once in his difficulties, but almost continually, and as it were in daily communications. Admonish such an one not to think highly, but to think unto soberness, for he saith most truly who hath said, Pride deserves reproach. Let the examples of the holy Fathers be mentioned, who have fled from the most fatal and the most fallacious curiosity of visions and miracles. St. Augustine, in his Confessions, glories in our Lord that He was delivered from it.'[1]

Neither these words of Gerson, nor words spoken and written by many of the Saints and spiritual masters, give any encouragement to visions or apparitions of any kind, and they most emphatically reprobate all pretences or imitations of this kind on the part of those who are not virtuous, and who are given up to spiritual pride and ambition. At the same time, whilst we must hold that due severity should be used in paternal correction when needed, harshness is sure to do more harm than good to most people. It is not wise, I think, to assume or pretend a harshness towards really devout souls whether in a convent or in the world. Young people who are being trained to virtue see through that kind of thing, and are often obliged for the sake of appearances to submit and look mortified, when in reality they are only amused at the simplicity of their guides. There ought to be no sham work encouraged or tolerated in these spiritual matters, and in that case I may ask how any honest spiritual father can treat with harshness those whom he knows to be holy before God. Let us therefore consider the matter in a mild, kind, and charitable manner, according to the sentiments and teaching of St. John of the Cross, in whose every line we can detect the spiritual refinement and attraction of his Divine Master. We have one point brought out clearly, and illuminated by reference to the writings of St. John of the Cross, by Joly in the 'Psychology of the Saints'.

[1] 'Treatise on Heroic Virtue,' vol. iii, p. 355

MYSTICAL PHENOMENA—VISIONS

(3) 'More than anyone else St. John of the Cross has laboured to impress upon men the real teaching of Catholic tradition, that phenomena of this kind do not constitute sanctity. We may go further, and say that in those centres which produce Saints, and where Saints are most honoured, these occurrences always, in the first instance, create distrust and suspicion. What is feared is that they are either caused by disease, or that they will end by producing it, on account of the too great strain to which they subject the mental and physical organization of the person who experiences them. According to the teaching of St. John of the Cross, the least unfavourable judgment that can be passed on them is that no one should show animus against or ill-treat persons subject to these states. All that is necessary is to warn them of the dangers they run, and gently to turn their attention to other things.

'We read in the "Ascent of Mount Carmel"[1] that these souls should be led by the way of faith, and be taught by degrees, to disregard these supernatural impressions. They should learn to strip themselves of them for the sake of their own greater profit in the spiritual life. It should be explained to them that this way is the better one, and that one single action, one single movement of the will, proceeding from charity is of more value, and is more precious in God's sight, than all the good put together which they may derive from their revelations. What is more, many who have never received these gifts have become incomparably more holy than those who have received them, in abundance, from heaven.'[2]

(3) They do not constitute Sanctity.

---

[1] ii. 22.   [2] 'Psychology of the Saints,' pp. 75, 76.

CHAPTER II

CORPOREAL APPARITIONS OR VISIONS

The meaning of corporeal apparitions

1. A CORPOREAL vision or apparition is an extraordinary manifestation, under a material and corporeal form, of an object, which our external senses could not otherwise perceive. As to the manifestation of the object, the corporeal vision is the same as the imaginative and intellectual visions; but it is distinguished from them in this, that in it the object falls under the observation of the sense of sight or of one or more of the other senses; whilst in the imaginative vision the object is represented in the phantasy, and in the intellectual vision the object is presented to the intellect. The manifestation must be in some extraordinary manner, because it could not otherwise be distinguished from natural vision.

These corporeal visions are also apparitions, because in them the objects themselves, or at least their species, make an organic impression upon our senses. Although the objects appear also in some way in the imaginative and intellectual manifestations, these are called more properly visions than apparitions.

I think, with M. Maréchaux, that the simplest and most practical method in dealing with a subject so indefinite and complicated as apparitions is to enumerate and to study one by one the objects of the different apparitions recorded in Sacred Scripture, in the history of the Church, and in the lives of the Saints, and I shall therefore adopt this method of dealing with the subject.

2. Scaramelli says that all beings who exist in heaven, in hell, in purgatory, and upon this earth may be objects of corporeal vision. God appeared to men as revealed in many places of Holy Scripture, and the apparitions of our Lord and Saviour are established on the same authority. Then we learn from the annals of the Church that the Blessed Virgin, the Angels, and the Saints in heaven have often appeared to men here on earth, and have been seen by them. The souls in purgatory have appeared in like manner, so have the lost souls, but only rarely. The demons have frequently and undoubtedly often appeared, and we have many examples of such apparitions. Cardinal Bona testifies that we have no example of the apparition of infants who have died without baptism. Even amongst the living, men have appeared to their fellow-creatures in an extraordinary manner, and in different places at the same time.[1]

2. The beings who appear, or the objects of visions or apparitions.

The various ways in which these apparitions have taken place in the past, as attested by sufficient evidence, may gain our attention and interest as strange things of the other world and appertaining to the world of spirit, as they never fail to gain the minds of young and old, even though I may have nothing new to tell. Yet these apparitions may be often considered from many points of view, and the answering of many difficulties in connection with

[1] Voss, 'Compend. Scaramelli,' p. 355.

them, together with whatever explanation I can collect together from authentic sources, may serve to encourage the timid and the doubtful, and to strengthen the piety and devotion of the faithful admirers of all the ways of God, whether manifested in the ordinary or in the extraordinary sphere of His dealings with mankind.

3. The theophanies, or the manifestations or apparitions of God

3. Since God is a pure Spirit, and the adorable Trinity surpasses all created intelligence, it may be asked how He can appear to us. It seems to be certain that He cannot by Himself be the object of any sensible or corporeal apparition; it does not appear to be certain that He cannot be the object of an intellectual vision in this life. The question is, however, discussed by St Thomas, who teaches that it is not impossible for a man living in this mortal flesh to see the essence of God, not by a permanent intuition, but only by a passing illumination. He thinks that Moses and St. Paul were raised up in ecstasy to such a supereminent vision. Benedict XIV. makes known to us very clearly the state of the question, and what we may hold with regard to it. He says:

'There is a question among theologians whether any man during this life can see the essence of God. The question relates to a mere man, for it is of the certainty of faith that Christ our Lord saw the essence of God while He was in this world from the instant of His conception, for He was blessed from the instant of His conception. The common opinion among them is that a man during this life cannot naturally attain to the clear vision of God, for while the soul is in the body it naturally knows only what has material form. It is manifest that by nature and the similitude of material things there can be no clear vision of God, and that the knowledge of God which is by similitude is not the knowledge of God in His essence, or of the essence of God

'The same theologians admit everywhere that God may in an extraordinary way, and by a special privilege, raise men in this mortal life to the clear vision of Himself, for God, the Author and Lord of nature, can release whom He pleases from the law of working and understanding by the help of the senses, either by restraining the external senses so that they shall not act, or by giving to the intellect the light of glory, either transiently or permanently as He gave it to Christ Whether this was so in the vision of St. Paul as it was in that of Moses, of which we read in Num xii. and Exod. xxxiii., is still a question among theologians. The opinion of St. Augustine is generally accepted, who inclines to the affirmative, and herein he is followed by St. Thomas, not so, however, as that Moses and Paul saw the essence of God as to all mysteries, and had the full vision as to all things so as to become blessed, but so as that their vision was intermediate between the vision of the blessed and the vision of the prophets—not permanent, but transient' The learned Pontiff then adds these significant words 'It is rather strange, therefore, that Silvius in his commentary on St. Thomas, and Noel Alexander in his commentary on the Epistle to the Corinthians, in other respects faithful disciples of St. Thomas, should in this instance have departed from his teaching.'[1]

[1] 'Treatise on Heroic Virtue,' vol iii, pp. 293, 294

Without discussing the question, I find that a recent writer, Dom B. M. Maréchaux, has come to the conclusion that, with two or three illustrious exceptions, the general rule remains, that no *mortal man can see God*. This vision, should it be fully imparted, would at once detach the soul from the body, and fix it for ever in eternal beatitude.[1]

It is certain, however, that God has deigned to appear and to manifest Himself in a sensible form. This is proved by all the *theophanies*, or apparitions of God, mentioned in the Old Testament. God appeared to Adam after his fall; He appeared to Noe, Abraham, and Jacob; He spoke to Moses from the burning bush, and said, *I am who am*, and He manifested Himself on Sion. It may therefore be asked, How are these frequent apparitions to be explained? I know no better explanation than that given by Benedict XIV with regard both to the sensible or bodily visions, and to the intellectual visions of God as recorded in Holy Writ. He says:

(1) *The apparitions of God in the Old Law not personal*

(1) 'According to the general opinion of theologians, the apparitions of God under the Old Law were not personal, but, as they say, impersonal; for God Himself did not assume a body and appear, but He did that by the ministry of Angels who represented Him, as Durant proves, where he shows how it may be said that God appeared, although an Angel appeared bodily, and how it is that Angels might say, *I am the Lord thy God*, although the prophets usually say, *Thus saith the Lord*. Thyræus agrees with him when he says of the visible appearance of God under the Old Testament, that God

[1] 'Le Merveilleux Divin,' p. 247.

Himself never assumed a body. And when it is said in the Old Testament that He was visible, all these visible apparitions were accomplished by the ministry and service of Angels, who formed and assumed bodies and represented God. For bodies which became visible to human eyes—I mean aerial bodies—ought to be easily made and formed, and to admit of human colour, and, when they are laid aside or dissolved, to leave nothing behind which the eyes of the bystanders can discern, so the same author proves in the same place.

'The Angels, who are called ministering spirits, form also voices, by which we say that God sometimes spoke under the Old Testament

'All this is fully treated of by Thyræus in his work, who also examines at great length whether God, in the revelation of the intellectual speaking, speaks Himself or by the ministry of others; and—after premising that there are species in these intellectual visions, apparitions, revelations, and speeches, which are images of the objects revealed, that there is also light in which the illuminated intellect has cognizance of the objects; and, again, that the species are of two kinds: either they are newly granted or existed before, but in the speech of God receive a new application; likewise that a new light above nature is added to that which is natural and connate, or is not added, but is helped by a certain natural industry of him who speaks—concludes that the new species which God reveals are bestowed by Him alone, not by Angels. This he also asserts of the light which is newly communicated to the intellect, and that the Angels make a new application of the species already existing, and enlighten the intellect when no new light is bestowed.'

The same Benedict XIV. says that Peter Cunæus is of opinion that, when the Sacred Scriptures say God appeared, we are not to understand them to speak of an Angel as the legate of God, but, rather, of the Divine Word or the Second Person of the Holy Trinity, who made Himself even then in human form visible to the Patriarchs He is followed by Bernard Lamg, and lately by Father Graveson. But we must not abandon the first opinion, as it is one widely maintained by the Fathers and the scholastic theologians. Therefore, having alleged the Fathers, Cardinal Bona thus proceeds 'Whatever Divine manifestations or appearances of God we read of, they were accomplished by Angels, through whose ministry they came to our Fathers The ancient Fathers are singularly agreed in this, and the chief of the schoolmen do not dissent from their judgment.'[1]

(2) The adoration given in cases of such apparitions explained

(2) The difficulty which arises out of this teaching is to explain how it was that the Saints of the old law—Abraham, Moses, and others—gave supreme adoration to those who appeared to them, as that does not seem to have been right if they were only Angels. In answer to this difficulty, we may say, in the first place, that the word 'adoration' is often used in Sacred Scripture in a wide sense, and signifies in general profound respect and reverential submission. Secondly, it may be observed that the Angels did not appear to the Patriarchs and Prophets, when they came, in their own proper person, in the same way as when they represented the person of God.

[1] 'Treatise on Heroic Virtue,' vol iii, pp 289-292.

In this latter case the majesty of the Most High surrounded them · they were as the legates of God, and God manifested His glory through them, so that it was God Himself in His representatives that was recognised and honoured by the Patriarchs and Prophets on those occasions Their vision went far beyond the Angel who stood before them in dazzling splendour, and formed words in their ears. It penetrated to Him who acted and expressed Himself through their ministry. Even in case of a false apparition or a diabolical one, the danger of idolatry may be easily avoided according to the following teaching of St. Bonaventure. He proposes the question ' whether *latria* may be given to the enemy of Christ'; and he replies : ' It is possible to give *latria* to the enemy of Christ in two ways—absolutely or conditionally. If absolutely —that is, meaning to the apparition—then, I say, it cannot be done without sin, nor is it excusable on the ground of ignorance, for there are three means of avoiding the error. The first is the warnings of Holy Scripture, which frequently says that many will come deceitfully in the name of Christ. The second is interior prayer, by which man ought to have recourse to God, that his heart may be enlightened. The third is to suspend his own belief, for a man ought not to believe every spirit, but to prove them if they are from God. For he who is ready to believe them is light of heart, and perhaps even proud when he thinks himself qualified to receive such visions and revelations But if he worships conditionally, this may take place in two ways either the condition is habitually considered or actually applied If actually applied—that is, by saying, "if Thou art really God or Christ"—they do not worship Lucifer, but, rather, Christ, for the adoration is not given but on condition, and is referred to Him to whom is referred the implied adoration. But, if that condition be only under a habitual consideration, in this way it is not sufficient to avoid the sin of idolatry."[1] It would appear, therefore, from this teaching that the condition should be actual and explicit before offering up our adoration to God in such visions and apparitions.

(3) In the New Testament the Divine apparitions were by personal intervention.

(3) Under the New Testament, as well at the transfiguration as at the baptism of Christ, it is to be admitted that the Father and the Holy Ghost manifested themselves by a personal intervention. We cannot suppose that it was Angels who acted in these scenes without detracting from the importance of these manifestations, in which the Holy Trinity affirmed its presence and indissoluble unity. It is according to order that Angels should be the intermediaries between God and the Patriarchs, but we cannot suppose them in that capacity between God the Father and His only begotten Son, and between the Son and the Holy Ghost. It is true they fulfilled ministerial offices towards our Saviour, but it was as servants to His sacred humanity.[2]

4. The apparitions of our Saviour.

4. Let us now pass to the apparitions of our Saviour in His sacred humanity. I need not write of the visibility of our Lord from His birth till His death, nor am I called upon in this place to treat of His apparitions in various forms after His resurrection and before His ascension. What we have

[1] Apud Benedict XIV., 'Treatise on Heroic Virtue,' vol. iii., p. 344.
[2] 'Le Merveilleux Divin,' p. 249.

to notice with regard to this subject is that when Christ appeared after His resurrection and before His ascension His apparition was personal, though immediately after His resurrection He appeared to the disciples as a stranger on the way to Emmaus, and as the gardener to Magdalene; for Christ by His mere will could cause His body, without a new miracle, to change the senses of the beholders After Christ's ascension into heaven it is most probable that His apparition to St. Paul, of which that Apostle speaks, was personal[1] This vision took place some years after the ascension; and as the Apostle says that Christ was seen by him as He was seen by Cephas and James and by the other Apostles, and as he proves from this vision and apparition of Christ that he was not less an Apostle than the others—*And I not an Apostle?* he says; *have I not seen Christ Jesus our Lord?*—all this tends to show that this vision and apparition was personal

The vision of Christ to St Peter, which is related by St. Ambrose and others, is also considered by many as personal. This is that vision or apparition which is said to have occurred when St Peter, at the request of the Christians, was retiring from Rome to escape from the fury of the heathens at the gates of the city he saw Christ enter it, and said to Him, 'Lord, whither goest Thou?' Christ answered, 'I come to be crucified again' Peter understood the Divine answer to mean his own crucifixion. Christ could not be crucified again—He had put off His mortal body; but Peter understood that Christ was to be crucified in His servant, and

---

[1] 1 Cor xv. 3.

so willingly returned, and glorified our Lord by his crucifixion and martyrdom. The Church erected in memory of this apparition, called *Domine, quo vadis?* marks the traditional site of the occurrence. It is probable, according to some authors, that this apparition of Christ was personal. Here, however, in giving a theological statement of the nature of the apparitions of Christ since His ascension, I may quote the opinions of standard theologians, as expressed in the words of Benedict XIV. :

'Be it as it may, whether the apparition to St Paul was personal, and how far that was so which occurred to St Peter, theologians inquire whether Christ descended from heaven to earth St Thomas thinks it not improbable that Christ left heaven for a time and descended to earth, although we read in the Scriptures that Christ ascended into heaven and sitteth at the right hand of God, and will descend on the day of the last judgment, as we read in Acts i. and ii. Yet this proves only that heaven is the peculiar and permanent abode of Christ, where, as in His own kingdom on His own throne, He dwells and sits ; but it is not to be inferred that He remains there ever immovable John Major is of opinion that Christ, since His ascension into heaven, has never left the heavenly courts, and yet has sometimes appeared on earth in visible form by the true presence of His body, being indeed in two places at once, as they say, quantitatively and circumscriptively. Suarez says that it is simply and absolutely true that Christ after His ascension has been sometimes on earth, but uncertain whether He was then absent from heaven or not [1]

[1] 'Treatise on Heroic Virtue,' vol iii , pp 297, 298

According to Maréchaux, it is probable our Saviour has not descended from heaven to appear to anyone since His ascension, if we except the apparition to St. Paul. He quotes St. Theresa in saying · 'I have understood from certain things which our Saviour has confided to me that since His ascension He has not descended from heaven, and that we do not find Him personally except in the Blessed Sacrament of the Altar.'

This author then says 'This is the case. We possess our Saviour in the Blessed Sacrament; that is sufficient for us. There is no need to possess Him otherwise. And this brings us to give a few words of explanation on certain apparitions of our Lord, under species and forms strange and unusual in the Sacrament of the Altar'

'There are many instances,' says Benedict XIV., 'of these apparitions on record. At one time is seen in the Sacred Host a man, at another part of man, at another an infant, at another blood. . . St Thomas discusses the question, and shows that such an apparition may take place in two ways · first, on the part of the beholders, in whose eye a change may be wrought, so that they expressly see flesh, or blood, or an infant, there being no change in the Sacrament, secondly, by a change in the Sacramental species themselves. He says that it may happen in the first manner when one sees the apparition and others see it not, and the second is when, under the species, all see a body, flesh, blood. and that not for an hour, but for a long time. Moreover, he says that Christ remains in the Sacrament in the first way as well as the second. In the first there is no change in the Sacrament; in the second, dimensions continuing, which are the foundations of the other accidents, the Body of Christ must be said to remain in the Sacrament. No deception results either in the first or second way from the apparition, for the apparition is granted in order to make manifest that Christ is truly in the Sacrament.' He afterwards quotes the words of Cardinal de Vitry, who says: 'But since the incomprehensible and marvellous depth of this Sacrament exceeds all understanding, we are commanded to believe, forbidden to discuss. God, therefore, to strengthen the faith of the weak in this Sacrament, has shown forth the truth of it by various miracles. Indeed, the likeness of flesh and blood has been frequently seen in the Holy Sacrament through the power of our Lord. And I with my own eyes have seen it in the Monastery of Prémontré, at Braine in France.'[1]

We may therefore assert that all the apparitions of our Saviour since His ascension, that may be called personal, were in the presence of the Blessed Sacrament, in which He is truly, really, and substantially present. This is especially to be noticed with regard to the vision of Margaret Mary Alacoque, when Christ showed her His Sacred Heart with the words *Behold this Heart which has loved men so much.* The three remarkable visions in which He appeared to her and showed her His Sacred Heart all took place in the presence of the Blessed Sacrament. Apart from this presence, when the Saints are said to have seen our Lord, we have to understand the vision as spiritual, in the sense that our Lord raised up the souls in the same

[1] 'Treatise on Heroic Virtue,' vol. III., pp. 300-302.

way as He did St. Stephen, and transported them in spirit to heaven, where they enjoyed the sight of our Lord. St Stephen *saw the heavens opened, and the Son of Man sitting on the right hand of God* This manner of vision will suffice to account for the truth of these visions which St Theresa and many other Saints narrate. They saw our Saviour, and He really appeared to them in this way.

I may sum up with Dom B. M Maréchaux by stating that we can distinguish three visions of our Saviour the vision of Him in His true body, the vision in an assumed body or in a body not His own; the purely spiritual vision, not external. The first is not in the usual order of things, as St Theresa says that there is no reason to believe that our Saviour descended from heaven to show Himself in His true body The second does not appear to us possible. It would weaken the proof of the resurrection, as it would afford a strong argument in favour of unbelievers who assert that the resurrection was not real, and that our Lord's apparitions after the resurrection were only fantastic and imaginative, or that His risen body was only an appearance of a body, and not real It is, absolutely speaking, possible for Christ to appear in the form of a body not His own, yet, for the reason here assigned, we may hold that this has never yet happened But the third kind of vision is possible—that is, the spiritual vision which the Saints have often experienced This in the presence of the Blessed Sacrament is intelligible, and a species of vision which may be called the most advantageous and the most likely when our Lord desires to manifest Himself in this special manner to His chosen servants. When the vision of our Saviour is external, sensible, and palpable, we must attribute it, as we have done the apparitions of God, and in the same sense, to the operation of the Angels whom our Saviour may send as His representatives and legates to men.[1]

[1] 'Le Merveilleux Divin,' pp 255, 256

CHAPTER III

THE APPARITIONS OF THE BLESSED VIRGIN AND OF SPIRITS

1. MANY theologians teach that, like our Saviour, the Blessed Virgin has not appeared personally here on earth since her assumption into heaven, but that her image has been represented by angelical operation in the apparitions that are recorded of her in the lives of the Saints and in Church history. Although there is an analogy between the Mother and the Son, nevertheless, the same reason does not exist for the apparitions of the Blessed Virgin not being personal as that assigned for the impersonal nature of the apparitions of our Saviour. He remains with us in the Blessed Sacrament, and a reason like this cannot be assigned for the impersonal nature of the apparitions of the Blessed Virgin It is true, according to our human way of regarding things, that Mary, as Queen of Heaven, may be represented by heavenly messengers and ministers, yet she is our Mother also, and a mother loves to visit her children personally. It would certainly offend Christian piety to say that the Blessed Virgin herself did not appear at La Salette or at Lourdes, but that it was an Angel who took her place. I only name these two as examples of

1. The apparitions of the Blessed Virgin

many other apparitions on record. Then, with regard to Lourdes, we have very strong evidence that the Blessed Virgin really appeared there in person. We have the approbation of the Church given to the liturgical office in which it is declared that the Mother of God and of men, she who was conceived Immaculate, appeared eighteen times to Bernadette on the rocks of Massabielle. The Church, after examining carefully all the circumstances of this apparition, tells us that it is she, the Blessed Virgin, who appeared, and all Christian people from every part of the world visit without ceasing that miraculous grotto, and repeat with one unanimous voice of love and enthusiasm it is she who appeared, and through whose intercession so many miraculous cures have been wrought, and so many Divine favours have been bestowed, at that holy shrine, to the edification of the entire Church, to the admiration of the non-Catholic world, and to the greater honour and glory of the Mother of God We are not to be understood, therefore, as in any way detracting from the reality and truth of this apparition, which we may take as a typical one, by the answer which we give to the following questions and its explanation.

How was this apparition effected? Did the Blessed Virgin descend from heaven in body and in soul? Did she quit for one moment the heavenly court? Were the blessed deprived of her presence? We may answer, No, she did not leave; she multiplied her presence. Remaining all the time in her place in heaven, she was transported in spirit, with a body assumed, to earth, and appeared here among her children. This, according to

Maréchaux, seems to be a solution to all difficulties. It has been proved beyond doubt that the Saints whilst living here on earth have sometimes appeared in two places distant from each other at the same time. They were in one of these places in their real body, and in another in an assumed body; for though it be true that a spirit can be in many places at the same time, it is not certain that a material body has this power. We may therefore say of this apparition of the Blessed Virgin, that, whilst remaining in heaven in her glorified body, she was transported in spirit to the earth with a body in which she had clothed herself for the occasion.

There certainly was something of the representative nature in some of her terrestrial visitations, because sometimes she appeared sad and in tears, and we know that in her state of glory she is not subject to sadness or tears or sorrow.

There is not the same difficulty in supposing the Blessed Virgin to assume the form and representation of a body in these apparitions as in the case of our Lord. It is true she rose from the dead, and she was assumed body and soul into heaven. But after her resurrection she did not remain here on earth for a time, and appear to men to prove the reality of her resurrection. This Christ did, as the Resurrection was to be the great proof of His religion and His teaching, and man should never have occasion to say that either during life or at death or after death did He assume a phantom body or appear in any such representative form, but always, as I have said, either in His own real body or where that body was really present; or otherwise through

His representative Angels, as in the *theophanies* of old.

Apparitions of Angels

2. We are here on earth surrounded by a world of spirits, so that they form, as it were, a luminous atmosphere between ourselves and God. They transmit to us the Divine orders, and often, as we have said, something of the Divine radiance; and in transmitting these things they have become intimately mixed up with our lives. Their spiritual action on the sensible world is continual; it is both discreet and efficacious, and is often hidden under the veil of natural causes. It is reasonable to hold that material elements are put in motion by spiritual operators, and faith itself sanctions by its authority the belief in the existence and in the intervention of spirits both good and bad in this world.

Since by nature the Angels are incorporeal, it is necessary that they assume bodies whenever they wish to manifest themselves to our senses. There is no doubt that they can assume strange bodies and appear in them. They have power over material elements, and these they can adopt and easily shape into the form of a human body, without, however, contracting any substantial union with them. They can form and dissolve these representations or images by their own natural power. It is certain that under certain circumstances determined by God they clothe themselves in these material forms and appear to men. The Sacred Scriptures narrate numerous apparitions of Angels in human form, and, according to Suarez, to call into doubt the reality and truth of these apparitions would be to go against faith.

MYSTICAL PHENOMENA—VISIONS

(1) Angels appeared immediately from the beginning of the world to the first parents of the human race. In diverse ways they dealt with the Patriarchs, as we read in Genesis. The Law was delivered to the Jews, not by the ministry of men only, but by that of Angels also, as we read in Acts vii.

In the New Testament mention is made of very many apparitions of Angels. Thus, we read that Zachary the priest, when he saw the Angel by the altar of the Temple, *was troubled, and fear fell upon him.*[1] The Blessed Virgin at the salutation of the Angel was troubled at his saying, and thought within herself what manner of salutation this should be. Of the shepherds we read, *that the Angel of the Lord stood by them, and the brightness of God shone round about them, and they feared with a great fear. . . And suddenly there was with the Angel a multitude of the heavenly army, praising God, and saying, Glory to God in the highest, and on earth peace to men of goodwill.*[2] Angels comforted our Saviour in the wilderness and in the Garden of Olives. They appeared to men at His nativity, at His resurrection, and at His ascension. They watched over and protected the infant Church, and liberated Peter from prison, and we have authentic testimony in the Lives of the Saints of the apparitions of Angels in every age of the Church.

(2) The evil spirits can also appear, and have often appeared. We are told that the devil can transform himself into an angel of light. In the Garden of Eden he entered into the body of the serpent, and, as by an instrument moved, struck, and modulated, and in a certain way imitated, as

Marginalia: (1) Apparitions of the good Angels. (2) The apparitions of devils.

[1] St Luke i. 12.   [2] St Luke ii. 9, 13, 14

well as he could, the human voice, according to the explanation of St John Chrysostom, Procopius, and St Augustine, quoted by Cornelius à Lapide in his commentaries upon Genesis. He then spoke to Eve —who thought that the serpent had obtained the function of speech, not by nature, but by some supernatural operation, as St Thomas says—and asked why she did not eat of the fruit in the midst of Paradise She replied that God had forbidden it on pain of death. He said, *No, you shall not die the death. For God doth know that in what day soever you shall eat thereof, your eyes shall be opened, and you shall be as gods, knowing good and evil*[1]

In the New Testament, too, Christ our Lord suffered Himself to be tempted by the devil, that to overcome his temptations He might be a mediator, not only by His help, but also by His example, as St. Augustine says. In that temptation, mentioned by St. Matthew and also by St. Luke, the devil appeared to our Lord, and showed Him the kingdoms of the world, promising to give them to Him if He would fall down and adore him Arauxo says that this apparition of the devil was accomplished by his assuming an aerial body He can create apparitions by an aerial body, condensing the air, so that it shall assume a human form, and resemble him whom he wishes to represent. It is evident that he has created such apparitions, as when in the figure of a man he tempted Christ fasting in the wilderness

Of *ideal* visions and apparitions which are wrought by the power of the devil Cardinal Bona speaks, and what he says tells us in some way how

[1] Gen III 4

the thing is done 'The devil, too, has his prophets and dreamers, whose imagination he influences, representing and suggesting many things to it' And again 'They transform themselves into the likeness of living persons, and place spectres before men's eyes or before their imaginations, and images and resemblances of things and persons, and, as the poets say of the fabulous Proteus, turn themselves into all forms that they may seduce and destroy wretched mortals.'[1]

3 According to Catholic faith, there are three places in which the souls of those who have departed out of this world are detained—in heaven, in hell, and in purgatory. Hence, we have to consider these apparitions according to their several states, and give a few words of explanation on the nature of these apparitions.

<small>3 The apparitions of souls of the departed</small>

(1) The Sacred Scripture furnishes us with many examples of apparitions, either imaginative or even sensible from those of the other world. We read that Samuel appeared to Saul,[2] and this strange apparition, on account of its connection with the witch and her enchantment, may call for a short explanation, which I here give in the words of Benedict XIV

<small>(1) The apparitions of the Saints</small>

'There is a question whether it was the soul of Samuel that appeared, or only a spectre resembling Samuel. St Augustine discusses the subject, and seems to say that either opinion may be maintained In Ecclus xlvi. 23 it is said, in praise of Samuel, that after his death *he made known to the king and*

---

[1] Benedict XIV, 'Treatise on Heroic Virtue' vol III, pp. 302-304
[2] 1 Kings xxviii.

showed him the end of his life. And as it could be no praise to Samuel that the devil, assuming his appearance, should speak to Saul and deceive him, persuading him that he was what he was not, hence it is, many conclude, that the soul itself of Samuel, at the bidding of God, assumed an aerial body and appeared, although the witch had had recourse to enchantment. For as God appeared to Balaam in the practice of enchantments, not because of His enchantments, but anticipating and hindering their effect, so, while the witch had recourse to enchantments, God anticipated them, sending the soul of Samuel and hindering their effect. But it is not said how far the witch had carried on her enchantments, for it may be maintained that she had not begun them, but that God anticipated the witch, who was preparing to have recourse to enchantments, at the request of Saul, and called Samuel by His own power. We do not read that the witch had made use of enchantments to call up Samuel, but that when Saul asked the woman to bring up Samuel, saying, *Bring me up Samuel,* Samuel appeared, and it is there added *When the woman saw Samuel, she cried out with a loud voice, and said to Saul, Why hast thou deceived me?* as if astonished at the appearance of Samuel before her enchantments.[1]

Then, in the Old Law mention is also made of the apparition of Onias the priest and of Jeremias the prophet long after their death, who showed themselves in visions to Judas Machabæus, and encouraged him to fight against the impious enemies of his country. In the New Testament it is recorded

[1] 'Treatise on Heroic Virtue,' vol. iii, pp. 288, 289.

that Moses appeared beside our Lord on Mount Thabor, and was seen by Peter, James, and John.

The Lives of the Saints contain very many marvels of this kind, narrated by their biographers in such a way that we do not notice any very remarkable or exceptional character in the various apparitions we read of The marvels are narrated by witnesses worthy of credit, either by the Saints themselves, or by those who received the account of these visions and apparitions from the Saints themselves, or from others who heard them from the Saints' own lips. As Benedict XIV. has wisely remarked on the kind of evidence on which the truth and reality of the visions of Saints rest, 'Visions and apparitions cannot be proved but on his word, or by his writings, to whom they are said to have been granted. Confessors and spiritual directors whose depositions are received always derive their knowledge thereof from the person to whom the vision or apparition has been granted. Virtues, increase of virtues, and many of the qualifications, by the help of which heavenly visions are distinguished (in the recipients), may be ascertained from other witnesses; but as some of them can be proved only by the testimony of spiritual directors, a cause of beatification and canonization full of visions and apparitions cannot be brought to a prosperous issue without the testimony of spiritual directors to the nature of these visions and apparitions, and unless, moreover, there be clear evidence of their goodness, prudence, and experience.'

The souls of the just or of the blessed can enter into visible communication with the living, either by way of dreams or by assumed aerial bodies in the same manner as the Angels can appear. We have not sufficient grounds for stating that the Angels come in their place to represent them. It is becoming and reasonable that they should be sent as the representatives of our Lord and the Blessed Virgin, because of the supreme dignity of the King and Queen of Heaven. They appear as messengers and ministers from the court of heaven sent by our Lord, but we cannot assign any reason for their appearing in any such capacity on the part of any of the Saints. Besides, it is as easy for us to suppose the apparition of the Saint himself as of an Angel in his place. It is true that St Thomas teaches that souls separated from their bodies have not by themselves the power to put material things in motion, nor, therefore, to form bodies. But the souls of the blessed, by the power with which God has invested them, can have and can use this power.

(2) The apparitions of the souls in purgatory

(2) Dom B. M. Maréchaux holds for certain that, in case of any visible communication taking place by the special permission of God between the souls in purgatory and the living, Angels are always the intermediaries. Certain mysterious notices for prayers on behalf of the souls in purgatory are cited as coming from Angels rather than from these souls themselves. There is, we know, a great difference between the souls of the blessed and the souls in purgatory: the former are free, and we can understand how God may confide certain missions to them; the latter are in prison, and, in our way of regarding things, prisoners are not allowed to go out during the period of their detention. It is, therefore, a rare thing and a privilege doubly exceptional for any of the souls in purgatory to be allowed

to appear to the living. It ordinarily belongs to the Angels to carry to us the messages of these holy prisoners, when it pleases God to favour them or us in that way. Notwithstanding this reservation, the same author allows that on rare occasions God has permitted these souls to appear sometimes to the Saints and to pious people, for we all know that God can permit this, and has permitted it, for His own wise designs.

(3) The apparitions of the damned are the rarest of all. The rich man who, according to the Gospel parable, died, and was buried in hell, and begged Abraham to send Lazarus to admonish his brother living on earth, fully recognised that it was easier for Lazarus than it was for him to pass over the great abyss which divides the two worlds. St Bonaventure says expressly, according to the testimony of Cardinal Bona, that the just sometimes return to earth, but the damned never. St. Thomas does not speak so absolutely; he grants that the damned can, although it has very seldom happened, show themselves for the instruction of, and to inspire fear into, the living. When this has occurred, they have appeared in some hideous form by which they could be recognised. In many cases when people thought the apparitions were of the damned souls, it was probably the devil who appeared and personated them.

(3) The apparitions of the damned

4. The enumeration of these different apparitions and their nature, which are given according to the principles of sound theology, may enable many to judge rightly of the phenomena of spiritism, and to acknowledge their diabolical character. The end for which God sends these special favours and

4. The end for which these favours and visions are granted

visions to men is explained to us by St. John of the Cross in the following manner

'I have much to say of the end which God has in view, and of the ways He employs when He sends visions to raise up the soul from its tepidity to the Divine union with Himself. This is treated of in all spiritual books, and I shall therefore confine myself here to the solution of the question before us That question is this Why does God, Who is most wise, and ever ready to remove every snare and every stumbling-block from before us, send us these supernatural visions, seeing that they are so full of danger and so perplexing to us in our further progress?

'To answer this, we have three principles to take for granted The first is thus expressed by St Paul *Those that are ordained of God.*[1] The second is expressed by the Holy Ghost saying of wisdom that it *ordereth all things sweetly*[2] The third is an axiom of theology *God moveth all things in harmony with their constitution.* According to these principles, then, it is evident that God, when He elevates the soul from the depth of its own vileness to the opposite heights of His own dignity in union with Himself, worketh orderly, sweetly, and in harmony with the constitution of the soul As the process by which the soul acquires knowledge rests on the forms and images of created things, and as the mode of the understanding and perception is that of the senses, it follows that God, in order to raise it up to the highest knowledge, orderly and sweetly, must begin with the lower senses, that He may thus raise it up in harmony with its own constitution to the

[1] Rom xiii 1 [2] Wisd viii 1

supreme wisdom of the spirit, which is not cognizable by sense. For this reason he leads the soul first of all through forms, images, and sensible ways proportionate to its capacity, whether natural or supernatural, and through reflections upwards to His own supreme Spirit. This is the cause of His sending visions and imaginary forms, and other sensible and intelligible means of knowledge. Not because He would not in an instant communicate the substance of the Spirit, provided that the two extremes, the human and Divine—that is, sense and Spirit—were ordinarily able to meet together and to be united in a single act without the previous intervention of many disposing acts, which orderly and sweetly concur together, one being the foundation and the preparation for the other, as in natural operations, where the first subserves the second, that the next, and so onwards. Thus, the way in which God leads man to perfection is the way of his natural constitution, raising him up from what is vile and exterior to that which is interior and noble.'[1]

The corporeal visions, when granted, are ordinarily imparted to beginners in the way of perfection. Sometimes, however, they may be imparted to sinners, and often to the perfect. They are not to be taken as signs of sanctity and perfection, but, rather, as signs of weakness and frailty of soul. Those favoured in this way should receive their visions with humility and turn them to spiritual advantage, always remembering that sanctity does not consist in visions, and sensible feelings and manifestations, but in the practice of virtue and the

[1] 'The Ascent of Mount Carmel,' book ii, chap xvii

advancement in Christian perfection. Nor are we to judge that the visions are unreal and diabolical from the fact that the recipient is imperfect and weak in virtue. They need not always suppose grace and perfection in the recipients in the same way as mystical union, ecstasy, and rapture, because they are given by God in order to make the soul more perfect.

CHAPTER IV

IMAGINATIVE AND INTELLECTUAL VISIONS

1 An imaginative or ideal vision consists in the interior representation of some object, which in the phantasy or imagination, either by combined species or species recently infused, and illustrated with light from above, is so formed that the said power sees its object with greater clearness than if it were beheld by corporeal vision This is the explanation or definition of imaginative visions given by Voss. It may perhaps be described in a simple manner, by saying that an imaginative vision is a sensible representation confined entirely to the imagination, and which presents itself supernaturally to the mind with the liveliness and clearness of a real physical thing It is well described by St John of the Cross.

'Under the designation of imaginative visions I include everything which may be supernaturally represented to the imagination by images, forms, figures, or impressions, and these of the most perfect kind, which represent things and influence us more vividly and more perfectly than it is possible in the natural order of the senses. For all these impressions and images which the five senses represent to the soul, and which establish themselves within in a natural way, may also have their place there in a

1 Imaginative or ideal visions

way that is supernatural, represented therein without any intervention whatever on the part of the outward senses The sense of fancy and memory is, as it were, a storehouse of the intellect, where all forms and objects of the intellect are treasured up, and thus the intellect considers them and forms judgments upon them.

'We must, therefore, remember that as the five outward senses propose and represent to the interior senses the images and pictures of their objects, so in a supernatural way, without the intervention of the outward senses, may be represented the same images and pictures, and that much more vividly and perfectly And thus by means of images God frequently shows many things to the soul, and teaches it wisdom, as we see throughout the Holy Scriptures. He showed His glory in the cloud which covered the tabernacle, and between the Seraphim which covered their faces and their feet with their wings. To Jeremias He showed a rod watching, and to Daniel a multitude of visions.'[1]

The imaginative visions of the mystical order and those of the natural order both take place in the imagination; this is the only relation of analogy between them They differ in all other respects The first are ordinarily produced suddenly without any presentiment, and they vanish just as quickly. Imaginative visions of the natural order, on the contrary, proceed from the exercise or labour of the mind; they result from preceding thoughts, or respond to some desire on which the soul is intent, and they disappear gradually.

The objects of imaginative visions can be the

[1] 'The Ascent of Mount Carmel,' book ii, chap. xvi

same as those of the corporeal visions—God, our Saviour, the Blessed Virgin, the Angels and Saints, etc

2 That these visions, like corporeal visions, may be subject to illusions does not need proof, because they can be produced by the devil or proceed from some bodily disposition. Father Baldelli, as quoted by Benedict XIV, gives us some explanation as to how this may happen

Imaginative visions subject to illusions

' Neither is it difficult to believe that not only ideal visions, but also bodily visions, may proceed from the devil, for he is able to change the images and excite the animal spirits, neither is he without means of making people see erroneously with the eyes and external senses, as, in fact, he does in the case of witches and necromancers And there is no doubt that, as some men by means of some natural secret impose upon the senses of others, and as many conjurers cause one thing to appear for another, so, and much more, can the devil, either by carrying from a distance many real bodies and sensible objects, or by producing them through their causes, or by deceiving by means of aerial bodies the external senses, and thereby causing the suspension of the senses, and changing the images presented to the internal senses, and causing those apparitions which occur in dreams, as Cajetan explains, and those who treat of superstitions. But it may appear difficult to some how visions result from bodily causes, if we had, in reference to ideal visions the experience of dreams, which are nothing else but fantastic apparitions, caused, for the most part, by the motions and concourse of diverse phantasies, by the vapours which cause sleep ; and for the bodily visions the experience of maniacs, madmen, and persons suffering from fever, who, owing to their several indispositions, say they see and feel what in fact they neither see nor feel.'[1]

St. Theresa explains how our Lord communicates Himself to a soul by an imaginative vision, and I shall give only one extract from her writings, which may serve to throw some light on the nature and character of this kind of vision. She writes:

'We now come to *imaginary visions*, in which it is said that the devil can more easily enter than in the preceding ones, and so it is the case. But when they come from our Lord they seem to me to be in some manner more profitable than others, and more conformable to our nature, with the exception, however, of those which our Lord discovers and makes known in the last mansion, for none of the other visions can equal these.' The Saint makes use of a similitude to explain her meaning, 'that of a jewel of great value and virtue in a casket of gold.' From this similitude she goes on to show how our Lord represents Himself to the soul whom He loves by this kind of vision. 'He clearly shows her His most sacred humanity in the way He pleases, either as He appeared when He was in the world, or as He was after His resurrection; and though this vision is effected with a quickness which resembles that of a flash of lightning, yet this glorious image remains so fixed into the imagination that I consider it impossible ever to blot it out, till the soul behold it there, where she shall possess it for ever. Though I call it an image, yet we must not have an idea that it seems as if it were painted in the

[1] 'Treatise on Heroic Virtue,' pp. 309, 310.

eye of the beholder; rather is it most truly endowed with life. Sometimes He discourses with the soul, and reveals great secrets to her.'[1]

3. An intellectual vision is the certain manifestation of an object to the intelligence, without any impression on the senses or imagination. It is the most perfect and the highest form of vision. These visions take place in that faculty of the soul where appear the things that have no bodily form, and where they are seen under the one aspect of being. Objects which by their nature are above sensible things, such as God, an Angel, the soul, and those things which fall under the senses, when considered as to their truth, the mind contemplates independently of any sensible representation either exterior or interior; and this operation is called intellectual, because it belongs entirely to that faculty which apprehends beings inasmuch as they are intelligible, whether they be simple or composite, infinite or limited, substances or modes; in so far as they are perceptible by the mind they are presented under the one common aspect, namely, that of being and of truth. It is for this reason that this kind of vision is the most excellent and the most spiritual, because by a vision of this kind man here on earth is enabled to understand and receive knowledge after the manner of the Angels and Saints in heaven; not through the senses or the imagination, but by the simple act of the intelligence illumined by a special Divine light.[2] On this we may remark that, according to the natural mode of knowing, the intellect has to derive all its know-

3. Intellectual visions.

[1] 'The Interior Castle': Sixth Mansion, chap. ix.
[2] See Lejeune, 'Manuel de Théologie Mystique,' p. 272.

ledge from the senses or the imagination, but, as Suarez says, and with him all other theologians, man can be elevated by a supernatural action to a contemplation of truth without being obscured by the images of the imagination. The action of the imagination is not so essential to knowledge that it may not be chained up or dispensed with by God

St. Theresa, referring to these visions, says that it is a very difficult matter to speak about, because it is exceedingly deep, and that the 'imaginative visions' are more easily explained.[1] And in her Life she narrates that, when giving an account of her vision to her confessor, she found it very difficult to explain it She says: 'I made use of several comparisons whereby to make myself understood, and yet, in my opinion, there is none which properly explains this kind of vision, for as this is one of the highest kind, according to what that holy and spiritual man, Father Peter of Alcantara, told me, as well as other great and learned men, so we cannot find words in this world to express it; at least, we who know so little cannot, though learned men may make themselves better understood'[2]

(1) The obscure intellectual vision

(1) Mystical authors distinguish two kinds of intellectual visions—one obscure, the other clear and distinct. We cannot better describe these than in the words of St. Theresa herself. She describes the obscure intellectual vision with which she had been favoured in the words quoted in Part III, p 384, to which I refer the reader It appears also, from her experiences, that intellectual visions, instead of passing quickly, like imaginative visions,

[1] 'Interior Castle' Sixth Mansion, chap x
[2] Her Life, chap xxvii

lasted for several days, and sometimes for a whole year.

(2) In the intellectual obscure vision the soul is certain of the presence of the object, but without any detailed perception of its intimate nature. In the intellectual distinct and clear vision the soul is not only certain of the presence of the object, but is able to penetrate into its nature, so that it believes it sees God, or that God enlightens it by a Divine clearness and illumination. St. Theresa describes these two modes of intellectual vision in the 'Interior Castle' as follows, although in this place she signifies that the intellectual obscure vision may pass away in an instant:

'It happens, when our Lord is pleased, that the soul, being in prayer and in perfect enjoyment of her senses, is on a sudden seized with a suspension, in which our Lord reveals great secrets to her, which she thinks she sees in God Himself, for these are not visions of the most sacred humanity. But though I say *she sees*, yet she sees nothing; for it is no imaginary, but a very intellectual vision, in which is discovered how all things are seen in God, and how He contains them in Himself. This is of great benefit to us; for though it passes away in an instant, yet it is deeply engraven in the soul, producing great self-confusion, and discerning more clearly our malice in offending God.'

Writing, evidently, of the clear and distinct intellectual vision, she says:

'It happens, likewise, that God very suddenly, and in a manner which cannot be expressed, discovers to us in Himself a certain truth which seems to obscure all those which are in creatures, clearly manifesting that He alone is truth which cannot deceive. Herein is fully comprehended what David says in the Psalm: *Every man is a liar* —words which could never be so understood, though we should often hear it said that God is the infallible Truth. I remember how Pilate asked our Lord in His Passion, and said: *What is truth?* and how little we in this world understand this supreme truth. I would willingly enter into more particulars, but they cannot be expressed. . . .

'Our Lord bestows these favours on a soul because, being His true spouse, and being now resolved to accomplish His will in everything, He is pleased to give her some knowledge of the means whereby she is to accomplish it, and of His greatness likewise It is not necessary for me to say any more. These two I have mentioned because they seem to me very profitable in teaching us that in such cases there is no ground for fearing, but, rather, reason to praise our Lord for giving them, for in my opinion the devil and our own imagination have little access here, and hence the soul enjoys great pleasure and satisfaction.'[1]

4 Intellectual visions cannot be the work of the devil

4 The question is asked in connection with intellectual visions as to whether they can be the work of the devil. The answer given is, that they cannot. This third kind of vision is distinct from the second, and is pure intelligence without the aid of images, and cannot occur in this life without being from God, Who alone can interrupt the connection and natural order of the faculties Nevertheless, if it should happen to be united with this order, it may proceed from some other cause

---

[1] 'The Interior Castle'. Sixth Mansion, chap x

besides God. The knowledge received through this kind of vision, according to St. John of the Cross, consists in a certain contact of the soul with the Divinity, and it is God Himself Who is then felt and tasted, though not manifestly and distinctly, as it will be in glory. But this touch of knowledge and of sweetness is so deep and so profound that it penetrates into the inmost substance of the soul, and the devil cannot interfere with it, nor produce anything like it—because there is nothing else comparable with it—nor infuse any sweetness or delight which shall at all resemble it. This knowledge savours in some measure of the Divine Essence and of everlasting life, and the devil has no power to simulate anything so great.

' Nevertheless, the devil is able to produce certain pretended imitations of it by representing to the soul a certain grandeur and sensible fulness, striving to persuade it that this is God; but he cannot so do this that his influence shall penetrate into the interior part of the soul, renew it, and fill it with love profoundly, as the knowledge of God does. For there are some acts of knowledge and touches of God, wrought by Him in the substance of the soul, which so enrich it that one of them is sufficient, not only to purge away at once certain imperfections, which had hitherto resisted the efforts of a whole life, but also to fill the soul with virtues and Divine gifts Such is the sweetness and deep delight of these touches of God, that one of them is more than a recompense for all the sufferings of this life, however great their number.'[1]

These intellectual visions properly belong to those

[1] 'The Ascent of Mount Carmel,' book ii, chap xxvi

who have reached perfection, and who have been raised up to the state known as spiritual matrimony. It is very seldom that God imparts such visions to the less perfect souls Then, as we have before said, these are not so evanescent as imaginary; they may last for weeks and months, and for a whole year, as in the case of St. Theresa, who had for many years an intellectual vision of our Saviour by her side and witnessing all her actions.

In the vision or apparition purely intellectual no deception can take place, as Cardinal Bona says. 'In this there can be no error, no deception; the rest are liable to errors and illusions.' And again 'No diabolical illusion can disturb the purely intellectual vision, whether the representation of things to the intellect be through species infused by God, or considered in the judgment upon those things which is formed by the light coming down from the Father of lights; for when these two do not depend upon the sense and imagination, no creature can interfere therein.'[1]

5. How to discern visions and apparitions

5. Before concluding the explanation of the subject of visions and apparitions, it will be naturally expected that some rules be given for discerning true and Divine visions from those that are false, natural, or diabolical, and for this purpose I select the following from the work of Benedict XIV., already so often quoted

(1) Visions from natural causes

(1) 'In order to ascertain whether the visions and apparitions be natural, we must diligently inquire whether they were preceded by any natural causes from which they might have proceeded. To sick

[1] Apud Benedict XIV, 'Treatise on Heroic Virtue,' vol III, p. 304

and delirious persons, to those who are afflicted with melancholy, to those who are disturbed by vehement thoughts and affections, it may easily happen that they think they see what does not exist, and that certain objects appear which do not, and which they usually speak of as things seen by them and revealed to them from heaven Bartholomew Medina gives this rule in these words: "The physical temperament must be taken into account, as well as health and occupation, for many sick and delirious persons, through excessive strain of the mind, wander, and think they see and hear sometimes what they never could have heard or seen We must inquire also into the prevailing inclination of his mind, and whether he was greatly under the influence of love or hatred. We must inquire carefully whether he who has visions is subject to melancholy or wasted away, for they who are afflicted with jaundice, with old age, and who are wasted away, are very often deluded. And hence it is that old men, when decrepit, become foolish . . ."

'Cardinal Bona speaks to the same effect · "The physical system, upon which, in general, the state of the mind depends, must be considered. For they are easily deceived who have but weak health, whose imagination is disturbed and vehement, who suffer from bile, which usually disorders the fancy and impresses various images on the disturbed senses; so that while they are awake they may seem to dream, and think that they see and hear what they cannot see nor hear. Long abstinence, frequent fasts, immoderate vigils, dryness of the brain, and the dispersion of the animal spirits, cause *many phantasms to appear, to which the deluded soul obstinately clings, as if they were Divine revelations.'"[1]*

(2) Diabolical visions

(2) Preternatural visions and apparitions, as we have said, may come from God or from the devil. Doctors have given many signs whereby we may distinguish between diabolical visions and those that are Divine. Gerson thus writes: 'This is the principal and chief test among the tests of our spiritual coin. All interior warnings, all strong impressions, all revelations, all miracles, all ecstatic love, all contemplation, all rapture, and, lastly, all interior and exterior workings, if preceded, attended, and followed by humility, if mixed up with nothing destructive of it, have with them a sign that they come from God or a good Angel; nor can ye be deceived.' With him agrees Tanner, who, in speaking of the visions of women, writes thus: 'Even female pretence cannot be long concealed, for where there is no foundation laid of the most profound humility, whatever is built thereon will quickly fall, and not without bringing disgrace; but when there is genuine humility, especially necessary in all who cling to God alone with a pure, simple, and most chaste affection, of whatever sex they may be, they are neither deceived nor can deceive.' In the dialogues of St. Catherine of Siena we thus read: 'This is necessary, that in my visions my soul be more and more humbled.' And again: 'The truth always makes the soul humble, delusion proud.' And Cardinal Bona: 'There is no greater proof of true visions than humility.'

'The second test by which visions of a good

[1] Apud Benedict XIV, 'Treatise on Heroic Virtue,' vol iii, pp 321, 322

spirit are discerned from things of an evil spirit is the fruit and the good works which result from these visions or revelations, for, as it is written in the Gospel *An evil tree cannot produce good fruit*, and, *By their fruit you shall know them.* Therefore, when we see that in these visions and revelations the mind is illuminated, wicked men are converted to a good and devout life, and that this happens in many persons, and perseveres long, then it is a most certain sign that such visions and revelations which have sent forth and produced such fruit have come rather from the Holy Spirit, and not from the devil, who cannot do such things; yea, things wholly at variance with this result from his visions, or, rather, illusions. These have usually caused men to err from the Catholic faith and good morals.

'Besides, it is said that the apparitions of Angels and devils differ in form. An Angel has but one— the human; the devil many—either men or beasts He never appears as a dove or lamb, because these mystically denote the Holy Ghost and Christ. . . . With respect to the human form, if the devil assumes it, it is for the most part black, deformed, maimed, unusual, and such as shows that the evil spirit lurks beneath it. The form of a brute or a monster is adapted only for the devil; for the souls of the dead, although of the damned, when by the permission of God they appear to the living, assume that form by which they are known.'[1]

(3) 'Cardinal Bona enumerates the characteristics of the visions, apparitions, and revelations of St. Theresa, saying that they serve as a test for the value of others. In the first place, then, as he there

(3) Characteristics of good visions exemplified in St Theresa

[1] 'Treatise on Heroic Virtue,' vol. III, pp 328, 331

speaks, she was always afraid of diabolical illusions, so that she never asked for or desired visions, but, rather, prayed God to lead her in the ordinary way, wishing only for this, that the Divine will be done in her. In the second place, though the devil usually bids those things to be kept secret which he reveals, she always heard from the Spirit that appeared to her that she might communicate with learned men In the third place, she obeyed her directors most carefully, and after her visions advanced more and more in charity and humility. In the fourth place, she more readily spoke to those who were incredulous, and loved those who persecuted her. In the fifth place, her mind was tranquil and joyful, and in her heart was a fervent desire of perfection. In the sixth place, He Who spoke interiorly to her reprehended her imperfections. In the seventh place, when it was said to her that if she desired of God what was just she should without doubt obtain it, she desired many things, and always obtained them. In the eighth place, whoever conversed with her, unless an evil disposition stood in the way, were stirred up to the love of God. In the ninth place, the visions and apparitions took place for the most part after long and fervent prayer, or after receiving the Eucharist, and kindled in her the most fervent desire of suffering for God. In the tenth place, she subdued the flesh by disciplines and haircloth, and rejoiced in tribulations, calumnies, and infirmities. In the eleventh place, she loved solitude, disliked all intercourse with the world, and tore herself away from every human affection. In the twelfth place, both in prosperity and adversity she preserved the same tranquillity of mind. Lastly, learned men observed nothing in her visions and apparitions inconsistent with faith and Christian religion, or anything blamable whatsoever.'[1]

H. Joly, speaking of this same Saint, writes ' St. Theresa was so perfectly conscious in herself of the effect of these states (ecstasies, visions, revelations) that she not only describes them for us, but also analyzes, explains, and comments upon them. Her observations are often of a deeply metaphysical nature, and she draws many very clear and precise psychological distinctions. She does not deny the existence of false visions, for she has experienced them herself; but she is on this account all the more alive to the contrast between the true and the false, and the better able to distinguish between them. "Therefore," she says, "there is an immense difference between them, and I do not doubt that even a soul which has arrived at only the prayer of quiet is perfectly well able to distinguish one from the other These visions have all their characteristic marks—the impress, as it were, of their author. I do not think that a soul can be deceived, provided it is humble and simple, and that it does not desire to be deceived. It is sufficient for a person to have only once seen our Lord to be perfectly able to recognise a vision caused by the devil. The latter may begin by causing a certain kind of pleasure, but it will be in vain, as the soul rejects it with a sort of instinctive horror. It sees that the love which is offered is not chaste and pure, and the enemy is soon detected and exposed. Therefore I say that the devil cannot injure a soul that is at all experienced "[2]

[1] 'Treatise on Heroic Virtue,' p 352
[2] 'The Psychology of the Saints,' p. 109

CHAPTER V

DIVINE LOCUTIONS OR SUPERNATURAL WORDS

<small>1 The various ways in which God speaks to us</small>

1. God speaks to us both internally and externally in many ways (1) He speaks to us externally both naturally by His creatures, when they cry out with a silent voice, *He made us, and not we ourselves*,[1] and supernaturally by His words contained in Sacred Scripture and transmitted to us by tradition. (2) He speaks to us externally by the ministers of His Church and by pious books, expounding the Word of God, either written or transmitted, according to His saying *He that heareth you heareth Me*[2] (3) He speaks to us internally both naturally by the dictates of conscience—*The light of Thy countenance, O Lord, is signed upon us*[3]—and supernaturally by supernatural motions, which are indeliberate on our part and which are effected in us without us, and incite us to believe and work in a salutary manner; and these acts are called supernatural illuminations and inspirations—actual graces. (4) He speaks also to His chosen ones by a proper locution, such as can be had here on earth, not as by a precise inspiration, but by words formed and expressed. It is of this way which is extraordinary that we treat, and as defined it can be understood as distinct from visions, which

---

[1] Ps xcix. 3   [2] St Luke x 16.   [3] Ps. iv 7.

MYSTICAL PHENOMENA—LOCUTIONS

offer to the mind realities or images for contemplation, while locutions are formal words which express truths or desires. If the locution discovers something hidden and secret it is called a revelation; if it foretells a future event it is called prophecy. Of these we shall treat in the following chapters. This extraordinary locution may be either vocal, imaginative, or intellectual, and these we shall now explain.[1]

2. Vocal locution takes place when words are addressed to the external sense of hearing, and resound in the ears. These sounds or vibrations are miraculous, and they resemble the sounds or vibrations of human speech. As to how the sounds are caused does not call for any minute explanation.

Divine vocal locution

In the case of our Lord and the Blessed Virgin, supposing on any extraordinary occasions that they are really and personally present, as they have their own bodies, these words can be spoken according to the usual modes of speech. In the case of locution of the Angels and of souls separated from the body, we may notice that these spirits do not use the human organs of speech, but they can easily produce vibrations or sounds in the air and imitate human words, and this can be understood as possible in the same way that it is possible for the soul itself to act upon the material body to which it is united

Sometimes these heavenly locutions are heard without the person pronouncing them being seen Thus, at the baptism and transfiguration of Christ the words were heard. *This is My beloved Son in Whom I am well pleased.*[2] And in the Temple, when Jesus prayed, *Father, glorify Thy Name*, a voice was heard coming from heaven, saying, *I have*

---
[1] Schram, vol II, p 236 [2] St Matt. III 17, XVII 5

both glorified it, and will glorify it again,[1] but no one saw the speaker of these heavenly words. Sometimes the words are heard and at the same time the speaker is seen, as happened to the shepherds on the night of the Nativity. They saw the Angels, and heard them singing *Glory to God in the highest and on earth peace to men of good will*.[2] In this and in other similar cases of the apparitions of Angels or Saints, the vision and locution are united in the same fact; but it may happen that the words be heard and the speaker be seen, and this without an apparition or vision, as, for example, when words come forth from the Blessed Sacrament or from images. Such a locution was that with which St. Thomas of Aquin was favoured when he heard the crucifix say to him 'Bene de Me scripsisti, Thoma' (Thou hast written well of Me, Thomas). These locutions, whether they happen in one or the other way, not only excite in the mind great attention, but also great emotion of holy affections in the heart, and this is a sign of their supernatural character.[3]

As it is certain that the devil can produce in the same manner as an Angel sounds like the human voice and human speech, it is necessary to observe circumspection with regard to these phenomena, and persons who experience them, or may have to deal with them, ought to be guided by the same rules of prudence and reserve which are prescribed for cases of corporeal visions.

Imaginative locutions

3. For the reason assigned by Maréchaux, it seems preferable to use the word 'imaginative'

[1] St John xii 28 [2] St Luke ii 14.
[3] Voss, 'Comp Direct Ascet,' p 384.

rather than 'imaginary' in speaking of these supernatural favours, visions, locutions, and revelations. In ordinary conversation the latter word means something fictitious or opposed to the reality. But visions, locutions, and revelations are not fictitious, but very real, if they come from God.

Imaginative locutions are words which are framed in the phantasy, and although they sound not in the ears, they are as clearly and articulately perceived by the recipient, even as if heard by the ears. God can, by Himself or through an Angel, represent on the phantasy the species of the words which He wishes to speak, and illumine them immediately by His heavenly light, so that the imaginative faculty vividly apprehends these words, and impresses them thus apprehended on the sensitive faculty In such a way, without being heard by the ears, they produce the same effect on the internal sense as do the ordinary words perceived by hearing, only with this difference—that the effects of these are natural; but the effects of the former are supernatural and fruitful of holy works [1]

These words, whether formed by God or an Angel in the imagination of the person who is praying or contemplating, are so ordained and disposed that sometimes they seem to descend from heaven, sometimes they seem to be uttered near at hand or at a distance, and sometimes they seem to rise up in the interior of the heart or soul. In whatever way these locutions are heard, they are always excited by God in the phantasy by the composition or combination of the species that make them perceptible.

[1] Ita Voss, 'Compend Scaramelli,' p 386

They are heard sometimes in sleep whilst the soul is at rest and free from all care;[1] sometimes they are heard by those awake when engaged in prayer or contemplation.[2]

St Theresa explains in chapter xxv. of her Life how these words and speeches are to be understood which God communicates to the soul without any voice or sound being heard. I can only give space for one extract.

'They are,' she says, 'certain words very distinctly formed in the soul, which, though not heard with the corporeal ears, are understood much more expressly and clearly than if they were so heard; nor can the soul avoid understanding them and giving her whole attention to them, and it is useless to resist, however much we may strive. When in this world we do not wish to hear, we can stop our ears, or else attend to other things, in such a way, that though we may hear the words, yet we shall not understand them. But when God speaks to the soul, there is no remedy whatever, but we are made to listen to the words whether we will or no, and the understanding is obliged to be very attentive in order to comprehend them. Thus, whether we wish or no, God wishes we should understand Him, and because He is all-powerful, that which He resolves must be done, and so He is known as the true Lord of us all. Of this truth I have had much experience, for the resistance I made continued almost two years on account of the fear I had, and even now I feel this fear sometimes; but resistance is of little use.'[3]

This locution is called imaginative—not as if it

---

[1] St Matt i 20   [2] Zach i 9, Acts x 15
[3] Her Life, chap xxv

were solely the operation of the imagination, because the intellect is also employed in it as well as the imagination ; but it is so called because of the first and principal impression which God makes by means of this locution, which is not on the external senses nor on the intellect, but on the imagination. It can be effected by impressions on the phantasy similar to those impressed by external words or sounds, and this is the manner in which God speaks in these kind of manifestations. The Angels, without supplying new species or representations to the phantasy, can excite it, nevertheless, in some way by the external senses, so that without words or sounds the intellect is able to gain knowledge from the phantasy, when excited and moved in that way, just as if words had been used to impress the imagination, though no words have been used. The Angels may concur in this locution either in their own name or in the name of God and as His ministers. Their office is limited in this to applying the active forces of the imagination to the passive, and thus bringing about some movement of that power, sufficient to enable the intellect to apprehend what is communicated to the imagination. It seems that Angels of their own natural power cannot supply species to the phantasy representing the locution, just as they cannot supply the species of colour to a person born blind. By extraordinary and miraculous power imparted to them the Angels could effect this, according to some authors, and I see no difficulty in the way of admitting that God can use them as His agents and living instruments in supplying the species of the various locutions which God imparts to His favoured servants here on earth.

We are told that the devil also, by applying what is called the *active* to the *passive* within the range of natural things, can effect upon the imagination the impressions of words and sounds, without the external senses being acted upon by these. This we know is possible, because a like result happens by a continuation of natural causes in persons who are deranged or asleep.

St. Theresa signifies that these locutions can come from the devil, and she gives us some signs by which diabolical locutions may be detected. She says

'When these things come from the devil, they not only produce no good effects, but they even produce evil effects. Besides the great dryness they leave behind them, they give the soul much trouble likewise; from the delusions of the devil no sweetness whatever remains in the soul, but she feels much terror and great disquiet. . The truth is that when these things come from the devil it seems that all blessings hide themselves, and even fly from the soul, so unquiet and in such disorder does she remain, without feeling any good effect And though some good desires may seem to be excited in her, yet they are not strong or effectual The humility the devil leaves behind is false, unquiet, and without sweetness, and I think anyone who has experienced "the good Spirit" will understand this.'[1]

4 Locutions and visions in dreams

4. These locutions may take place sometimes during sleep and in dreams. I only mention dreams here in passing, because it will not be necessary to give the subject any lengthy consideration It is rarely that God makes known His secrets to men in dreams, and Divine dreams announcing future events

[1] Her Life, chap xxv

are not sent but for some great cause which concerns the public welfare. It is, however, certain that dreams have been sometimes sent by God God warned Abimelech, King of Gerar, in a dream, not to touch the wife of Abraham. Jacob in a dream saw the mystical ladder and the Angels ascending and descending God appeared in a dream to Laban, and bade him not to deal harshly with Jacob And there are many other examples in the Old and New Testament of God speaking to men through a dream From the New Testament we may select for an example the communication made to St Joseph after our Saviour's birth. Joseph, the husband of Mary, as we read in St. Matt. ii. 13, had a locution in a dream. *Arise, and take the Child and His Mother, and fly into Egypt . . . For it will come to pass that Herod will seek the Child to destroy Him.* And at another time in Egypt, after the death of Herod, an Angel appeared to him in sleep, and said *Arise, and take the Child and His Mother, and go into the land of Israel for they are dead that sought the life of the Child*

The following remarks from Benedict XIV will be sufficient to explain how dreams are to be regarded in their relation either to locutions or to visions or revelations ·

'If the question should arise concerning a vision, apparition, or revelation, alleged to have taken place during sleep, we must not neglect carefully to inquire into those natural causes from which dreams proceed. . . . Great caution must be had in the matter of dreams, according to the commentator on Climacus, who says " Great prudence must be shown in dealing with these things which are usual in sleep, and rather to be set aside altogether, because they are uncertain; for they are few who can discriminate between them. And as the greater portion is fortuitous and accidental, owing to the varied and disorderly movements of the animal spirits, and of the sensible species through the recesses of the brain, the Holy Scriptures rightly bid us to heed them not, as it is written in Lev. xix. 26. *You shall not divine and observe dreams*, and in Jer. xxix. 8. *Give no heed to your dreams which you dream*, and in Eccles. v. 6. *Where there are many dreams there are many vanities.*'[1]

'Thyræus lays down seven tests by which we can know that dreams cannot be Divine. The first is the confusion of matter which occurs in dreams; the second, their falseness; the third, their trifling character; the fourth, their wickedness; the fifth, their uselessness; the sixth, their superfluousness; the seventh, the impiety of those who dream. He then shows it to be necessary that the contrary of this should be found in those dreams which may be admitted as Divine, but it is necessary in reference to the present question—that is, in regard to the cause of canonization—"that what is revealed in sleep should be such as that the certain knowledge of it can be derived to men only from God, and the movement of the mind such as God alone can produce."'

'Cardinal Bona more clearly says that those dreams are from the devil which suggest useless superstitions and vain things, which move people in any way to evil, which reveal secret things only to gratify curiosity, or make an ostentatious show of knowledge, which foretell future events, but which

[1] 'Treatise on Heroic Virtue,' vol. iii., p. 326

the issues prove to have been false, which are disordered and confused, and which immediately vanish away. And, on the other hand, the proofs of Divine dreams are the subjects themselves, which thereby become known if they are such as can be revealed only by God, such as the secrets of hearts, the hidden mysteries of faith, future contingencies dependent on free will He adds that God, when He sends dreams, enlightens the mind and moves the will so that it shall firmly cling to them, and certainly know that they proceed from God, nor does it at any time forget them. He concludes that a more certain proof is derived from the subject of the dream than from the manner in which it occurs, for God sometimes sends them in a state of the profoundest repose, sometimes with great bodily uneasiness; sometimes He sends a dream without the understanding thereof, sometimes the understanding; sometimes He manifests things clearly and openly, sometimes obscurely and in riddles.'[1]

5. Finally, God speaks to devout souls by intellectual locutions. By an *intellectual locution* we are to understand that which God makes to the soul by words perceived and understood only intellectually, and independently of the external sense of hearing and the internal sense of phantasy or imagination It may happen by a very special privilege that God may speak to the soul in a manner purely intellectual and independently of any species acquired from sensible things, or any application to the phantasy of the species or images impressed upon it This is done by species immediately infused by God into the mind itself, after the manner in which

5. Intellectual locutions

[1] 'Treatise on Heroic Virtue,' vol III, pp 340, 341

souls separated from the body understand, or after the manner of understanding of the soul of Christ, which possessed the vision of God even when Christ was a wayfarer, or, again, after the manner of the locutions of God with the Angels or of the Angels with each other. St. Theresa describes how it is that God speaks to the soul without articulate words. 'To me it seems,' she says, 'that our Lord is here pleased that our soul should have some knowledge of that which passes in heaven; and that as the blessed understand one another there without speaking, so also it should be here, that God and the soul might understand one another, and this for the sole reason that His Majesty is pleased they should do so without any artifice being used to make known the love which these two friends bear each other. Just as in the world when two persons love one another dearly, and have a good understanding, they seem able to understand each other, without any signs, by only looking at one another. This ought to be our case, since without our knowing expressly how these two lovers look earnestly at each other in the face, as the spouse in the Book of Canticles saith to her beloved; for so, I think, I have heard it mentioned there.[1]

6. St. John of the Cross distinguishes three kinds of intellectual locutions—namely, *successive*, *formal*, and *substantial*. It is not certain that St John of the Cross restricts these subdivisions to intellectual locutions. Scaramelli, who quotes St. John of the Cross, gives these three kinds as a division of imaginative locutions. According to Lejeune, many authors, and among them Philip of the Most Holy

[1] Her Life, chap xxvii

Trinity and St Liguori, understand the division to apply to all supernatural locutions, whether vocal, imaginative, or intellectual Schram places the classification of St John of the Cross under intellectual locutions, and it is certain that the kinds of locutions explained by St John of the Cross may be applied above all to intellectual locutions

In describing these locutions, we cannot do better than call in the aid of this eminent and holy writer, who can explain his own meaning better than any of his commentators. 'I shall pursue the same course,' he says, 'with the third kind of apprehensions, the supernatural locutions of spiritual men, which are effected without the instrumentality of the corporeal sense. These locutions, notwithstanding their rarity, may be comprised under three designations *successive*, *formal*, and *substantial* words By *successive* words I mean certain words and considerations which the mind self-recollected, forms and fashions within itself. By *formal* I mean certain distinct and definite words which the mind receives not from itself, but from a third person, sometimes while in a state of self-recollection, and at other times while not. By *substantial* I mean other words which are also formally in the mind, sometimes while it is recollected, and sometimes while it is not. These words produce and effect in the innermost soul that substance and power of which they are the expression.' The Saint devotes several chapters of 'The Ascent of Mount Carmel' to explaining these in the order he has named them.

(1) St. John of the Cross thus describes suc-[1] cessive locutions

[1] Successive locutions

'At all times when successive words take place, it is when the mind is collected and absorbed by some particular subject; and while attentively considering the matter which occupies its thoughts, it proceeds from one part of it to another, puts words and reasonings together so much to the purpose, and with such felicity and clearness discovers by reflection things it knew not before, that it seems to itself as if it were not itself which did so, but some third person which addressed it interiorly, reasoning, answering, and informing. And in truth there is good ground for this notion; the mind then reasons with itself as one man does with another, and to a certain extent it is so. For though it be the mind itself that thus reasons, yet the Holy Ghost very often assists it in the formation of these conceptions, words, and reasonings. Thus, the mind addresses itself to itself as if to some third person.'

He then shows how the Holy Ghost may teach a truth which the mind puts into words:

'For as the intellect is then united and intently occupied with the truth of that whereof it thinks, as the Holy Spirit is also united with it, the intellect in this communion with the Divine Spirit, through the channel of that particular truth, forms successively within itself those other truths which relate to the matter before it, the Holy Ghost, the Teacher, opening the way and giving light. This is one way in which the Holy Ghost teaches us. The understanding being thus enlightened and instructed by the great Teacher, while perceiving these truths, forms at the same time the words in question about those truths which it receives from another source. We may apply to this the saying of Isaac. *The voice* indeed is the voice of Jacob, but the hands are the hands of Esau.[1] He who is in this state cannot believe that the words and expressions do not proceed from some third person, not knowing how easily the intellect can form words about conceptions and truths which it derives from another person

'These interior successive locutions furnish occasions to the evil spirit, especially when persons have an inclination or affection for them. For when they begin to recollect themselves, the devil offers to them materials for discursive reflections, suggesting thoughts and expressions to the intellect, and then, having deceived them by things that appear to be true, casts them down to the ground Such is his dealing with those who have entered into a compact with him, tacit or expressed. Thus he converses with some heretics, especially with heresiarchs; he informs their intellect with most subtle thoughts and reasonings, false, however, and erroneous.

'It appears, then, that these successive words may proceed from three sources from the Holy Spirit, moving and enlightening, from the natural intellect; and from the evil spirit suggesting.

'The evil locutions are occasionally hard to distinguish, for though they dry up the love of God in the will, and incline men to vanity, self-esteem, or complacency, still, they beget at times a certain false humility and a fervent affection of the will founded on self-love, which requires for its detection great spirituality of mind. This the devil brings about the better to conceal his presence. He always labours to move the will so that men shall esteem these interior communications and make

[1] Gen xxvii. 22

much account of them, in order to induce them to give themselves up to them, and occupy themselves with what is not virtue, but, rather, an occasion of losing what virtue they may have.

'Let us, therefore, abide by this necessary caution in order to escape all perplexity and delusions never to make any account of these locutions, from whatsoever source they may come, but learn how to direct our will courageously to God in the perfect fulfilment of His law and holy counsels, which is the wisdom of the Saints, content with the knowledge of those truths and mysteries, in simplicity and sincerity, as the Holy Church sets forth ; for these are sufficient to inflame our will without thrusting ourselves into deep and curious investigations, when the absence of danger is a miracle. It is with reference to this that St. Paul exhorts us *not to be more wise than it behoveth to be wise.*[1] Let this suffice on the subject of successive words.'[2]

(2) Formal locutions or words

(2) 'The second kind of interior locutions are formal words uttered in the mind, sometimes supernaturally, without the intervention of the senses, whether in a state of recollection or not. I call them formal words, because the mind formally perceives they are spoken by a third person, independently of its own operations. For this reason they are very different from those of which I have just spoken. They differ from them, not only because they take place without any effort of the mind, but sometimes even when the mind is not recollected, but far from thinking of what is uttered within it. This is not so in the case of successive words, for these always relate

[1] Rom. xii. 3.
[2] 'The Ascent of Mount Carmel,' book ii., chap. xxix.

to the matter which then occupies the mind. The locutions of which I am now speaking are sometimes perfectly formed, sometimes not, being very often, as it were, conceptions, by which something is said at one time in the way of an answer, at another by another mode of speaking Sometimes it is one word, at another two or more, and occasionally successive words, as in the former case, for they continue in the way of instruction to the soul, or of discussion with it. Still, all takes place without the active participation of the mind, for it is as if another person were speaking, as we read in Daniel, who says that an Angel instructed him and spoke This was formal successive reasoning and instruction. The Angel says *I am now come forth to teach thee.*[1]

'When these locutions are no more than formal, the effect on the mind is not great. They are in general sent only to instruct and enlighten us on a particular subject, and it is not necessary for this purpose that they should have another effect different from that for which they are sent. And so whenever they come from God they effect their object in the soul; for they render it ready to accomplish what is commanded, and enlighten it so that it understands what it hears They do not always remove the repugnance which the soul feels, but rather increase it, and this is the operation of God, the end of which is the more perfect instruction, humiliation, and profit of the soul This repugnance is in general the result when great and noble deeds are commanded, and great promptitude and facility, is the result when vile and humiliating things are enjoined.

[1] Dan ix 22.

Thus, when Moses was commanded to go to Pharao and deliver the people of Israel, he felt so great a repugnance for his task that God was obliged to command him three times and show him signs. And after all this was not sufficient till God gave him Aaron as his partner in the work, and a partaker of his dignity. . . .

'We must not make much of these formal locutions any more than of the successive; for over and above the occupation of the mind with that which is not the legitimate and proximate means of union with God—namely, faith—there is also the too certain risk of diabolic delusions. We can scarcely distinguish at times what locutions come from a good, and what from an evil, spirit. And as the effects of them are not great, we can hardly distinguish them by that test; for sometimes the diabolical locutions have a more sensible influence on the imperfect than the Divine locutions on spiritual persons. . . .

'I content myself with saying that the real and secure teaching on the subject is, not to give heed to them, however plausible they may be, but to be governed in all by reason, and by what the Church has taught and is teaching us every day.'[1]

(3) Interior substantial locutions.

(3) 'The third kind of interior locutions are the substantial words. Though these are also formal, inasmuch as they are formally impressed on the soul, they differ from them in this: the substantial locutions produce a vivid and substantial effect in the soul, while those locutions which are only formal do not. Though it be true that every substantial locution is also formal, yet every formal locution is not substantial, but only that which really im-

---

[1] 'The Ascent of Mount Carmel,' book ii., chap. xxx.

presses on the soul what it signifies. Thus, if our Lord were to say formally to a particular soul, "Be thou good," that soul would immediately be good, or, "Love thou Me," that soul would at once have and feel the substance of love—that is, a true love of God, or, again, if He were to say to a timid soul, "Be not afraid," that soul would on the instant become courageous and calm. For *the Word of God*, saith the wise man, *is full of power*.[1] Thus, what the locution meaneth is substantially accomplished in the soul. This is the meaning of those words of David: *He will give to His voice the voice of power*.[2] Thus also dealt He with Abraham, when He said unto him *Walk before Me, and be perfect*.[3] Abraham was then perfect, and ever reverently walked before God.

'This is the power of His word in the Gospel by which He healed the sick and raised the dead by a word only Such, too, are his substantial locutions they are of such price and moment as to be the life and strength and incomparable good of souls, for one locution of God does for the soul far more at once than that soul has done for itself in its whole past life.

'The soul is not called upon to do or attempt anything with regard to these locutions, but to be resigned and humble. It is not called upon to undervalue or fear them, nor to labour in doing what they enjoin; for God by means of these substantial locutions works in and by the soul Himself. And herein they differ from the formal and successive locutions The soul need not reject these locutions, for the effect of them remains

[1] Ecclus. viii 4.   [2] Ps. lxvii 34.   [3] Gen xvii 1

substantially in the soul, and full of blessings; and therefore the action of the soul is useless, because it has received them passively. Neither need the soul be afraid of illusions here for these locutions are beyond the reach of the intellect or the evil spirit. The devil cannot passively produce this substantial effect in any soul whatever, so as to impress upon it the effect and habit of this locution, though he may by his suggestions lead those souls in whom he dwells as their lord, in virtue of their voluntary compact with him, to perform deeds of exceeding malignity. For he is able to influence these easily because they are united to him voluntarily in the bonds of iniquity We see by experience that even good men suffer violence from his suggestions, which are exceeding strong, but if men are evilly disposed his suggestions then are more efficacious

'But the devil cannot produce any effects resembling those of the Divine locutions, for there is no comparison possible between his locutions and those of God. All his are as if they were not in presence of the Divine, and their effects as nothing compared with the effects of God's locutions. This is the meaning of those words of the prophet: *What hath the chaff to do with the wheat? . . . Are not My words as a fire, and as a hammer that breaketh the rock in pieces?*[1] Thus, the substantial locutions conduce greatly to the union of the soul with God; and the more interior they are, the more substantial are they, and the more profitable. Blessed, then, is the soul to which God sends His locutions *Speak, Lord, for Thy servant heareth.*'[2]

[1] Jer xxiii 28, 29
[2] 'The Ascent of Mount Carmel,' book ii, chap. xxvi

CHAPTER VI

ON REVELATIONS

1. IN treating of visions and locutions, we had to speak of revelations frequently, for much that concerns visions and locutions concerns revelations also, as Benedict XIV. tells us. Nevertheless, after the example of mystical writers, it must be considered of sufficient importance to explain many things which peculiarly belong to revelations, and to this purpose the present chapter will be devoted

A Divine locution which manifests something before hidden or secret is called a Divine revelation, which may be defined. 'An enlightenment of the mind, by which God manifests something secret or unknown, either past, present, or future, and instructs a person either for his own salvation or the salvation of others.' The word 'revelation' originally means an unveiling—a manifestation of some object by drawing back the covering by which it was hidden. Hence, we commonly use the word in the sense of 'bringing to light some fact or truth not generally known.' But it is especially applied to manifestations made by God, Who is Himself hidden from our eyes, yet makes Himself known to us.

What is meant by revelation

2. Three degrees of revelation.

2. 'God discloses Himself to us in three ways. The study of the universe, and especially of man, the noblest object in the universe, clearly proves to us the existence of One Who is the Creator and Lord of all. This mode of manifestation is called natural revelation, because it is brought about by means of nature, and because our own nature has a claim to it. . . . But God has also spoken to man by His own voice, both directly and through prophets, Apostles, and sacred writers. This positive (as opposed to natural) revelation proceeds from the gratuitous condescension of God, and tends to a gratuitous union with Him, both of which are far beyond the demands of nature. Hence, it is called supernatural revelation, and sometimes revelation pure and simple, because it is more properly a disclosure of something hidden. The third and highest degree of revelation is in the Beatific Vision in heaven, where God withdraws the veil entirely, and manifests Himself in all His glory. Here on earth, even in spiritual revelation, *we walk by faith, and not by sight;*[1] *we see now through a glass in a dark manner, but then* (in the Beatific Vision) *face to face;*[2] *we shall see Him as He is.*[3]

3. Canonical and private revelations.

3. Of Divine revelations, some are canonical and some private. The canonical revelations are those contained in Holy Scripture and Divine tradition, and which are proposed by the Church to be believed by faith; private revelations are those which are made to a particular person, whether it be to the common utility of the Church or not. We have

---

[1] 2 Cor. v. 7. [2] 1 Cor. xiii. 12.
[3] St. John iii. 2. See 'A Manual of Catholic Theology,' vol. i., p. 3.

MYSTICAL PHENOMENA—REVELATIONS

not to treat here of canonical revelations, which are the foundations of our faith, and through which the mysteries of religion have been manifested to us. 'The dignity and perfection of Christian revelation require that no further public revelation is to be made. The Old Testament dispensation pointed to one that was to follow, but the Christian dispensation is that *which remaineth* (2 Cor. iii. 11; *cf* Rom x 3 *et seq.*, Gal iii 23 *et seq.*), an *immovable kingdom* (Heb. xii. 28); perfectly and absolutely sufficient (Heb. vii. 11 *et seq*), not shadow, but the very image of the things to come (Heb. x. 1). And Christ distinctly says that His doctrine shall be preached until the consummation of the world, and declares. *All things whatsoever I have heard from My Father I have made known unto you* (St John xv. 15). And, *When He, the Spirit of Truth, is come, He will teach you all truth* (St. John xvi 13). The Apostles also exhort their disciples to stand by the doctrine which they received, and to listen only to the Church (2 Tim. ii. 2 and iii. 14). And the epistle ascribed to St. Barnabas contains the well-known formula · "The rule of light is to keep what thou hast received without adding or taking away" Moreover, the Church has always rejected the pretension of those who claim to have received new revelations of a higher order from the Holy Spirit —*e g.*, the Montanists, Manicheans, Fraticelli, the Anabaptists, Quakers, and Irvingites.

'The finality of the present revelation does not, however, exclude the possibility of minor and subsidiary revelations made in order to throw light upon doctrine or discipline. The Church is the judge of the value of these revelations We may mention, as instances of those which have been approved, the Feast of Corpus Christi and the devotion to the Sacred Heart of Jesus."[1]

4 Revelations as distinct from visions and apparitions

4. Scacchus, as quoted by Benedict XIV, writing of revelation as distinct from vision, says 'that it is a revelation as often as anything, till then unknown, is made known to men, and, although in every vision some manifestation takes place, that, however, is not sufficient to constitute a revelation; for he who sees does not at times understand what he sees; when he understands, he is said to have a revelation. The example of the vision granted to St. Peter related in the Acts is given as an illustration, which St. Peter did not at first understand; but when afterwards he went to Joppa, and was in the house of Cornelius the centurion, where he found many Gentiles who were waiting for him to hear the word of God, he understood the vision of the linen sheet. Peter had before seen and heard, but this vision assumed the nature of a revelation only when Peter understood it.' Another author quoted by Benedict XIV., Arauxo, thus speaks: 'Visions and revelations refer to the same thing, with this only difference, that revelation presupposes vision, and contains in addition the understanding of that which is seen, according to the words: *For there is need of understanding in a vision.*'[2] I may add that a revelation is distinguished from a vision in another respect, namely, that it is made to a person by locution, whilst a vision is strictly to be understood of that which is seen, and a vision becomes a revelation when it is accompanied by a Divine locution, when that locution causes the vision to be under-

[1] See 'A Manual of Catholic Theology,' vol 1, p 14
[2] Dan x 1.

stood. Again, we have in this place to restrict revelations to the manifestations of secrets, past, or absent, or present, which are unknown; this we do in order to keep revelation distinct from prophecy, which extends to future things.

5. As we have said that visions and apparitions are of three kinds—namely, natural, diabolical, and heavenly or Divine—so we may say the same of private revelations. Benedict XIV. gives us briefly an explanation of these three kinds:

5. Division of private revelations.

'Those are natural which result from natural causes, from abundance of bile, from bodily weakness, from excessive watching, from an injured brain, from a turbid or over vehement imagination.

'Those are diabolical which proceed from the devil, for the devil reveals not only what is evil, but sometimes what is good, in order to deceive the unwary or withdraw them from a greater good, or urge them to evil, as St. Gregory explains it upon these words of Job: *The beasts of the field shall play.* Many things relating to these diabolical revelations have been collected by Larrea, by Martin del Rio, and by Philamarini, among which may perhaps be those said to have been made to heretics, both in ancient and modern times, unless they are to be attributed rather to their lying. Those are well known which have been published by Cerinthus, Montanus and his prophetess, also Luther, Carlstadt, Thomas Munzer, and the Anabaptists.

'Finally, those are heavenly and Divine private revelations by which God sometimes illuminates and instructs a person for his own eternal salvation, or that of others.'[1]

[1] 'Treatise on Heroic Virtue,' vol. iii., p. 369 *et seq.*

6. The existence of Divine private revelations

6. Schram gives us some proofs from Holy Scripture to establish the truth and reality of Divine private revelations from the very beginning of the Church. He first gives us the observation of Estius on the fourteenth chapter of the First Epistle of St. Paul to the Corinthians. Estius says that St. Paul, in speaking of the gift of prophecy in this place, does not confine it to predictions concerning future events, but means it to refer also to Divine inspirations concerning what is secret, whether future or not, such as explanations of difficult and obscure texts of Scripture, or explanations which serve to promote Christian doctrine and piety. The word 'prophet' is applied in this sense in the Acts to those of whom it is said *Now there were in the church which was at Antioch, prophets and doctors, among whom was Barnabas, and Simon who was called Niger*, etc.[1] It is also in this sense that the four virgin daughters of Philip did prophesy.[2] It was also by private revelation that their father Philip explained to the eunuch of Queen Candace the passage of the prophet Isaias which led up to his baptism.[3] It is of this manner of prophesying or of Divine private revelations concerning hidden mysteries that St. Paul speaks when he says *Despise not prophecies*. And that he speaks of private revelations in the fourteenth chapter of the First Epistle to the Corinthians is shown from verse 3, when he says: *He that prophesieth speaketh to men unto edification, and exhortation, and comfort*, and in verse 26, when he says: *How is it then, brethren? When you come together, every one of you hath a psalm, hath a doctrine, hath a revelation,*

[1] Acts xiii. 1 [2] Acts xxi. 9 [3] Acts viii. 29

hath a tongue, hath an interpretation: let all things be done to edification All this is interpreted as signifying the revelation of occult mysteries.

The same author, Schram, confirms this doctrine, and establishes it as appertaining to every age of the Church from two definitions of the Council of Trent One of which declares that without a special revelation of God no one can know whether he is among the elect. The other which declares that no one can with infallible certainty know whether he can persevere to the end in good [1] From this he concludes that the Council supposes a private revelation may be made concerning the secret mystery of predestination, and consequently it may be made about other truths of less moment. Pope Gelasius is quoted as saying that revelations of this kind are not to be rejected, but to be approved.

Benedict XIV. refers to the centuriators of Magdeburg, who, in their hostility to private revelations beyond the limits of the canonical books, have endeavoured to get rid of them altogether; and to Melancthon, who accounted them fabulous and superstitious, and he quotes Gravina as proving clearly against the former—(1) That Divine, private, and particular revelations must be admitted on valid evidence drawn from ecclesiastical history, (2) that many of the heretics have attempted in vain to get rid of these true revelations; (3) that many impostors pretended to them; (4) that the question turns upon this, how it may be rightly examined into and considered, what are the private revelations which may be attributed to God as their Author? [2]

---

[1] Council Trent, Sess VI, chaps xii and xvi
[2] 'Treatise on Heroic Virtue,' vol iii, p 372.

7. Signs by which heavenly revelations may be distinguished

7. Cardinal Torquemada, in the prologue to the revelations of St. Bridget, mentions the signs by which a heavenly revelation is distinguished from that which is demoniacal. These are his words: 'The first sign is when they are approved by the judgment of great and experienced men. The second is derived from the effects which they leave behind in the soul of him to whom they are granted, when devotion and humility increase in him, and the glory of God is promoted by these revelations. The third is derived from the subject-matter, when all that is said is found to be true. The fourth is derived from the form of them when they are consistent with Holy Scripture. The fifth is derived from the character of their subject, namely, approved sanctity. Suarez wisely observes that in revelations we must begin by an accurate investigation, whether that which is said to be revealed be contrary to the Catholic faith or good morals, so that when its agreement with Holy Scripture and with good morals is established, then only occurs the opportunity of testing its other characteristics, which would be altogether unseemly and superfluous if that foundation failed us. This must be the first proof, afterwards, when it shall have appeared that the matter is not contrary to the Catholic faith, other conjectures and signs are to be brought forward.'

Benedict XIV, in elucidation of this condition, goes on to explain as follows:

'The agreement, then, of revelation with the sacred writings, with Divine and Apostolic traditions, with the morality and definitions of the Church, is the chief test of Divine private revelations; not that any revelation is to be immediately regarded as heavenly and Divine because it is in harmony with the sacred writings, Apostolic traditions, the morality and definitions of the Church, but as soon as anything appears therein inconsistent with these, it is to be rejected as lies and illusions of the devil. The Apostle says in his Epistle to the Galatians : *If an Angel from heaven preach a gospel besides that which we have preached to you, let him be anathema.*[1] And, again, he writes to the Thessalonians : *Hold the traditions which you have learned ;*[2] and to the Hebrews : *Be not led away with various and strange doctrines.*[3] We must say the same of revelations which contain anything at variance with the unanimous teaching of the holy Fathers or of theologians; for the unanimous voice of the Fathers cannot be in error in distinguishing the matters of faith.

'In the Council of Trent it was specially forbidden, under pain of anathema, to interpret the Holy Scriptures contrary to the unanimous sense of the holy Fathers; and when theologians with great consent teach that any doctrine is derived from principles of faith in the matters of faith and morals, they furnish a strong presumption that to contradict it is heretical, or very nearly so. . . . But it must be observed that the consent of the Fathers is not to be understood mathematically, so that not one of the Fathers of all ages shall be wanting, but morally, so that the consent shall be of all, or nearly all. Cardinal Perron therefore thus explains the unanimous assent of the Fathers in his learned reply to the King of Great Britain : "It is thus we are to understand the unanimous consent of the Fathers,

---

[1] Gal. i. 8.   [2] 2 Thess. ii. 14.   [3] Heb. xiii. 9.

when the most eminent of each nation agree in maintaining a certain proposition, so that none of them, who, always orthodox, always agreed with the orthodox, dissent from the rest."[1]

Benedict XIV. continues the subject, and refers to other matters to be considered in treating of revelations. 'Moreover,' he says, 'what we have said of revelations inconsistent with the sacred writings, Apostolic tradition, the unanimous consent of Fathers and theologians, is necessarily to be considered when we treat of revelations by which evil is encouraged; or if good be encouraged, it is so done as to be a hindrance to some greater good; also if the revelations contain lies or contradictions, if curious and useless things be revealed, if the matter revealed could have been discovered by human reason, if anything be revealed which, though it does not exceed the Divine power, is yet not conformable with the wisdom of God and His other attributes—for instance, if a person says that it has been revealed to him that the world moves in a straight line, that an Angel is to be annihilated and then created anew, if anything be revealed as about to happen which does not.'[2]

These are in general the tests by which we have to examine revelations in order to decide whether they be true and from God, or false, or from natural or diabolical sources, and they regard the subject-matter of the revelations.

With regard to the persons to whom revelations are said to be made, we have to observe all those things which we have mentioned as necessary to be

---

[1] 'Treatise on Heroic Virtue,' vol. iii., p. 372 *et seq.*
[2] *Ibid.*, pp. 375, 376.

MYSTICAL PHENOMENA—REVELATIONS

examined in cases of persons to whom visions and apparitions occur. Many circumstances attending Divine revelations are enumerated by Cardinal Bona: 'In order to ascertain whether a revelation be from God, we must see whether it has those conditions which the Apostle St. James attributes to the wisdom revealed of God, saying: But the wisdom that is from above first, indeed, is *chaste*—that is, pure and removed from all carnal and earthly pleasure; then *peaceable*—always calm, and contending with no one; *modest*, and quiet in manner, gesture, and conversation; *easy to be persuaded*—that is, easily yielding to the judgment of others; *consenting to the good*, acquiescing in their opinions; *full of mercy and good fruits*—that is, good works, and dispensing liberally to all the needy; *without judging*, as many do, who discuss the conduct and acts of others, interpreting them ill; *without dissimulation*—without guile and fraud, simple and sincere. These are the marks and characteristics of true wisdom; these are the virtues by which a Divine revelation moves men. But if those things which are revealed tend to strife and contention, to worldly cares and vanity, to pride and obstinacy, they proceed without doubt from a carnal and worldly wisdom, which does not receive the things of the Spirit of God or from the evil spirit.'[1]

8. Both Benedict XIV. and Schram, with other mystical writers, propose and answer some important particulars or questions with regard to private revelations. The first of these is whether these revelations can be the object of faith. In solving this question, we have to distinguish between the

[1] 'Treatise on Heroic Virtue,' vol. iii., p. 386.

person to whom the revelation is made and others to whom the revelation is afterwards made known.

(1) With regard to persons to whom the revelation is made

(1) Are they to whom a revelation is made, and who are certain it comes from God, bound to give a firm assent to it? The answer to this question is in the affirmative. 'The only question among theologians is this whether the matter of a private revelation be objects of Divine theological faith. Some, indeed, think that he to whom a revelation is made neither can believe nor is bound to believe such a revelation with Catholic faith—that is, that by which we are made Christians—seeing that it is not contained in the habit of the formal object of the same, but is from another special light from above, either of a particular faith, or of a prophecy, or of discerning of spirits. Arauxo adopts this opinion. Others say that a private revelation, even with reference to the objects revealed, ought to be believed by him to whom it is made with Divine theological faith; and, consequently, whatever God reveals is a material object of Divine faith, for the first truth-revealing is the proper and proximate ground of assenting to everything God reveals, whether to a private person or to the whole Church, and whether the revelations have regard to the general or private good. Of this opinion is Cardinal Gotti.'[1]

If the revelation is not certain, but only probable, then, according to Hurtado, we must distinguish 'between a private revelation concerning some good to be done or evil to be avoided, and a revelation of release or dispensation, as they say, in a mattter of precept; and with respect to the first, he says that

[1] 'Treatise on Heroic Virtue,' vol. III., p. 390

everyone may abound in his own sense, and so may give credit to even a probable revelation on account of its matter when there is no danger, but otherwise with respect to the second.' Jerome Savonarola, in his compendium of revelations, seems to have spoken to the same effect when he thus wrote in defence of them: 'Seeing, then, what I have said is contrary neither to faith, nor to good morals, nor to natural reason, and is very likely to be true, as I have shown at different times by many arguments, and that, moreover, it leads men to live religiously, as I have found by experience, it follows that he cannot be charged with levity who gives belief readily thereto.'

John Salas was of opinion that probability of a revelation sufficed so that one might give credit to it, and so conform his own actions and those of others to what is thus revealed. This opinion cannot certainly be held in the case of a revelation of release or dispensation in a matter of precept, and it would be erroneous in any case to teach that Divine faith could be given to that which is only probably revealed. Benedict XIV. reminds us that, 'if we are speaking of that Divine faith with which many say that he to whom a private revelation is made is bound to believe, the opinion which allows a probability of Divine revelation to be sufficient is utterly condemned.' The Holy Council of Trent thus speaks: 'As no religious man ought to doubt of the mercy of God, of the merits of Christ, of the virtue and efficacy of the Sacraments, so everyone, while he considers his own weakness and indisposition, may be in fear and alarm with respect to his state of grace, for no one can know with a certainty of faith, where there is no possibility of error, that he has attained to the grace of God. But,' continues the learned Pontiff, 'if the probability of a revelation were alone sufficient, we might, by interior and repeated acts of contrition, believe with Divine faith that we have attained to the grace of God, for this may be derived with the greatest probability from the universally revealed proposition that the contrite obtain grace, and from another sufficiently probable, that we are truly contrite. Therefore, among the propositions condemned by Innocent XI, March 2, 1679, the twenty-fifth is this "The assent of faith supernatural and profitable to salvation co-exists with a knowledge only probable of a revelation—yea, even with the fear wherewith one fears that God may not have spoken"'

(2) With regard to others

(2) What is to be said of others to whom the revelations are directed or to whom they are not directed? To this Benedict XIV. replies as follows·

'This differs from the foregoing; that has reference to him to whom the revelation is made, but this relates to other persons—namely, those to whom the revelation is directed and those to whom it is not Cardinal de Lugo teaches that he to whom that private revelation is proposed and announced ought to believe and obey the command or message of God if it be proposed to him on sufficient evidence; for God speaks to him, at least, by means of another, and therefore requires him to believe. Hence it is that he is required to believe God, Who requires him to do so.

'As to others to whom the revelation is not directed, both Cardinal de Lugo and Arauxo maintain that they are not really bound to believe such a revelation ; nor, if they believe, is such an assent that of Catholic or Divine faith, because it does not rest on Divine testimony, which is the formal and proper ground of Divine faith ; it does not resolve itself proximately into a revelation made to a private person, for that does not appear, but for the account of him who speaks of it, nor into a mediate revelation, as it is called, for it is not directed to them, nor does God speak to them. It resolves itself only into the human testimony of him who relates to others his own private revelation. Therefore, as the formal object of Divine faith is wanting therein, the assent can only be that of a human faith."[1]

9. The second question which is here proposed for consideration is in the words of Benedict XIV : 'What is to be said of those private revelations which the Apostolic See has approved of, those of the Blessed Hildegarde, of St. Bridget, and of St. Catherine of Siena ?' He answers this question and quotes authorities in support of his teaching in a manner not surpassed by any other author

9. The meaning of the approbation of the Church given to some private revelations

'We have already said,' he writes, 'that these revelations, although approved of, ought not to, and cannot, receive any assent of Catholic, but only of human faith, according to the rules of prudence, according to which the aforesaid revelations are probable, and piously to be believed. We then alleged some authors, we now allege others in addition. Melchior Cano thus speaks of not giving the assent of Catholic faith to these revelations "Because to believe or not to believe those things which Bridget and Catherine of Siena saw does not concern

[1] 'Treatise on Heroic Virtue,' vol III, p 394.

the Church, those things are by no means to be referred to the faith."

'Cardinal Cajetan teaches that we must cling to the Catholic revelations which were made to the Apostles and Prophets as the foundations of our faith, but to private revelations that were made to the Saints, although approved, (we cling) as probable. We cling to the Catholic revelations as necessary, so that he shows himself a heretic who obstinately opposes any one of them. But we cling to the revelations made to the Saints, whose doctrine the Church accepts as probable. So St. Augustine and St. Thomas have written, and experience continually testifies. . . . To the same effect is the form of approbation of the revelations of St. Bridget, by Cardinal Torquemada "All and singular of them" —he is speaking of the books of the revelations— "I have accurately examined, according to my ability, and find none of them, piously and modestly understood, to be at variance with the Holy Scriptures or the sayings of the holy Fathers, but I find every one sufficiently consonant and conformable thereto, and all of these piously and modestly to be received, and that they may be read in the Church of God in the same manner that the books of many other Doctors, histories of the Saints, and legends, are licensed to be read to the faithful. Wherefore Vasquez well observes 'The revelations of St. Bridget have been sanctioned, and as pious and without superstition may be prudently received by the people.'"

'So also the Fathers of Salamanca. From this, then, it follows that anyone may, without injury to the Catholic faith, give no heed to these revelations

MYSTICAL PHENOMENA—REVELATIONS

and differ from them, provided he does so modestly, not without reason, and without contempt. . . . Theologians and mystics acknowledge that private revelations, however approved and received, although they ought to be believed by those to whom they are given, among others the opposite'[1]—that is, the same obligation does not bind them. Whenever, therefore, the Church takes under her protection these revelations, she does not make herself responsible for the facts or for the doctrine which they contain, and in approving, for example, of the revelations of St. Hildegarde, St. Bridget, St. Catherine of Siena, and St. Theresa, she does not thereby impose them as an obligation upon the faithful, but only recommends them to the respect of the faithful, and authorizes their publication and reading.

By a decree of March 13, 1625, Urban VIII. prohibited the publication of private revelations without the approbation of ecclesiastical authority. The same decree imposes on all great reserve even in private conversation relative to supernatural facts which are not very authentic. The excessive credulity of some Catholics in this respect may do harm to the cause of religion, because it is the Church that is blamed very often by the enemies of religion for the caprices and eccentricities of pious but too credulous individual Catholics.

10. There is one more important question proposed and answered by Benedict XIV. which deserves consideration, as it may serve to solve many difficulties, and confirm what has been said with regard to the manner in which private revela-

10. Whether a holy soul may be mistaken with regard to its revelations.

[1] 'Treatise on Heroic Virtue,' vol. iii., p. 395 *et seq.*

tions have to be received by the faithful, and the credence to be given to them. The question is, 'Whether a Saint may have revelations, not from the Holy Spirit, but resulting from his own individual judgment and reasonings, so far as his intellect, influenced by pious dispositions, and imbued with opinions on any subject connected with religion, judges that he has the Divine Spirit, when, however, he is in invincible error.

'We have already said, when speaking of the prophetic spirit, that sometimes the holy prophets, when consulted, from the frequent practice of prophecy, utter some things of their own spirit, suspecting them to proceed from the spirit of prophecy. In the same way it may happen that a Saint may think, from preconceived opinions and from fixed ideas in the imagination, that certain things are revealed to him by God which yet God does not reveal. So speaks Hurtado. He gives an instance in the revelations of St. Bridget, who says it was revealed to her that, when Christ our Lord was scourged and crucified, His loins were girt with a veil; the contrary is taught by many of the holy Fathers, whom Suarez quotes and follows. Certainly there are not wanting those who write that the loins of our Lord were covered with a veil when He was crucified and scourged, and men learned in profane history show that those who were crucified were stripped of their garments, but had their loins covered. This is the opinion of Menochius, Tostatus, and Salmeron. And Hurtado thinks that the revelation of St. Bridget proceeded on the ground of this opinion, or might have done so.

'The Bollandists in the margin to the Life of Mary

Magdalene de Pazzi, show that raptures may be above nature and in their substance Divine, but in their circumstances conformed to the ideas naturally received, which God leaves in the state they are in, since it was of no moment in the end He had in view. They instance those revelations of holy women in which Christ appeared nailed with three nails to the cross, sometimes with four; and also those in which St. Jerome stands with a lion, or St. James appears in the dress of a hermit. They think, indeed, that these most fervent meditations on the Passion of Christ, and these devout affections towards St. James and St. Jerome, proceeded from God, but that the Holy Ghost would not give a new and certain revelation as to the number of nails by which Christ was nailed to the cross. But neither had St. Jerome in his lifetime a lion as his companion—for it is not true that he met a lion roaring loudly, with a thorn in his paw, that he wiped away the corrupted matter and bound it up, and that the lion thus cured would never afterwards leave him; this happened not to St. Jerome, but to the Abbot Gerasimus—but he is painted with a lion because as a lion he roars against the heretics, as we read in the annals of Cardinal Baronius. And St. James, when he was on earth, did not wear the habit of a pilgrim, but is so painted that we may know that it is he in whose honour pilgrimages are so frequently made to the Gallician shores.

'In the heart of St. Clare of Montefalco, the instruments of the Passion of Christ and the three nails by which He was nailed to the cross appear miraculously formed. Cornelius Curtius, an Augustinian, shows from reason, authority, and pictures that the nails were not three, but four. He says that he has seen the heart of the Blessed Clare, and adds

'"Will you decide that the crucifixion was so because that holy woman's meditations on the crucifixion assumed that form? I think not, if you have common-sense. Those instruments were engraven on her heart, not to delineate the Passion of Christ, but to make known to posterity the fervent love of Clare. The Bollandists, taking this into consideration, say that it pleased not God to adapt and correct the images in the mind of Clare according to the rule of the truth known to Himself, for that had no reference to the spiritual good which He procured for her by that miracle."[1]

[1] 'Treatise on Heroic Virtue,' vol III, p 402 *et seq*

CHAPTER VII

REVELATION OF THE SECRETS OF SOULS

1. THERE are three kinds of secrets relative to souls—the secret of conscience in this life; the secret of the state of souls after death; and the secret of predestination, which is in God. According to the providential order of God, these three secrets are inviolable. We could not suppose a revelation of them which would not overthrow all the conditions of our existence here below. It may happen in some particular cases, and for His own particular designs, that God may lift the veil that hides these secrets; but instances of this kind have been ever rare, and we should not admit, except with very great reserve, those revelations which regard the state of souls and of consciences.

Three kinds of secrets of souls

Dom B. M. Maréchaux writes in explanation of these three secrets, and of the manner in which we have to regard their revelation, in his work entitled 'Le Merveilleux Divin.' We shall adopt his explanation and his teaching on these secrets.

(1) The human soul during the present life is perhaps the most mysterious creature in the whole universe. In its quality of spirit it enjoys the privilege of shutting itself up in a secrecy impenetrable to all except God. At present it is in a

(1) The secret of consciences

state of trial and of spiritual formation; it has to prepare itself from childhood for another life, and no one can know what may be the result of its life of trial as a wayfarer in this world. It is true it shows itself in many ways. It shows itself in the exterior man, according to the words of Holy Writ · *A man is known by his look, and a wise man, when thou meetest him, is known by his countenance. The attire of the body, and the laughter of the teeth, and the gait of the man, show what he is* [1] From such external signs you can judge of the character of the man, of his tastes, his qualities and his vices, but you cannot know what goes on in the depths of the soul.

· Even an Angel, whose vision, wholly spiritual, is far more perfect than ours, cannot fully penetrate this mysterious creature He can detect the smallest motions of passion, and the most subtle imaginations which impress themselves upon us, he can explain the circumference of the interior fortress and have a clear knowledge of all its surroundings, but he cannot enter the interior castle itself, which is reserved for God alone. God glories in having the key of souls: *I am He*, He saith, *that searcheth the reins and hearts.*[2]

The two things in us which are hidden even from the knowledge of the Angels are our interior thoughts and the state of our conscience. But in these there is a difference in degree as to the secrecy. Our thought is of itself hidden, but it tends to manifest itself As soon as it is formed it seeks for an expression of itself; and this suffices to give to the Angels or to the devil, at least, a conjectural

---

[1] Ecclus xix 26, 27   [2] Apoc ii 23

knowledge or view of it. It is not the thought proper, but, rather, the interior word, which is formed and expressed somehow in the imagination or brain, which becomes perceptible to the angelic vision, before it is expressed in words But this knowledge even in the Angels is not more than conjectural, and it has always in it a conjectural element.

The state of conscience does not manifest itself even in that way. It may be called the secret of secrets, the mystery of mysteries. Is such a soul in the state of sin or in a state of grace? God alone knows with certain knowledge. The soul itself does not know the secret of its own state. The soul, it is true, may know by certain signs its interior state, and be able to have what is called a moral certainty with regard to that state, and by the same signs an Angel may establish a presumptive knowledge of its state, but the depth of the soul is hidden

We may therefore conclude that, if the Angels may be able to come to some knowledge of our thoughts in the way we have mentioned, they cannot in the same way come to the knowledge of the state of our conscience, unless God reveals it to them. Every revelation, therefore, of this kind must come from God, either directly from Himself, or indirectly through the ministry of His Angels, to whom He may manifest that state.

Such revelations are very rare. It often happens that God grants to Saints and holy persons the gift of *discernment of spirits*. This gift does not mean that the recipient can know the interior conscience, but only the different movements which agitate and trouble the soul, and the way of its proper direction in the spiritual life By means of this light spiritual directors are enabled to guide a soul safely through the many and intricate difficulties which beset it in the way of salvation; but it does not enable them to penetrate into the very interior of the soul itself. The intuition or view of conscience or of the state of soul is a gift very rare, even in the annals of sanctity. We cannot wonder at this when we are assured that the soul does not know its own state, according to the words: *There are just men and wise men, and their works are in the hands of God, and yet man knoweth not whether he be worthy of love or hatred*[1]

<small>(2) The state of the soul after death</small>

(2) Immediately after death the state of souls is declared by judgment. The judgment is unknown to men. The Angels and demons know the result of that judgment, and minister in its execution. They know, therefore, which souls go to heaven, which to purgatory, and which to hell. They are, therefore, able to inform men of the state of the departed souls, but this they cannot do without a special permission from God, which is seldom granted. It is true we read in the Lives of the Saints that many of them were informed by a Divine light of the state of some souls in whom they had been interested, and for whom they had suffered and prayed, and God bestowed this favour upon them for their consolation, and to incite their zeal still more for the salvation of souls. We must not, however, too easily believe that such a favour is granted to ordinary mortals. It is, and will always remain, an exceptional favour As a rule, all pretended communications of our spirits with those of the dead are to be regarded as false, and this is

[1] Ecclus. ix 1

MYSTICAL PHENOMENA—REVELATIONS

especially the case when the communications are said to be frequent.

We read often in an author otherwise pious and orthodox[1] the recital of many visions relative to the state of souls after death. We read, amongst other things, that, of those who depart out of this world in any given moment, only three are saved. This is said to strike terror into people. But what are we to think of such visions? To arrive at such a conclusion, it would be necessary to believe that the elect of God are not only relatively few in number, but very few indeed, and the doctrine is simply terrible. A vision of this kind, if accepted at all, must be explained, or explained away, rather, according to the teaching of Holy Scripture, as interpreted by the Fathers and by orthodox commentators. The words of our Saviour, *Many are called, but few are chosen*, taken in their strictly literal sense, would lead us to the conclusion that, of the thousands of souls that appear every moment before the tribunal of God, more than three certainly go to purgatory or to heaven. St. Augustine teaches that though the elect are a small number relatively to the reprobate, yet they are a considerable number considered in themselves; and this is the conclusion to be arrived at from the texts of Holy Scripture.

There are many theologians, and amongst them Suarez, who hold that the majority of adult Catholics will be saved. (Baptized children dying before they come to the use of reason are, of course, all saved.) Some theologians even hold that the majority of mankind, including heathens, heretics,

[1] P. de Saint-Jure, 'Connaissance et Amour de Notre Seigneur Jésus-Christ,' livre iii., chap. xxii. 2.

etc., will be saved. Father Joseph Rickaby says in his Conference entitled 'The Extension of Salvation': 'But as to what proportion of men die in sanctifying grace, and what proportion in mortal sin, nothing is revealed, nothing is of faith, and nothing is really known to theologians. If ever you find a theologian confidently consigning the mass of human souls to eternal flames, be sure he is venturing beyond the bounds of Christian faith and of theological science You are quite free to disbelieve his word; I do not believe it myself.'[1] A vision or revelation has not been granted to settle this theological speculation or to manifest to us this hidden mystery known only to God.

If it be right to disapprove of visions that are calculated to frighten people, and are not otherwise well founded, it is equally right and advisable to warn people against certain revelations which represent the salvation of persons who have lived bad and sinful lives. The pious and wise Cardinal Bona says that we have good reason to suspect that such revelations are illusions of the devil, who endeavours thereby to encourage sinners to sleep in their criminal habits, and to make them believe that in the end, by some wonderful means, they will be saved. Without doubt, the mercy of God is infinite, and in His mercy He may bestow His graces in the last hour upon sinners. But He Himself has told us that as a man lives so shall he die. This is understood as the general rule of Divine providence

(3) The secret of predestination

(3) It remains that we speak of a secret even

[1] See 'The Saved and Lost,' a study by Rev. N Walsh, S.J,

more profound than that of the state of consciences or of souls departed, a secret in the presence of which St. Paul exclaimed: *O the depth of the riches of the wisdom and of the knowledge of God! How incomprehensible are His judgments, and how unsearchable His ways!*[1]

If, as according to the same Apostle, it is only the spirit of man that *knoweth the things that are in him; so the things that are of God, no man knoweth but the Spirit of God.*[2] Man, even in regard to the things that are in him, is subject to illusions; how little, therefore, can he pretend to know of the secrets that are in God—those secrets that are hidden even from the highest Angels!

Such, for example, is the secret of predestination. Is such a soul predestined to enter heaven? God knows, and He alone knows, and this secret cannot be revealed but by Him, and that by a special and particular revelation. Some Saints, after a long life of suffering and of labour for God, received from Him a revelation that they were numbered amongst the predestined; but this singular favour is also rare even amongst the Saints. As a general rule, no matter how much God consoles His servants, no matter howsoever He gives them foretastes of His Spirit, and instils firm confidence into their hearts, He does not manifest to them the secret of their predestination. It would be necessary to be a great Saint to support such a revelation: in the generality of cases certitude as to their salvation would beget negligence; uncertainty, on the contrary, begets vigilance and maintains humility. So teaches St. Thomas of Aquin; but it may be objected

[1] Rom. xi. 33. [2] 1 Cor. ii. 11.

that uncertainty causes sometimes unbearable agony.
To this the author of the 'Imitation of Christ'
replies 'A soul may be tormented by the thought
of the uncertainty of its salvation Ah ! it may say
to God, if only I knew that I was of the number
of the predestined ! An interior voice answers,
That which you would do, do, and your salvation is
assured.'[1] Wise and profound saying, well calculated to comfort any souls who may be troubled in
that way. If the secret of predestination has not
been revealed except rarely, theologians hold for
certain that the secret of reprobation has never
been revealed, and will never be revealed. The
reason of this is because the soul, as long as it is in
this life, is in the way of salvation. God knows, it
is true, at the present moment the souls that will go
to hell, but none of them will go there except
through its own fault ; therefore the knowledge of
God does not impose any necessity upon them, no
more than does the view or sight of one man impose
a necessity on the movements of another. Every
revelation with regard to the reprobating of a soul
must be regarded as conditional or as a threatening
warning. It is true the reprobation of Antichrist
is asserted in Sacred Scripture, but even he will
make free election of his own wickedness, and in
his hatred of God he will freely bring upon himself
all the consequences of his choice.

Let us, therefore, be on our guard against revelations which pretend to make known the secret of
predestination or that of reprobation. It is in the
order of providence that salvation be given as the
prize of our race or course in life, according to the

[1] 'Imitation of Christ,' book i., chap xxv. 2

comparison used by St. Paul:[1] that it be as the harvest which crowns the labour of a whole year, according to the idea frequently expressed in the Scriptures.[2] It is by the free and persevering efforts of man prevented and sustained by grace that, in the order of salvation, the promises and designs of God will be realized.[3] Thus far Dom Maréchaux.

2. I shall only call attention to one particular revelation in connection with the above doctrine on the secrets of the soul—namely, the revelation attributed to Margaret Mary Alacoque regarding the grace of final penitence to be granted to souls who communicate on the first Friday of nine consecutive months.

[2. The revelation with regard to the devotion of the nine Fridays, in honour of the Sacred Heart.]

In the 'Handbook of the Apostleship of Prayer' the following reference is made to the revelation and to the promise of final perseverance:

'Among the records made by Blessed Margaret Mary of the promises of the Sacred Heart, revealed to her in favour of those who shall be devoted to it, are the following words, which contain what is generally called the twelfth or great promise: *One Friday, during Holy Communion, He said to His unworthy servant, if she does not deceive herself: "I promise thee, in the excessive mercy of My heart, that its all-powerful love will grant to all those who communicate on nine consecutive first Fridays of the month the grace of final perseverance; they shall not die in My disfavour, nor without receiving their Sacraments; for My Divine Heart shall be their safe refuge in this last moment."*

---

[1] 1 Cor. ix. 24.   [2] 2 Tim. ii. 6; St. Jas. v. 7.
[3] See 'Le Merveilleux,' p. 103 *et seq.*

'That these words are among the authentic writings of Blessed Margaret Mary is certain. It is also certain that they were neither condemned nor censured by the Church after the close examination to which all her writings were submitted in the process of her beatification ; and though this must not be taken as implying that the Church authoritatively declares this particular revelation to have been a fact, it implies that there is nothing in it opposed to Catholic faith '[1]

I may add to this explanation a few words of Nicholas Lancizzi, quoted by Benedict XIV, that may assist us in solving the difficulties that sometimes arise from the publication of apocryphal revelations 'We must know that when pious persons, abstracted from the senses, speak, they frequently speak of their own understanding, and are sometimes deceived. This is certain, and persons experienced in these things know it, and it is clear from authentic ecclesiastical histories, and I could name some holy women, canonized by the Apostolic See, whose sayings and writings in rapture, and derived from raptures, are filled with errors, and therefore not allowed to be published '[2]

From what has been said above concerning the secret of predestination, and from the doctrine of theologians as already explained in this work, we have to say that such a promise as that just quoted cannot be taken in a strictly literal sense As a matter of fact, it is well known that some have died without the last Sacraments who had observed the devotion of the nine Fridays, as it is called. These

[1] 'Handbook of the Apostleship of Prayer,' p 127.
[2] 'Treatise on Heroic Virtue,' vol III, p. 403

were not necessarily sinners, for even Saints as well as sinners meet with sudden deaths. It cannot be supposed that their Communions were not worthy Communions, because this would be to assume a revelation of the secret of conscience of these individuals, and to fall into a great sin against charity by rash judgment. Then, again, the promise of the grace of final penitence, and the words, 'They shall not die in My disgrace,' taken in a literal sense, clearly signify a revelation of the secret of predestination, and this, we know, cannot be admitted. To state that this promise is a true revelation giving assurance of the salvation of those (for the words mean salvation) who communicate on the first Friday of nine consecutive months is clearly not in accordance with the Church's teaching on the uncertainty of the state of grace and of predestination, and is therefore not to be received or understood in this literal sense. If the promise be admitted as a true revelation, it must be regarded as conditional, and subject to an explanation, such as I shall give presently concerning the scapular of Mount Carmel.

It will be understood that what I here state concerning this particular promise, which has never received the approbation of the Church, need not imply the least disapproval of the devotion of the nine first Fridays, as practised by religious and devout seculars, after the example of Blessed Margaret Mary Alacoque, who, we are told, adopted a custom, suggested by our Lord, of making a novena in honour of the Sacred Heart of Jesus, receiving Communion each first Friday of the month for nine consecutive months. Rev. Father Gautrelet, S J., in his 'Manual of Devotion to the Sacred Heart of Jesus' (the best manual I have ever read on the subject), expresses in careful theological language and in a modified form the fruit to be derived from this practice in the following words: 'Our Lord gave her grounds of confidence, that whosoever adopted this practice should have the grace of final repentance, and receive the Sacraments of the Church before death.'[1]

The promise of the Blessed Virgin to St Simon Stock

3. As thus expressed, and understanding it as a conditional promise, it may be admitted with the same interpretation and explanation as that which is given of the promise of the Blessed Virgin made to St. Simon Stock, with regard to the salvation of those who wear the brown scapular of Mount Carmel, which I here subjoin:

'It is a dogma of faith, that no one here on earth can be certain of grace or predestination without a special revelation from God, and it is not received by those who wear the scapular. We may, however, piously admit the general revelation in favour of the salvation of such souls if all other conditions, both general and particular, be observed. The general conditions are the observance of the Commandments and all Christian duties. The particular conditions are those rules prescribed for the members of the sodality. The wearing of the scapular is then a sign of salvation and predestination, in the sense that it is an emblem or token of a special protection of the Blessed Virgin, by which the members of the sodality may be enabled more securely to keep the Commandments, and more safely to obtain their eternal beatitude. No more than this

---

[1] 'Manual of Devotion to the Sacred Heart,' p. 34

is meant when it is said that the wearing of the scapular is a sign of salvation, a pledge of predestination. Then it will be said that there is nothing extraordinary or special in it, if it is only a promise that the members of the sodality will be saved if they keep the Commandments and piously live good lives, as all Christians who do this can be saved without the scapular or the aid of any sodality. Although this is quite true, we must at the same time remember and conclude that we obtain a special privilege by being enrolled in Mary's scapular, inasmuch as this is a sacred badge and pledge of her special protection, which she extends to her clients to enable them to keep the Commandments, to live a holy life, and to die well. And this is the special virtue which we attribute to the wearing of the scapular, according to the promise made to St Simon, and which may be extended to all those who have enrolled themselves in her congregations and confraternities as children of Mary.'[1]

4 I have further to remark concerning the revelations made by God to Margaret Mary Alacoque, that the fact that one of the promises attributed to her needs some explanation to bring it into harmony with the principles of sound theology should not be regarded as a reason for in any way discrediting the others, or the substance of the revelations made to her concerning devotion to the Sacred Heart On the contrary, as I have said in a former work, the visions and revelations of this great Saint have all the signs and conditions required for true and Divine manifestations ·

'(1) They were beyond the power of nature, and

[1] 'The Creed Explained,' p 151

she was not asleep or insane when she received them.

'(2) They were not false, because the subsequent spread of the devotion to the Sacred Heart, which was revealed to her, depended upon contingent causes, namely, the free will of men, and her revelations and visions in this respect were afterwards known to be verified by facts

'(3) Her visions and revelations were not diabolical, but from God. (i.) The object, namely, the devotion to the Sacred Heart of Jesus, was good and pious, (ii.) she herself was virtuous and discreet, for she has been canonized by the Church; (iii.) her virtue suffered no diminution by reason of these supernatural favours, as is evident from the history of her life, (iv.) prudent directors and confessors believed in the truth and reality of her revelations. This is sufficiently proved from the fact that she was guided in regard to them by the advice of Father de la Columbière, the greatest spiritual director of his day in France.'[1]

[1] 'Convent Life,' p. 219.

CHAPTER VIII

ON PROPHECIES

1. PROPHECY is the foreknowledge and foretelling of future events. It sometimes extends to past events, of which there is no recollection, and to present events distant in place and hidden, and to the inward thoughts of the heart, so that he is a prophet who divinely knows those things which are removed from sense and the natural knowledge of men, and is able to make them known. After treating of visions and revelations, it is clear that a Divine manifestation of hidden present mysteries or past events comes under one or other of these, and to avoid unnecessary repetition we shall therefore understand by prophecy that which it is in its strict and proper sense, the revelation of future events, according to the words of St Gregory on Ezechiel: ' Because, then, that is prophecy which announces future events; when it speaks of what is past or present it loses the name of prophecy.' ' Prophecy consists in knowledge, and in the manifestation of what is known. And knowledge, indeed, of its own nature goes before; for no one can speak of anything unless he has knowledge of it. But as graces *gratis datæ* are manifestations of the Spirit for the profit of others, hence it comes to pass that in prophecy

[1] The meaning of prophecy

manifestation must be added to knowledge...
Moreover, in the estimate of grace *gratis data* manifestation must be said to be more excellent than knowledge, as Cardinal de Lauræa shows at length According to St. Thomas, as prophecy belongs to the knowledge of what is beyond natural reason, it follows that it requires a certain intellectual light, transcending the natural light of reason. Wherefore the knowledge of the prophets, if it be considered with reference to God, comprises in a certain sense a Divine and uncreated action, which is called revelation, or the speech of God; but considered with reference to the prophet—that is, so far as it is vitally elicited from his intellect through that light, and there remains it is said to be a vision or hearing, according to the diverse ways it has respect to God as revealing and speaking.'[1]

<small>The manner in which the prophetic representation may be effected</small>

2. In order to know, a prophet needs the representation of the event in some way to his mind. This representation can be effected in three ways, as we have explained when writing on visions and revelations 'Firstly, according to the exterior perception of the senses, as if the bodily eye beheld anything, or the ear heard, and thence the species of things pass to the imagination and the understanding Secondly, by the inward sense, as, when nothing outwardly appears, something is represented to the imagination, and thence passes to the understanding, whether through God infusing into the imagination wholly new species of things, the objects of what the eye has not seen nor the ear heard, or disposing in a new way that which exists already habitually

[1] Benedict XIV, 'Treatise on Heroic Virtue,' vol III, pp. 139, 140

MYSTICAL PHENOMENA—PROPHECIES

therein, and which has been admitted through the senses. Thirdly, by a representation altogether intellectual, when God, without the motion or the help of the interior or exterior senses, produces in the intellect new intelligible species, or modifies or disposes the old, which have been received through the senses, so that they shall represent intelligible truth without the aid of images in the thoughts. This third is the most perfect form of prophecy, and the second form, namely, the imaginative, is more perfect than the first, namely, that by which representation is effected by the external senses. These degrees are not to be so distinguished one from another, as that in any one of them the knowledge of a prophet consists solely in external or internal sensation; but it must always reach to a judgment of the understanding, and they are distinguished so far as that, in the highest, the intellectual knowledge does not commence in the senses, nor does it depend on them, but flows rather from the understanding to the senses; whilst in the other two the knowledge and the representation are derived from the senses, either from the internal or the external simultaneously, on which they depend, and from which they derive their designation.

Both St. Thomas and Suarez tell us that prophecy is either purely intellectual or sensible. In the former case the prophetic communication is given directly to the intellect without the intervention of any sensible image. 'This seems to happen very rarely,' remarks the Rev. A. J. Maas, 'and in the Sacred Scriptures we know of no other instance except that of St. Paul.'[1] Cardinal Bona adds that it is still a

---
[1] 2 Cor. xii. 2. 'Christ in Type and Prophecy,' vol. i., p. 91.

subject of debate between the scholastic and mystic theologians, how a purely intellectual vision, without the intervention of image in the thought, can be effected in the soul united to the body in this mortal life.[1]

<small>3. Those through whom prophetic revelation is made</small>

3. Prophetic revelation is made by means of the Angels. An Angel speaks to Agar, Angels address Lot, an Angel speaks to Abraham, and says: *I will multiply thy seed.* In the new Testament we read that the Angel appeared to Zachary, saying : *I am Gabriel, who stand before God, and am sent to speak to thee, and to bring thee these good tidings.*[2] The same Gabriel was sent to the Blessed Virgin, and revealed to her deep mysteries concerning the Incarnation and Redemption. No one can therefore deny that there is prophecy which is angelic, and that most true. Cardinal de Lauraea, as quoted by Benedict XIV., says that it is not out of the course of things for God Himself to speak to the prophet, teaching him what he is to make known, namely, by speaking to him, as another man would speak to the prophet, or appearing to him in the form of man. And the same author quotes Cardinal Torquemada as saying : 'It must be remembered that God speaks in two ways : either He speaks Himself, or His words come to us through the Angels. For unless the Angels in speaking to us assume for a time an aerial body, they could not become visible to our outward senses.' In the same way proceeds Torreblanca : God usually breathes His power into men by means of an Angel, who assumes a body, or only

---

[1] Benedict XIV., 'Treatise on Heroic Virtue,' vol. iii, pp. 141, 142

[2] St Luke i. 19.

a spiritual appearance. But we must not therefore deny that God can, if He will, directly Himself illuminate the minds of men.

4. The various kinds of prophecies are given by Schram and by Benedict XIV. in almost the same words. Benedict XIV. writes:

4. Division of prophecies.

'Prophecy may be considered in many ways, either with reference to the illumination, or to the object or thing known, or to the means by which the representation is made known, or to the way in which knowledge is conveyed. With reference to the illumination, it is perfect or imperfect; the first is, when not only the matter revealed, but also the revelation itself, is known, and that it is God Who makes it. This only is called absolutely and simply prophecy. The second is that when, although a truth is made known, it is yet not so certainly nor sufficiently perceived from whom the revelation proceeds, and whether the prophetic or the individual spirit speaks. This is called the prophetic instinct, wherein it is possible, because of the manner of it, that a man may be deceived.

'With reference to the object, it may be a prophecy of denunciation, or foreknowledge, or predestination. The first is when God reveals future events, which He knows not in themselves, or in an absolute decree, but in the order of their own causes, and in conditional decrees which may be hindered from taking effect by other decrees which are absolute. Wherefore the meaning of the revelation is, not that such things will absolutely come to pass, but only from the influences of causes determinate for that end. In these is involved the condition, unless hindered from above, though the prophets do not express it, but seem to speak absolutely. The second is that when God reveals future events, depending on created free-will, which He sees as things present in eternity. The third is when He reveals what He alone will do, and sees them present in eternity and in the absolute decree. With reference to the means or the species by which the objects revealed are represented, prophecy is divided into that of the intellect, the imagination, and the body, according to our foregoing observations.

'Finally, with reference to the way in which the knowledge is conveyed, prophecy is divided into that which takes place when the senses are not suspended, and this retains the general name of prophecy, and that which takes place when they are so suspended, this is called rapture.

'What we have stated in the foregoing section may be read in so many words in the work of the Fathers of Salamanca, who are throughout consistent with what St. Thomas teaches. For he inquires whether the prophets always knew what they uttered in prophecy, and answers that the true prophets, whose minds are Divinely inspired, not only know what is revealed to them, but also that they are revealed by God, as it is written *The Spirit of the Lord hath spoken by me.*[1]

'The holy Doctor likewise explains that division of prophecy into prophecy of the predestination of God, foreknowledge, and denunciation, and having proposed the question whether prophetic vision takes place when the senses are suspended, he teaches that there is no suspension of the senses when any-

[1] 2 Kings xxiii 2.

thing is represented to the mind of the prophet through sensible species; nor is it necessary that the senses should be suspended when the mind of the prophet is illuminated by an intelligible light or informed by intelligible species, but it is necessary that the senses should be suspended when the revelation is wrought by forms of the imagination.'[1]

5. Speaking on the subjects or recipients of prophecy, this author says: 'The subjects of prophecy are good Angels, devils, men, women, children, heathens, or Gentiles; nor is it necessary that a man should be gifted with any particular disposition in order to be a subject of prophecy, provided his intellect and senses be adapted for making manifest these things which God has revealed to him. Though moral goodness be most profitable to a prophet, yet it is not absolutely necessary in order to obtain the gift of prophecy. As to the Angels this is clear, for they by their own natural penetration cannot foreknow future events which are undetermined and uncertain, neither can they know the part which they have not seen themselves, and which has left no memorial behind, as theologians generally maintain against Durandus, nor the secrets of the heart of another, whether man or Angel. When, then, God reveals to an Angel what is future, past, and present, that he might reveal it to a man, according to what we have written, the Angel becomes a prophet. . . . As to the devil, though he certainly cannot foretell future events, yet nothing hinders but God may make use of him to manifest what is future, past, and present, though hidden. Therefore, as narrated by St. Luke, when

5. The subjects or recipients of prophecy.

[1] 'Treatise on Heroic Virtue,' vol iii, pp. 146-148

the devil saw Jesus he fell down before Him, and, crying out with a loud voice, said: *What have I to do with Thee, Jesus, Son of the most High God?*[1] For Jesus commanded the unclean spirit to go out of the man.'[2]

There are instances of women and children prophesying in Sacred Scripture. Mary, the sister of Moses, is called a prophetess; Anna, the mother of Samuel, was endowed with the gift of prophecy. Elizabeth, the mother of John the Baptist, by a revelation from God, recognised and confessed Mary the Mother of God. Samuel and Daniel as boys prophesied; Balaam, a Gentile foretold the advent of the Messias and the devastation of Assyria and Palestine. St. Thomas, in order to prove that the heathens were capable of prophecy, makes use of the instance of the Sibyls, who make clear mention of the mysteries of the Trinity, of the Incarnation of the Word, of the life, Passion, and resurrection of Christ, to whom, though heathens and women, God had given the gift of prophecy in reward of their virginity, as St. Jerome thinks. It is true the sibylline poems now extant became in course of time interpolated; but, as Benedict XIV remarks, this does not hinder much of them, especially what the early Fathers referred to, from being genuine and in no wise apocryphal.

We may add, before finishing the question of the subject or recipient of the gift of prophecy, that though God once made use of an irrational animal, namely, an ass, to rebuke Balaam,[3] yet has He

---

[1] St. Luke viii 28
[2] 'Treatise on Heroic Virtue,' vol iii , pp. 144-150
[3] Num xxii. 28

MYSTICAL PHENOMENA—PROPHECIES

never made use of an irrational or inanimate creature to manifest future events, or things present which are hidden.

6 'We must say,' observes Benedict XIV, 'that no mere man had prophetic knowledge habitually, or in his own power, before he received any actual revelation or motion of the Holy Ghost by inspiration or the word of God. We say that no mere man ever had prophetic knowledge in this way, that we might except Christ our Lord, Who in virtue of the hypostatic union had in this life blessed and supreme knowledge, whereby He knew all truths which can be revealed by prophecy to men, and so could, of His own proper and habitual or abiding knowledge, prophesy, without waiting for any revelation or the word of God. Again, it is certain that no prophet, Christ always excepted, however great, nor even one who received many revelations, has received the gift of prophecy to be habitually with him, so as to have the knowledge of secret things or be able to prophesy at will.' Thus, Eliseus once said *The Lord hath hid it from me, and hath not told me.*[1] . . . St. Thomas teaches that the prophetic light is in the soul of a prophet after the manner of a passion or passing impression, and thus the mind of a prophet is always in need of a new revelation, like a disciple who, having not yet mastered the principles of his art, requires to be taught each of them separately. . . . Calmet says: "Lastly, if the Spirit of God were always present with the prophets, why, then, are those expressions so common in their writings, *The Spirit of the Lord*, or, *The hand of the Lord, came upon me?*" These are most evident proofs,

[6. The gift of prophecy not a habit or permanent quality of the soul]

---
[1] 4 Kings iv. 27.

says St. Jerome in his commentaries on Ezechiel ii., that by reason of human frailty and bodily necessities the Holy Spirit at times withdrew Himself from them.'

I may now with Benedict XIV. sum up what has been so far written concerning prophecies; that it is of the essence of true prophecy that the prophet should not only know what is revealed to him, but also that it is God Who reveals it, that no natural disposition is required for prophecy, that union with God by charity is not requisite in order to have the gift of prophecy, and thus it was at times bestowed upon sinners; and, finally, that prophecy was never possessed habitually by any mere man.[1]

7. What credence is to be given to private prophecies

7. That the spirit of prophecy exists in the Church might easily be proved both from Sacred Scripture and the acts of canonization of the Saints We shall not labour this point, therefore, but proceed to speak of the credence due to private prophecies. Cardinal Cajetan inquires whether all who are believed to be prophets are to be listened to in those things which they say they receive in the spirit of prophecy. His reply, as given by Benedict XIV, is this

'Human actions are of two kinds, one of which relates to public duties, and especially ecclesiastical, such as preaching, celebrating Mass, pronouncing judicial decisions, and the like, with respect to these the question is settled in the canon law, where it is said that no credit is to be publicly given to him who says he has invisibly received a mission from God, unless he confirms it by a miracle or a special testimony of Holy Scripture. The other human

[1] 'Treatise on Heroic Virtue,' vol. iii, pp 158-160

actions are those of private persons, and speaking of these, he distinguishes between a prophet who enjoins or advises them, according to the universal laws of the Church, and a prophet who directs them without reference to those laws; in the first case every man may abound in his own sense, so as to direct his actions according to the will of the prophet; in the second case the prophet is not to be listened to, for good and evil in human actions are considered in their agreement or disagreement with Divine and human, especially ecclesiastical, laws. To this effect writes the Apostle: *Extinguish not the spirits, despise not prophecies; but prove all things, hold fast that which is good.* . . .[1] Calmet says in one place: "The Lord Jesus Christ, having cautioned us against the craft of false prophets and the workers of false miracles, bids us (St. Matt. vii. 15) judge of them by their visible worth and doctrine. If an Angel from heaven were to teach otherwise than the Apostles did, St. Paul pronounces him anathema.[2] Miracles are of no force, the fulfilment of oracles is nothing, if they be not in harmony with the true and holy doctrine taught by the ancient prophets."[3]

8. The same rules which are given to decide whether visions or revelations are from God equally apply to prophecies. Benedict XIV. lays down several rules, and applies them in their relation to causes of beatification and canonization. A summary of these rules will suffice for our purpose, namely, to enable us to judge of prophecies and of their Divine origin in any particular case that may come under our observation:

8. Tests or rules by which Divine prophecies are to be recognised given by Benedict XIV.

[1] 1 Thess. v. 19.   [2] Gal. i. 8.
[3] See Benedict XIV., vol. iii., pp. 192-194.

(1) The recipient of the gift of prophecy should be good and virtuous as a rule. Prophecy as a grace *gratis data* may at times be bestowed upon sinners, but it is more frequently bestowed upon the just. Calmet observes: 'We readily admit that a good and modest life is not necessary as an evidence of true prophecy, for there are well-known instances of some wicked men whom God made use of as instruments to publish His oracles, as we have seen in the case of Balaam and Caiphas, but these instances are rare.' Cardinal Bona says the same, and adds: 'For the most part, therefore, the gift is bestowed by God upon holy men.'

(2) The prophecy must be conformable to piety and Christian truth. This rule is given us by God Himself: *If there arise in the midst of thee a prophet, or one that saith he hath dreamed a dream, and to foretell a sign and a wonder, and that come to pass which he spoke, and he say to thee: Let us go and follow strange gods, and let us serve them: thou shalt not hear the words of that prophet or dreamer, for the Lord your God trieth you, that it may appear whether you love Him with all your heart, and with all your soul, or no. Follow the Lord your God, and fear Him . . . And that prophet or forger of dreams shall be slain.*[1]

(3) The prediction should be beyond human knowledge, such as secret thoughts and future contingencies. Calmet says: 'It belongs to prophecy to make known with a certain clear and assured confidence matters which are entirely secret, although they have no connection otherwise with natural and secondary causes. The astronomer

---

[1] Deut. xiii. 1-5.

does nothing against the laws of nature when he foretells an eclipse of the sun, nor the philosopher when he predicts certain effects which depend upon causes whose existence he has ascertained. But if we hear a prophet foretell a certain fortuitous event which depends on causes not controlled, and which operate either way, and if it appear also that this was revealed by him many ages before; if he have announced the birth of a man, his name, victories, acts, and death, if he announces some marvel altogether at variance with the present circumstances, then I look upon it as more than human, and refer the whole to God.'

(4) The manner of predicting and its effect upon the prophet should be attended to. Cardinal Bona writes 'False prophets speak when their minds are disturbed, because they cannot endure the assaults of the devil, who moves them But they whom God moves speak with gentleness, humility, and modesty' This he confirms by the authority of St John Chrysostom, who says 'It is peculiar to a false prophet to be disturbed in mind, to suffer violence and compulsion, to be driven, to be drawn, to be hurried away like a madman. But it is not so with the true prophet, he in sobriety of mind, modestly and temperately, and knowing what he says. speaks all things.'

(5) We have to ascertain whether that secret thing which the prophet revealed be such as it was revealed, and whether the contingent future event occurred in the way he foretold it. The rule is derived from Deuteronomy *And if in silent thought thou answer· How shall I know the word that the Lord hath not spoken? thou shalt have*

this sign: Whatsoever that same prophet foretelleth in the name of the Lord, and it cometh not to pass: that thing the Lord hath not spoken, but the prophet hath forged it by the pride of his mind; and therefore thou shalt not fear him.[1]

There are some limitations to this rule: (1) If the prophecy was not absolute, but containing threatenings only, and tempered by conditions, namely, with a condition expressed or understood, as exemplified in the prophecy of Jonas to the Ninivites, and that of Isaias to King Ezechias. (2) There is no contradiction in this, that the revelation be true and from God, and the human explanation of it false, for man may interpret it otherwise than God understands it. It is by these limitations we have to explain the prophecy of St. Bernard regarding the success of the Second Crusade, and that of St. Vincent Ferrer regarding the near approach of the General Judgment in his day. These two, I admit, involve delicate questions and require lengthy explanations. I shall confine myself to a few words. St. Bernard preached the Second Crusade and predicted its success, and confirmed the prediction by numerous miracles; but the only success really promised to that crusade, materially so disastrous, appears to be the salvation of many souls who had given their lives for the faith. St. Vincent Ferrer announced the Day of Judgment, and said that he was the Angel of the Apocalypse, and he worked a wonderful miracle of restoring to life a dead person under the eyes of the unbelieving University of Salamanca; all his hearers understood him as speaking

[1] Deut. xviii. 21, 22.

of the General Judgment, and the event showed that his words referred only to the particular judgment, and that he was only the angel or messenger of this particular judgment, to give warning to his hearers.

(6) *When a prophet speaks or announces something through the prophetic instinct which is not revealed to him, he should correct his mistake* St. Gregory, having said that holy prophets, through the frequent practice of prophesying, predict something of themselves, and believe that they are therein influenced by the spirit of prophecy, adds that between true and false prophets there is this difference · 'True prophets, if at any time they utter anything of themselves, quickly correct it, instructed through the hearers by the Holy Ghost. But false prophets both utter falsehoods and, strangers to the Holy Ghost, persevere in their falsehood.' We have an instance of this in Nathan, a most famous prophet of the Lord David was thinking of building the Temple of God, and Nathan, as we read, said to him: *Go, do all that is in thy heart, because the Lord is with thee.*[1] But that very night the Lord commanded the prophet to return to the King, and say that the glory of building the Temple was reserved, not for him, but for his son.[2]

[1] 2 Kings vii 3
[2] 'Treatise on Heroic Virtue,' vol iii, chap viii

CHAPTER IX

ON THE GIFT OF MIRACLES

1. Miracles in relation to mystical theology

1. I do not find the subject of miracles treated in any of the works on mystical theology that have come under my observation. It is a subject that belongs properly to natural theology or to dogmatic theology, and in introducing a chapter on the subject in a manual of mystical theology I am influenced by two considerations: (1) The gift of miracles may be classed among the mystical phenomena, (2) this gift, considered in relation to exalted sanctity, calls for some explanation and direction for the guidance of devout souls. I shall not, therefore, be expected to write a treatise on the subject of miracles, nor is it within my scope to treat of the possibility of miracles, their existence, and their continuation throughout all ages, nor of miracles regarded as the motive of the credibility of the Christian religion. All these questions are dealt with satisfactorily and exhaustively in natural and scholastic theology, in our catechetical books of instructions, and in the valuable volumes on miracles published in English, especially Cardinal Newman's two essays on miracles and Bishop Hays' treatise on miracles. These works are complete both for all doctrinal purposes and for the refutation of all

objections that human malice or human ingenuity can invent against the Scriptural miracles or the approved ecclesiastical miracles in post-Scriptural times. I have therefore to deal with the subject only inasmuch as it comes under the two considerations above mentioned and in matters connected with them.

2. We have, according to regular order, first to define what is meant by a miracle, and to give the division of miracles. According to St. Thomas, ' Miracles are effects wrought by the power of God alone in things which have a natural tendency to a contrary effect, or to a contrary way of proceeding '

The Rev. B. Boedder, S.J., referring to this definition, gives the following exposition of the teaching of St Thomas: 'After having given his definition, the Angelic Doctor, by way of further explanation, indicates two series of facts, which at first sight would seem to be miracles, but are not miracles in the sense in which Catholic theologians use the term.

' The first series is formed by the hidden effects of nature (*ea quænatura facit nobis tamen vel alicui occulta*) These are natural effects, the natural cause of which is unknown. That cause may be either some hidden force or forces of nature acting by themselves, or it may be forces of nature applied by the natural faculties of man in an artificial way, or it may be forces of nature utilized by pure spirits, supposing they act only with their natural faculties All these effects are wonderful and marvellous, but not miracles.

' The second series is made up of actions which are Divine, but occur regularly in the *ordinary* natural or supernatural course of things (*ea quæ*

Deus facit nec aliter nata sunt fieri nisi a Deo). Such actions are: (1) The creation of each individual human soul, which takes place through purely Divine power as often as the substratum of a human body has been duly prepared by natural causes. . . . The creation of a human soul, then, though a purely Divine action, is neither a miracle nor a supernatual action, in the strict sense of the word. It is not a miracle, because it is in harmony with the ordinary course of things; it is not a supernatural action, because it is necessary for the completion of human nature. Also, the first creation of pure spirits and of matter, though most marvellous, does not come under the category of miracles, because by that creation the very foundation of created nature was laid. (2) Christians believe also in other actions, transcending not only the faculties of creatures, but even the exigencies grounded on their nature and their faculties, and therefore strictly supernatural actions, yet not miracles. Such actions are the *infusion* or *increase of sanctifying grace* through the Sacraments of the Church and through acts of perfect contrition. Such are also all *illuminations* and *inspirations* of the Holy Ghost, by which men are prepared and helped to the performance of saving and meritorious works. These actions are not miracles, because they follow the ordinary course of constant supernatural influence of God upon rational creatures, in accordance with the general direction of His Providence in the present order of things towards a supernatural beatitude.

'To express this clearly, modern theologians define a miracle to be a *sensible, unusual, Divine, and supernatural work.*

'(1) A miracle is defined a *sensible work*, because the definition does not extend beyond those extraordinary supernatural facts which imply changes perceptible through the senses.

'(2) A miracle is defined an *unusual work*, because it is opposed to the ordinary course of nature, or to the ordinary way in which corporal things under similar circumstances act and react on one another. The mere frequency of a miracle in comparatively few spots of the globe does not take away its character of being an *unusual work*. To use the words of St. Thomas: "If daily some blind man were made to see, this would nevertheless be a miracle, because opposed to the ordinary course of nature."

'(3) A miracle is called a *Divine work*, because it is due to a special positive agency of God. The co-operation of even the holiest and most wonderful of the Saints in the miracles which they are said to work does not extend beyond acting as impetrators or as instrumental and ministerial causes.

'(4) A miracle is called not only a *Divine*, but also a *supernatural work*, because it is not one of those Divine works which complete the natural existence of corporeal things, man included. To this work belong the first creation of the world and the continual creation of individual souls.

'*Note.*—In the language of Scripture miracles are often called *signs, prodigies, virtues*. The word *sign* refers to the intention God has in working miracles. He wills thereby to speak to man in a sensible way. The name *prodigy* points to the wonder excited in human minds by the sight of miracles, whilst the word *virtue* implies that they are manifestations of *power*, supreme and Divine.'[1]

3. The division of miracles

3. The same author gives us the division of miracles as commonly accepted in Catholic schools, and mentioned by St Thomas, and his explanation of the various kinds is both clear and precise

'Miracles are divided into miracles *above nature*, *beside nature*, and *against nature*.

'*Above nature* are those miracles which are worked in material subjects, in which in the ordinary course of nature similar effects never occur. Thus, it never happens naturally that a dead and decomposing body rises to life again Therefore, the resurrection of Lazarus was a miracle above nature

'*Beside nature* are those miracles that occur in material subjects, in which, through the forces of nature, either left to themselves or artificially applied, similar effects do occur Here an effect is known to be miraculous by its occurring at a prophesied time, or simply upon the word of a thaumaturgus, and that in cases in which similar effects could not have been obtained through natural forces otherwise than gradually, and with no certainty about the success. Thus, the fact that in Egypt, upon the word of Moses, all the first-born of men and beasts died in one night, whilst the Israelites were spared, was a miracle beside nature. Such a miracle, also, was the sudden withering of the hand of Jeroboam when he stretched it out against the prophet of God, and the blindness of the sorcerer Elymas, caused upon the prediction of St. Paul

'*Against nature* are the miracles which happen in material subjects that naturally tend to a contrary

---

[1] 'Natural Theology,' p 413 *et seq*

effect, and are not prevented from producing their effect by any natural cause. Thus, the preservation of the three companions of Daniel was a miracle against nature ; also the going back of the shadow on the sundial of Achaz.

'This is the division of miracles which is substantially to be found in St. Thomas. The term "nature" which is taken as the standard of this division, means the whole of corporeal substances, and their forces acting under Divine concurrence, either by themselves alone or under some artificial direction of rational creatures. We may note that the miracles *against nature* come in no way against the essence or against the final end of natural substances, but only against the course of action these substances would take, if God had not decreed from eternity for special reasons to interfere with it.

' But how to combine the division with the definition? The definition says that every miracle is *supernatural* or *above nature*. In the division, on the contrary, only one class of miracle is marked as being *above nature*. The solution is to be found in the fact that in the definition the miraculous effect is considered as it exists in the concrete, with all its circumstances, knowable to a diligent observer. When thus viewed, every real miracle must be pronounced to be supernatural, or a Divine effect. But a miraculous effect, though manifestly Divine when viewed adequately, may be taken into consideration inadequately, and the question asked : How does this effect stand to the efficiency of mere natural forces, abstraction being made from all particular circumstances ? This consideration leads to the result that some miracles are *above nature*, others *beside nature*, others, again, *against nature*. Therefore the definition is not opposed to the division, because in the definition the miraculous effect is viewed as happening under all the peculiar circumstances under which it does happen; whilst the division of miracles is made by comparing the effect with the forces of nature, abstracting from concrete circumstances.'[1]

4. The gift of miracles is one of the graces *gratis data* enumerated by St Paul[2] Speaking of this gift, Benedict XIV. establishes three things. (1) That the gift of miracles includes the grace of healing mentioned by the Apostle; (2) that the gift or grace of miracles abides in the Church, (3) that it is not given as a habitual gift to any mere creature, man, or Angel.

(1) 'Suarez says that the grace of healing signifies only what the word imparts—that is, the marvellous healing of bodily diseases; and the working of miracles includes all other marvellous works which are beyond nature, and the object of which are men and sensible things. This is also the doctrine of St. Thomas, who proposes the question, whether there be a grace *gratis data* for performing miracles, and, having resolved it in the affirmative, urges this objection: the miraculous restoration to health takes place by Divine power, therefore the grace of healing ought not to be distinguished from the working of miracles; to which he thus replies. "The grace of healing is mentioned separately, because thereby some benefit is conferred upon man, namely, of bodily health,

[1] 'Natural Theology.' Boedder, pp 419-421
[2] 1 Cor xii 4

over and above the general benefit which is shown in all miracles, namely, that men may be led to the knowledge of God." [1]

(2) The learned Pontiff Benedict XIV., speaking on this subject, says that 'there is the grace of miracles in the Church; for the Holy Spirit furnishes the Church with those things that are profitable to salvation. Wherefore as knowledge Divinely received comes to the knowledge of others by the gift of tongues and the grace of speech, so by the operation of miracles it confirms the word spoken, that it may be believed, as it is written in St. Mark,[2] *and confirming the word with signs that followed.* Thus St Thomas and Silvius proceed to observe "God sufficiently furnishes the Church with those things which are necessary to the salvation of the people; but it concerns the salvation of the elect, not only that the wholesome doctrine be laid before them, whether by the gift of tongues or the grace of speech, but also that it be confirmed so as to become credible It is fitting that this confirmation should be effected by miracles, for those who see them wrought see that they are done by God alone, and are beyond the power of created nature They are then led by Divine help to embrace supernatural truth, in confirmation of which they are wrought, and they are also strengthened firmly to maintain what they have embraced. Therefore, as the grace of speech is necessary to put the faith before infidels, so the working of miracles is necessary also for the confirmation of the faith recently preached." [3] It is

(2) The gift or grace of miracles in the Church

---

[1] 'Treatise on Heroic Virtue,' vol iii, p 128
[2] St Mark xvi 20
[3] 'Treatise on Heroic Virtue,' vol iii, pp 129, 130

in this sense that the Church, through the Vatican Council, has declared. 'In order that our faith be reasonable, God has added to the inward help of the grace of the Holy Spirit external proofs for His manifestation, namely, Divine deeds, above all miracles which show the omnipotence of God in a glorious light, and which are at the same time the surest tokens of Divine manifestation, and of the most convincing kind for man.'[1]

By these words the Vatican Council has shown the Christian conception of a miracle, its character and aim. They are visible tokens which show to us the power of God and His immediate influence on the course of natural events; they imprint upon the revelation of natural and supernatural doctrines the seal of undeniable truth.

The Gospel bears testimony to the innumerable miracles of our Lord, and it also narrates that our Saviour referred to them in order to demand faith for His utterance: *Believe you not, that I am in the Father, and the Father in Me? otherwise, believe for the very work's sake*[2] And, again. *If I had not done among them the works that no other man hath done, they would not have sin.*[3] Our Divine Saviour promises expressly that this gift, the working of miracles, would not die with His death, but would continue in His disciples *Amen, amen, I say, he that believeth in Me, the works that I do he also shall do, and greater than those shall he do.*[4] And at the last meeting with His disciples, after His resurrection, He repeated solemnly *And these signs shall follow them that believe in My name they shall*

---

[1] 'Conc Vat.,' cap iii, de Fide   [2] St John xiv 11
[3] St. John xv 24   [4] St John xiv 12

MYSTICAL PHENOMENA—MIRACLES

cast out devils; they shall speak with new tongues; they shall take up serpents, and if they drink any deadly thing, it shall not hurt them; they shall lay their hands upon the sick, and they shall recover.[1] It is very difficult after such plain utterances to comprehend how certain people, who acknowledge the holy writings as the Word of God, can deny the possibility of miracles after the death of Christ and the Apostles.

(3) Benedict XIV. says: 'This grace of miracles is not anything that habitually abides in the soul; for the principle of working miracles extends to everything that can be done supernaturally, and is therefore nothing less than the Divine omnipotence, which can be communicated to no creature nor to any mere man. If, indeed, the power of working miracles were always abiding in those who had the grace of miracles, they would be at all times able to work miracles when they pleased, which is not the case. The Apostles ask, *Why could we not cast him out?*[2] Christ replied, *But this kind is not cast out but by prayer and fasting.* Again, Eliseus could not raise up the son of the Sunamitess to life by means of his staff.[3] Wherefore the grace of miracles consists in this, that when God bestows it upon anyone He sometimes moves him to do something which issues in a wonderful work; sometimes He makes use instrumentally of contact with anything belonging to such a person, sometimes prayer or devout invocation of His name, a word, or any other outward sign. Thus speaks Silvius. We said that the grace of miracles is habitually communicated to

(3) The gift of miracles not granted as a habit to any mere man.

---

[1] St. Mark xvi. 17, 18.   [2] St. Matt. xvii. 18.
[3] 2 Kings iv. 31.

no mere man; to Christ, indeed, as man, or to His humanity, was granted a perpetual and constant working of miracles, because He was able of His own free will to work miracles as often as He judged it convenient. For this He had the ever-ready concurrence of the Divinity, although there was in His humanity no permanent quality which could be a physical cause of miracles, as is well observed by Suarez.'[1]

<small>3. Relation of the gift of miracles to sanctity</small>

5. The same learned Pontiff tells us sufficient with regard to miracles in their relation to sanctity of life, when speaking of their estimate in the cause of the beatification and canonization of the Saints. He says

'It is the common opinion of theologians that the grace of miracles is a grace *gratis data*, and therefore that it is given, not only to the just, but also to sinners . . . Our Lord says that He knows not those who have done evil, though they may have prophesied in His name, cast out devils in His name, and done many wonderful works. And the Apostle said that without charity he was nothing, though he might have faith to remove mountains. On this passage of the Apostle, Estius remarks: "For as it offers no contradiction to the Apostle that a man should have the gift of tongues or prophecy, or knowledge of mysteries, and excel in knowledge, which are first spoken of, or be liberal to the poor, or give his body to be burned for the name of Christ, which are afterwards spoken, and yet not have charity; so also there is no contradiction in a man having faith to remove mountains, and being without charity."'

[1] 'Treatise on Heroic Virtue,' vol III, p 130

6. I speak here of the miracles of the Saints, and the miracles that occur frequently at holy places and holy shrines in every age of the Church, and I know no better way of showing how the real miracles are verified than by giving the rules of investigation observed by the Church in the process of beatification or canonization of the Saints. The question concerning the miracles of the servants of God is divided into two parts, each of which is examined separately. The first is, whether the actual existence of the miraculous facts produced in the process has been thoroughly proved before the Commissioners. Secondly, whether these facts be really supernatural and true miracles, the work of God and of good Angels. On these two questions Bishop Hay writes as follows

'The discussion of the first of these brings on a review of the whole process, wherein the proceedings of the Commissioners, the witnesses, their qualifications, their depositions, and all the circumstances, are canvassed, and the promoter of the faith himself urges every objection he can imagine against them All must be thoroughly solved by the solicitors for the case; and if they fail to satisfy the judges, the miracle is rejected as not proved. If the facts be indubitable, then the court proceeds to examine the other question, whether the facts so proved are supernatural and true miracles.

'In examining this point, three different classes of miracles are distinguished. Some are of such a stupendous nature as evidently to surpass all created power, and show themselves at once to be the work of God, and these are of the first order. Others less astonishing may, for anything we know, be within the power of those created intellectual beings, whose knowledge and power far exceed ours; and these are of the second order. Others, again, are in substance natural events, which may be produced by the assistance of art, but from the concurrence of circumstances, and the manner in which they are performed, become truly miraculous; and these are of the third order.

'Now, when any miracle of the first order is produced, and the fact is undoubtedly proved, it needs no further discussion; it carries on the face of it the proofs of its Divinity, and shows itself at once to be the immediate work of God, and such the raising of a dead person to life is always considered.

'In miracles of the second order, which are plainly preternatural—that is, above all the efforts of human power—the question is, to discern whether they be the work of God or the operation of the evil spirits. In deciding this, the fact is examined by the rules of the criterion for the purpose. It requires five principal qualities to constitute in the judgment of the court a Divine miracle. They are as follows: First, "The reality of the effect." The power of evil spirits is limited, that of God has no bounds; the wonders produced by the devil are at best but vain appearances, which absorb the attention or deceive the senses; but a true miracle produces a real effect. Secondly, "The duration." Effects of enchantment are only momentary; those of true miracles are permanent. Thirdly, "The utility." God Almighty does not employ His power in vain. Frivolous events and changes, which merely produce fear or wonder, are unworthy of the attention of a reasonable man, much less do they deserve that the

MYSTICAL PHENOMENA—MIRACLES

Divine wisdom should make use of a particular order of His Providence to produce them. Still less can it be supposed that Almighty God will act in a miraculous manner to exhibit things unbecoming, ridiculous, or favourable to any unjust or wicked design. Fourthly, "The means used." Prayer, invocation of the holy name of God, of the Blessed Trinity, and of the Saints, are the means of obtaining true miracles from God; false wonders are obtained by having recourse to the devil, to superstitious spells, shameful artifices, or extravagant actions. Fifthly, "The principal object." Almighty God can have no other ultimate end in all He does than His own glory and our real happiness. The confirmation or advancement of piety and Christian justice, and the sanctification of souls, are the only supreme motives ultimately worthy of His goodness and His infinite wisdom. Miracles of the second order must be attended with all these qualities before they can be admitted in this court as Divine, and the absence of any one of them would effectually discredit the case for ever.

Miracles of the third order, as cures of diseases, are examined in the strictest manner; and it must necessarily be proved, to the conviction of the judges, that they were attended with all those circumstances which evidently show that the operation was Divine. The circumstances indispensably required are: First, that the disease be considerable, dangerous, inveterate, and such as commonly resists the power of known medicines, or, at least, that a cure by their means would be long and difficult. Secondly, that the disease has not come to a crisis, after which it is natural to expect a mitigation of the symptoms and a cure. ³Thirdly, that no ordinary natural remedies have been applied, or that such time has elapsed that they could have no influence in the cure. Fourthly, that the cure be sudden and instantaneous, that the violent pains or imminent danger cease at once, instead of diminishing gradually, as we see in the operations of nature. ⁵Fifthly, that the cure be perfect and complete. ⁶Sixthly, that the health recovered be permanent, and not followed by a speedy relapse.

'The concurrence of all these conditions and circumstances must be proved with the utmost clearness, before the miraculous character of the facts can be admitted; and in this investigation there is the greatest rigour used.'[1]

These rules may be applied by Bishops, priests, and people within their own sphere, and they may be guided by them in giving or withholding their belief in the miracles which they may witness or which may be brought under their notice.

7. *Miracles not expected by pious people without sufficient cause.*

7. When pious people pray to God and to the Saints to aid them in all their necessities, great and small, temporal and spiritual, it should not be supposed that they, on all these occasions ask for or expect miracles. They pray in the true sense of the petition in the Lord's Prayer: 'Give us this day our daily bread.' They know that God may grant their requests by natural means as well as by miracles, but it is not for them to judge what are the proper means to be employed. To God they are both equally easy, and our religion assures us that sometimes He uses one, and sometimes the other; sometimes He procures the sanctity and perfection of His

[1] Bishop Hay on 'Miracles,' chap. xv.

servants by ordinary though supernatural means, and sometimes He employs extraordinary and miraculous means for His purpose, as He in His wisdom judges proper. But it cannot be denied that it is most becoming the Divine goodness and wisdom to use the means for attaining His end which are most proper and most conducive thereto.

p 640

CONCLUSION

SUMMARY OF ADMONITIONS AND DIRECTIONS

p 642

CONCLUSION

SUMMARY OF ADMONITIONS AND DIRECTIONS

1. IN the course of this work the admonition given by spiritual writers 'not to be too credulous or too incredulous' has been repeated more than once for the benefit of those who may have to direct souls that are favoured by the extraordinary graces and gifts of which we have treated. The admonition is repeated now for the last time. I may repeat also that the ordinary supernatural life, as taught in the 'Manual of Ascetical Theology,' is the surer and the safer way to heaven. This ordinary supernatural life and its perfection is supposed before, and is the very foundation of, the extraordinary supernatural favours. Yet these favours are not essential to it, nor altogether confined to it, if we except the higher degrees of contemplation. When, however, God condescends to call souls to contemplation, they are bound to correspond to that call, and, though infused contemplation and the gifts of which we have written may be regarded as graces *gratis datæ*, they are to be regarded also as signal tokens of the Divine love for such souls, and serve indirectly and efficaciously to promote their greater sanctification.

When persons are favoured by the gift of infused

contemplation, or by visions, locutions, and revelations, it is evident that they are being led by extraordinary means in the way of their spiritual life, that the way itself is extraordinary, and one that is beset by many dangers, on account of the delusions and snares to which souls are exposed along that way. Hence the necessity of guidance and of a great caution and vigilance.

<small>2 More women than men favoured with mystical gifts</small>

2. It has been said that more women than men are favoured with these extraordinary gifts, and frequent warning seems to be necessary in their case against delusions, deceptions, hysteria, and hallucinations, to which they are more subject or exposed than are men. Divine favours can always be recognised and distinguished from such errors and diseases, if we carefully attend to their nature and qualities as explained by mystical theologians, and the truly saintly persons themselves are often the best judges of real Divine gifts and their counterfeits. The warning is necessary, because, as H. Joly well remarks, 'human nature is ever the same In the present day, as in every age, there are persons with diseased minds, who, instead of dreaming of earthly love and greatness, become enamoured of the melancholy joys of an imaginary intercourse with Angels and with the Deity. They are to be met with in all pious circles. Priests, whom they torment with their scruples and general unreasonableness, know them well. Why should we hide the fact that there are some in convents, since St. Theresa and St. Jane de Chantal tell us that they found many in their own communities? They are constantly warning us against that evil system, which begins by unrestrained enjoyment of certain sensible spiritual joys,

is continued by a half-voluntary depression of spirits, is increased by want of nourishment, followed by growing physical weakness, until it ends in a kind of ecstasy which contains nothing but danger.' 'The error we are endeavouring to correct,' says this author, 'consists in supposing that, because this innocent but melancholy imitation of sanctity exists, therefore it is the habitual state of real saints.'[1]

We have therefore to observe that it would be a great mistake to reject genuine cases of true and extraordinary sanctity because the extraordinary phenomena of the Saints have been imitated or abused by some fanatical and deluded souls. Speaking of these supernatural and extraordinary favours, it is asserted and admitted that more women than men have received them, and women more than men are often enriched with the greatest treasures of heaven. Such, says Scaramelli, is the experience of all times, and it is also evident to reason. St. Theresa says somewhere in her writings that more women than men are enriched by God with these extraordinary graces. That, she said, she had herself discovered, and her opinion was confirmed by that of St. Peter of Alcantara, who also brought forward the best reasons to establish his opinion. His reasons are the same substantially as those which Father Baker assigns, when treating on the same particular point. He, as well as other mystical writers, considered it a point of importance and well worthy of notice. He writes as follows

'Both history and fresher experience do assure us that in these latter times God hath as freely (and

[1] 'The Psychology of the Saints,' p. 93

perhaps more commonly) communicated the Divine lights and graces proper to a contemplative life to simple women, endowed with lesser and more contemptible gifts of judgment, but yet enriched with stronger wills and more fervent affections to Him than the ablest men. And the reason hereof we may judge to be, partly because God thereby should, as is most due, reap all the glory of His most free graces, which if they did usually attend our natural endowments would be challenged as due to our own abilities and endeavours, and partly also, because as substantial holiness so the perfection of it, which is contemplation, consists far more principally in the operation of the will than of the understanding. And since women do far more abound, and are far more constant and fixed in affections and other occupations of the will than men, no marvel if God doth oft find them fitter subjects for His graces than men.

'And for this reason it is (besides that women are less encumbered with solicitous business abroad, their secular employments being chiefly domestical within their own walls) that they do far more frequently repair to the churches, more assiduously perform their devotions both there and at home, and reap the blessings of the Sacraments plentifully (upon which grounds the Church calls them the devout sex). . . . Notwithstanding all this, true it is that the contemplations of men are more noble, sublime, and more exalted in spirit—that is, less partaking of sensible effects, as raptures, ecstasies, or imaginative representations, as likewise melting tendernesses of affection, than those of women.'[1]

[1] 'Holy Wisdom,' p. 136.

ADMONITIONS AND DIRECTIONS

3. It is not to be wondered at, therefore, if more women than men are favoured by the extraordinary favours of the mystical life; at the same time, that it may not be supposed that such favours are natural rather than supernatural, and therefore to be suspected, or that they are confined to women or characteristic of the devout sex, let us bear in mind that the number of canonized men Saints is large compared with that of women. There are human and ecclesiastical reasons by which this can be accounted for, and we can never conclude from the percentage of canonized Saints anything certain as to the number of real Saints. The canonized Saints are only very few compared with the number of uncanonized Saints, a small handful of those who have been brought under the public notice of the Church and of the faithful, and whom God, for His own wise ends, wished to be distinguished by special honour in the Church, and to be held up for the special veneration and imitation of the faithful. Nevertheless, my argument is that, since more men than women have been canonized, it cannot be said that visions, locutions, revelations, and miraculous gifts, and the like, are peculiar to devout women. These are examined into in the process of canonization, and examined with the greatest care and minuteness in the case of all Saints not Martyrs, and we may therefore say that, of the approved visions, revelations, manifestations, and the extraordinary phenomena of the supernatural life, more belong to men than to women. I do not say that all Saints have been mystics, or that to be a Saint one must be favoured with mystical phenomena; but it is certain that in the lives of nearly all the

3. More men canonized than women

Saints we read of those extraordinary favours and graces, and, furthermore, as we have seen, these things are always taken into consideration in the process of their beatification and canonization. And, therefore, in the case of men more often than in the case of women, gifts and works of the extraordinary and exalted nature treated of in mystical theology have undergone the rigorous examination of the Church, and have been authentically published to the world as true and incontestable after such examination.

<small>1 The necessity of prudent spiritual direction in the mystical life</small>

4. In reviewing the various subjects treated in this work, whilst admiring and praising the wonderful ways of God in dealing with His privileged children, we must be impressed oftentimes with the difficulties and dangers to which these souls are exposed, and with the consequent necessity of careful and prudent spiritual direction. Confessors and directors have, therefore, a very important, and sometimes a very arduous, duty to perform in their official capacity when dealing with cases that are unusual and extraordinary. These cases are, however, not so unusual as is commonly imagined. Perhaps they are not easily known That may be, but on reading what theologians tell us on these matters, and examining carefully the signs that accompany the various kinds of contemplation and its several degrees, it is possible to detect even in our busy times some such cases. Sometimes and more frequently this may be in religious houses, but sometimes also in the world, and oftener, perhaps, amongst very simple and illiterate people. I have in my mind at present one such holy person. She does not know nor does the world know of her

exalted state; and I have in my mind more than one person of the class of those who are not illiterate, and who yet, without discursive prayer, are able to spend hours of the greatest happiness in contemplation before the most Holy Sacrament.

With regard to mystical phenomena outside contemplation, I can only repeat what I have already written in another work with regard to such phenomena, and which may be useful at the close of this work also for the guidance of confessors and penitents, and which may serve as a summary of the admonitions which mystical authors frequently repeat.

Concerning visions, revelations, and suchlike supernatural manifestations, we subjoin the following directions :

5 In the first place, souls thus favoured should not be supposed all at once to be under a delusion, neither should these visions and the like be taken all at once as coming from the Holy Ghost. Virtue does not consist in them, but in good works, and in the increase of grace and charity, for revelations have sometimes been made to the bad—Balaam, Caiphas, and others. Those who receive such favours should not, therefore, regard themselves as Saints. At the same time, we must have great respect for such manifestations, according to the advice of St. Paul *Extinguish not the Spirit. Despise not prophecies; but prove all things hold fast that which is good.*[1]

5 Summary of directions with regard to mystical phenomena outside contemplation

How are true revelations and visions to be distinguished from false ones ?

To guard against deception and error in such

[1] 1 Thess v 19-21

matters, it is necessary to pray and to investigate the case carefully. Humility is also required, because God has hidden these things from the wise and prudent, and revealed them to little ones.[1] We should therefore consider, first, the person who makes the revelation, secondly, the person to whom the revelation is made; and, thirdly, the nature of the thing revealed, and its effects or results.

(1) From whom does the vision or revelation come? Whether from a good or a bad spirit. A good Angel, we are told, begins by exhorting to what is good, and perseveres in it; a bad Angel at first urges to good, and then inclines to evil. The good Angel in the beginning causes fear, but immediately brings consolation and comfort, the bad stupefies in the beginning, and leaves desolation. Also, we must inquire as to the form in which the Angel appears. Because if in the form of a beast or a monster, or in human shape, but somehow curious or deformed, he is to be considered a bad Angel.

(2) The person who receives the vision. The disposition of the persons should be considered, whether bilious [2] or melancholy, because such persons are given to imaginations and fancies. Whether in bad health or the brain in any way affected; also age has to be taken into consideration, because if very old there is danger of lightness of head, and if very young there is danger of lightness of heart. It will also help if we can know a person's predominant inclination or hobby. St. Leo says that the devil takes occasion of doing harm from what

ADMONITIONS AND DIRECTIONS

he perceives to occupy a person's mind. Because if affected with strong inclinations towards what is supposed to be revealed, then the vision may easily proceed from one's self or from the devil. This may be known in the case of a penitent, who, when forbidden by the confessor to think of or to pay any attention to such things, grows sad and begins to speak against the confessor. In such a case the vision is from the evil spirit, because he who is guided by the Spirit of God is not made sad by the command of a confessor, but will try to conform to it. It is also of importance to consider whether the person is educated, to whom does he confess, whether he is affected by singularity of penances and devotions not approved by his superiors, whether a novice or one advanced in virtue. Above all, we have to consider whether he is obedient to superiors and to his confessor; because if he fail in this he certainly exposes himself to the danger of error and deception. In separating himself from the guidance of his confessor, he impedes the medium through which God ordinarily communicates His will even in regard to His extraordinary gifts. It is also a sign of deception if he speak to others of his revelations or visions, as this would show pride and vanity. Frequently asking conference on the subject with confessors and spiritual directors, long accounts of his visions and apparitions and apprehensions, are also signs of deception. Of those deceived in this way, Gerson says: 'Expertis credite nominatim Augustino et Bonaventuro, *vix est alter pestis vel efficacior ad nocendum vel insanabilior.*'

(3) The revelations and visions themselves and

their effects. As to the revelations, visions, etc., themselves, we have to notice:

1. Whether they contain anything false, because in this case they cannot proceed from the Spirit of Truth. Therefore it is necessary to consider whether the revelation or vision is conformable to Scripture, to faith and morals, to theology, and to the doctrines and traditions of the Church.

2. Whether it is necessary or concerns a matter of grave importance, because revelations that teach useless and trifling things are delusions.

3. The revelation that makes known the faults of others and their sins is very much to be suspected, especially if an interior or exterior voice be heard telling such things.

4. If the revelation suggests something good even, but extraordinary and singular, it is open to suspicion, as, for example, to fast for a long time on bread and water.

As to the effect of these manifestations or communications, we have to inquire:

1. Do they incline the soul to virtue, to good works, to an efficacious desire and determination to suffer for Christ, to contempt of one's self, and to self-knowledge?

2. Do they bring peace, light, and certainty, and do they leave after them an increase of the love of God and deep reverence for Divine things? Are they accompanied by the Cross and by mortification, and do they tend to the manifestation of the faith and the utility of the Church?

3. Finally, we have to consider whether the holy fear of the Lord is preserved in the soul, that fear which makes it more cautious and vigilant in its

obligations, lest God should be displeased with it. This is one of the best effects, according to the words of St. Paul to the Philippians *Work out your salvation in fear and trembling.* If, on the contrary, there arise in the soul too much confidence and facility, without circumspection or holy fear, the supposed communications are the work of the evil spirit, for this spirit takes away from the soul the fear of God, that it may lead it into sin, as it happened to Eve when the devil said to her · 'Ye shall not die the death.'[1]

6. We have now to bring to a close our long and sometimes difficult exposition of the mystical life of the soul on earth. We have studied contemplation in itself and in its various degrees as the end and principal object of that life. As a preparation for contemplation we have had to treat of prayer, mortification, active and passive purifications; and in order to the completion of our work it was necessary to explain the various ways in which the mystical life manifests itself externally, and the mystical phenomena whereby God makes known to us from time to time the exalted and heroic sanctity of His Saints and servants. We have now to remind our readers, for the last time, that whosoever wishes to attain to the perfection and to the full use of contemplation must do so by perfecting himself in all virtues, and especially in the theological virtues. Some may in the very beginning of the spiritual life experience a foretaste and a faint view of the contemplative life, but the solid, useful experience of that life can only be obtained after a man has

[1] 'Convent Life,' p 216 *et seq* Remarks taken chiefly from Cajetan de Alexandris ('Conf Mon,' cap viii, s iii)

within him some degree of perfection in the virtues. 'Christ is not only the Door, but the Doorkeeper, and without His leave no man can come in, as He Himself saith. *No man cometh to the Father but by Me*;[1] that is to say, no man cometh to the contemplation of the Godhead but he that is first of all reformed by perfection in humility and charity to the likeness of Jesus in His humanity.'[2]

They have also to keep in mind that it is habitual grace which unites the soul to God, and which enables it to merit and to obtain in due time its eternal beatitude. Charity also unites the soul to God as to its object, and it is by its acts that an increase of grace here and of glory hereafter is chiefly merited Contemplation, however, supposes grace and its union as its foundation, and it includes charity as its component part; therefore it regards God and is ordained to Him as to its object, and it unites the soul with God as with its beginning, its object and its end, and this is the most complete and perfect which a wayfarer here on earth can have with God, Who is our origin and our destiny.

Finally, all should frequently reflect upon our Lord's words *He that shall persevere to the end, he shall be saved.*[3] Perseverance is necessary for all, and even the most exalted and most favoured souls have to be constantly reminded of this truth. Bishop Ullathorne well remarks.

'The soul that has been once illuminated with the light of contemplation, though but for a short time, can never forget it, nor can ever be the same as before.' A higher and a purer standard of good is

---

[1] St John xiv 6. [2] 'Scale of Perfection,' p 146
[3] St Matt x 22 and xxiv 13

implanted in the mind and in the conscience. To turn to evil would be much more fearful and loathsome than before, the rending of the conscience would be more terrible. To abandon God after the light of His countenance had shone with sweetness and power on the soul would be a spiritual apostasy, to which the words of St. Paul are but too applicable: *It is impossible* [that is to say, very difficult] *for those who were once illuminated, have tasted also the heavenly gift, and were made partakers of the Holy Ghost, have, moreover, tasted the good word of God, and the powers of the world to come, and are fallen away, to be renewed again to penance.*[1] Such falls after true contemplation must be rare indeed. The causes are more numerous where a pretension to the gift is false, a mere delusion of the imagination rather than a union of mind and heart with the Divine light, generating conceit in place of humility. But true contemplation brings with it such a knowledge of God and of self, generates so much charity and humility, and inspires such a horror for sin, that the soul is drawn ever closer to God and further from selfishness.'

Prayer is the great means of perseverance, and to it I therefore direct the attention of the readers as a concluding recommendation. From the portion of the work which treats of this subject I may claim, with the learned and pious Bishop just quoted, that three paramount instructions may be gathered. 'First, in every kind of prayer, whether vocal, meditative, aspiratory or contemplative, whilst the manner is different, the spirit is the same. All prayer has one final end, our beatitude in God, and

[1] Heb. vi 4-6

all should be exercised in spirit and in truth. Secondly, every kind of prayer leads to interior recollection according to each one's gift and disposition; and when this recollection ascends to contemplation the summit of prayer is reached; there is nothing between the soul and God but His own gifts; it is a certain foreshadowing within the brevity of time of the eternal contemplation of God. Thirdly, the greatest fruits of prayer are not visible in the time of prayer, but only a certain light, refreshment, and consolation. Even this is often withheld for the correction, or the probation, or the discipline of the soul; but the memory of that refreshment is a great encouragement in time of trial. The great reward of prayer is reserved for eternity, and the generous soul will say: Give me now thorns, and keep the crown for eternity.'[1]

[1] 'Christian Patience,' p. 206.

INDEX

Acts of devotion of the contemplative soul to the Blessed Virgin, 78

Admiration accompanies contemplation, 29, effect of, 144

Admonition concerning the prayer of recollection, 382

Angels, apparitions of, 530

Anguish and *Thirst of Love*, the sixth degree of contemplation, 420

Apparitions, corporeal, 512, the beings who appear, 513, *theophanies*, or apparitions of God, 514, in the Old Law not personal, 516, in the New Law by personal intervention, 520, adoration to be given in such cases, 518, apparitions of our Saviour 520, in the Blessed Sacrament, 523, three visions of our Saviour distinguished, 525, apparitions of the Blessed Virgin, 527, at Lourdes, 528, of Angels, 530, of good Angels, 531, of devils, *ibid*, of Saints, 533, of souls in purgatory, 536; of the damned, 537, no authentic example of the apparition of an infant who has died without Baptism, 513, the end for which these apparitions and visions are granted, 537 See Visions

Appetite, sensitive and rational, 93, 94, appetency, 95

Approbation of the Church given to private revelations, meaning of, 589

Aridity, 285

Athanasian Creed, 58, Cardinal Newman's estimate of, 60

Attention required for vocal prayer, 194, degrees of, 195

Benefits of the passive purification of the spirit, 364

Bodily diseases as purifications, 326 See Mortifications

Bossuet and *Fénelon*, controversy between See Quietism

Breviary, 191

Causes of contemplation See Principles

Charity, fraternal, the fruit of contemplation, 149, *perfect charity* towards God the fruit of contemplation, 152

Christ, apparitions of, 520, 523, 525

Confessors not to be too credulous or too incredulous about visions and other mystical phenomena, 508, 643

Conscience, purity of, 256, examination of, 271

Contemplation in general, 1

Contemplation place assigned to it in the mystical life, 19, its definition and explanation, 28, contemplation of the faithful Catholic distinct from that of the philosopher 30 description of, by Benedict XIV., 34; distinction between thought, meditation, and contemplation, 35, various species of ordinary, 37, extraordinary, 38; extraordinary and the graces *gra-*

[657]   42

tuitously given, 39, 41, the gift of, sanctifying, 41, points in which ordinary and extraordinary contemplation agree and differ, 42, 43, forms or divisions of contemplation, by Richard of St Victor, 45, cherubic and seraphic contemplation, 46, objects of, see Objects, system of contemplation according to Richard of St Victor, summarized by Archbishop Vaughan in his 'Life of St Thomas of Aquin,' 85, causes and principles of, 90 (see Causes and Principles), contemplation may be desired and prayed for, 110 conditions to be observed in praying for it, 112, contemplation and the uncertainty of grace, 120, effects and fruits of, 142 (see Effects and Fruits), not a permanent habit, 156, its duration, 157, experience of St Theresa and other Saints, 160, contemplation and meditation alternate 161, the gift sometimes withdrawn, 163, reasons of withdrawal, 165, contemplation, preparation and dispositions for, 168 (see Preparation for Contemplation and Dispositions required for Contemplation), degrees of, see Degrees, contemplation by distinct and indistinct acts, 371

Degrees of contemplative prayer, 371, the degrees of contemplation and the names used vary according to different mystical authors, 373, the classification of the degrees diverse, 375 the classification and nomenclature adopted, 377 First Degree. *The Prayer of Recollection*, 380, admonition concerning, 382; described by St Theresa, 383 Second Degree, *Spiritual Silence* holds a middle place between the prayer of recollection and the prayer of union 385, spiritual silence, its causes and effects, 386, special directions concerning, 387, remarks of St Francis de Sales applied to this degree, 389 Third Degree, *The Prayer of Quiet*, 390, St Theresa's description of, 391, the soul active in this state, 393, in what sense called passive, 396, Quietism condemned by the Church, 406 Fourth Degree, *The Inebriation of Love*, 409, imperfect and perfect, 410, effects of, 413 Fifth Degree, *Spiritual Sleep* described, 414, its effects, 415, the pure spiritual light giving rest to the soul, 416, liquefaction and spiritual sleep (St Francis de Sales), 418 Sixth Degree, *The Anguish and Thirst of Love* 420, of beginners, of proficients and of the perfect, 421, 422 Seventh Degree, *The Mystical and Simple Union of Love*, 427 its meaning, 428, various grades of union, 432, the prayer of simple union, *ibid* whether the powers of the soul are suspended during it, 433 whether senses of the body are suspended, 435, difference between this and the prayer of quiet, 436 its effects, 437, the Divine touches of the soul, 439 Eighth Degree, *Ecstatic Union*, 444 (see Ecstasy) Ninth Degree, *Rapture*, 448 (see Rapture and Ecstasy), *spiritual espousals* belong to this degree, 456 (see Espousals) Tenth Degree, *Perfect Union or Spiritual Marriage*, 464 (see Marriage, Spiritual)

Delight the effect of contemplation, 145

Desolation, 286, the great, described by Father Baker 317

Devil the cause of purifications, as an agent, 305, apparitions of, 531

Diabolical temptations against the theological virtues, 306 against the moral virtues, 309, how to regard such temptations, 310, obsession, 317, possession, 321

Direction, need of, in the mystical life, 509, 643, 648, summary of

directions with regard to mystical phenomena, 649
Direction, spiritual, need of, in time of purification, 302, directions of St Paul of the Cross on the purification of the spirit, 365
Dispositions required for contemplation, 169, natural, *ibid*, moral, 172, retirement and solitude, 173
Divine illumination, why called 'night,' 342
Divine mysticism, 11, diabolical mysticism, 12
Doctrinal mystical theology, 10
Dreams, 501, locutions in dreams, 562
Duration of contemplation, 157

Ecstasy its nature and character, 445, proceeds from three sources, 447, distinction between ecstasy and rapture, 448, different kinds of, 449, natural, diabolical, and Divine 450, some characteristics of Divine ecstasies 455, whether acts of an ecstatic are meritorious, 456, whether ecstasies and raptures occur in a state of perfect union or spiritual marriage, 478
Effects of contemplation, 142, elevation and suspension of mind, 143, admiration, 144, joy and delight, 145, effects of passive purification of the senses, 300, of purification of the spirit, 350
Effects of the inebriation of love and of spiritual sleep See Fourth and Fifth Degrees of Contemplation
Effects of the mystical and simple union of love, see Seventh Degree of Contemplation, of spiritual espousals, 458, of spiritual marriage 481
Emotions or passions, 93 in relation to contemplation, 98
Errors of quietism and semiquietism, 399, 400
Espousals spiritual, between God and the soul, 456, effects of, 458

Eucharist, Holy, the object of contemplation, 72
Examination of conscience, 271
Excellence of mental prayer or meditation, 201
Experience of St. Theresa and other Saints as to the duration of contemplation, 160
Experimental mystical theology, 8

Faculties of the soul, 35, sensitive, 91, their relation to contemplation, 96, the intellect, 101, the will, 102, memory in relation to contemplation, 104
Faith, whether private revelations the object of, 585
False mystics—Michael Molinos, Francis Malavallus, 62, 63, 398
Favours, extraordinary, always gratuitous, 82
Fénelon and Bossuet, controversy between See Quietism
Fruits of contemplation, 147, humility, 147, fraternal charity, 149, perfect charity towards God, 152 love shown in suffering, 153, the active love of the Saints, 154, of the passive purification of the spirit, 364

Ghost, Holy, a new mission of, by spiritual marriage, 477
Gifts of the Holy Ghost defined and explained, 128
Gifts of the Holy Ghost the principles and sources of contemplation, 130, gifts of understanding and wisdom in relation to contemplation, 34, 131, 132, knowledge, 133, counsel, 134, fortitude, 135, piety or godliness, 136, the fear of the Lord, 137, gift of prophecy, see Prophecies, of miracle, see Miracles, gifts, mystical, more often granted to women than men, 644
Gluttony, spiritual, 291
God and His attributes as the objects of contemplation, 49, the notion and image of God present in the soul described by Cardinal Newman, 51, how the image may be adapted to contemplation, 53, the attri-

butes of God the object of contemplation, 55, knowledge of God by way of *affirmation* and *negation*, 56, manner of His presence in the contemplative soul, 118, the cause of passive purifications, 290
God, apparitions of, 516, 520
Gospel of pain, 248
Grace gratuitously given and extraordinary contemplation, 39, 41, 138
Grace, sanctifying, the principle or cause of contemplation, 116
Grace, actual, the principle of contemplation, 124

Habit, contemplation not a permanent, 156
Heart, purity of, 259
Humanity, sacred, of Christ the object of contemplation, 62, 65
Humility the fruit of contemplation, 147

Illuminative state or way, 16
Imagination, purification of, 263
Inebriation of love. See Fourth Degree of Contemplation
Incarnation, mystery of, as the object of contemplation, 62, 64
Infants dying without Baptism, no authentic example of their apparition, 513
Inflammation of love, 357
Intellect in relation to contemplation, 104-106
Intellectual motions towards God circular, straight, and oblique, 87, note
Intercourse with seculars, 177
Intuition as applied to contemplation, 31

Job, holy, example of, 323
Joy the effect of contemplation, 145

Knowledge of God by way of *affirmation* and *negation,* 56, how to know ourselves, 277
Knowledge of salvation, whether certain in a state of perfect union or spiritual marriage, 479

Laws according to which God bestows His extraordinary favours not understood by us, 82
Lazarus, example of, 325
Life, active, 20, contemplative and mixed, 21, contemplative more perfect than the active, 22, mixed more perfect than either active or contemplative, 22, active and contemplative exemplified in St Theresa and St John of the Cross, 24, character or distinct feature of each kind of life, 25
Liquefaction and spiritual sleep, 418
Locutions, Divine the various ways in which God speaks to us, 556, vocal locutions, 557, imaginative locutions, 558, locutions in dreams, 562, *intellectual locutions,* 565, three kinds of, 566, successive locutions, 567, formal locutions, 570, substantial locutions, 572
Love shown in suffering, 153, the active love of the Saints, 154, the purification of, its degrees, 355, inflammation of, 357, wounds of, 359, languor of, 361, love of *chaste desire (concupiscentiae)* and of *benevolence,* 403, inebriation of, see Fourth Degree of Contemplation, anguish and thirst of, 420, the mystical and simple union of, see Seventh Degree of Contemplation

Marriage, spiritual, tenth degree of contemplation, explained, 464, its nature in a mystical sense, and its difference from spiritual espousals, 467, in what sense a stable and permanent state, 479, twofold vision of our Lord in this state, 473, two things essential to this union, 475, *graces of,* a new mission of the Holy Ghost, 477 whether the soul is in this state impeccable, *ibid.,* whether ecstasies or raptures occur in this state, 478, whether certain knowledge of salvation in this state, 479, effects of, 481

INDEX

Mary, the Blessed Virgin, the object of contemplation, 76, acts of devotion to, 78, promise of, to St. Simon Stock, 606, apparitions of, 527

Meditation and contemplation alternate, 161

Memory in relation to contemplation, 104, purification of, 265

Mental prayer or meditation, excellence of, 201, necessity of, 202, true notion of, 204, importance of a proper method, 207, internal affective prayer, 216, distinction between affective prayer and meditation, 216, affective prayer as a preparation for contemplation, 218, an outline of the acts of the will in prayer, by Father Baker, 222, when a soul can pass from meditation to contemplation, 224

Methods of meditation Ignatian, 208, Sulpician, 210, Father Faber's estimate of the two methods, 213, 214, method of prayer of Father Baltazar Alvarez, 219

Miracles in relation to mystical theology, 624, definition and meaning of, 625 division of, 628, above nature, *ibid*, beside nature, *ibid*, against nature, *ibid*, the gift of, 630, includes the grace of healing, *ibid*, exists in the Church, 631, not a permanent habit in any mere man, 633, relation of this gift to sanctity, 634, how true miracles may be distinguished from false, 635, not to be expected without sufficient cause, 638

Mortification its definition and explanation, 229, its division, 232, its necessity, 232, 234, its utility, 237

Mortification, bodily, a preparation for contemplation, 238, due measure of, 239, remarks of St Theresa on, 241, considered in order to the canonization of Saints, 242, general rules for the practice of, 244, 'The Gospel of Pain,' by Rev Father Tyrrell, S.J, 248

Mystic, the, dies and is born again, 98, false mystics, 62, 63, 398

'*Mystical,*' meaning and application of the word, 3

Mystical life, some general observations on, 15

Mystical theology its definition and subject-matter, 4, division of, 8, 11, necessity of, 10, natural phenomena in relation to, 14, in relation to sanctity, 643

Mysticism, extraordinary phenomena of false and true, contrasted, 453

Necessity of vocal prayers for beginners, 190, for religious, 191, of mental prayer or meditation, 202

Nights, dark, described by St John of the Cross, 254, why the Divine illumination is called 'night,' 342

Nine Fridays, devotion of, 603, the twelfth promise with regard to final perseverance not to be understood in a strictly literal sense, 604

Objects of contemplation, primary and secondary, 48, God and His attributes as the objects of contemplation, 49 (see God), the Most Holy Trinity the object of contemplation, 58, the Incarnation and the sacred humanity of Christ objects of contemplation, 62, the Holy Eucharist the object of contemplation, 72, the Blessed Virgin the object of contemplation, 76, the heavenly spirits the objects of contemplation, 77, all supernatural works the objects of contemplation, 79, state of the Church militant the object of contemplation, 81, graces, Sacraments, all supernatural things, the objects of contemplation, 82

Obsession, diabolical, 317

Passion, sacred, of Christ the object of contemplation, 63, 66

Father Baker's instruction on this subject, 69; instruments of, represented in the heart of St Clare of Montefalco, 593
Passiones concupiscibiles et irascibiles, 94
Passions or emotions, 93
Phenomena, mystical, distinct from contemplation, see *Visions, Locutions, Revelations, Prophecies, Miracles,* they do not constitute sanctity, 511
Possession, diabolical, 321
Prayer as a preparation for contemplation the meaning of prayer, 180, as described by Father Baker, 183, in relation to Christian perfection, 185, division of, 186, public and private, of praise, thanksgiving, and petition, 188, vocal prayer, its necessity and utility for beginners, 190 for religious - the Breviary, 191, short ejaculatory prayers, 192, as a means to contemplation in ancient times, 193, attention required for, 194, voluntary vocal prayers recommended. 197, necessity and utility of, illustrated by the example of St Pius V, 198, *Mental Prayer,* see Meditation, see also Mortification and Purifications, Prayer of Contemplation, its Degrees, see Degrees, Part III
Preparation for contemplation, 169
Principles of contemplation on the part of man, 90, the sensitive faculties, 91, the emotions or passions, 93, relation of the sensitive faculties to contemplation, 96, relation of the emotions or feelings to contemplation, 98, the superior faculties of the soul as the causes or principles of contemplation, 101 intellect, will, and memory as principles of contemplation, 104, 106
Principles of contemplation on the part of God, 116, sanctifying grace, 116, the virtues, 122, actual graces, 124, the gifts of the Holy Ghost, 128, the graces *gratis datœ,* 138
Prophecies. meaning of, 609, that in which the prophetic representation may be effected, 610, those through whom prophetic revelation is made, 612, division of, 613, the subjects or recipients of, 615, this not a permanent habit or quality of the soul, 617, what credence to be given to private prophecies, 618, tests or rules by which prophecies may be known as Divine, 619
Purgative state or way, 16, purgations, see Purifications
Purifications, active and passive, explained, 253, *active* consist in four kinds of purity, namely, of *conscience,* of *heart,* of *spirit* and of *action,* 254 *et seq,* 269, purification of the imagination, 263, of the memory, 265, *passive, of the senses,* 280, three things experienced in this, 283, God the efficient cause of, 290 reasons for these purifications, 294, their severity, 295, not always a sign of vocation to contemplation, 299, effects of these purifications, 300, secondary cause of, 305 purifications from the devil as agent *ibid,* from natural causes— example of holy Job 323, example of Lazarus 325, bodily diseases and sickness, 326, loss of friends, 328, persecutions from men, 329 whether one may justify himself or complain, 332, value of patient suffering 334
Purification of the spirit, 338, its material cause, *ibid,* its formal cause, 339, its efficient and its final cause, 341, described by Bishop Ullathorne, *ibid,* when it takes place, 345, temptations of the soul in this state, 349, effects of this purification, 350, manner in which the soul should act, 353, the purification of love, its degrees, 355, the inflammation of love, 357, the wounds of love, 359, the

languor of love, 361; fruits and benefits of this state, 364, directions of St Paul of the Cross with regard to this state of purification, 365

Quiet, prayer of, 390 See Third Degree of Contemplation

Quietism, history and errors of, 399, semi-quietism, history and errors of, 400

Recollection, prayer of, 380

Remarks, concluding, on the degrees of contemplation, 484

Retirement in relation to contemplation, 173, in relation to charitable intercourse, 176

Revelations what is meant by revelation, 575, degrees of, 576 canonical and private, *ibid*, distinct from visions and apparitions, 578, division of private revelations, 579, the existence of Divine private revelations, 580 signs by which they may be known, 582, whether the object of faith, 585, with regard to the persons to whom they are given, 586, with regard to others, 588, meaning of the approbation of the Church given to them, 589, whether holy souls may be mistaken in them, 591, 604 revelations of secrets of souls, see Secrets of Souls, 595, revelations about the devotion to the Sacred Heart made to Blessed Margaret Mary Alacoque, 603, 607, the promise attached to the devotion of the *Nine Fridays* not to be understood literally, 604, the promise of the Blessed Virgin to St Simon Stock explained 606

Scapular, brown, of Mount Carmel, 606

Secrets of souls, three kinds, 595, the secret of conscience, 595, secret of the state of souls after death, 598, secret of predestination, 600

Senses, passive purification of, 280

Sickness, duties in time of, 327

Silence, spiritual, second degree of contemplation, 385, causes and effects, 386, special directions concerning, 387; remarks of St Francis de Sales applied to this prayer, 389

Sleep, spiritual, fifth degree of contemplation, 414

Solitude in relation to contemplation, 173, in relation to charitable intercourse, 176

Souls, lost, apparitions of, 537, souls in purgatory, apparitions of, 536

Spirit, purity of, 263

State of the blessed in heaven, and their glory, the object of contemplation, 79, state of the Church militant the object of contemplation, 81

States of perfection—purgative, illuminative, and unitive, 16, three kinds in the spiritual life —active, contemplative, and mixed, 20

Suffering, love shown in, 153, value of patient suffering, 334

Summary of directions with regard to mystical phenomena, 649

Suspension of mind effect of contemplation, 143

System of contemplation of Richard of St Victor, 85

Temptations, diabolical, 306, how to be resisted, 310, not to be sought for nor promoted, 313 that assail the soul in the state of the passive purification of the spirit, 349

Theophanies, or apparitions of God, 516

Touches, Divine, of the soul See Seventh Degree, 437

Trinity, the Most Holy, the object of contemplation, 58 doctrine of, *ibid*

Union, ecstatic, eighth degree of contemplation, 444

Union, mystical and simple, seventh degree of contemplation, 427

Union, explanation of, by St John of the Cross, 442

Union, perfect, of spiritual marriage, two things essential, 475
Unitive state or way, 16
Utility of vocal prayer for beginners, 190; for religious, 191; of short ejaculatory prayers, 192

Vanity to be avoided, 270
Virgin, the Blessed, as the object of contemplation, 76; acts of devotion to, 78
Virtues the principles of contemplation, 122
Vision, St. John's, 77; vision of our Lord to the soul in the state of spiritual marriage, 473
Visions, notion of, 498; different kinds of, 500; they do not exclude each other, 501; their order, 502; not hallucinations, 503; true miracles, 504; not to be desired, 506; confessors not to be too credulous or too incredulous in these matters, 508; they do not constitute sanctity, 511; *corporeal*, see Apparitions, 512; *imaginative* or *ideal*, 541; subject to illusions, 543; *intellectual*, 545; obscure, intellectual, and clear, 546, 547; cannot be the work of the devil, 548; how to discern visions and apparitions, 550; those from natural causes, 550
Visions, diabolical, 552; characteristics of good visions exemplified in St. Theresa, 553
Vocation, Divine, special, required for the mystical state, 18; general rules for knowing the Divine call to contemplation, 225

Warning against being too much occupied with self, 274
Weariness, 283
Will in relation to contemplation, 104, 106; free will in contemplation, 109
Women more than men favoured with mystical gifts, 644
Women, fewer, than men canonized, 647
Words, Divine. See Locutions
Works: the supernatural works of God the object of contemplation, 79
Wounds of love, 359; how they act on the soul, 424

THE END

R. & T. WASHBOURNE, 4, PATERNOSTER ROW, LONDON